For Ozlem,

With hope that this volume may connect you and Beth — and your shared stunning values and practices in contemporary society.

Nanette

Gender in Judaism and Islam

Common Lives, Uncommon Heritage

Edited by Firoozeh Kashani-Sabet and Beth S. Wenger

NEW YORK UNIVERSITY PRESS
New York and London

NEW YORK UNIVERSITY PRESS
New York and London
www.nyupress.org

References to Internet websites (URLs) were accurate at the time of writing.
Neither the author nor New York University Press is responsible for URLs that
may have expired or changed since the manuscript was prepared.

LIBRARY OF CONGRESS CATALOGING-IN-PUBLICATION DATA
Gender in Judaism and Islam : common lives, uncommon heritage / edited by Firoozeh
Kashani-Sabet and Beth S. Wenger.
pages cm
Includes bibliographical references and index.
ISBN 978-1-4798-5326-7 (cl : alk. paper) -- ISBN 978-1-4798-0127-5 (pb : alk. paper)
1. Women in Judaism. 2. Women in Islam. 3. Feminism--Religious aspects--Judaism 4.
Feminism--Religious aspects--Islam. 5. Women and religion. I. Kashani-Sabet, Firoozeh,
1967- editor. II. Wenger, Beth S., 1963- editor.
BM729.W6G46 2014
296.082--dc23
2014024573

New York University Press books are printed on acid-free paper,
and their binding materials are chosen for strength and durability.
We strive to use environmentally responsible suppliers and materials
to the greatest extent possible in publishing our books.

Manufactured in the United States of America

10 9 8 7 6 5 4 3 2 1

Also available as an ebook

*For all the Jewish and Muslim women
striving for mutual equality and understanding*

CONTENTS

Acknowledgments   ix

Introduction   1
  Firoozeh Kashani-Sabet and Beth S. Wenger

PART I. COMPARATIVE PERSPECTIVES   13

1 Jewish and Muslim Feminist Theologies in Dialogue:
  Discourses of Difference   17
  Susannah Heschel

2 Jewish and Islamic Legal Traditions: Diffusions of Law   46
  Amira Sonbol

PART II. LIMITS OF BIOLOGY:
BODILY PURITY AND RELIGIOSITY   69

3 Scholarly versus Women's Authority in the Islamic Law of
  Menstrual Purity   73
  Marion Katz

4 Gender Duality and Its Subversions in Rabbinic Law   106
  Charlotte Elisheva Fonrobert

5 Gender and Reproductive Technologies in Shia Iran   126
  Soraya Tremayne

PART III. CRIMES OF PASSION:
FORMATIVE TEXTS AND TRADITIONS   151

6 Not a Man: Joseph and the Character of Masculinity in
   Judaism and Islam   155
   Lori Lefkovitz

7 Dishonorable Passions: Law and Virtue in Muslim Communities 181
   Catherine Warrick

8 Legislating the Family: Gender, Jewish Law, and Rabbinical
   Courts in Mandate Palestine   203
   Lisa Fishbayn Joffe

PART IV. CULTURAL DEPICTIONS
OF JEWISH AND MUSLIM WOMEN   237

9 A Literary Perspective: Domestic Violence, the "Woman
   Question," and the "Arab Question" in Early Zionism   241
   Andrea Siegel

10 An Autobiographical Perspective: Schools, Jails, and
    Cemeteries in Shoshanna Levy's Life Story   268
    Orit Bashkin

11 An Artistic Perspective: The Women of Bahram Beizai's Cinema 311
    Hamid Dabashi

Afterword: Common Ground, Contested Terrain   341
   Joan W. Scott

Glossary   349
About the Contributors   351
Index   355

ACKNOWLEDGMENTS

The idea for this anthology emerged after we convened a conference on the theme of Gender in Judaism and Islam at the University of Pennsylvania in the spring of 2010. The stimulating dialogue and new ideas that arose from that daylong discussion convinced us that the issues deserved more sustained exploration. The essays that comprise this volume include both expanded versions of papers delivered at that conference as well as contributions that we solicited in the months that followed. We are deeply grateful to all the authors in this anthology, for it is their innovative scholarship that has made this project so vital and engaging. This volume has been a collaborative effort, and it is a pleasure to have the opportunity to acknowledge all those who helped bring it to fruition.

We thank the School of Arts and Sciences of the University of Pennsylvania for supporting us with a Mellon Cultural Diversity Grant, which allowed the Jewish Studies Program and the Middle East Center to sponsor the conference that sparked this volume. We also appreciate the many schools, departments, and programs across Penn that cosponsored the event, including the History Department, Law School, Religious Studies Department, Near Eastern Languages & Civilizations Department, School of Nursing, Alice Paul Center for Research on Women, Gender, & Sexuality, and the Women's Studies Program.

We were extremely fortunate to have superb staff members and students who helped to make the conference a success. The gathering would simply not have been possible without the expert administrative skills of Chrissy Walsh of the Jewish Studies Program, and James Ryan and Jinhee Song of the Middle East Center. Also providing valuable assistance were Fatima Abdrabboh and Agatha Kowproski, students in Penn's Law School, who helped with many of the conference details. We further appreciate the members of our organizing committee—Talya Fishman, Nili Gold, Kathryn Hellerstein, Arthur Kiron, Joseph Lowry,

Eve Troutt Powell, and Brian Spooner—who helped refine our objectives during the planning process.

We thank scholars Yael Feldman, Susan Kahn, and Brian Spooner who presented papers during the conference but were unable to contribute essays to the volume. Although their work does not appear here, their participation helped to shape many of the ideas contained in the pages that follow.

While the initial conference inspired the creation of this volume, so much of its development took place in subsequent months. Almost half the essays that appear in this anthology were solicited after the conference, as we began to conceive the best ways to bring new perspectives to issues of gender in Jewish and Islamic Studies and to foster connections between these two emerging fields. We appreciate very much the helpful suggestions offered by the two anonymous readers for NYU Press; their insights have made this a better book. We also owe a very special thanks to James Ryan, currently a doctoral candidate in Middle Eastern history in Penn's History Department. Jim joined the project in its final months, and his expert editorial assistance and careful attention to detail allowed us to complete the volume in a timely fashion.

We are deeply grateful to our editor at NYU Press, Jennifer Hammer, who has believed in this project from the beginning and has provided unflagging support throughout the process. We thank also our copyeditor at NYU Press, Usha Sanyal, whose work has greatly improved the volume. Martin Tulic created the index for the book and we appreciate his thoroughness in identifying key themes and ideas.

Creating this anthology has been a genuine pleasure and an intellectual passion. Working on this project has not only made us aware of the high caliber of scholarship evidenced by all the contributors, but has also reminded us how mutually beneficial it can be to draw connections between Jewish and Islamic Studies and how important it remains to foster new perspectives on gender in both these fields.

Firoozeh Kashani-Sabet and Beth S. Wenger

Introduction

FIROOZEH KASHANI-SABET AND BETH S. WENGER

Tensions have run high in recent years between Jewish and Muslim communities, from the United States to the Middle East. Yet a close look at women who have embraced Islam and Judaism reveals striking parallels, illuminating the ways in which these women have negotiated similar power dynamics in their religious and social lives. This volume examines two of the world's most ancient cultures and religions—Judaism and Islam—through the prism of gender. Bringing these two distinct, yet interconnected, traditions into dialogue around issues of gender opens up fresh perspectives and invites new avenues of interpretation. This book includes the work of scholars from a variety of disciplines working in the fields of Islam and Judaism. It addresses diverse topics ranging from gendered readings of texts, legal issues in marriage and divorce, ritual practices, and social realities to religious questions, and women's literary expressions and historical experiences. It also explores feminist influences within Muslim and Jewish communities, and touches upon issues affecting Jewish and Muslim women in contemporary society. Moreover, the volume focuses attention on the theoretical innovations that gender scholarship has brought to the study of Muslim and Jewish experiences.

Given the current geopolitical context, which most often represents Islam and Judaism as at odds, it is particularly useful to consider the connections and commonalities between these two cultures and religious civilizations. Jewish and Islamic histories have long been interrelated. Both are cultures born in the Middle East and rooted in texts and traditions that have often excluded women. Over the centuries, the experiences of Jewish and Muslim women have been shaped by the ways in which their texts demarcated the biology of gender and the structures by which their cultures defined women's roles. At the same time, both groups have recently seen a resurgence in religious orthodoxy among women, as well as burgeoning feminist movements that challenge traditional religious structures. In American society, Jews and Muslims operate as minority cultures, carving out a place for religious and ethnic distinctiveness. For all these reasons, the time is ripe for a volume that explores the relationship between these two cultures through the lens of gender.

Islam emerged as a religion in the tradition of Judaism and Christianity, but one that shares many more legal precepts with the former. The Judeo-Christian tradition, as implied by the term itself, has been the subject of copious scholarship, whereas connections between Judaism and Islam have just begun to take shape, particularly in the field of gender history.[1] Within the individual fields of Islamic and Jewish Studies, there is by now a substantial literature on gender. Yet there are still relatively few works that examine these two traditions together. One useful volume, *Daughters of Abraham: Feminist Thought in Judaism, Christianity, and Islam* edited by Yvonne Yazbeck Haddad and John L. Esposito, seeks to uncover a feminist vein in each of the three monotheistic traditions, offering feminist readings of traditional texts and teachings.[2] Likewise, another anthology, *Eve and Adam: Jewish, Christian, and Muslim Readings on Genesis and Gender*, focuses on how the three traditions grapple with issues of gender, focusing specifically on interpretations of the Book of Genesis.[3] Jan Feldman's *Citizenship, Faith, & Feminism: Jewish and Muslim Women Reclaim Their Rights* puts forward an engaging exploration of feminism and women's rights, but much of its methodology is rooted in survey techniques, and it deals specifically with Orthodox women in Israel, Muslim women in Kuwait, and women of both faiths in the United States.[4] This volume follows in the attempt to engage in comparative work on gender in Judaism and Islam, but it differs from these recent treatments in its range, thematic emphasis, and breadth. By considering religious texts, legal discourses, historical experiences, and representations in literature, film, and autobiography, as well as an examination of feminism in Judaism and Islam, it offers a far-reaching exploration of the distinctive aspects and interconnectedness of these two rich traditions.

While both fields regularly produce important new works about gender, it is important to recognize the distinct environments in which Jewish and Islamic Studies function. Certainly, Jews enjoy greater privilege in the West and thus scholars of Jewish Studies do not confront the charged climate of Islamophobia that scholars of Islam occasionally face. In matters of gender, the current political and social climate also presents unique challenges for Islamic Studies, as charges of backwardness and fanaticism in Islam's treatment of women are far more pervasive than in similar discussions surrounding Orthodox Jewish women. At the same time, the field of Jewish Studies has grappled with its set of questions, particularly in scholarship about Zionism and Israel. Several chapters in this volume use gender as a means to problematize Israeli and Zionist discourses, examining, for example, a legal system that denies women full marriage equality in family law. Two chapters employ gender as an analytical framework to explore complex relationships between Arab and Jewish cultures in ways that prompt new approaches to Zionist history. Recognizing that Islamic and Jewish Studies each confronts its particular collection of political and intellectual challenges, this volume puts the two fields in dialogue in ways that enrich both arenas of scholarship.

The experience and meaning of gender and religiosity within the context of two monotheistic faiths offer analytical tools for studying the lives of Muslim and Jewish women. Both Judaism and Islam have long traditions of religious scholars (usually men) debating the meaning of sacred texts and arguing over the application of religious laws. Yet at the same time, neither tradition precludes any member of its faith from accessing God directly, and both share the notion that prayer is a religious act available to all. In this way, Islam and Judaism have never completely allowed the religious (male) elite to have exclusive access to holy texts, leaving openings for ordinary men as well as women to direct their religious lives, albeit to different extents, depending on time and place. In recent years, feminists from both traditions, many of them highly educated and capable of textual exegesis, have begun to offer new readings of foundational religious literature that address the ways that women are discussed in sacred texts and contemplate the many absences where women do not appear at all. The sorts of questions they ask spark the conversations that the scholars in this volume have initiated.

Many chapters of this book consider legal issues, from the ancient period through contemporary times. Because Islam and Judaism derive their civil and religious practices through complex systems of legal interpretation, many of the contributors have chosen to explore the ways that women's experiences have been shaped by those legal decisions, as well as the ways that women have found to subvert legal doctrines. Thus, this volume considers subjects as varied as the tensions inherent in traditional laws governing menstruation, the consequences of allowing rabbinical courts to govern family law in Palestine and Israel, debates about honor killings in the Arab World, and the legal wrangling over reproductive technologies in contemporary Iran.

Much of this volume is concerned with issues of religious practice and religious law, but at the same time many of the chapters reveal the interplay between the religious and secular arenas, and the impact of both on gendered experience. Anthropologists have long argued that the practice of religion can at times differ markedly from the theology of religion, and many of this volume's contributors pay particular attention to the realities of lived religion as they diverge from or at least modify the dictates of religious law.[5] The boundaries between the secular and the religious worlds have always been highly fluid, and in fact newer scholarship has made a convincing case that the two categories should not be considered as either firmly bounded or starkly oppositional.[6] Some of the authors demonstrate the need to consider religious law and ritual practice in proper social and historical context, noting the variables across time, space, and cultures. By examining lived religion alongside religious doctrines, this volume sheds light on women's experiences beyond the dictates of religious mandates.

This book considers not only religious, but also national and ethnic identities. Particularly in Part 4, the contributors examine the representations and self-representations of Islamic and Jewish women in literature, film, and autobiography. In considering these modes of cultural production, this volume reaches beyond religion as an isolated category to explore the ways in which political struggles, migrations, and shifting national ideas have influenced women's experiences and been reflected in cultural expressions. Chapters in Part 4 of the book examine different sorts of texts from those considered by other contributors to this volume—not the foundational religious texts or the legal discourses surrounding their implementation, but rather the representations of women and by women that give voice to their historical experiences.

The first pair of chapters speak to the ways in which the body and the biology of gender have produced legal texts that often denigrate women's status in Judaism and Islam. Susannah Heschel begins by tracing the historical background of women's roles and rights in the two traditions and then treats the ways that both groups of women have been the subjects of the gaze of outside observers. She focuses particularly on contemporary expressions and dilemmas of Islamic and Jewish feminism, including concepts of the divine, equality under religious law, relationships to sacred texts, and approaches to patriarchy and sexuality. Amira Sonbol offers an Islamic counterpoint to Heschel's discussions, with a particular focus on the legal and doctrinal roots of both traditions and highlighting the shared cultures of the two groups. Sonbol points to the commonalities within Jewish and Islamic legal traditions and emphasizes the need to interpret religious law in social context and with particular attention to lived experience. She calls for a more nuanced reading of legal texts and for more careful consideration of the processes of historical change.

As in other subfields of gender history, the bodies of women and the biological determinants of gender have shaped legal and social norms. Both Jewish and Islamic texts devote considerable attention to the bodily differences of women and men, often to support the patriarchal precepts of their religious communities. Analyses of Islamic and Jewish law indicate the ways that male scholars of both traditions have used gender and biological differences to subordinate women. In Part 2 of the book Marion Katz discusses notions of bodily pollution and religiosity by evaluating Islamic injunctions on menstruation. On the one hand, the laws of menstruation were dictated by religious law and adjudicated by learned elite (men); at the same time, women possessed greater familiarity with their own bodily functions, and thus had some power in this particular legal arena. The application of religious laws governing menstruation reflected this inherent tension, as authority was sometimes vested in the hands of male legal scholars but other times rested with women themselves. Women's ability to draw legal conclusions about menstruation was empowering in many ways unanticipated by male scholars. Katz traces this ongoing tension beginning in the classical period as she considers the different approaches taken within distinct schools of Islamic legal tradition.

Charlotte Fonrobert also focuses on issues of the body, but within Jewish traditions. Rabbinic legal discourse can be described as being dedicated to the construction and reinforcement of gender duality at almost every turn. From the Mishnah onward, rabbinic law is fundamentally concerned with whether one is considered a man or a woman. Fonrobert sheds light on the preoccupation with this duality by focusing on the rabbis' conscious concerns about potential deviations from their heteronormative project by repeatedly considering unruly bodies, bodies that are dually sexed (*androginos*) or not (yet) sexed (*tumtum*). The content of such texts is easily dismissed as marginal to the project of rabbinic law since the rulings apply only to a tiny percentage of the population. Yet rather than giving in to tendencies that undermine the margins of discourse, Fonrobert demonstrates that the intense rabbinic preoccupation with those who defy heteronormative categories indicates precisely that gender classification lay at the very heart of the rabbinic worldview.

Together, Katz and Fonrobert help to explain the ways in which women skirted around the legal frameworks of Islam and Judaism, which were created and defined by male scholars. Women found ways to defy legal authorities, as male jurists could only understand certain biological matters theoretically and not experientially. Soraya Tremayne gives the debate on religion, gender, and biology a modern twist by exploring the controversies surrounding the use of assistive technologies in the field of reproductive health. Tremayne focuses on the use of reproductive technologies within the theocratic regime of Shia Iran. She demonstrates the crucial role of religious scholars in allowing the use of reproductive technologies and in determining population policies. Religious authorities in Iran have also allowed third party gamete and embryo donation and surrogacy. Tremayne argues that without the backing of the senior clerics, these technologies would not have been permissible or accepted by many who used them. Yet as a result of their use, these technologies have had unanticipated consequences for gender relations. The implementation of Iran's current population policies has resulted in smaller family sizes, a drastic increase in female education, and a rise in the age of marriage for both men and women. These changes have transformed the structure of family life and the relationship between women and men. Women have also gained powers in other spheres beyond their reproductive life, and often no longer conform to the ideal Islamic role model. At the same time, Islamic ideology, through its legal and political structures, has tried to restrict women to their traditional roles as mothers and wives, and men have often resisted deviations from traditional means of reproduction. These tensions are played out daily within the confines of the Islamic Republic of Iran.

The third part of the book explores some of the formative texts and legal traditions within Islamic and Jewish cultures. Lori Lefkovitz brings a literary approach to her careful reading of the story of Joseph and highlights the differences and similarities in the biblical and Qur'anic versions. Joseph, a revered figure in both Islamic and Jewish literature, has been embraced as a heroic character by those traditions, whether in scriptural texts or in subsequent renditions of the tale. Lefkovitz approaches the Yosef (of Jewish tradition) and Yusuf (of Islamic tradition) as textual twins and compares the models of masculinity that each figure provides, finding in Yosef a more insecure masculinity when compared to the confident masculine figure embodied by Yusuf. In following the construction of the Joseph characters from their scriptural origins through their contemporary iterations, Lefkovitz demonstrates just how powerful these biblical narratives remain in the shaping of Jewish and Islamic cultures.

The two remaining chapters in Part 3 move from scriptural texts to consider the legal framework of Islamic and Jewish societies by examining the ways in which "crimes of passion" have been adjudicated in family courts within the two religious communities. Catherine Warrick investigates the social context of honor killings in Muslim communities. Honor killings are a poorly understood and contentious tradition popularly linked to Islam in the views of some Muslims (and many if not most non-Muslim observers). But many Islamic legal scholars contend that the practice is not rooted in traditional sources and has no basis in shari'a or state law. There have been some claims that this practice has tribal and anthropological roots. Honor killings remain a source of significant conflict and contention within Islamic societies. Many authorities, particularly religious officials in government, denounce honor killings as impermissible according to Islamic law and consider them a form of homicide. But, as Warrick explains, many Islamist leaders insist that they can be understood or excused, if not desired, as a means to regulate women's behavior and morality. The defense of honor killings remains a way to maintain male hegemony and to control women, but it also reflects a desire on the part of Islamists to create a shari'a-based legal system, or at least subvert the legal system in nations where such a system does not prevail; in this respect, the expressed support for honor killings represents a means to challenge the legitimacy of existing regimes in several Arab countries.

Lisa Fishbayn Joffe also considers the role of religious law, but in Israeli rather than in Islamic society, exploring the long-lasting consequences of the decision made in the British Mandate period to confer exclusive jurisdiction over family law cases involving Jews to state-supported rabbinical courts. She argues that the decision to leave family law in the hands of the rabbis was not only a result of the struggle between Orthodox and secular parties—an ongoing tension within Zionism before and after the creation of the state of Israel—but also an outgrowth of the British colonial policy of indirect rule as a method of governing multicultural states. While British rule during the Mandate period did bring about some improvements in women's status, the power over family law that was entrusted to the jurisdiction of rabbis and religious courts created obstacles to gender equality that remain in place to this day. By giving religious authorities sole power to regulate marriage and divorce, the agreements forged in the pre-state period have institutionalized gender inequities and created formidable legal impediments to more egalitarian approaches to family law. Joffe's exploration of the origins of this legal system in Mandate Palestine thus has important implications for understanding the current state of family law in modern Israel.

Part 4 of the book shifts the focus to cultural expressions within Jewish and Islamic communities, using them to reveal historical experiences and cultural ideals. In an effort to demonstrate the interwoven nature of the Woman Question and the Arab Question, Andrea Siegel focuses on the specific motif of domestic violence, which appears in a limited but highly revealing subset of Hebrew stories that employ representations of violence against women in the early years of Zionism. In an era that was permeated by the volatile combination of nationalism and anti-Semitism, one way that Jewish writers commented upon possibilities for Jewish-Arab coexistence in Palestine was through stories that explored the urge to use force—upon one's family member, neighbor, or oneself. Domestic violence was certainly not any more or less prevalent in Jewish families of the era than in other ethnic or religious groups, but as Siegel explains, her project is to uncover the narrative *function* of domestic violence in the Zionist attempt to feel at home in the "old-new homeland." Siegel begins by examining two pre-1929 Hebrew short stories on the Arab Question that incorporate domestic violence plots. She concludes by highlighting the function of domestic violence in the most significant pre-state Hebrew literary work, Yehuda Burla's multivolume novel *Daughter of Zion* (1930–1931). That work effectively dismantles Zionist hopes for productive Arab-Jewish coexistence in Palestine.

The question of religion and gender took on added complexity in some of the predominantly Islamic states of the Middle East that were home to significant Jewish communities. Some of these cultural and religious tensions were played out in modern Iraq, which struggled to forge a national identity for its diverse citizenry. Orit Bashkin provides a model for the ways that gender analysis offers new perspectives on Arab-Jewish identities in Iraq and in Israel. She does this by analyzing and contextualizing one case study—the life story of an Iraqi Jewish woman, Shoshanna Levy, who was born in Baghdad in 1938 and, like most other Iraqi Jews, left for Israel in the early 1950s. Using Levy's autobiography, Bashkin offers a compelling reading of Jewish-Iraqi gendered identity as well as the tensions between Arab and Zionist national discourses that were embodied, and in some cases, subverted by Iraqi Jews and Jews from other Arab lands. Her chapter considers the interplay of national and gendered identities through the life story of Shoshanna Levy.

At the beginning of her life in Israel, Shoshanna lacked the ability to communicate; as an Arabic speaker, she did not possess the language skills to converse with the predominantly Ashkenazic, Israeli, Hebrew-speaking elites. As an adult writing in Hebrew in the 2000s, having by then mastered the Hebrew language, her autobiography reveals the complex strands of Arab-Jewish culture and the struggles of a Jewish woman from the Arab world to establish a new life and a new identity as a Mizrahi Jew in the state of Israel. While Bashkin focuses on a specific life story, a generation of Mizrahi women from different Arab lands shared similar experiences, and she extracts their larger meanings from this autobiography.

The dynamics of religion in women's lives have taken on new meaning in the Islamic Republic of Iran. Hamid Dabashi discusses the work of the acclaimed Iranian filmmaker Bahram Beizai, focusing particularly on the female characters that are central to his films. Dabashi explores the myths that lie at the heart of Beizai's characters, noting that the women are consistently portrayed as noble workers, farmers, essentially as "earth mothers." Dabashi also dissects the meanings of the interactions of female characters with men and other family members. While he pays particular attention to the mythological motifs inherent in all of Beizai's films, Dabashi also powerfully suggests the ways that this filmmaker weaves that mythology together with contemporary social issues, challenging fundamental issues of gender and power in modern Iranian culture.

The chapters in this part share an understanding of the ways that patriarchy has entrenched itself in Jewish and Islamic communities beyond the interpretation of texts and religious laws. Analyses of film, art, and culture, in particular, bring to light the tensions experienced by women and men as they grapple with modern concepts such as equality and citizenship, and demonstrate their constant struggles to break out of the gender stereotypes that have been reinforced through religious and social practices. Whether being expected to embrace machismo culture or the role of dutiful mother and wife, men and women alternately embrace and reject their religious and cultural traditions in an effort to meet their personal and societal obligations.

Joan Scott concludes the volume with an afterword. Scott reflects upon the diverse issues treated in this book and points to the ways in which they have complicated our understanding of Jewish and Islamic gendered experiences. She notes that this volume has resisted casting

Jews and Muslims as cultural opponents and has instead emphasized the interconnectedness of their histories, particularly in the arena of gender. As Scott observes, feminism itself has the power to provide a nuanced approach to both these cultural traditions, whether in the interpretation of ancient texts or in the challenges encountered in contemporary society.

This volume stands as a new contribution to two evolving arenas of scholarship. The fields of Jewish and Islamic Studies, both relatively new to the academy, have been significantly reshaped by scholarship on gender. Beyond merely including women in the discussion, new works on gender have sparked the reconceptualization of both fields, providing innovative theoretical approaches and prompting rereadings of traditional texts and reconsiderations about religious cultures. As part of an ongoing effort to reevaluate religious and ethnic culture through the lens of gender, this book adds new comparative dimensions and brings to light original scholarship gathered from archives around the world. It demonstrates the ways that the politics of gender has forced a reassessment of religious laws and legal practices as well as a new examination of basic concepts such as marriage, motherhood, and maternity in Judaism and Islam.

At a time when current political and cultural events often position Judaism and Islam as inherently oppositional, it is worthwhile to explore the relationship and interconnectedness of these two cultures. We hope this volume will be a catalyst for further discussion about religious communities and will spark new comparative work in gender studies.

NOTES

1. The notion of a Judeo-Christian tradition has been challenged by many scholars, but the literature on this subject remains far more substantial than works on Judaism and Islam. See, for example, Arthur A. Cohen, *The Myth of the Judeo-Christian Tradition* (New York: Harper & Row, 1969); Henri A. Krop, Arie L. Molendijk, and Hent de Vries, eds., *Post-Theism: Reframing the Judeo-Christian Tradition* (Leuven: Peeters, 2000); Robert Gordis, *Judeo-Christian Tradition: Illusion or Reality* (New York: Judaica Press, 1965); Fuad Shaʿban, *For Zion's Sake: The Judeo-Christian Tradition in American Culture* (London: Pluto Press, 2005).

2. Yvonne Yazbeck Haddad and John L. Esposito, eds., *Daughters of Abraham: Feminist Thought in Judaism, Christianity, and Islam* (Gainesville: University of Florida Press, 2001).

3. Kristen E. Kvam, Linda S. Schearing, and Valarie H. Ziegler, eds., *Eve and Adam: Jewish, Christian, and Muslim Readings on Genesis and Gender* (Bloomington: Indiana University Press, 1999).

4. Jan Feldman, *Citizenship, Faith, & Feminism: Jewish and Muslim Women Reclaim Their Rights* (Waltham, Mass.: Brandeis University Press, 2011).

5. See, for example, Clifford Geertz's groundbreaking work, *The Interpretation of Cultures: Selected Essays* (New York: Basic Books, 1973); for a general survey, see Fiona Bowie, *The Anthropology of Religion: An Introduction* (Malden, Mass.: Blackwell, 2000).

6. See, for example, Charles Taylor, *A Secular Age* (Cambridge, Mass.: Belknap Press of Harvard University Press, 2007); Craig Calhoun, Mark Juergensmeyer, and Jonathan VanAntwerpen, eds., *Rethinking Secularism* (New York: Oxford University Press, 2011).

PART I

Comparative Perspectives

In matters of gender, Judaism and Islam share similar modes of interpreting religious law and, in more recent years, have confronted parallel challenges in fighting for women's equality. Yet these two traditions are by no means identical; they possess unique characteristics and exist in different religious and political environments.

Susannah Heschel and Amira Sonbol explore the intersections and divergences of Judaism and Islam on questions of gender in the following two opening chapters. Neither author attempts a comprehensive analysis of the complexities of gender relations within the two traditions; rather, each reflects on the interconnectedness of women's issues as they operate and are challenged within their separate religious structures.

Susannah Heschel considers, among other subjects, the nuances of feminism. "Liberation," she argues, has meant different things to Muslim and Jewish women. Heschel traces the origins of women's rights among both groups, noting that while the rights of Jewish women were bound up—and often sublimated—within Western Enlightenment attitudes toward Jews and the broader campaign for Jewish emancipation, considerations of Muslim women's rights often came as part of—and remained second to—the resistance to colonialism. Still, Jewish and Muslim feminists found their voices through these cultural conflicts.

As Heschel emphasizes, both Jewish and Muslim women became subjected to the gaze of outsiders; for generations, women of both faiths have been stereotyped and used to measure, for example, how "civilized" Jews really were in nineteenth-century Western Europe or to determine the fanaticism of contemporary Muslims—a matter often gauged through the popularity of women's traditional dress. Heschel proceeds to discuss a range of pressing religious and social issues, from women's access to religious power and their struggles to influence and take control of religious authority, to their rights to study and interpret sacred texts, and, as women, to bring about genuine transformations within their respective traditions.

Amira Sonbol also considers the parallels between Islam and Judaism, focusing particularly on religious law, its interpretation, and its implications for Muslim and Jewish women. She emphasizes the similar legal processes in the Jewish and Muslim worlds, where common practices originated in sacred scriptures and then were subject to various interpretations through the centuries. She stresses the dissemination of oral traditions that allowed for greater communal interplay in enforcing and determining religious rulings.

Sonbol demands that scholars pay attention to the function of narrative as it inflected oral interpretations of law and influenced later written codes and treatises. Emphasizing the human dimension of interpretation, she shifts the focus from scholars and religious experts to the communities in which they lived and practiced their traditions. Sonbol aims to recall the orality that was at the root of religious laws, reclaiming the very lived experiences and social contexts that produced them. Only in appreciating the lived tradition of religious law, she argues, will Jewish and Muslim women be able to effect real change in their respective communities.

Neither Heschel nor Sonbol makes a case for the sameness of Islamic and Jewish traditions. Rather, they encourage shared readings of gender in Judaism and Islam and point to common challenges and questions. Their chapters exemplify the power of comparative approaches to yield fresh insights for both religious communities.

1

Jewish and Muslim Feminist Theologies in Dialogue

Discourses of Difference

SUSANNAH HESCHEL

Islamic and Judaic Feminist Theologies: The Context

Although Christians have developed the most important and influential feminist theologies, it is Jewish and Muslim feminists who have the most in common with each other as they struggle to achieve equality within their respective religions, both of which are rooted in legal systems.[1] Jews and Muslims work within religious systems of civil and ritual legal jurisdiction that center around revealed scripture and oral traditions that for centuries have been the nearly exclusive domain of male scholars and judges. Jews and Muslims also share some customs; for instance, both indicate religious membership through hair and head coverings.[2] While head coverings for women are not an explicit requirement of Islamic or Jewish scriptures, but based instead on custom and tradition, they have become increasingly important in recent decades, usually in conjunction with secularization efforts and political movements.[3] Yet here the two religions diverge in gendered fashion: Jewish identity is signified through Jewish men and their head coverings, whereas Islamic identity is signified through Muslim women and their head coverings. Political liberation movements—whether overturning

colonial rule or establishing an independent Jewish State of Israel—
have led both Jewish and Muslim women to intensify their "modest"
attire of long sleeves and skirts, hats, scarves, wigs, or veils, even as their
presence in the public sphere has finally been legitimated.

What, then, constitutes women's "liberation" for feminists in Islam
and Judaism? Is it the freedom to intensify their religious devotion,
or the freedom to achieve equality with men as figures of religious
authority, or the freedom from religion altogether? Muslim and Jewish feminists have directed their attention to different issues. Muslim
feminists have focused on family law—marriage, divorce, inheritance,
and protection from physical abuse—whereas Jewish feminists have
centered primarily on public worship—study and interpretation of
Jewish legal texts and scripture, and laws regulating Jewish divorce.
Not all these concerns are new, or developed in isolation. Having
lived under Muslim rule for many centuries, Jewish religious customs
and even Jewish religious laws were at times influenced by Islamic
practices. Recent scholarship by Gideon Libson has revealed that as
early as the Geonic period, sixth to eleventh centuries, Jewish legal
authorities living in Muslim lands were pressured to liberalize aspects
of Jewish law affecting women.[4] For instance, Jewish divorce laws
were liberalized because Islamic divorce laws were considerably more
sympathetic to women, which attracted Jewish women converts seeking expeditious divorces.

While Islam may have been more liberal in certain respects, this is
not always recognized in contemporary comparisons of the two religions. Modern-day Americans at times regard Islamic law as dangerous
(and outdated?), and some states have pending legislation preventing
any influence of sharia, Islamic law. In 2011, nearly half the state legislatures in the United States were considering, or had passed, legislation that prohibited judges from considering sharia, Islamic law, when
issuing judgments. Unfortunately, Judaism and Islam's mutual appreciation for each other has deteriorated in recent decades. Contemporary feminism has not seen a strong coalition of Jewish and Muslim
feminists, and more often there is antagonism as some Jewish groups
have funded Islamophobic organizations and at times portrayed Islam
as a religion intrinsically hostile to Jews and Judaism and oppressive to
Muslim women.[5] Calling attention to the parallel feminist efforts, and

revitalizing collaboration, should become our joint goal. Most importantly, feminist critique of any religion should not be manipulated into a denunciation of that religion, given the reality of misogyny and patriarchal domination in all religions.

Anti-Jewish and Anti-Muslim Attitudes

Both religions have long faced political critiques regarding their legal systems. During the nineteenth century, as Europeans debated the political emancipation of the Jews, Judaism itself came under scrutiny for its suitability to the modern age. They questioned whether Jewish law permitted Jews to join the military and whether Judaism was an "Oriental" religion, given the role it prescribed for women. When Muslims migrated to European countries after World War II, there were similar debates regarding Islam's alleged "Orientalism," as well as its compatibility with European society, and whether European culture was intrinsically "Christian" or multicultural. Within the United States, Islam came under sharp scrutiny after September 11, 2001; questions were raised about whether Islamic jihad (struggle on behalf of religion) ordered Muslims to wage war against non-Muslims, whether Muslim women were oppressed by their religion, and whether Islam was suited to democratic culture. Such questions epitomized the veil as a symbol of American suspicion regarding Islam: Were Muslims seeking to dominate the West, just as they dominated their women? Were Muslims placing the West under surveillance, gazing at non-Muslims from an unseen, hidden place, just as veiled Muslim women could see but remain unseen? For instance, in their study of the semiotics of the veil, Christina von Braun and Bettina Mathes argue that the anxiety of the West over Muslim women's veiling is actually about unveiling and revealing, not only the unveiling of women's bodies, but the revelation of God's commands.[6] While the veil was originally common in Christianity and was subsequently appropriated by Muslims, the West came to equate the liberation of women with unveiling and unmasking. Von Braun and Mathes link those cultural attitudes to theological convictions: in Christianity, God is not concealed but is revealed in the body of a man, whereas Islam forbids any bodily image of God or of the Prophet Muhammad.

Was Muslim treatment of women a sign of the retrograde nature of Islam, a backward religion that has failed to modernize? *What Went Wrong?* asked the title of a 2002 book by Bernard Lewis, a prominent scholar of the Islamicate world. Other scholars and political policy organizations have sought to explain Islam's alleged failure to enter the modern world.[7] In a 2003 report for the Rand Corporation, "Civil, Democratic Islam: Partners, Resources, and Strategies," political scientist Cheryl Benard urged the promotion among Muslims of Western-style historical-critical approaches to scripture in order to encourage a less "fundamentalist" reading of the Qur'an. A critical response by anthropologist Saba Mahmood argued that Muslims should not be expected to follow Western models of religious modernization, and that the failure of Muslims to assimilate into Western countries lies with the West's skewed understanding of secularism, one that is so deeply rooted in Christian assumptions that it is inapplicable to the Muslim world.[8]

While Mahmood has been notably sympathetic to religious Muslim women, identifying agency in their piety, books critical of Islam's sexism written by Muslim women, based on their own experiences, have achieved considerable popularity in the West. Irshad Manji and Ayaan Hirsi Ali are two of the best-known authors of diatribes against Islam's treatment of women.[9] Neither distinguishes between Islam as a religion and the customs promoted in the countries in which they were raised— Manji in Kenya, Ali in Somalia. Nor do their books explore comparative dimensions with the sexism of other religions, nor historical explanations for the sexism that is certainly present in all religions. As a result, it is not always clear to all readers if the books are intended as a critique of Islam's sexism or of Islam.

Islamic feminism arrived in the United States in recent decades during the flourishing of feminist efforts to reconsider the role of gender in Judaism and Christianity, but came to widespread public attention only after the September 11 attacks and the rising concern over terrorist attacks committed in the name of Islam. As a result, Muslim feminists were frequently separated from the already well-established Christian and Jewish feminist debates and instead viewed in isolation, often to corroborate entrenched negative stereotypes of Islam. Thus, Muslim feminists experienced the conundrum of presenting a critique of Islam's sexism and a simultaneous defense of its religious legitimacy in a Western, democratic context.

This conundrum is similar to the one faced by earlier generations of Jewish feminists who sought change in women's status within Judaism during an era (nineteenth-century Europe) in which the political rights and social equality of Jews were not yet fully established. Criticizing Judaism in that era—or Islam in this era—they fear would reinforce already negative images of their respective religions in popular culture, giving fodder to anti-Semites or Islamophobes. As early as the Middle Ages, some Christians had criticized Judaism for not including women in central religious rituals (prayer quorums or rites of covenant), and some Christian theologians pointed to women's inferior status within Judaism as an area of difference in the nineteenth and early twentieth centuries.[10] Using its treatment of women as evidence, Judaism was denigrated as "oriental" and "primitive," placing Jewish feminists in a difficult position, similar to the one Muslim feminists in the United States and Europe face today. Both felt trapped in a political maze in which feminist criticism of Islam and Judaism gave fodder to Islamophobes and anti-Semites.

Rarely these days do we hear discussions of Islam and its existence in Western society without hearing negative comments about its treatment of women. Feminist theology may be dormant in modern Christian and Jewish circles, but it is a heated and passionate topic in relation to Islam. Yet the denigrations of Judaism and Islam in the Christian culture of the West are different: Judaism has long been coded as a legalistic and oppressive religion, characterized by narrow-mindedness, hypocrisy, and superciliousness, whereas Islam, which has long been viewed as a throwback to Judaism's legalism,[11] is often presented today as a religion seeking the violent overthrow of Christianity, the West, and democratic freedoms.

This political maze is fueled by a historical cultural anxiety in Christian Europe that viewed Judaism and Islam as inferior but nonetheless powerful forces that threatened to disfigure and degenerate European power. Calls to liberate Europe from Jewish influence became particularly shrill with the rise of racial theory in the second half of the nineteenth century, and reached a peak in Nazi Germany's effort to exterminate the Jews. Military opposition, particularly from the Ottoman

Empire, was translated as an Islamic threat to Christian Europe. As Albert Hourani once put it, Judaism was the theological challenge to Christianity, while Islam was the military challenge.[12]

Historical Origins of the Struggle for Women's Religious Rights

Historians debate the origins of both Muslim and Jewish feminist movements. Calls for the liberation of women within the two religions were heard during the nineteenth and early twentieth centuries as both Jews and Muslims were facing problems of political liberation—Muslims seeking the overthrow of European colonial domination and Jews seeking political emancipation as a colonized body within Europe. In both cases, wider political contexts influenced the nascent women's rights movements. The Egyptian Muslim leader Qasim Amin (1863–1908), an advocate of modernization and Western culture, is often heralded as the first Arab feminist. He insisted on women's rights, particularly in education, and also demanded an end to women's veiling and seclusion. Egypt had declined and fallen under Western domination, Amin argued, in part as a result of its suppression of women.[13] Yet by linking women's rights with his advocacy of modernization, and making the removal of the veil an affirmation of Western culture, Amin inadvertently transformed the veil into a decisive marker of Islamic identity in opposition to the West and to modernity. This in turn led to Islamist movements that revered the veil as central to Islam and a symbol of Muslim resistance to Western culture. Moreover, as feminist scholar Leila Ahmed pointed out, Amin's agenda was ultimately not feminist—empowering women and overturning patriarchy—but rather the substitution of Western androcentrism for Egyptian androcentrism.[14]

Jewish Enlightenment and, later, socialist critics of Jewish communal and religious structures often fought for women's rights, but like Amin, not always for the sake of empowering women. Within the Jewish context, support for women's rights was similarly intertwined with the position of Jews in relation to European (Christian) culture. Jewish socialists and Zionists, for example, had other political goals, and positions of political leadership were firmly in men's hands. Moreover, the emancipation of "Jews" was sometimes limited to men: While Jews were permitted entry into German universities in the early nineteenth century, for example, women (Jewish and Gentile) were excluded until the 1890s. Some European feminist organizations did not admit Jewish women as members, and some Jewish communities did not permit women to vote in communal elections until the 1920s. Early Jewish efforts to redress gender imbalance attempted to enhance women's educational opportunities and position within the Jewish community, creating social service and charitable organizations run by women, rather than overturn male domination. The Jüdischer Frauenbund (Jewish Women's Organization) was founded in Germany in 1904 by a social worker, Bertha Pappenheim, and strove to win voting rights for women within Jewish communal affairs, but offices of communal leadership remained in the hands of men.[15] Within the United States, Rebecca Gratz founded the nineteenth-century Sunday School movement that created new roles for women in Jewish education, even as the rabbinate remained a male institution until the 1970s and 1980s.

While women's rights within the larger Jewish and Muslim societies were the focus of early feminist activity, equality within the religious sphere has become central to Jewish and Muslim feminists in recent decades. Religious questions began by challenging aspects of religious law, particularly women's rights within marriage and divorce. Soon, however, the issue of authority came to the fore: Who had the right to determine matters of religious law, which had traditionally been firmly in the hands of men, both in Islam and Judaism? Those questions, in turn, led to theological challenges: Can there be equality for women within a religion whose texts, institutions, and even its God have been consistently male since its inception? Is a feminist Islam or a feminist Judaism a contradiction in terms? Are changes in religious law and the addition of women's scriptural commentaries going to create fundamental alterations in the religion or merely mask an incorrigibly masculinist religion?

The Orientalism Factor

In other words, women have long served as a template for Jewish and Muslim apologists seeking acceptance in European and American societies, and as lightning rods for those seeking to exclude Jews and Muslims. The treatment of women became an index for the degree of "orientalism" marking Judaism in the nineteenth century, and of "fanaticism" and "irrationality" marking Islam in more recent decades. Charges that Judaism was an "Oriental" religion were used to justify the exclusion of Jews from full membership in European society, and movements to reform traditional synagogue services were motivated in part by the desire to undermine that "Oriental" image of Judaism as stagnant, primitive, and non-European. Yet this also carried a Jewish challenge to European self-understanding as a Christian society. Thus the resistance aroused by Judaism (and later by Islam) was a response to demands for a reconfiguration of European self-perception: a dislocation of its adherence to Christianity and a rejection of Christianity's own Jewish roots, at times symbolized via Europe's gender identity. Recent claims that Europe is being "Islamicized" and becoming a "Eurabia," thus losing its Christian identity, are heightened by debates over legislation banning Muslim women's body coverings from public sight. Control of the gaze over the female body—that is, protection of the power of the male gaze—means rejecting the possibility of being viewed by Muslim women who keep themselves from being viewed. The Christian concern to control this gaze is revealed, for example, in the angry nineteenth-century theological responses to Jewish scholarship on Christian origins, and in the writings of European travelers to Muslim countries who spoke of the denigrated status of Muslim women. In their study of the veil, von Braun and Mathes argue that Western denunciations of Muslim women's veiling as oppressive to women function as a projection of Western anxieties: "[T]he physical violence to which the veiled Muslim woman is believed to be subjected is an expression of the symbolic violence to which the exposed Western woman is subject—a form of violence which she can neither prove nor make visible without being taken for a liar. Thus condemned to self-deception, she identifies and combats this violence in the face of 'the other woman.'"[16]

Such projections and the anxieties to which they give rise are not new. The decline of the Ottoman Empire and the rise of European colonialism diminished the sense of a Muslim military threat, but they did not diminish anxieties over Islamic sexual influences over the West. In a revealing passage of his memoir, *Tristes Tropiques*, published in 1955, the noted anthropologist Claude Levi-Strauss wrote,

Now I can see, beyond Islam, to India, but it is the India of Buddha, before Muhammad. For me as a European, and because I am a European, Muhammad intervenes with uncouth clumsiness, between our thought and Indian doctrines that are very close to it, in such a way as to prevent East and West joining hands, as they might well have done, in harmonious collaboration. . . . If the West traces its internal tensions back to their source, it will see that Islam, by coming between Buddhism and Christianity, Islamized us at the time when the West, by taking part in the crusades, was involved in opposing it and therefore came to resemble it, instead of undergoing—had Islam never come into being—a slow process of osmosis with Buddhism, which would have Christianized us still further, and would have made us all the more Christian in that we would have gone back beyond Christianity itself. It was then that the West lost the opportunity of remaining female.[17]

The alleged "Islamization of the West" was not a military conquest, but a sexual and religious misfortune, according to Levi-Strauss, preventing the West from being fully Christianized and female. Islam is so powerful and so dangerous, the statement implies, that it can alter Europe's gender. Such fears were present in the medieval Christian notion of a "feminized Orient" that led by the sixteenth century to a belief that Oriental men are effeminate.[18] Thus, contemporary fears of a "Eurabia" are not new, but have a long history in European Christian culture.

Jewish scholars have not always shared these views. On the contrary, when it came to Islam, European Jews saw both Europe and Islam differently. Long aware of the good treatment they received in Muslim Spain in contrast to their persecution in Christian Spain, their welcome by the Ottoman Empire in contrast to pogroms and anti-Semitism in Central Europe, Jews developed an affinity for Islam. Indeed, it was Jewish scholars who created the field of Islamic Studies in the nineteenth century and flocked to it. Gustav Weil went to Egypt in the 1830s to teach and study and examine Arabic manuscripts; in 1833 Abraham Geiger published a widely praised book delineating the rabbinic parallels to the Qur'an; in the 1860s the Hungarian linguist Arminius Vambery wrote highly popular travelogues about his years in Turkey, Persia, and Central Asia; Ignaz Goldziher was warmly received at al-Azhar

University in the 1870s; Josef Horovitz was professor of Arabic at a Muslim University for seven years, from 1907 to 1914.[19]

These Jewish scholars demonstrated close parallels between Islam and Judaism: that the Qur'an draws from rabbinic literature; that the hadith, like the Talmud, has chains of attribution to teachers of earlier generations; that both Judaism and Islam insist on strict monotheism, reject anthropomorphism, and place religious law at the center of their religious traditions. Indeed, synagogues were built in Moorish architecture because Islam was able to signify Judaism in Europe, whereas Gothic architecture masks Judaism as Christianity. In these and other ways, Islam became a template for presenting aspects of Judaism to the European Christian audience. In so doing, Jewish scholars promoted a very conservative element: they praised what they saw as the strong family values in Islam, its strict sexual morality, its women in their proper subservient position—all this in an era when Jewish women in Europe were agitating for a change in their status. Thus the Jewish identification with Islam had an antifeminist undertone.

Contemporary Relations

In recent years, however, what once united us often divides us. The growth of an ugly and very public anti-Semitism in Muslim countries may not have arisen because of the Qur'an, but neither have Islamic religious leaders quenched it. Tensions over the state of Israel have exacerbated the problem. The simultaneous rise of a Jewish polemical literature claiming that Islam is a religion of violence and anti-Semitism, the extensive Jewish financial support of Islamophobic organizations,[20] and claims that Islam is a religion with a death culture have created the spectacle of Jews embracing Muslim feminists in an alliance to attack Islam. When Muslim and Jewish feminists examine shared problems and concerns we find much in common and insights that can be mutually beneficial. Feminist comparisons of the two religions can lead us to greater insights and more subtle interpretations. Both groups of feminists negotiate with a massive body of religious law and commentaries that have been composed over centuries; develop new interpretations of scripture that provide a basis for women's rights within the family and society; and struggle with figures of authority who are invariably men, and communities that are not always sympathetic to feminist complaints and demands for change. As someone who has been active for decades in Jewish feminist concerns, I am appalled that some Jewish groups have embraced Muslim feminists as critics of Islam while ignoring criticisms of Judaism articulated by Jewish feminists. I have found that both of us, Muslim and Jewish feminists, worry about our religions that allow men to dominate as our prophets and judges, legal authorities and scriptural interpreters; why we say that "God is neither male nor female, He is above gender." At times we become cynical, aware that men are the subjects, women the objects of religion, aware that we are relegated to the back of the prayer house, whether literally or metaphorically, not for our sakes but for the sake of men whose spiritual needs inevitably take precedence over ours. Ultimately, we wonder if we can have a viable, vibrant spiritual life as feminists of faith. At the same time, we are conscious that our critique of sexism in Judaism and Islam can be easily manipulated by those who wish to defame our religions for their own political ends.

An Orthodox rabbi once explained that feminism was the result of plumbing and electricity: Because women now have so much free time, they want to enter the male domain and study rabbinic texts. Of course, it is not study for its own sake that women seek. Jewish women began to master rabbinic texts because we wanted to bring about a transformation of Judaism and in many ways we have succeeded. Women are now ordained rabbis, and a century after mixed seating was introduced in liberal synagogues, women have equal ritual status in virtually all non-Orthodox congregations in the United States and Great Britain. For Muslim women, the immediate goals have focused less on leading prayers or abolishing the separate seating arrangements at mosques than it has on studying classical Islamic texts. Indeed, in recent years there has been a remarkable and much-studied massive grassroots movement among Muslim women to study the Qur'an with women teachers—the so-called "mosque movement" described by anthropologist Saba Mahmood.[21] The goal of those women, as interpreted by Mahmood, is to learn prescribed Islamic religious behavior and the cultivation of an inner spiritual life: how to be a good Muslim and shape a Muslim society. In those women's study groups at mosques, there is no attention to historical-critical

methods, of course, nor to feminist theory; the approach is pious and
the assumption is that the Qur'an is the word of God and therefore
inherently just and right. However, simply by engaging in Qur'an
study at mosques, women can exert agency within themselves, Mahmood argues, and attain tools to exert agency within their families.
Indeed, these women's commitment to Islamic piety is impressive and
has parallels among ultra-Orthodox Jewish women, as Tamar El-Or
and Rivka Neriya-Ben Shachar have shown.[22] Yet there are also narrow constrictions on the lives of women willing to live within the
constraints of religious legal systems developed and regulated by men.
According to Mahmood, these Muslim women say that they want
to know God's will and believe that God is pleased that they wear a
veil. Their certainty seems to be derived not only from a study of the
divinely revealed Qur'an but also from their private religious experiences at prayer. El-Or describes ultra-Orthodox women as "educated
but ignorant," trained through study not to question the rubrics of
their pietistic communities and the male authority regulating them.
The agency of women in pietistic circles may have increased through
their knowledge of sacred scriptures, but their inner subjectivity, guiding their choices of how to spend their lives, may well be suppressed.

Feminisms, God, and Law

Pietistic circles, whether within Judaism or Islam, claim to know God's
will and strive to fulfill it. In so doing, they are not only acting in accordance with divine command but also attempting to give God pleasure.
Hoping to please God through piety can become a dangerous theological and political position. In her recent book, *For Love of the Father*,
psychoanalyst Ruth Stein argues that the homoeroticism fostered by the
religiosity of fundamentalist groups such as the one led by Mohammad
Attah, viewed suicidal conflagration as a way to give God an orgasm.[23]
Piety can become a justification for violating social boundaries, even
life itself. All religious communities today confront the fanatics within:
those who will murder, torture, and bring world destruction because
they respect no limits. Yet the desire to know and love God can also be
a path to protesting the injustice and exploitation that often conceal-
themselves in religious garb.

There are additional elements to the relationship with God that feminist analysis has called to our attention. The urge for intimacy with an exclusively male God through prayer and study is not only about achieving power or agency or piety or virtue. We as women enter a male realm of texts and piety permeated with a male homoeroticism that is denied but not entirely repressed. Homoeroticism pervades the male-God relationship and the male-male relationships of study houses and communal worship.[24] Religious women in mosques form relationships with other women, outside the family, a horizontal empowerment that offers support and encouragement, though no political or legal change of status. By contrast, religious men enjoy a "vertically phallic eros," as Ruth Stein writes, a phallicism by proxy, because God is the phallus of these men, their source of power and authority, inner well-being, and purification.[25] The heterosexuality that is demanded by religious communities thus has to be created within that homoerotic field of religion, posing difficulties for men as well as women. How do we as women, lesbian and straight, function in that kind of homoerotic religious realm?

Muslim feminists have identified such problems within Islam. Fatima Mernissi has argued that women and men are kept separate because heterosexual love is perceived as too dangerous to the social order established by God. Indeed, she argues that it is not feminism but heterosexuality, the bonds between women and men, which is perceived as the real threat to Islam, since heterosexual love disrupts the homosocial and homoerotic order of male-dominated religions.[26] Her argument applies easily to the male-only rabbinic order of Judaism as well.

Indeed, many efforts to liberalize Jewish religious practice have been to de-eroticize Judaism in order to promote women to positions of authority and leadership. As Judaism began to liberalize in the nineteenth century, the focus on bodies and their associated rituals were abandoned—laws concerning sexual purity and immersion in the mikveh fell into disuse, along with observance of kosher food laws, body movements during prayer in synagogues, as well as hair coverings for women and men, and ritual fringes and hair sidelocks for men. The suppression of physicality and the erotic that it often engendered did not necessarily lead to gender equality, but it created a new array of problems for women.

Jewish feminism in many circumstances has encouraged equality for women under the guise of male imitation. For example, to qualify for the rabbinate in Conservative Judaism, women rabbinical students have to take on the ritual obligations of men—such as putting on tefillin (phylacteries) daily—as if religious Jewish women, who had never put on tefillin, had not really been religious all these centuries. Putting on tefillin is ambiguous: does it empower women or does it reconfirm the perception that Judaism is a male phenomenon and women striving for piety must imitate male acts? In a different venture, in recent decades Jewish feminists, while critical of the Jewish legal regulations governing sexuality, have been reviving the mikveh (ritual bath immersion) as an important spiritual experience for women. At the same time, they often disregard or reject outright the strict laws regulating the separation of wives from husbands for the period of niddah—menstruation plus seven days. The affirmation of mikveh as a space for women's spiritual inspiration divorces the affirmation of women's bodies from the male regulations that have "owned" them since biblical law.

Women may have parity with men in many non-Orthodox religious settings, at least heterosexual women, but they still encounter patronizing attitudes and inequities in pay and responsibility, as well as homophobia. Recent studies indicate that women rabbis, for instance, are not paid salaries equal to those of men, and that startlingly few women stand in positions of high authority within secular Jewish organizations. On the other hand, since the 1970s numerous institutions have been established in which women are able to receive formal instruction in rabbinic texts. One important result is that women now interpret issues of Jewish law and provide advice for women, particularly on matters of family law and menstrual purity, within Orthodox and non-Orthodox settings.

Similarly, the mosque movement is creating prominent women who serve as teachers, legal advisors, and preachers throughout the Muslim world, sometimes with the title of Sheikha. Dr. Su'ad Saleh, professor of jurisprudence in the women's division of al-Azhar University, issues fatwas, religious judgments, and has applied for years to be recognized as a Muftiyah, a member of the official board of muftis, but has been voted down each time[27]—but at least she receives the dignity of a vote; a haredi (ultra-Orthodox) woman would never even come

JEWISH AND MUSLIM FEMINIST THEOLOGIES IN DIALOGUE >> 31

into question as a possible member of a bet din (court of Jewish law), head of a yeshiva, or as a Hasidic rebbe. In the modern Orthodox world, however, there have been important developments, with women acquiring sophisticated textual abilities in rabbinic literature at women's yeshivot, and functioning as halakhic advisors to women. Recently, the title of Rabbah had to be withdrawn from the modern Orthodox Sara Hurwitz, who has served for years as madricha ruhanit, a spiritual counselor, of a synagogue in New York. But it is clear that the title will be restored in a few years and women will be ordained Orthodox rabbis in our lifetime, an extraordinary achievement. In fact, there are no impediments within sharia or halakha to a Muftiyah or a Rabbah; the impediments have been political, cultural, and traditional, not based on religious law. Still, it is a rare moment when a woman leads public worship at a mosque.

If the impediments to women in religion are extralegal—theological and sociological—then feminists must examine how patriarchy came into existence in Islam and Judaism and how it has retained such a tenacious hold. Moreover, how are we as feminists to understand God, prophecy, revelation, tradition, the nature of interpretation, spiritual life, prayer, ritual, religious leadership, and communal institutions, if they are all defined by men?

Parallel Feminist Explanations of Religious Patriarchy

Jewish and Muslim feminists have arrived at explanations for patriarchy that often sound quite similar. For Fatima Mernissi, patriarchy is the fault of the Jews, of pagan Arabs, and the failure of Islam to conquer fully the pre-Islamic "jahiliyya mentality."[28] Blu Greenberg views rabbinic law as improving the status of women over the prevailing Greco-Roman era.[29] Leila Ahmed argues that the Qur'an promotes an equality lost during the Abbasid Empire, as Islam was influenced by Byzantine Christianity and Sasanian Zoroastrianism as it conquered Syria and Iraq: "Islam's ethical vision . . . is stubbornly egalitarian, including with respect to the sexes."[30] The problem is not Islam per se, but external influences; not the Qur'an, but the way it came to be interpreted. Early Islam, Ahmed argues, saw women participating in the public realm, both on the battlefield and in positions of religious authority.

The Malaysian Muslim feminist, Zainah Anwar, calls for a return to the revolutionary spirit of Islamic origins;[31] similarly, Rachel Adler notes that even in the Bible, God places the covenant above the law that He proclaimed.[32] Ziba Mir-Hosseini calls for a distinction between divine revelation and human interpretation of the Qur'an; Judith Plaskow notes that women were present together with men at the moment of the revelation at Mt. Sinai, and that women must now engage in the interpretation of that revelation according to their experience and understanding.[33] Amina Wadud simply declares that patriarchy is *shirk* (heresy);[34] Susannah Heschel declares that sexism cannot be the will of God.[35]

For Mernissi and Asma Barlas, the only weapon for human rights and women's rights in the Islamic world is religion—there can be no meaningful change without the Qur'an.[36] Yet Amira Sonbol has pointed out that it is not always religion that is the problem, but those aspects of Islam granted power by an individual government; Jordan, she says, took the most patriarchal laws of the Hanafi and Malikite legal systems, making personal status laws ultimately a construct of the modern state, even if they are expressed via sharia.[37] We see similar problems in Egypt and in the state of Israel: the secular prime minister, David Ben Gurion, made a political deal with the Orthodox rabbinate, granting Orthodox rabbis exclusive control over Jewish marriage and divorce. Jewish law governing contracts and business, for example, is not enforced; there are no mashgichim (religious supervisors) in the banks. So who exactly is responsible for men bribing women to grant them a divorce, religious leaders or the state that empowers them? The line between state and rabbis, the secular and the religious, is not clear. Indeed, as Amnon Raz-Krakotzkin has argued, the distinction of the religious and secular into separate political realms is inappropriate: "Secularization meant the nationalization of religious-messianic conceptions, not their replacement. God excluded from the discourse, yet divine promise continued to direct political activity and to serve as a source of legitimacy."[38]

For some feminists, it is the experience of piety that is central, while for others it is the theological coherence of the religion that matters. We agree, however, that patriarchy is a politics of sexual differentiation that privileges males. But just how intrinsic is patriarchy to our religion? Most Muslim feminists seem to agree that the Qur'an does not endorse patriarchy. There are three aspects to the argument: Tawhid, divine unity, means that sovereignty is indivisible, so that male privilege or men as rulers over women is *shirk*. God is just and never transgresses another's rights. Second, when men transgress women's rights they commit *zulm* (injustice through exploitation). If we read the Qur'an as advocating patriarchy, we ascribe *zulm* to God. Third, God is unlike anything created so that the pronoun "He" is a faulty linguistic convention. These three points can be easily applied to Judaism, since its theological assumptions are so close to those of Islam; Jewish counterparts to the insistence on divine unity and uniqueness, and the prohibition against injustice are central to Judaism as well as Islam. Unlike Christianity, neither Islam nor Judaism has the problem of a divinity that is also a male human.[39]

Muslim feminists, like Jewish and Christian feminists, often rely on an argument from origins. As the Malaysian Muslim feminist Zainah Anwar writes, "At the time of the Revelation, Islam's message was revolutionary in spirit and gave women rights not available in most cultures of the era. It is time to reassert this revolutionary spirit."[40] In an analogous fashion, Bernadette Brooten has demonstrated that in the ancient synagogue, women served as leaders and did not sit on a women's balcony.[41] So why are we doing it today?

The search for the origins of patriarchy in religion can lead to blame: Christian feminists claiming Jesus as a feminist and blaming Jewish influence on early Christianity for the patriarchy within the religion. Recent scholarship by Gideon Libson has demonstrated that Jewish women benefited from Islam's influence on Jewish law; during the Geonic period, the rabbis decreed that a woman who has lost her ketubah (marriage certificate) would receive a "mohar," a monetary sum based on the ketubot of her kinswomen.[42] Since that custom "is unattested anywhere in the Talmudic literature," it is likely that "the source of the Geonic practice of allowing a woman who has lost her ketubah deed to receive an increment of the ketubah money . . . must be sought in Islamic law or in the practice of Arab society as bound by the law of Islam."[43] The Geonim also came to allow a woman to sue for divorce in a Jewish court, like her Muslim counterparts, instead of having to wait for a man to issue a divorce.[44] Because Islamic law was more liberal than Jewish law, some Jewish women were drawn to convert in order to divorce their husbands.

Amina Wadud argues that patriarchy was introduced into Islam "from the satanic notion of *istikbar* (thinking of oneself as better than another)."[45] Sexism contradicts our understanding of God, and the sexism of the Bible and Talmud is the primary argument against accepting it as divine revelation. Can God will an inferior status to women? Or do we have to concede that scripture is just and right and good because it is revealed by God? The Ash'ari school within Islam holds that justice is derived from revealed texts and is not subject to external verification. The Mu'tazilite school, by contrast, argues that our notion of justice is innate, rational, and exists independently of scripture. That is, as Ziba Mir-Hosseini writes, justice cannot be religious; it is religion that has to be just.[46] Notions of the humane, of justice, do not arise solely by reading the text, and the conflict between the text and the humane is not textual in origin, nor is it resolved by appeal to texts, though textual support may be a crucial political and rhetorical device in bringing about change. Rachel Adler has pointed out that sometimes contradiction stands at the heart of Judaism: in the metaphor used by the prophet Hosea, God takes back Israel as his wife, despite her adulterous desertion and in violation of God's own law, in Deuteronomy, that a man may not remain with a wife who has committed adultery. Adler suggests reading the text as "a struggle within the divine consciousness, in which God is torn between the maintenance of law and its constructive violation."[47] It is the very contradiction within the metaphor, she writes, that stands at the theological heart of the prophetic message: "the metaphor that preserves the covenant breaks the law."[48] Religion and justice may stand in contradiction, but the humane must always triumph.

Of course, we should also remember the magnificent words of Mary Daly, who rejected the need for precedent and said, in response to claims that Jesus was a feminist, "Fine. Wonderful. But even if he wasn't, I am."[49]

Reading Scripture

Radically new ways of reading the Bible, such as that of Rachel Adler, involve not only an encounter with the scriptural text, but also an encounter with centuries of men's interpretations. For Muslim

feminists, the issue is reading the Qur'an by means of Qur'anic principles: arriving at a sound theological understanding of God means
understanding the Qur'an as divine self-disclosure: how God describes
God in the Qur'an. Feminists have to unpack the history of interpretation to expose and eradicate patriarchal misinterpretations, not an easy
hermeneutical task, as Elisabeth Schuessler-Fiorenza, in particular, has
pointed out.[50] Feminists work to expose the textualization of misogyny by questioning the politics of the text. What are the most effective hermeneutical techniques to read religious texts? On this point,
Jewish feminists today are frequently more radical and experimen-
tal than Muslim feminists. For example, a Mishnah in Ketubot, the
laws of marriage contracts, tells us that all wives are obliged to weave
wool, even if they can afford servants to do it. One feminist approach,
by Tal Ilan, reads the passage this way: "The idea that keeping busy
with spinning and weaving protects a woman's chastity and also demonstrates a woman's diligence and high quality originates in classical
Greece. . . . [Women] helped support their households and worked in
professions in which they had special knowledge and training."[51] She
enumerates what rabbinic Judaism permits women: selling dough, tex-
tiles, olives, working as innkeepers, hairdressers, professional mourn-
ers, and midwives. By contrast, Miriam Peskowitz asks what is concealed by the text: by mandating weaving, the rabbis are reassuring
husbands that their wives are under control and not betraying them.
But the law in the Mishnah, Peskowitz writes, "effectively hides from
view the very men whom it privileges and whose advantages it will
extend. This position hides both the husband who controls and owns
the wife's labors, and the rabbis who imagine themselves as legisla-
tors, but who were, simultaneously, husbands themselves. It makes an
economy of discipline and control seem benevolent, and for a woman's
own good."[52] Laws about wives are simultaneously about husbands,
and their goal is empowering and protecting their privileges under
the guise of concern for women, marriage, and the family. Such an
approach to religious texts is rare in Islamic feminism. Instead, they
tend to follow the example of Tal Ilan, looking for positive statements
about women or precedents of women's actions that are mentioned
in the Qur'an and hadith, rather than exposing the underlying power
politics at work.

Sexuality

Interpretation is crucial not simply as a matter of communal author-ity, but as a vehicle for women's minds. At issue, as Leslie Adelson has described in a different context, is the meaning of a woman's mouth. If the vagina represents sex, then the mouth represents gender.[53] In a famous essay, "Castration or Decapitation?," Helene Cixous points out that under patriarchy, women are undermined less through sexual dis-advantage than by the rejection of their minds.[54] The denial of wom-en's participation in the intellectual adventure of shaping Judaism and Islam, the muzzle on the mouth, is the legacy we are trying to overcome.

Women's sexuality has at times been demonized, and at other times respected and even valorized in both traditional and modern Islam and Judaism. However, the two religions construct eroticism in differ-ent ways. For example, sexual intercourse is forbidden in both religions when a woman is menstruating, but rabbinic law demands an addi-tional seven "clean" days following menstruation before intercourse may be resumed, and during that entire period of time, absolutely no physical contact between wife and husband is permitted, lest it lead to arousal and sexual relations. Even a friendly handshake is considered dangerous during the days of forbidden sexuality.

Qur'an 2:22 reads: "And if they ask you about menstruation, say: It is an impurity. So keep away from women during their menstruation and do not approach them until they are clean. Once they get clean go to them as Allah commanded you. Allah loves the repentant and loves those who purify themselves." According to a hadith, however, physi-cal contact during menstruation is permitted: "The Prophet instructed 'Ā'isha while she was menstruating, 'Uncover your thigh.' She said: And I did so, and he placed his cheek and his chest against my thigh. I leaned over him till he warmed up, for he ached from the cold." This stands in contrast to Judaism's prohibitions, which attempt to prevent lust from overcoming a married couple, leading them to violate the law. Islamic tradition seems to assume that no man would want to have intercourse with a menstruating woman, so there is no danger of physi-cal, even intimate contact. The comparison also raises the specter of the erotic dimension: Islamic law assumes that erotic desire can be held safely in check, or that a menstruating woman exudes no erotic appeal.

Jewish law, by enacting stringent regulations forbidding physical contact or erotic arousal, assumes or even creates the desire and arousal. For example, a wife who is "niddah" (impure by reason of menstruation or childbirth) may not pour wine into her husband's glass in his presence because that is considered arousing to the man.

Given the massive attention in both Judaism and Islam to regulating sexual relations, Fatima Mernissi may be correct that women and men are kept separate because heterosexual love is considered too dangerous and threatening to the religious order.[55] The matter becomes even more complex when we recognize that the religious texts and traditions of both Judaism and Islam have been developed over the centuries by conventicles of male religious scholars, studying and praying together day after day for their entire lives. Not only do they achieve male hegemony over scriptural interpretation and legal adjudication, but they also create an arena of homosociality among themselves and in their relationship with God, informed and enlivened by homoerotic tensions. Carving out a system of mandated heterosexual marriage within that homosocial realm was no simple task.

Both religions understand that women, like men, have strong sexual desires that must be held in check, and both consider husbands obligated to satisfy their wives' sexual needs. Yet while the woman must be satisfied both physically and emotionally, according to the medieval Hebrew text, *The Holy Letter*, it is her mouth as the portal of her mind that remains the constant problem.[56] Traditional Jewish and Muslim cultures may have had a positive, even lusty attitude toward heterosexual relationships and at times tolerated or even celebrated homosexual relationships, but both have long been stringent about maintaining boundaries excluding women's intellectual and spiritual participation in the religious community.

For that reason, women's study of religious texts has assumed a central position in feminist theology. Within the Jewish world, numerous institutions, formal and informal, have sprung up since the 1980s that offer training to women in rabbinic texts and classical commentaries. Women now hold doctorates and professorships in the field of Jewish Studies and a vast literature of Jewish women's studies has come into being. Access to texts that were once the exclusive preserve of men is now available to women. As a result, more and more women now serve as advisors on matters of Jewish law, particularly in areas where women have often experienced discrimination or humiliation, such as marriage and divorce regulations and the laws of menstrual purity.

Within Islam, a similar movement is emerging, of study groups for women that often meet in mosques and now carry the moniker, "mosque movement." As in Judaism, Muslim women are especially concerned with examining Qur'anic passages that deal with family law, including sexual relations, inheritance and property, and women's rights. In both cases, women are certainly empowered in relation to men by knowing, firsthand, the religious texts pertaining to their lives, without having to ask male authorities what the texts say. On the other hand, such pietistic study does not include the kinds of historical-critical methods that constitute the world of academic scholarship, nor the theoretical frameworks of postmodernism, feminism, or other theories that would reconfigure the texts and challenge them. The advent of the so-called Arab Spring, with its widespread political activism among women, has brought new calls by women to reconsider both religious and secular laws, particularly in the context of democracy.

In addition to acquiring knowledge, study of religious texts is also a religious experience and an entry into a formal structure of religious authority and control; the question is whether the women who are entering those studies are being further subjugated or are being empowered. Analyzing Haredi (ultra-Orthodox) women taking special classes for women in Jewish religious texts, the anthropologist Tamar El-Or concluded that the study program kept those women "educated but ignorant." That is, they were taught texts to justify their subjugated role in relation to men and to increase the piety that made them accept that role.

Analyses of the mosque movement, particularly Saba Mahmood's recent book, *Politics of Piety*, raise questions about how to study religious experience. Too often social scientists have transformed religious piety into something political, psychological, or sociological, Mahmood notes, and the authentic voice of religious experience is lost. Women's agency is not suppressed by religious communities, Mahmood argues, but is enhanced by the power women acquire from firsthand knowledge of the religious traditions that govern the lives of their families and communities, and by meeting with like-minded women at the mosque.

Piety has also been a powerful tool for women to bring about social change, as the Christian temperance movement in the United States, for instance, illustrates. As feminist scholars, we want to respect that the religious experience of women can be empowering, yet we also argue that while these women may attain agency through their piety and study, what of their subjectivity, their mouths and minds? How will social and legal transformation come about if their piety requires acquiescence to male institutions and intellectual structures?

The intensive study of religious texts by women is one of the most notable feminist developments we have in common as Muslims and Jews. But are the virtues cultivated—humility, shyness, modesty, as Mahmood reports—useful to women? Does modesty help us fight for child custody in a divorce battle? Is shyness what Jewish women needed in Auschwitz? Unfortunately, Mahmood ignores the long tradition of feminist theology, such as Valerie Saiving's argument that virtue is class- and gender-dependent, that humility ought to be cultivated by the men who run this world, whereas virtue for women would be self-esteem and a little hubris.[57]

Apologetics also intervenes in other ways. In feminist scholarship, Jewish women are often presented as the best Jews, the most loyal, the last to assimilate. In reading texts, we are at most offering feminist strategies for dealing with male-authored ideas; ultimately, we have to recognize that all the classical rabbinic texts and medieval philosophical and mystical literature were composed by men.

Conclusion

The feminist movement is foremost about women's rights and empowerment. At the same time, it is clear that gender operates on many levels, from institutional organizations to imagined fantasies. The position of women within a religion symbolizes its understanding of God and also organizes its complex relationship to the larger societal context. Gender also plays a key role in how a religion, especially a minority religion, is perceived by those who stand outside, as the quote from Claude Levi-Strauss illustrates. Finally, as much as a religion may provide theological, social, and political teachings, it also enters the realm of the intimate in the lives of its adherents, regulating experiences of sexualities, bodily functions, marital relationships, and emotions ranging from love to disgust.

Just as Islam and Judaism became tools used by Europe to configure its gender identity, the oppression of women sometimes expresses a hidden aspect of the religious community's collective sense of itself. I want to conclude with the example of the agunah, the chained woman whose husband refuses to grant her a get (a certificate of divorce); only a husband can divorce his wife under Jewish law. Even if she has no contact with the husband, even if he has abandoned her, she remains locked in marriage to him and cannot free herself.

To be chained to a man and yet in exile from him is a situation that Jewish law could have remedied as easily as rabbis banned polygamy in the early Middle Ages. Instead, women who want a get from their husbands are frequently pressured to renounce alimony or child custody in exchange for a get.

The divorce laws that create the agunah function as a kind of stonewall around the lives of those Jewish women who continue to accept Jewish law as determinative, or who cannot, for family or social reasons, leave its rubrics. Perhaps the agunah persists because she represents something deeper, more existential, about our self-understanding as Jews as a people in exile. Jews are wanderers in a physical diaspora, but are also in a spiritual diaspora, linked to God yet distant and not yet redeemed by God. Can the sense of Jewish exile ever be overcome? The state of Israel was supposed to solve the national question, yet that question remains profoundly unresolved today. Jews have lived in exile for so long that it has become almost impossible to release ourselves from that state of being, whether through a political Zionism that does not involve isolation and exile, or from a cultural redemption that liberates women and transforms Judaism. Until then, the agunah remains a symbol for the collective Jewish existential experience of exile and a concrete example of women's lack of freedom regardless of piety, study, or acquiescence.

The context for Muslim women is different. Long accustomed to living under Muslim rulers, the migration of Muslims to Europe and the United States has posed new challenges to the transnational nature of Islamic identity. In addition, the widespread political challenges within the Islamicate world, with calls for democracy on the one hand, and the imposition of strict Islamic law on the other, have offered new and vastly different contexts for the interpretation of Muslim women's rights, identities, and voices of authority. In countries where the removal of women's head coverings was once viewed as a gesture of liberation from colonialism, veils are reappearing, even as women serve in the government and professions. The outcome of these rapid changes for the feminist movement will not be known for years.

Muslim women are wrestling with the word, with the text of the Qur'an, God's word, but it is a word that has been received and transmitted entirely by men. Women study the Qur'an to cultivate piety and also to earn respect, but what they imbibe, memorize, and repeat is, at least in the tradition of medieval rationalist philosophy, the word of God spoken in human language, divine revelation as modified for human comprehension.[58] Muslim women have become figures representing Islam as a whole, often used as symbols for what non-Muslims regard as Islam's alleged failure to modernize. A Muslim woman who covers her hair as a sign of religious identity and commitment may instead be viewed negatively, as a symbol for Islam as a regressive, oppressive religion. Thus, Muslim women are expected to bring change in their status as women within Islam as a prerequisite for winning acceptance for Islam in contemporary non-Muslim societies. For other Muslim women, hair coverings may represent an affirmation of identity or a protection of virtue in a male society. What was once a feminist effort to win greater religious engagement for women must guard against becoming a political effort to diminish the public expression of religious identity, hinder women's ability to move easily in the public sphere, or even serve as a tool of cultural imperialism.

Jewish and Muslim feminists are wrestling with the teachings and symbols of their religions, with what the text both conceals and empowers. For both, religious change has to be undertaken with an eye to the political consequences, which may not conform to goals that are feminist, nonviolent, and constructive. There is a hadith that says that the learned man's ink is as precious as the martyr's blood. Let us hope that the feminist movements, Jewish and Muslim, in the sweeping social and theological transformations they are creating, will fulfill the prophetic nature of that hadith.

NOTES

1. I would like to thank Mona Abaza for arranging important conversations for me with feminists in Cairo during February 2010. Riham Bazi, Allison Church, Heba Raouf, Bettina Mathes, and Christina von Braun have also been important interlocutors on these issues and I am grateful to them. My gratitude as well to Eliana Piper, my assistant through the Presidential Scholar program at Dartmouth College.

2. Faegheh Shirazi, *The Veil Unveiled: The Hijab in Modern Culture* (Gainesville, Fla.: University Press of Florida, 2001).

3. Susannah Heschel, "Sind Juden Männer? Können Frauen jüdisch sein? Die gesellschaftliche Definition des männlichen/weiblichen Körpers," *Der Schejne Jid: Das Bild des 'jüdischen Körpers' in Mythos und Ritual*, ed. Sander L. Gilman, Robert Jütte, and Gabriele Kohlbauer-Fritz (Vienna: Picus Verlag, 1998), 86–96.

4. Gideon Libson, *Jewish and Islamic Law: A Comparative Study of Custom during the Geonic Period* (Cambridge, Mass.: Harvard University Press, 2003).

5. Wajahat Ali, Eli Clifton, Matthew Duss, Lee Fang, Scott Keyes, and Faiz Shakir, *Fear, Inc.: The Roots of the Islamophobia Network in America*, Report of the Center for American Progress, published August 26, 2011.

6. Christina von Braun and Bettina Mathes, *Verschleierte Wirklichkeit: Die Frau, der Islam und der West* (Berlin: Aufbau Verlag, 2007).

7. Bernard Lewis, *What Went Wrong? Western Impact and Middle Eastern Response* (New York: Oxford University Press, 2002); Dan Diner, *Lost in the Sacred: Why the Muslim World Stood Still* (Princeton: Princeton University Press, 2009).

8. Saba Mahmood, "Secularism, Hermeneutics, and Empire: The Politics of Islamic Reformation," *Public Culture* 18: 2 (2006), 323–347. She is responding to the Rand Corporation report by Cheryl Benard, "Civil Democratic Islam: Partners, Resources, and Strategies" (2003).

9. Irshad Manji, *The Trouble with Islam: A Muslim's Call for Reform in Her Faith* (New York: St. Martin's Press, 2004); Ayaan Hirsi Ali, *Infidel* (New York: Free Press, 2007).

10. For a discussion of Christian theological anti-Judaism, especially within Christian feminism, see Judith Plaskow, "Feminist Anti-Judaism and the Christian God," *Journal of Feminist Studies in Religion*, 7, 2 (Fall 1991), 99–108; Katharina von Kellenbach, *Anti-Judaism in Feminist Religious Writings* (Atlanta, Ga.: Scholars Press, 1994); Susannah Heschel, "Configurations of Patriarchy, Judaism and Nazism in German Feminist Thought," *Gender and Judaism*, ed. T. M. Rudavsky (New York: NYU Press, 1995); idem., "Jüdisch-feministische Theologie und Antijudaismus in christlich-feministischer Theologie," *Feministische Theologie und die Verantwortung für die Geschichte*, ed. Leonore Siegele-Wenschkewitz (Munich: Christian Kaiser Verlag, 1988).

11. Suzanne Akbari, *Idols in the East: European Representations of Islam and the Orient, 1100–1450* (Ithaca, N.Y.: Cornell University Press, 2009).

12. Albert Hourani, *Islam in European Thought* (Cambridge: Cambridge University Press, 1991).

13. Qasim Amin, *The Liberation of Women*, 1899; reprinted in Qasim Amin, *The Liberation of Women; and, The New Woman: Two Documents in the History of Egyptian Feminism*, trans. Samiha Sidhom Peterson (Cairo: American University in Cairo Press, 2000).

14. Leila Ahmed, *Women and Gender in Islam: Historical Roots of a Modern Debate* (New Haven: Yale University Press, 1992).

15. Marion Kaplan, *The Jewish Feminist Movement in Germany: The Campaigns of the Juedischer Frauenbund, 1904–1938* (Westport, Conn.: Greenwood Press, 1979).

16. Christina von Braun and Bettina Mathes, *Verschleierte Wirklichkeit. Die Frau, der Islam und der Westen* [Veiled Reality: Women, Islam and the West]. (Berlin: Aufbau Verlag, 2007), 228–229.

17. Claude Levi-Strauss, *Tristes Tropiques*, trans. John and Doreen Weightman (New York: Penguin Books, 1992),143. Originally published in 1955.

18. Akbari, *Idols in the East*, 284.

19. Susannah Heschel, "German-Jewish Scholarship on Islam as a Tool of De-Orientalization," *New German Critique* 117 (Fall 2012), 91–108.

20. Wajahat Ali et al., *Fear, Inc.*

21. Saba Mahmood, *Politics of Piety: The Islamic Revival and the Feminist Subject* (Princeton: Princeton University Press, 2005).

22. Tamar El-Or, *Educated and Ignorant: Ultraorthodox Jewish Women and Their World* (Boulder, Colo.: Lynne Rienner, 1994); Rivka Neriya-Ben Shachar and Azi Lev-On, "Gender, Religion, and New Media: Attitudes and Behaviors Related to the Internet among Ultra-Orthodox Women Employed in Computerized Environments," *International Journal of Communication* 5 (2011), 875–895.

23. Ruth Stein, *For Love of the Father: A Psychoanalytic Study of Religious Terrorism* (Stanford: Stanford University Press, 2010).

24. See the brilliant analysis by Howard Eilberg-Schwartz, *God's Phallus and Other Problems for Men and Monotheism* (Boston: Beacon Press, 1994).

25. Stein, *For Love of the Father*.

26. Fatima Mernissi, *The Veil and the Male Elite: A Feminist Interpretaiton of Women's Rights in Islam*, trans. Mary Jo Lakeland (New York: Basic Books, 1987).

27. See the interview with Su'ad Saleh in the film documentary by Brigid Maher, *Veiled Voices* (2009).

28. Mernissi, *The Veil and the Male Elite*, 81.

29. Blu Greenberg, *On Women and Judaism: A View from Tradition* (Philadelphia: Jewish Publication Society, 1981).

30. Ahmed, *Women and Gender in Islam*, 63.

31. Zainah Anwar, "Introduction: Why Equality and Justice Now," in *Wanted: Equality and Justice in the Muslim Family*, ed. Zainah Anwar (Selangor, Malaysia: Musawah, 2009), 7.

32. Rachel Adler, *Engendering Judaism: An Inclusive Theology and Ethics* (Philadelphia: Jewish Publication Society, 1997).

33. Ziba Mir-Hosseini, *Islam and Gender: The Religious Debate in Contemporary Iran* (Princeton: Princeton University Press, 1999); idem., "Towards Gender Equality: Muslim Family Laws and the Shari'ah," in *Wanted*; Judith Plaskow, *Standing Again at Sinai: Judaism from a Feminist Perspective* (San Francisco: Harper and Row, 1990).

34. Amina Wadud, "Islam beyond Patriarchy through Gender Inclusive Qur'anic Analysis," in *Wanted*, 102.

35. Susannah Heschel, "Introduction," *On Being a Jewish Feminist: A Reader* (New York: Schocken Books, 1983).

36. Asma Barlas, *"Believing Women" in Islam: Unreading Patriarchal Interpretations in the Qur'an* (Austin: University of Texas Press, 2002).

37. Amira Sonbol, *Women of Jordan: Islam, Labor, and the Law* (Syracuse, N.Y.: Syracuse University Press, 2003).

38. Amnon Raz-Krakotzkin, "A National Colonial Theology—Religion, Orientalism and the Construction of the Secular in Zionist Discourse," *Tel Aviv Jahrbuch fuer deutsche Geschichte* 30 (2002), 312–326.

39. Asma Barlas, "The Qur'an, Sexual Equality, and Feminism," paper presented at the University of Toronto, January 12, 2004, p. 5. Accessed on the internet: http://www.asmabarlas.com/TALKS/20040112_UToronto.pdf

40. Anwar, "Introduction," in *Wanted*, 7.

41. Bernadette J. Brooten, *Women Leaders in the Ancient Synagogue: Inscriptional Evidence and Background Issues* (Chico, Calif.: Scholars Press, 1982).

42. Libson, *Jewish and Islamic Law*, 161.

43. Ibid., 164.

44. Ibid., 313.

45. Wadud, "Islam beyond Patriarchy," 102.

46. Mir-Hosseini, "Towards Gender Equality," in *Wanted*, 26.

47. Adler, *Engendering Judaism*,164.

48. Ibid., 163.

49. Mary Daly, *Beyond God the Father* (Boston: Beacon Press, 1973), 73.

50. Elisabeth Schuessler-Fiorenza, *Bread Not Stone: The Challenge of Feminist Biblical Interpretation* (Boston: Beacon Press, 1984).

51. Tal Ilan, *Jewish Women in Greco-Roman Palestine* (Tübingen: J. C. B. Mohr [Paul Siebeck], 1995), 186.

52. Miriam Peskowitz, *Spinning Fantasies: Rabbis, Gender, and History* (Berkeley: University of California Press, 1997), 101.

53. Leslie A. Adelson, *Making Bodies, Making History: Feminism and German Identity* (Lincoln: University of Nebraska Press, 1993), 39.

54. Helene Cixous, "Castration or Decapitation?" trans. Annette Kuhn, *Signs* 7, 1 (Autumn 1981), 41–55.

55. Fatima Mernissi, *Beyond the Veil: Male-Female Dynamics in a Muslim Society* (London: Al-Saqi Books, 1985).
56. *The Holy Letter: A Study in Medieval Sexual Morality Ascribed to Nahmanides,* trans. Seymour Cohen (New York: Ktav, 1976).
57. Valerie Saiving, "The Human Situation: A Feminist View," *Journal of Religion* 40, 2 (1960), 100–112.
58. Travis Zadeh, *The Vernacular Qur'an: Translation and the Rise of Persian Exegesis* (Oxford: Oxford University Press, in association with the Institute of Ismaili Studies, London, 2012), 178–213.

2

Jewish and Islamic Legal Traditions

Diffusions of Law

AMIRA SONBOL

I have been teaching a seminar titled "Women and Law" for many years; every time we discuss Rachel Biale's *Women and Jewish Law*[1] students are surprised at the similarities between Jewish and Muslim laws dealing with women and gender. Not only are the laws similar, but social outlooks, the conservatism of the religious classes, and the attitudes of the women themselves seem to be shared by people of the two faiths. This is not surprising, for as the essays in this book show, the lives of Jewish and Muslim women have many parallels. Notwithstanding modern conflicts between Jews and Muslims, historically the two peoples have shared cultures, exchanged ideas, and lived together throughout the area extending from the Euphrates and Iraq all the way to early modern Spain. The origins of the legal systems in both societies have their roots in the ancient Middle East and the histories of the two communities illustrate that they were in constant contact through long periods of time. Only in the modern period, with the rise of the Arab-Israeli conflict, has there been an unwillingness to recognize these truths. For women working to change family laws and achieve greater dignity and a semblance of gender equality, it is essential that the commonalities between the histories of women be studied to illustrate the human production of law. If for no other reason, this needs to be done in order to break the power of the religious discourse that presents the laws guiding gender relations as holy edicts not to be questioned.

Culture and Legal Production

Perhaps, it is in the process of legal production that we find the greatest, if not the best known, similarities between the two communities; for both were dependent on written traditions, authoritative interpretations, oral transmissions into and out of the traditions, and dissemination and practice of law within particular and differentiated environments. Commonalities of origins, means of transmission and social orality, and communal cultural similarities within comparable environmental conditions, all mean that legal production would exhibit similarities even without any theological parallels between the two traditions; yet such parallels do exist. When this process of legal production is deconstructed and clarified, it becomes possible to distinguish between scriptures and the laws produced on their basis over time and place. In other words, we should be cautious in seeing shari'a law or halakhic law as synonymous to holy edicts, for they are in fact the product of historical processes and human endeavor. It is people who determine laws, formulating them in keeping with time, place, and special issues. Ahmed Souaiaia's words regarding the production of Islamic law give a glimpse of the process:

> There is an undeniable link between classical Islamic law, as a product of the standardizing process mentioned by Juynboll for example, and the original primary sources. That link is the mediating oral authorizing traditions that allowed for the building of an ascriptive accretion of law shaped by the earliest of oral precedents. The historical evidence from Qur'an and Hadith literature, the numerous legal cases in inheritance and property laws, and the theoretical principle of abrogation all underscore the fact that Islamic law has in fact deviated from explicit enunciations of the Qur'an. This deviation has been accepted by some and criticized and rejected by others within the Muslim community throughout history, yet these deviations have remained part of the tradition.[2]

Once a legal conclusion is arrived at, supported by the *fuqaha'* (religious thinkers) and the state and applied in juridical decisions, it becomes standardized as "Islamic" and a tradition very hard to change. The resulting legal codes become a significant burden in any effort to reform or change gender laws and an effort needs to be made not only to contextualize but also to determine when a particular juridical decision was made into law and enforced so as to deconstruct what has become its unquestioned legitimacy.

Orality and the dynamics involved in the transmission of knowledge over space and time deserve focused attention, and particularly so in traditions and communities where the deployment of knowledge served a critical role in the spread and preservation of the religious tradition and the construction of law—as is the case for both Judaism and Islam. Hadith narration (sayings of the Prophet Muhammad), for example, is central to Islamic law and the whole science of hadith is intended to ascertain whether a particular tradition has enough validity and authenticity for acceptance, acceptance with caution, or rejection. But *'ilm al-rijal* (science of men), as the science of hadith is sometimes called, is based on determining the worthiness of any particular narrator—that is, whether he was a good Muslim—within the chain of narrators, whether he can be placed within the correct historical context in relation to the chain of transmitters, and whether the body of the hadith is consistent with the Qur'an. The dynamics of orality, context, and narration are not given as much importance; yet the very reasons for the narration and form of its delivery can tell us why a particular hadith is thought of, brought up, remembered, or the stories and words used to frame it within a dialogue communicated during a specific situation. Hence, narration and narratives, how and why the hadith came about and the language and idioms used in it are vital for understanding the production of this very important source of law. These considerations are as valid to Jewish law which, like Islamic law and probably influenced by Islamic law in its use of a system of *isnad* (chain of reference),[3] is highly dependent on narratives as part of the legal tradition. Simon Shoshan tells us:

> Narrative is perhaps the most ubiquitous and multifarious of all literary forms. Stories, be they epic poems or modern novels, hold prominent places in the literary canons of virtually every culture. Yet storytelling

is hardly the sole preserve of the belles lettres. Narratives are also an important feature of many other forms of discourse, including the study of law, medicine, history, and philosophy.[4]

This important observation calls us to consider narratives and their importance to religious discourse and legal production. It follows that narratives do not merely give the background to the production of law, but they actually enframe the law, providing the dynamics for the decision making that, once completed, becomes established and standardized outside its original context and purpose.

The interaction between the written word and oral tradition has characterized the history of the development of both Islamic and Jewish laws and continues until today. This is of particular significance for women and gender since for both communities, religious law continues to shape marriage and family even while most other areas covered by law follow modern Western law and find in natural rights a philosophical framework for what is referred to as secular matters like criminal or commercial law. Marriage and family are seen as belonging strictly to religious law. Given how globally widespread both these traditions are and the variety of communities to which Jews have migrated and countries to which Islam spread, interaction with the new and novel must have been a constant factor; hence, rejuvenation and change in law and legal practice brought in a diffusion of law from and to the peoples and communities in which these traditions spread. One should add that, perhaps due to these constant shifts, symbols and practices of particular significance were preserved wherever Jews settled and wherever Islam appeared, notwithstanding significant differences in language and customs. These include specific symbols ranging from religious requirements like fasting or praying, to religious rituals like male circumcision for both groups, the star of David or the crescent, ethics of charity, or particular forms of dress.

Relations between Arabs and Jews go far back in history. S. D. Goitein dates close relations between the two groups back to the ninth century C.E. and points out that numerous references to Arabs are found in "later books of the Bible, in Flavius Josephus and in particular in the vast literature of the Jews that developed in the first centuries of the Christian era, the Talmud and the *Midrash*."[5] The same can be said about references to Jews in Muslim sources, in the Qur'an, hadith, fiqh, and extensive literature. The Golden Age of Islam can also be said to be the Golden Age of medieval Jewish learning with great names like Moses Maimonides in Andalusia and the prosperous merchants of Cairo about whom S. D. Goitein wrote his classic work on Cairo's medieval Mediterranean society. Early Jewish converts to Islam, like Al-Husayn ibn Salam and Abu Musa al-Ash'ari, were contemporaries of the Prophet Muhammad and became his companions. As conversion increased with expansion and intermarriage, time and space brought in influences from the various peoples and areas into which Islam spread. This included Jewish practices, themselves very much a part of the culture of the period when the transformations were taking place. While these early connections may appear to have little relevance to the modern world, actually—and particularly for Muslim communities—events and legal acts said to have taken place in the early days continue to constitute legal reality. This is particularly so for women, due to the nature of state-sponsored patriarchy enforced by modern legal codes.

The Example of Stoning

If someone had suggested back in the mid-twentieth century that stoning would become a punishment enacted by law, few would have taken the proposal seriously. Yet even today in Nigeria and Sudan, women face judgments of stoning, and since the Iranian Revolution the punishment has been enacted against women many times, and in a few instances against men, in Iran, Pakistan, Saudi Arabia, and Afghanistan. Even in the Turkish heartland, society took it upon itself to punish a woman through stoning, as the horrific story of Cemse Allak in 2003 illustrates. Because of the publicity surrounding Cemse, who was left for dead for seven months after being stoned, the Turkish parliament enacted laws against honor crimes. At least in Cemse's case, the man accused of adultery with her was also stoned.[6] This was not true in the other cases, most of which involved accusations by men, deliberation by men, and execution by men, with clerics reading "God's Law" to assure God of vengeance. These were the words used in the famous stoning of Soraya in post-revolutionary Iran and applied more recently to prosecute Amina Lawal and Safiya Hussain in northern Nigeria.

Yet the Qur'an is the most important source of Islamic law, and there is no mention of stoning in the Qur'an:

> The woman and the man guilty of adultery or fornication, flog each of them with a hundred stripes. . . . Let no man guilty of adultery or forni-cation marry but a woman similarly guilty, or an unbeliever: nor let any but such a man or an unbeliever marry such a woman: to the believers such a thing is forbidden. (Al-Nur 24:2–3)[7]

These verses are very enlightening, given that there is no mention of stoning but rather an admonition that adulterers marry only adulter-esses. Moreover, the text seems to be talking about male and female adulterers in similar terms. So where do those using the law to enact stoning find support, and why is it that most men involved in adultery manage to evade punishment? They find support in the prophetic sunna (precedence, traditions) based on collections of hadiths (sayings), tra-ditions and acts of the Prophet that religious thinkers began to collect over one hundred years after his death. Hadith, based on the sunna, is considered to be the second source of law in the Islamic shari'a by all Muslim sects, although different sects may have somewhat different collections for historical reasons. In other words, the textualization of narratives built on stories passed down from generation to generation through chains of references provided elucidations as well as supple-mentary additions to the Qur'an, even though the Qur'an may not men-tion the material in these narratives. A good example here is of a hadith almost always cited to prove that the Prophet Muhammad did order stoning and hence set the precedent:

> Narrated Abu Huraira: A man from among the people, came to Allah's Apostle while Allah's Apostle was sitting in the mosque, and addressed him, saying, "O Allah's Apostle! I have committed an illegal sexual inter-course." The Prophet turned his face away from him. The man came to that side to which the Prophet had turned his face, and said, "O Allah's Apostle! I have committed an illegal intercourse." The Prophet turned his face to the other side, and the man came to that side, and when he confessed four times, the Prophet called him and said, "Are you mad?" He said, "No, O Allah's Apostle!" The Prophet said, "Are you married?"

He said, "Yes, O Allah's Apostle." The Prophet said (to the people), "Take
him away and stone him to death." Ibn Shihab added, "I was told by one
who heard Jabir, that Jabir said, 'I was among those who stoned the man,
and we stoned him at the Musalla (praying Place), and when the stones
troubled him, he jumped quickly and ran away, but we overtook him at
Al-Harra and stoned him to death (there).'"[8]

The narrative nature of the hadith is clear; the authority quoted is telling a story of an event he witnessed and a conversation that took place
between the Prophet Muhammad and Ma'iz. This story was not written
down immediately and passed through at least four generations of tell-
ers before being put down as text. That is one reason there are various
versions of the hadith depending on the source. In another narration,
for example, the Prophet is said to have said to the people, "[T]ake him
and do with him what he asks for," but when he ran away trying to get
out of punishment, the Prophet told them to stone him. The difference
in meaning and significance is important since it is one thing to tell
the people to stone a person and another to tell them to do what the
man asks for. The narrative itself and the details of the story line, when
scrutinized, show that the Prophet did not pass a judgment of stoning
against Ma'iz but rather fulfilled what Ma'iz himself wanted after his
insistence several times, during which the Prophet turned away from
him, avoiding the issue. Stoning was believed to purify—in Islam ablutions can be performed by touching stone if water is not available—and
was a way of cleansing the self from dishonor in a society that considered tribal and clan honor of paramount importance. Yet today, the
nature of the narrative, the story itself and its details, are bypassed, and
it is the fact that stoning did take place during the Prophet's time that is
used to give legal support to stoning.

The authenticity of hadiths has been debated by religious authorities, who developed a science to help determine their validity. Because
stoning was not mentioned in the Qur'an, the debates between various
fuqaha' regarding stoning seemed to focus on the issue of abrogation[9]
and whether there were lines of the Qur'an abrogated by others and
whether a hadith can be abrogated by the Qur'an.[10] The more conservative the interpreter, the more accepting he is of the abrogation of stoning hadiths. This is the case with Ibn Taymiyya (1263–1328) and other

medieval hadith collectors like al-Bukhārī and al-Tabari. It is also true of modern Wahhabis, the Taliban, and other Salafi groups. Muhammad Ibn Abd al-Wahhab (1703–1792), after whom the school of Wahhabism takes its name, is known to have demanded that people "do what is right" to the point of being coerced into it by force; those who refused were to be punished. He forbade people from committing sins and laid down the *hudud* (religious punishment) for them; these included "executing the sorcerer, whipping the drunk, cutting off the hand of the thief and stoning the married adulterer." The Wahhabi school followed the medieval theologian Ibn Taymiyya and with the growth in importance of the Wahhabi Saudi kingdom with its oil wealth, his conservative ideas spread far and wide, and with them these understandings of the shari'a. Scenes of stoning in Saudi Arabia and other countries where it is practiced, like Somalia and Iran, are reminiscent of the ritual of stoning the devil during hajj (the Muslim pilgrimage) where people throw stones/pebbles at a symbolic devil to prevent him from misleading them. It should be added that stoning has never been widespread and that Iran removed stoning from the Islamic Penal Code in 2012, though the threat and practice continue.

In other Muslim countries where tribalism was never the dominant structure, such as Tunis, Egypt, or Syria, stoning is not an issue. For example, in Egypt stoning has never made its appearance, and the imams of Egypt have stood strongly against the validity of stoning or hadith abrogation stories that are used to support stoning. Thus, we find that whereas the Meccan Imam Mālik ibn Anas accepted stoning as punishment based on early hadith of the Prophet, his contemporary the Imam al-Shāfi'ī who also accepted stoning, changed his mind once he moved to live in Egypt declaring that the shari'a applied in Egypt necessarily had to be different than a shari'a applied elsewhere because of the changed conditions. To Shāfi'ī, the punishment of stoning was abrogated in the Qur'an, leaving the statement "the fornicatoress and the fornicator— scourge each one of them with a hundred stripes" as the basis for punishment for adultery. Imam al-Shāfi'ī was clear about the need to interpret the shari'a according to the environment and context, and Cairo, where he migrated, was quite cosmopolitan compared to the tribal community where Imam Mālik lived. Methodologically, Mālik accepted that a hadith can be followed even if abrogation had taken place, while Shāfi'ī saw that only the Qur'an can abrogate the Qur'an. One should therefore not be surprised that Wahhabis accept Ibn Taymiyya's strict adherence to stoning, while modern Egyptian *ulama* refuse the very possibility of stoning as a judgment for adultery. Shaikh Muhammad Abu Zahra, one of Egypt's most important modern Azhari sheikhs, is known for his refusal of stoning, declaring it to be a Jewish practice that the Prophet instituted at first but that was abrogated by the Qur'an and replaced by a hundred lashes, a severe punishment indeed. Among the evidence Abu Zahra presents is the Qur'anic *aya* (verse): "if married and they commit adultery, they are due half of the punishment due free women." There is no half punishment for stoning. (Al-Nisa' 4:25)

The Prophet Muhammad is said to have ordered the stoning of Jews twice by some sources, although one particular case is the one always quoted:

> Narrated 'Abdullah bin 'Umar: The Jews came to Allah's Apostle and told him that a man and a woman from amongst them had committed illegal sexual intercourse. Allah's Apostle said to them, "What do you find in the Torah (old Testament) about the legal punishment of stoning?" They replied, "(But) we announce their crime and lash them." 'Abdullah bin Salam said, "You are telling a lie; Torah contains the order of Rajm." They brought and opened the Torah and one of them solaced his hand on the Verse of Rajm and read the verses preceding and following it. 'Abdullah bin Salam said to him, "Lift your hand." When he lifted his hand, the Verse of Rajm was written there. They said, "Muhammad has told the truth; the Torah has the Verse of Rajm." The Prophet then gave the order that both of them should be stoned to death. ('Abdullah bin 'Umar said, "I saw the man leaning over the woman to shelter her from the stones.")[11]

This hadith is probably the most famous one dealing with social issues that involves Jews in early Islam. The description of the stoning procedures differs little from the stoning punishment in the Torah:

> if this is proven, there is no excuse for the girl. They are to take the girl to her father's house and the men of her town are to stone her until she dies because she has committed a sin against Israel, so you will remove the evil from amongst you. If a man is caught sleeping with the wife

of another man, the two are to be killed, the man fornicating and the woman, so the evil is removed from Israel. If the girl is a virgin and engaged to a man, and a man found her in the town and fornicated with her, then take them both to the doors of that town and stone them until death. The girl because she did not scream down the town, and the man because he humiliated the woman of another man, so the evil will be removed from among you. (Deuteronomy 22: 20–24)

Here reference to cleansing and purification of the community are strong and explain why a man like Ma'iz could choose to be stoned.

If we go back to the discussion regarding abrogation and take this last hadith into consideration, it is evident that stoning could not have been a punishment condoned by Islam even though it was probably practiced by some tribes in Arabia. The verses of the Torah regarding stoning adulterers and its connection with purifying society from evil are echoed in words used about God's vengeance in stoning Soraya and other women today in the Islamic world. They are also echoed in the stoning hadith of al-Ghamidiyya who asked to be stoned for committing a sin and the Prophet's words following her stoning, when he addressed those who prayed over her (dead body): "She has made such a repentance that if it were to be divided among seventy men of Medina, it would be enough."[12] It is through true repentance that sins are cleansed in Islamic tradition. Those who stone adulterers do it on the basis that the Prophet did order stoning. Thus, as in the case of Ma'iz, it is the "news," or conclusion of the narrative that provides legitimacy for their actions. That this "news" is not supported by the Qur'an and is divorced from the context and details of the story is disregarded. Yet one can only point out that according to the narrative of events contained in the Prophet's hadith ordering the stoning of the Jewish couple, the stoning decision was based on the authority of Jewish scripture. This would lead to the conclusion that since no such verse exists in the Qur'an, or that if such a verse did exist but was abrogated, stoning could not be a punishment for adultery in Islam. It would also mean that Abu Zahra may be correct that stoning may have been a Jewish practice accepted by the Prophet in early Islam and that stoning was later abrogated.

This discussion, while technical, actually summarizes long debates that are important in themselves because they clarify the process of legal production. While much of what is applied is seen as synonymous to God's laws as found in scripture, in fact it is the human understanding of scripture that guides the actual debates and conclusions arrived at and hence human action. Deconstructing these debates, rereading sources and narratives with context and comparative methods in mind, could lead to a better understanding of the lived realities and the laws that were produced by social dynamics. This type of methodology is unrecognized by fundamentalist Muslim groups today who see the words of what they call the consensus of theologians as representing God's will, to be applied by any society that calls itself Muslim; otherwise the person is out of Islam, a *kafir* (apostate). It is one reason why these groups are today called *takfiriyyin*, or those who declared all others than themselves to be apostates. For those who continue to advocate and push for laws to implement stoning in Muslim countries, the question remains: why is it that Jewish communities today do not even consider such punishment even though the early experience of both Muslims and Jews with regard to adultery and punishment have close parallels?

On Marriage and Contracts

The treatment of a married woman is different from that of an unmarried woman in Jewish and Muslim law. While the Qur'an's textual punishment for adultery does not differentiate between the married and unmarried, "the woman and the man guilty of adultery or fornication, flog each of them with a hundred stripes," the *fuqaha'* differentiate between the married and unmarried: flogging and exile for the unmarried and stoning for the married. As explained earlier, the hadith literature provides the basis for these punishments and is used to stone and advocate stoning today. Various methods are used today to spread and deploy this fundamentalist discourse and establish it as a "truth" by making it familiar to the common reader; this includes inundating the Internet with stories of stoning and textually "editing" religious texts whether in hard print or in e-format. For example, bracketed phrases are often added to Qur'anic verses; the words are meant to explain meanings, but they actually add interpretations. A widely used web page on the Internet named Sahih International, for example, translates the Qur'anic verse dealing with stoning as follows: "The [unmarried] woman or [unmarried] man found guilty of sexual intercourse—lash each one of them with a hundred lashes" (Al-Nur 24:2).[13] The Qur'an does not mention married or unmarried, but the addition gives credibility to the idea that there is another punishment not mentioned in the Qur'an for the married woman or married man. Another interesting example of gendering through textual editing emerges in the interpretion of the first verse of Surat al-Nisa' (the "Chapter on Women" or the "Chapter for Women"; it can be read either way, each with its own significance). The line reads as follows: "We created you of one soul and of it created its spouse." (Al-Nisa' 4:1). This verse can be understood as a universal declaration of human and gender equality, a very powerful statement that can be seen to be at the heart and essence of Islam. To make sure that it is not understood as message of equality, and particularly since the word "soul" in Arabic is grammatically feminine and the word "spouse" is grammatically masculine, some recent translations of the Qur'an add the word Adam in brackets after the word "soul" and the word Hawwa/Eve in brackets after "spouse."

Discourses distinguishing between the married and unmarried, or positing the superiority of Adam over Eve, have parallels in Judaism and Islam. Judaism considers marriage sacred: "In patriarchal times the purity of marriage was pictured as jealously guarded (see the cases of Sarah and Rebekah; Gen. xii. 18, 19, xx. 2–7, xxvi. 10, 11)."[14] Similarly, and certainly by the medieval period, the sanctity of marriage, established by the Qur'an, was extended to ensure the legitimacy of children through *fiqh* (theology); five *maqasid* (objectives) for the shari'a were developed, namely preserving (*hifz*) religion (*din*), preserving life (*nafs*), preserving wealth (*mal*), preserving progeny (*al-nasl*), and preserving the mind (*'aql*). One should not be surprised at the development of this theology, which occurred with the growth in wealth of the Muslim communities during the golden age of the Abbasid period (roughly ninth to tenth centuries). Inheritance and wealth became a preoccupation of the *fuqaha'* and with it they also became concerned with patriarchal authority, to the serious detriment of gender relations. This theology, which combined the preservation of life with the preservation of one's lineage to ensure proper inheritance, presents a different philosophy from the Qur'an and practices during the time of the

Prophet and points to the importance of context and historical process in the production of law. Here the series of *ayas* enframing the subject of stoning are illustrative; they also show that focusing on only one verse in scripture and using it to reach conclusions, as interpreters often do, is problematic. Rather, scriptures should be read as a series of verses with both specific and wider meanings that are better understood from within the context of the times.

> And for those who launch a charge against their spouses, and have (in support) no evidence but their own, their solitary evidence (can be received) if they bear witness four times (with an oath) by Allah that they are solemnly telling the truth; 7. And the fifth (oath) (should be) that they solemnly invoke the curse of Allah on themselves if they tell a lie. 8. But it would avert the punishment from the wife, if she bears witness four times (with an oath). By Allah, that (her husband) is telling a lie; 9. And the fifth (oath) should be that she solemnly invokes the wrath of Allah on herself if (her accuser) is telling the truth. 10. (Al-Nur 24:2–14)[15]

These verses, referred to as verses of *mula'ana* (oath/damning) are explained by *fuqaha'* as being a way of ensuring progeny so that a woman would not foist a child on a man who was not its father.[16] Yet this text actually exonerates the wife and denies her indictment for the crime of adultery. But *li'an* is little known or understood today and hardly ever applied, notwithstanding its serious implications and particular advantage to women who are caught in this type of bind, namely, a husband refusing to admit paternity of the son she is carrying or to whom she gave birth. According to *li'an*, when a man refuses to acknowledge a pregnancy or child born to his wife as his, he confronts her with his charges; if she insists that this is in fact his child, they face off against each other, taking oaths against their mortal souls. Such oaths are a serious matter for believing Muslims and not invoked casually, and at each stage of the process, each party has a chance to reflect before taking the next oath. This goes on for five rounds for each of the two parties, after which the child is considered the wife's and the couple is permanently divorced with no possibility of reconciliation or remarriage. As for the child, he takes the mother's name and is not considered the man's child.[17]

The Qur'anic *ayas* involving *li'an* are supported by the Prophet's sunna through several versions of a hadith that tell of the Prophet ordering a man and his wife "to invoke curses on each other."[18] The following version of the hadith from Sunan Abu Dawood shows the multifaceted dimensions of the *li'an* system and its purposes. Here it is presented in summary:

HILAL IBN UMAYYAH . . . RETURNED FROM HIS LAND AND FOUND A MAN WITH HIS WIFE. HE WITNESSED WITH HIS EYES AND HEARD WITH HIS EARS. . . . [H]E WENT TO THE APOSTLE OF ALLAH . . . AND SAID . . . I CAME TO MY WIFE AT NIGHT AND FOUND A MAN WITH HER. I SAW WITH MY OWN EYES AND HEARD WITH MY OWN EARS . . . . [T]HE PROPHET SENT FOR HER.] . . . HILAL SAID: I swear by Allah, I spoke the truth against her. She said: He told a lie.

THE APOSTLE OF ALLAH (PEACE BE UPON HIM) SAID: Apply the method of invoking curses on each other. Hilal was told: Bear witness. So he bore witness before Allah four times that he spoke the truth.

WHEN HE WAS ABOUT TO UTTER A FIFTH TIME, HE WAS TOLD: Hilal, fear Allah, for the punishment in this world is easier than that in the next world; and this is the deciding one that will surely cause punishment to you.

HE SAID: I swear by Allah. Allah will not punish me for this (act), as He did not cause me to be flogged for this (act). So he bore witness a fifth time invoking the curse of Allah on him if he was one of those who told lies.

THEN THE PEOPLE SAID TO HER: Testify. So she gave testimony before Allah that he was a liar.

WHEN SHE WAS GOING TO TESTIFY A FIFTH TIME, SHE WAS TOLD: Fear Allah, for the punishment in this world is easier than that in the next world. This is the deciding one that will surely cause punishment to you.

SHE HESITATED FOR A MOMENT, AND THEN SAID: By Allah, *I shall not disgrace my people.*[19] So she testified a fifth time invoking the curse of Allah on her if he spoke the truth.

THE APOSTLE OF ALLAH (PEACE BE UPON HIM) SEPARATED THEM
FROM EACH OTHER, AND DECIDED THAT THE CHILD WOULD NOT
BE ATTRIBUTED TO ITS FATHER. NEITHER SHE NOR HER CHILD
WOULD BE ACCUSED OF ADULTERY. HE WHO ACCUSED HER OR
HER CHILD WOULD BE LIABLE TO PUNISHMENT. HE ALSO DECIDED
THAT THERE WOULD BE NO DWELLING AND MAINTENANCE FOR
HER (FROM THE HUSBAND), AS THEY WERE SEPARATED WITHOUT
DIVORCE.

HE THEN SAID: If she gives birth to a child with reddish hair, light buttocks, wide belly and light shins, he will be the child of Hilal. If she
bears a dusky child with curly hair, fat limbs, fat shins and fat buttocks he will be the child of the one who was accused of adultery. She
gave birth to a dusky child with curly hair, fat limbs, fat shins and fat
buttocks.

THE APOSTLE OF ALLAH (PEACE BE UPON HIM) SAID: Had there been no
oaths I should have dealt with her severely.

IKRIMAH SAID: Later on he became the chief of the tribe of Mudar. He was
not attributed to his father.[20]

From the above hadith, which expands on the Qur'anic *ayas* discussing *li'an*, we learn the approach to denial of paternity by the Prophet
Muhammad and how he applied it during his lifetime. His judgment
was to separate the spouses who invoked curses against each other and
attributed the child whose paternity was disputed to the mother; furthermore, the man was denied the possibility of ever getting his wife
back or claiming the child as his. In other words, in such a situation a
man has to be absolutely certain that the child was not his; there was no
going back. At the same time, by choosing to take the oath, the woman
was exonerated from dishonor and no punishment was inflicted against
her as would have happened if the case had been treated as *zina* (fornication). In the above hadith, as in the case of the man, each time the
woman took the oath, she was warned that her punishment for lying
would be more severe in the afterlife than it would be while she was
living. When it came to the fifth oath, it was pointed out to her that
this was her last chance and there was no going back. She chose to take
the oath and lie, as became obvious later once her child was born. Her
words explain her decision in doing so: "By Allah, I shall not disgrace

my people." As for the child, he was not held responsible for any of this and grew to become the leader of his tribe.

The *ayas* and hadith of *mula'ana* illustrate Islam's approach to infidelity as illustrated by the Prophet Muhammad's means of dealing with the issue. Even though the husband indicated he had seen and heard his wife with another man, the rules of the Qur'an that there be four witnesses to the act were not met. These rules are almost impossible to meet unless it is a case of intentional entrapment, which may have other complications of evidence reliability. That lying would mean suffering in hell after death was seen as enough of a stimulus to tell the truth, given confessions of *zina* recorded by historians and in the hadith literature. In this particular example, the woman, Hilal's wife, understood she was lying, but her tribe's honor, which would have suffered seriously from her act, was more important than her immortal soul; hence her decision to undertake the oath, even though she understood that eventually the truth would come out. The Prophet must have been aware of this and hence allowed her the choice even though her declaration that "By God, I will not dishonor my people" was tantamount to a confession of adultery.

Most importantly, paternity did not have to belong to the father, and illegitimacy was not an issue and certainly not a stigma borne by the child as became the case in medieval theology. It is the contractual commitment that seemed to be of importance, a contract of marriage to which both partners committed themselves, and when broken, the offender had to be punished. For both Jewish and Muslim law, all sexual activity had to take place within legal bounds; presumably that meant marriage, but concubinage was also regulated and recognized. The marital contract, *ketubah*, or *katb al-kitab*, that is, the marriage contract of Jews and Muslims respectively, have many similarities. Some of these are based on customs and practices that predated Judaism and Islam, being part of civilizations into which the two traditions spread and from which much of what became "contractual" in Islamic and Judaic tradition can be traced. Thus, marriage contracts from parts of modern-day Iraq during the Sumerian and Akkadian periods, as well as marriage contracts in Ancient Egypt, illustrate many of the conditional and contractual bases of marriage.[21] This connection is not well studied and the statement "Islamic marriage" seems to indicate the purely religious nature of marriage in Islam; the same can be said about Jewish marriage. In earlier articles, I have described premodern Muslim marriage as a *tabula rasa* in which the parties concerned not only included necessary information without which the marriage was considered invalid, but they also added specific items that the contracting couple expected out of the marriage; failure to fulfill these expectations constituted a breach of contract allowing dissolution or renegotiation. Today, the contract is a state document, officiated by a state servant and recorded in official records, and many alternative forms of marriage have appeared and been legitimized in different countries. The study of marriage as contract therefore provides a rich history of the processes, interactions, and diffusion of law and traditions. As a snapshot of this process, and only to illustrate what is meant by the diffusion of law, comparing marriage contracts and divorce records of various religious communities, for example the Jewish *ketubah* and the marriage contract of the Muslim communities, will illustrate a wider shared gender history and commonalities in women's search for legal change.

The Muslim marriage contract in pre-Islamic and early Islamic Mecca was an oral transaction and became a written document perhaps only as late as the Ikhshidid period. The early Muslim chronicler Ibn Hisham, who lived in the eighth century, relates the story of how the Prophet's father Abdallah married the Prophet's mother. As Abdallah walked following his father through the marketplace in Mecca heading to her house to ask for her hand in marriage, a woman-seer stopped him and asked him to marry her. He apologized, indicating that he had to follow his father to ask for someone else's hand in marriage. Later on, they met again and Abdallah was curious as to why she was no longer interested in marrying him. She answered that she had no need for him any more. What had interested her in him was a light that shone from him as he went to betroth Amina, the Prophet's mother, the light being an indication of the coming birth of the Prophet. Abdallah then traveled abroad to trade and died. His marriage to Amina was very short-lived but Muhammad was the result of the union.[22]

Ibn Hisham's story does not tell us what the contractual basis of the marriage was, but it seems that the betrothal and the marriage took place at the same time and if there was a written document, he does not refer to it. The story also tells us that it was not unusual for women to take the initiative to marry and choose their partners, and this is confirmed by the first marriage of the Prophet himself whose wife, Khadija, asked for his hand in marriage. Even though Meccan tribal society was patriarchal, the Prophet was actually first raised by his mother's tribe until her death and then he moved to live with his paternal grandfather. Islam emphasized marriage and the need to legalize a relationship and declare that a union was taking place. The type of union itself changed over time to become more of the type of contract considered prototypically Islamic today. But this process took time, and the product follows basic gender principles in the Qur'an such as the Islamic prohibition of incest or women contracting a marriage to more than one man simultaneously. Some central principles of Jewish marriage, including traditions of betrothal, also appear in Muslim contracts, which almost always indicate if it is the father officiating or another male in his place. I should add that depending on the location, such as Upper Egypt, for instance, mothers had the right to find marriage partners for their daughters if the father was deceased and they were given guardianship. This is for the Maliki *madhhab* only, however, and only in Upper Egypt. The same did not apply to Malikis in Alexandria, for example.

Major changes took place in marriage contracts over time among the Muslim, Jewish, and Christian communities living throughout the Middle East. Christians, like Jews, had their own laws and communities, but some traditions seem to be normative to the three groups. One such tradition that serves as a useful example, as it has existed over time within various communities, involves women's living expectations from the marriage and more specifically, their food and clothing. Tied to the living standard the bride was used to or was willing to accept, the obligation that the husband provide for the food and board seemed not to be taken for granted but was an item usually included in marriage contracts and marital laws. Perhaps this had more to do with the quality of food and clothing provided, for instance, than the obligation to support her, which *fiqh* indicates is the husband's responsibility. Notwithstanding, some marriage contracts indicate that the husband would provide food for a woman and her children if such children existed and/or indicate that the man would be living in the woman's house without paying her rent. This may sound natural since husbands were not automatically responsible for the wife's children and if he were the supporter he would be expected to pay the rent. However, why include what is obvious in a contract, and how do we explain court cases brought by wives against husbands who had not paid support, as well as husbands' refusal to pay since there had been no previous agreement? The following court case from 1074 Alexandria shows that the situation was not as simple as *fiqh* tells us, which is probably why women included the specifics of support in their contracts.

> The woman . . . claimed that her husband . . . owes her . . . as per her twenty-one year contracted marriage . . . and thus owes her forty-two seasons of clothing . . . winter and summer . . . she asked him for this and for her delayed dowry . . . he responded that . . . the delayed clothing is not his responsibility because of the time involved, because this was not required of him in the form of money and no court decision supports her request.[23]

The case went against the woman because of the length of time involved. It seems from this and similar cases that these contracts were central legal documents in which women included details of support, including the actual budget for their clothing and the class of food, housing, and even servants or slaves for the richer brides.

When documents and religious literature are read as sources for studying lived realities, it becomes clear how culture and traditions, not only religious discourses, influence practice, particularly as we understand these discourses today. The following divorce cases brought to the Alexandria courts illustrate precisely this point.

> 1. Wassili al-Qubruzi, the tailor, came to the Majlis al-Shar' al-Sharif to inform that his wife, Marusa bint Dimitri al-Rumi, does not listen to him and has gone out of his *ta'a* (obedience) . . . and asked that she be brought to court to talk to her about this. She came and the husband talked to her in the presence of her nephew . . . and the respectable Hussain Agha Bashi . . . and others present there. She refused to reconcile with her named husband and explained that he left her for three years without support (*nafaqa*). He offered the amount of eight thousand silver *nisf* as compensation but she refused and announced "I do not accept/want (*la aqbalahu*) and showed disobedience (*nushuz*) and willfulness (*'isyan*).

She was informed that she had no right to a *nafaqa* and no clothing allowance due her from her husband as long as she did not follow his wishes. She stood firm and the husband accepted her *nushuz*.[24]

2. In Majlis al-Shar'i . . . in front of *mawlana* (his honor) . . . the Christian woman named Maryam bint 'Abdel-Ahhad al-Siryani, vouched for by her father, asked her husband 'Ibriyan wild Habiyan the Copt who is present with her in court, to divorce her (*an yakhla'ha*) from his *'isma* and marriage knot (*'uqdat nikahi*) in return for her relinquishing her *mu'akhkhar sadaq* (delayed dowry) amounting to ten qurush and from her *nafaqat al-'idda* (alimony for period of *'idda*) and housing expenses [during the *'idda*] and from fifteen qurush left over from her previous *nafaqa* according to this earlier document. . . . He accepted and *khala'ha* (removed/divorced) her so she is divorced from him and cannot go back to him except with a new marriage contract and new dowry.[25]

Christians, like other minorities of the Ottoman Empire, belonged to their own religious communities or millets and were guided by the laws of these communities. Yet as we see from these two divorce cases, divorce was easily practiced among them and the language used, including an advance dowry, a delayed dowry, *khul'* (divorce at a woman's request) and *'idda* (waiting period after divorce during which a woman could not marry), and all aspects of the document are actually Islamic and found in Muslim marriage contracts and divorce documents of the same period. Similar circumstances occurred within the Jewish community, as the following case of adoption from Nablus shows us:

The Jewish woman Bayuda bint Maymun came before the Majlis al-Shar' al-Sharif al-Ahmadi, assembly of the *manif* religion, the Mahamadi, and declared that her husband died one year earlier and left her with a small son and that she is unable to support him, that she is very poor, and she gave the small boy to Sheikh Mahmud b. Ahmad. He received him from her *tasaluman shar'iyyan* (legally). His age is one year and six months. He gave him the name of Muhammad, and [took it] for his wife to breast feed him. This after *mawlana* (our lord) the Hanafi *qadi*, mentioned above, declared the conversion to Islam of the boy in accordance with his *madhhab* . . . after these procedures were completed, the *qadi* allocated [funds] for the wife of the said sheikh, her name being Laila bint Hassan, for the support of the orphan Muhammad, his food, support, and clothing, which is necessary, as well as all he needs legally. One piece of Egyptian silver is allotted from that day. The *qadi* permitted that this amount be spent from that day on when needed, and to fall back on whoever is responsible legally [meaning the state treasury].[26]

To conclude, there is much to be said about similarities in historical experience, culture, and lived realities within Muslim and Jewish communities. The cases presented in this chapter, a sample of similar extensive texts, underscore the need for a more nuanced interpretation of documents and greater consideration of historical change in the production of law. To change gender laws today, particularly in Muslim societies, it is essential that a comparative history of social processes be made, a history that illustrates the evolution of the production of law and the interaction between legal production and lived experience. The latter guides the production of law at least as powerfully as religious principles, which may continue to be at the heart of the law. But human relations evolve with changed contexts, technology, and socioeconomic conditions. Laws that have exhibited flexibility today can be used as methods and models to introduce rights and freedoms that are jeopardized by growing patriarchy and fundamentalism.

NOTES

1. Rachel Biale, *Women and Jewish Law: The Essential Texts, Their History and Their Relevance for Today* (New York: Schocken Books, 1995).
2. Ahmed E. Souaiaia (08-01-2004), *On the Sources of Islamic Law and Practices* (Kindle Locations 415-420). JLR. Kindle edition.
3. Gregor Schoeler, "Oral Torah and Hadith: Transmission, Prohibition of Writing, Redaction," in *The Oral and the Written in Early Islam*, ed. James E. Montgomery, trans. Uwe Vagelpohl (London: Routledge, 2006), 111–41.
4. Moshe Simon-Shoshan, *Stories of the Law: Narratives and the Construction of Authority in the Mishnah* (New York: Oxford University Press, 2012), 15.
5. S. D. Goitein, *Jews & Arabs: A Concise History of Their Social and Cultural Relations* (New York: Dover Publications, 1900), 5.
6. "'Honor Killings' Defy Turkish Efforts to End Them," *New York Times*, 13 July 2003 http://www.nytimes.com/2003/07/13/international/13TURK.html?ex=10591 77936&ei=1&en=cb3fb5cd8aa86dd2 and http://bianet.org/english/people/21434-honor-killings-in-turkey Accessed 14 October 2013.

7. Abdullah Yusuf Ali, trans., *The Meaning of the Holy Quran* (Brentwood, Md.: Amana Corporation, 1993), 865–867.

8. *Sahih Muslim*, vol. 17, no. 4196.

9. Abrogation involves God's command that certain lines of the Qur'an received by the Prophet be abrogated or replaced.

10. Jacob Neusner and Tamara Sonn, *Comparing Religions through Law: Judaism and Islam* (London: Routledge, 1999).

11. *Sahih Bukhari*, vol. 4, no. 829.

12. *Sahih Muslim*, vol. 16, no. 4207.

13. http://quran.com/24

14. Cyrus Adler, *Adultery in Jewish Law* (New York: Funk and Wagnalls, 1906), Kindle edition, location 13.

15. Yusuf Ali, trans., *The Meaning of the Holy Quran*, 865–867.

16. This is the usual explanation. For example, see http://www.ejabh.com/arabic_article_96799.html. This is a Question and Answer web page, increasingly used by Muslims as a source for fatwas (Ask the Mufti), and the answer is always to indicate that the intent is to protect the right of the husband and to ensure progeny. Accessed 14 October 2013.

17. Surat al-Nur (24:6–10) from Yusuf Ali, trans., *The Meaning of the Holy Quran*, 866–867.

18. *Sunan Abu Dawud*, Book 12, Number 2247, narrated by Ibn Abbas.

19. Emphasis in the text is my own.

20. *Sunan Abu Dawud*, Book of Divorce, vol. 6, no. 22471.21.

21. Please see the following article for a discussion of this subject and comparison of marriage contracts from ancient Egypt, Ottoman Egypt, and modern Egypt. Amira Sonbol, "History of Marriage Contracts in Egypt," in *The Islamic Marriage Contract: Case Studies in Islamic Family Law,* ed. Asifa Quraishi and Frank E. Vogel (Cambridge, Mass.: Harvard University Press, 2009).

22. Ibn Hisham, *Al-Sira al-Nabawiyya* (Beirut: Dar al-Kitab al-'Arabi, 1990), 178–179.

23. Alexandria Shari'a Court, 1074 H., vol. 51, 138–139, case 326.

24. Alexandria Shari'a Court, Mubaya'at, 1230 H., 120 repeat:281–908.

25. Al-Quds Shari'a Court, 1054[1604], 27–134:324–1.

26. Nablus Sijill, vol. 1, 22, 1066.

PART II

Limits of Biology

Bodily Purity and Religiosity

The combination of fear and awe surrounding women's reproductive capacities, and the desire to regulate them, has perpetuated scores of religious laws designed to control women's bodies in both Islam and Judaism. The three chapters in this section take different approaches to understanding the connections between power, the body, and sexuality in Islamic and Jewish cultures. Ranging from the ancient to the modern, they confront fundamental definitions of gender and ongoing questions of corporeal authority.

Both Judaism and Islam have developed complex legal systems to regulate ritual purity and impurity during women's menstrual cycles. Marion Katz tackles the intricate regulations governing Islamic laws of purity with a particular interest in deciphering those instances when authority in this arena lay with male religious scholars and when it was entrusted to women themselves (clearly the greatest "experts" in matters concerning their own bodies). As Katz explains, the issue remained contested as a subject of debate, with women's expertise carrying greater or lesser influence within different schools of Islamic thought. More than simply highlighting the variations in Islamic practices, Katz's work demonstrates cogently that in matters pertaining to their bodies, women's power and male religious authority often collided, causing constant tension over notions of bodily pollution and religiosity.

Charlotte Fonrobert confronts the most basic issues of gender as she considers the religious practices of ancient Judaism, which rigidly defined all of social experience according to fixed binary categories of male and female. She follows the extensive discussion carried on by the rabbis about how to construct regulations for those considered neither men nor women, but a combination of both. How could Judaism, with its clearly prescribed behaviors and obligations assigned to men and women, deal with the hybrid category of the *androginos*? As she explores the rabbinic dialogue surrounding the person defined as both man and woman, Fonrobert draws revealing conclusions about the very nature of ancient rabbinic culture. Any deviation from highly determined and clearly differentiated notions of male and female prompted enormous anxiety among the rabbis. The fact that they were so confounded and determined to regulate the category of the androgynous person sheds light on just how profoundly their entire conception of religion, and of lived experience, hinged on maintaining a fixed notion of gender duality.

From Fonrobert's discussion of ancient religious practices, Soraya Tremayne ventures into a consideration of modern reproductive technologies in Shia Iran. While Tremayne's chronological and thematic focus differs from the previous two chapters, she demonstrates how the corpus of ancient religious laws discussed by Fonrobert and Katz was mobilized and adapted to modern socioeconomic conditions in an Islamic theocratic state—sometimes with surprising and unexpected consequences for women. On the one hand, the respect for women as childbearers and mothers led to enhanced educational opportunities and a degree of empowerment over their own bodies, yet on the other, women still remained subject to Islamic laws governing the family, child custody, and other crucial matters. In what may seem an unexpected move to outside observers of Islam, Iranian clerics allowed for modern infertility treatments among married couples, including in vitro fertilization and third-party egg, sperm, and gamete donations, because of their concern with strengthening the family unit. As Tremayne argues, despite the state's progressive authorization of reproductive technologies, the stigma of infertility remained powerful within Iranian society, especially so in the case of male infertility, and sometimes led to episodes of violence and discord. The application of modern methods of fertility treatment within the bounds of Islamic law thus turns out to have contradictory consequences, allowing women greater control of their own bodies and a degree of advancement, but also reinforcing women's primary role as mothers and fortifying distinct and fixed gender roles in Iranian society.

The three chapters in this section point to the complex intersections between religious laws, the body, and gendered authority. For women, who have traditionally been defined in Islamic and Jewish cultures by their reproductive roles, the ability to exert control over their bodies and to delineate their social position independent of their biological functions remains an ongoing challenge.

3

Scholarly versus Women's Authority in the
Islamic Law of Menstrual Purity

MARION KATZ

In his handbook of Islamic legal regulations for Muslim women, the
Ḥanbalī preacher Ibn al-Jawzī (d. 597 A.H./1200 C.E.) makes the following pithy remark about the law of menstrual purity: "If a woman experiences irregularities in her menstrual period, she is obliged to present her
case to religious scholars every time it occurs. Since women's intellects
would be unable to comprehend an explanation of this here, we have
omitted it."[1] A woman's menstrual purity status can be vital for several
reasons. A woman cannot validly perform central ritual duties such as
prayer (ṣalāt) and fasting (ṣawm) while menstruating; she is also forbidden to have marital relations.[2] Ibn al-Jawzī's brisk assumption that no
woman can be expected to fathom Islamic law in an area so intimately
related to female biology epitomizes many feminists' darkest fears about
the nature of ritual purity. Not only do the regulations relating to menstrual pollution disproportionately exclude women from ritual activities, their very complexity is here seen to transfer menstruation from the
realm of women's bodily experience to that of male scholarly expertise.

Why should the law of menstrual purity be so forbiddingly abstruse?
Neither complex interpretive issues nor questions of authority arise
when a woman's menstrual cycle is normal and regular; classical Islamic
legal texts cast no doubt on a woman's ability to regulate her own ritual

(and, in conjunction with her husband, sexual) life under ordinary circumstances. Irregular bleeding, however, creates ambiguity about a woman's purity status. It raises the possibility that a given instance of vaginal bleeding is not in fact menstrual, and thus does not incur the same legal consequences. In such cases, legal authorities had to determine not only the criteria that could be used to resolve the ambiguity, but the identity—and the gender—of the parties who were authorized to make valid judgments in this area.

The Jewish law of ritual purity similarly requires that distinctions be drawn between different types of bleeding. On the one hand, the Bible distinguishes between menstruation and the "discharge of blood" occurring outside the normal cycle, or extending "for many days" (Leviticus 15:25). On the other, the Mishnah differentiates among different hues of blood, only some of which were identified as being menstrual and thus incurring the corresponding legal consequences. Charlotte Fonrobert has analyzed how these distinctions led to the production of "a certain kind of knowledge, an expertise, regarding women's blood."[3] Significantly, this was an expertise to be wielded by male scholars: "already in the Mishnah the rabbis are staged . . . as authoritative interpreters of women's bodies, as opposed to the women who are staged as the object of interpretation."[4]

As we shall see, in the Islamic case the situation was more complex. While the Mishnah offers vignettes of women approaching male scholars with cases of ambiguous bleeding and of single-sex gatherings of male rabbis discussing samples of blood,[5] an Islamic source of the formative period depicts the Prophet's influential widow 'Ā'isha inspecting samples sent to her by women of the community and advising them about their menstrual status.[6] While 'Ā'isha was a woman of extraordinary prestige, she was not regarded as unique in this regard. Nevertheless, in the formative period of Islamic law and long thereafter, the authority of women to establish and apply the criteria relating to menstruation was actively contested by Muslim legal authorities. The prolonged debate over this topic reflects both the fundamental recognition by Muslim thinkers that women were intellectually qualified to engage in the transmission of authoritative knowledge and in legal reasoning, and a countervailing tendency to treat women as the objects (rather than the subjects) of a legal discourse de facto dominated by male scholars.

Menstruation as an Issue of Ritual Purity

Most ambiguities in a woman's purity status arise from the distinction between menstrual bleeding (*ḥayḍ*) and pathological bleeding (*istiḥāḍa*), which is of abnormal duration or takes place outside the woman's regular cycle. Although this distinction might be regarded as a medical one, and Greek (and other) medical ideas circulated among Muslims from an early date, medical discourses did not provide the framework for the analysis of this issue by Muslim jurists.[7] On the one hand, ritual purity was an autonomous symbolic field largely distinct from issues of physical health and hygiene; on the other, the Prophet Muhammad himself was the source of authoritative knowledge about bodily well-being as well as of more narrowly religious knowledge. During the Prophet Muhammad's lifetime, he is supposed to have been approached by a woman who suffered from chronic bleeding. In response to her enquiry, the Prophet is reported to have declared that what she was experiencing was not actually menstruation but a hemorrhage from a vein within the womb.[8] A woman suffering from such a flux would not be permanently excluded from ritual activity, but could perform the minor ablutions (*wuḍū'*) and pray—as could, for instance, a person suffering from a chronic nosebleed. She could also, at least according to some authorities, have marital relations.

In fact, accounts of encounters between the Prophet and women who suffered from chronic bleeding suggest three different solutions to the problem of determining the woman's purity status. First, if the bleeding fluctuated in color and quantity according to a monthly cycle, the woman might be able to identify her menstrual periods by observing the blood. Second, if there was no discernible change in the bleeding, she could continue to abstain from prayer during the days of the month when she had menstruated when her cycle was regular. Finally, if she had never had a regular cycle or had lost track of it since the onset of chronic bleeding, she could follow the cycle predominant among "her women," or refrain from prayer and sex for six or seven days (considered to be the length of a normal period).[9]

To this point, the law is fairly straightforward, and places judgments about ambiguous bleeding within the comprehension and control of the affected woman. However, certain questions remain open. The statements attributed to the Prophet posit chronic bleeding, but they do not address the exact point at which bleeding should be deemed abnormally prolonged. Early jurists proposed various numbers of days as the maximum length of a normal menstrual period, most often ten, but also smaller and larger numbers—usually without any textual basis attributable to the Prophet.[10] These dicta were based (at least tacitly, and often explicitly) on claims about empirical data.

Even more complex issues are raised when the bleeding in question is not continuous but intermittent. What if, for instance, a woman bleeds for three days, stops for three more, and then bleeds for a further day? What if she has two apparent periods, but only twelve days apart? It is such cases of irregular bleeding that tested the interpretive ingenuity of religious scholars. Early scholars, particularly in Iraq, seem to have constructed increasingly complex solutions to the problem of distinguishing menstruation from abnormal bleeding in such cases. For instance, a report in an early source states that the Iraqi authority Sufyān al-Thawrī (d. 161 A.H./778 C.E.) was asked about a woman whose normal menstrual period was six days long. If she bled for two days and then stopped, what should she do? He answered that she should perform her ablutions and resume praying; if her bleeding resumed after that she should stop praying again until she reached a total of ten days. If the intermittent bleeding lasted for more than ten days, she should make up all the prayers for the days that fell after her normal six-day period (because it was retroactively categorized as abnormal bleeding, and thus she was not precluded from prayer).[11]

The complex ramifications to which such technical musings quickly led can be seen in a text as early as the *Kitāb al-Ḥayḍ (Book of menstruation)*, attributed to the Hanafi scholar Muhammad ibn al-Ḥasan al-Shaybānī (d. ca. 189 A.H./805 C.E.). Although now subsumed in a larger work, the section on menstrual purity is essentially a freestanding manual consisting of a large number of thought problems accompanied by the solutions attributed to Muhammad al-Shaybānī, his colleague Abū Yūsuf (d. 182 A.H./798 C.E.), and sometimes their teacher Abū Ḥanīfa (d. 150 A.H./767 C.E.), the eponymous founder of the Hanafi school.[12] This work focuses narrowly and systematically on a single technical question: How can menstruation be differentiated from chronic bleeding (*istiḥāḍa*) in those cases where a woman's period is interrupted by days without any flow of blood? Not only do the numerical permutations in the days of bleeding and purity for successive cases appear in a regular order, but the solutions themselves are blandly predictable.

The text attributes distinct underlying principles to al-Shaybānī and to Abū Yūsuf. In the case of a woman who has never menstruated before and experiences two individual days of bleeding separated by eight days without any flow, Abū Yūsuf is said to hold that the entire ten days is one menstrual period (that is, she is technically menstruating the entire time, even though she experiences no bleeding for eight out of the ten days). Al-Shaybānī, in contrast, argues that she has experienced no menstrual period at all, because each instance of bleeding is too short to constitute a menstrual period in itself, and they are separated by a larger number of days without flow (eight) than the total number of days of bleeding (two). In contrast, if the number of days of bleeding exceeded the number without, the entire ten days would be considered one menstrual period. His rationale for this criterion is that women's menstrual periods are ordinarily intermittent, rather than continuous; an interruption in the flow does not constitute abnormal bleeding unless it becomes unusually long.[13]

Al-Shaybānī also attacks Abū Yūsuf's principles on grounds of the counterintuitive nature of the results they yield, exemplifying the problem by modifying the first example so that the woman experiences nine days without flow after the first day of bleeding. In this case, Abū Yūsuf treats the first ten days as a menstrual period, and the eleventh day (which exceeds the maximum length of a period according to the school) as abnormal bleeding (istiḥāḍa). Al-Shaybānī points out that it is only the bleeding on the eleventh day that transforms the preceding nine days without flow into juridical days of menstruation; yet this is paradoxical, because the eleventh day is not deemed to be a day of menstruation, but of abnormal bleeding. How can a day of abnormal bleeding transform nine other days into days of menstruation? Using the hadith from the Prophet cited above, al-Shaybānī argues that the distinction between ḥayḍ and istiḥāḍa is not merely nominal and juridical, but physical. The blood of istiḥāḍa is deemed to be of a different nature and come from a different source (according to the Prophet, a vein near the opening of the womb). Here al-Shaybānī's approach seems far more naturalistic than Abū Yūsuf's, both because he tries to ground his model in what he clearly considers empirical data about normal menstruation (that it is often discontinuous) and because he asserts that *hayd* and *istihāda* are physical/ biological categories, rather than abstract juridical ones.[14]

The different approaches of the disciples of Abū Ḥanīfa are also reflected in an early source from outside the Hanafi school, the *Kitāb al-Umm* of al-Shāfiʿī (d. 204 A.H./820 C.E.), the eponymous founder of another school of Islamic law. Without attributing it to any named figures, al-Shāfiʿī discusses the first example from the *Aṣl* and the difference of opinion between Abū Yūsuf and Muhammad al-Shaybānī. He represents the conflict almost completely as one between the artificiality of Abū Yūsuf's system and the relative naturalism of al-Shaybānī's. He has his (unnamed) al-Shaybānī figure exclaim in exasperation, "Glory be to God![15] It is not permissible for someone who has made this kind of mistake to issue juristic opinions. He has made her pure in the days when she is bleeding and menstruating on the days when she is not!"[16]

Despite the significant differences between the models of Abū Yūsuf and al-Shaybānī, however, other examples demonstrate that both sets of rules generate artificial and counterintuitive conclusions about the purity status of a woman with irregular bleeding. Consider the following two cases:

Muhammad ibn al-Ḥasan said: If a woman used to menstruate regularly (*haydan maʿrūfan*) at the beginning of every [lunar] month for five days, and one time she menstruated for four days at the beginning of the month, then the bleeding stopped for five days, and then she bled [lit., "menstruated"] for a day after that, adding up to ten days—all of that is menstruation, according to Abū Ḥanīfa, Abū Yūsuf and Muhammad. If she were to experience bleeding for three days at the beginning of the month, then [the bleeding] stopped for nine days, and then she experienced it again for one, two, or three days, the menstrual period is the first three days and the rest of the bleeding is *istihāda*—according to the opinion of Muhammad. Abū Yūsuf said that five days at the beginning of the month are the menstrual period: the first three days when she experienced bleeding, and [the first] two days when she was not bleeding [lit., "of her purity"]; the rest is *istihāda*.[17]

In the first case, according to both sets of rules, the woman is considered to be menstruating for the duration of a five-day period in which she experiences no bleeding at all. It is impossible for her to know this, of course, until the bleeding begins again on the tenth day. Presumably, she is expected to have resumed prayer in the meantime; on the tenth day, she may deduce (presumably with the help of a jurist) that she was technically menstruating the entire time and regard her ritual activities retroactively as invalid. If she has fasted, for instance, she will plan to repeat the fast at another time. In the second case, both sets of rules dictate that the woman is actually pure during days when she is bleeding. The situation is further complicated if irregular bleeding is deemed to add up to a total exceeding the maximum ten days, in which case the bleeding is retroactively considered *istiḥāḍa*, the woman concludes that she was pure after all, and she is obligated to make up the prayers that she missed while she was bleeding.[18]

Later scholars produced even more perplexing scenarios in their attempts to trace the implications of this set of rules. The legal fiction that a woman might be juristically deemed to be menstruating on days when she experienced no bleeding opened the door to ever more complex and artificial calculations. Second-order ambiguities arose when it was necessary to decide whether calculations should be based on days of de facto bleeding and nonbleeding, or juristic menstruation and nonmenstruation (two different categories that often bore a very tenuous relationship to one another).[19]

A very different approach to the issue of irregular bleeding is attributed to al-Shaybānī's contemporary, the great legal scholar Mālik ibn Anas (d. 179 A.H./796 C.E.), the eponymous founder of the Mālikī school of law that came to predominate in North Africa and Andalusia. In the *Mudawwana*, the earliest and most authoritative collection of his reported legal opinions, he is said to have held that the lower limit for the duration of a menstrual period is one spurt (*dufʿa*) of blood. Thus, if a woman were to bleed briefly in the course of one day or night, she could then perform her ablutions and pray. If the woman then experiences a day or two of further bleeding, if it comes "soon" after the initial bleeding she should add it to the initial period of bleeding and consider them one menstrual period. As for the blood-free days in between, she is considered to have been pure. If it is a "long" time between the two bouts of bleeding, they are considered to be two separate menstrual periods.[20] According to the *Mudawwana*, Mālik did not specify the precise periods of time considered "short" or "long." Judging from other remarks attributed to Mālik that will be discussed below, it seems likely that he left it to the discretion of the individual woman to judge how much time had to elapse before new bleeding seemed to indicate the beginning of a new cycle.

If a woman has irregular bleeding over a period of time, according to Mālik, she adds up the days of bleeding and disregards the rest. When the days of bleeding add up to three more days than the normal length of her menstrual period, she can consider herself to be experiencing pathological bleeding (*istiḥāḍa*). If a woman continues to bleed for a period of months, she continues to perform *wuḍū'* and pray unless there is a change in the bleeding that convinces her that she is actually menstruating. Otherwise, all the bleeding is considered *istiḥāḍa* and she is not required to calculate monthly cycles during which to refrain from prayer. The *Mudawwana* comments on the requirement that the woman cease to pray if she notices a change in her bleeding that "women claim (*al-nisā' yaz'amna*) that menstrual blood does not resemble the blood of *istiḥāḍa* in smell or color."[21]

Although a certain amount of effort may be required to master these rules, their application is relatively easy. A woman can generally assume that if she is bleeding, she is menstruating and thus impure; conversely, if her bleeding ceases, she may perform her ablutions and pray. Only if her total days of bleeding in a month exceed a limit of days based on her own accustomed cycle need she take into account the possibility of pathological bleeding; once she has entered this category, she need not worry about the computation of a cycle, as only observable variations in her bleeding require that she deem herself to be menstruating. All in all, this is a system that preserves the maximum correspondence between the theoretical construct of ritual purity and the physical phenomenon of menstrual bleeding as observed or defined by the woman herself.[22]

Mālik's reluctance to assert juristic authority in this area independently of the observations or assertions of women was one that he is said to have explicitly articulated in connection to another, related question, that of the maximum duration of postpartum bleeding. The *Mudawwana* reports, "Mālik used to say about the woman with postpartum bleeding (*al-nafsāʾ*), 'The longest that bleeding can detain her [from ritual activity] is sixty days.' Then he withdrew that opinion at the end of our association with him and said, 'It is my opinion that women and experts should be consulted about this (*arā an yusʾala ʿan dhālika al-nisāʾ wa-ahl al-maʿrifa*) and she should refrain [from praying] for the longest [period they identify].'"[23] This opinion met with outspoken opposition from some authorities, even within the early Mālikī school. Interestingly, such disagreement is sometimes couched in terms that explicitly express distrust in the knowledge and reliability of women. "Ibn al-Mājishūn[24] said, 'One should not consult women about that today, because they are deficient in practice and lacking in knowledge (*li-taqāṣur aʿmālihinna wa-qillat maʿrifatihinna*). Women were asked about that of old (*qadīman*), and they said that its utmost limit was sixty to seventy [days].'"[25] Of the scholars retrospectively identified as the founders of the four classical schools of Sunni law, Mālik is the one who most clearly represents a naturalistic approach to menstrual purity with minimal divergence between the concrete observance of bleeding and the juristic status of menstrual pollution. By keeping the juristic category of menstrual purity closely tied to the de facto observation of bleeding, Mālik leaves it primarily within the purview of women, who are best positioned to make such observations.

The early Shāfiʿī compilation *Kitāb al-Umm*, whose critique of the Hanafi positions we have seen above, suggests evolution either in the thought of al-Shāfiʿī himself over the course of his career, or of the early Shāfiʿī school. Al-Shāfiʿī (d. 204 A.H./820 C.E.) studied with Mālik in Medina early in his career, subsequently engaged in polemics with Muhammad al-Shaybānī in Iraq, and had a contentious relationship with the Mālikīs in Egypt at the end of his life, when much of *Kitāb al-Umm* is said to have been composed.[26] Regardless of whether the tensions reflected in the text represent the evolving scholarship of one individual or the shifting consensus of a legal school, however, the text of *Kitāb al-Umm* suggests that more than geography was at stake in the debate. The remarks attributed to al-Shāfiʿī reflect sharp and explicit concern with the degree to which "menstruation" as a legal category was to be defined in terms of reports about the menstrual cycles of actual, living women.

The discussion begins with al-Shāfiʿī's observation that "some people" hold that a menstrual period can last no less than three days and no more than ten, with the consequence that any bleeding failing to conform to these standards is considered pathological and not associated with menstrual pollution. Al-Shāfiʿi challenges this doctrine by an appeal to empirical evidence:

> Al-Shāfiʿī said: One of the people who hold these opinions was asked, "What is your view (a-raʾayta) of a case where you say that something cannot occur and it is a known fact that it does occur? Don't you think that your opinion could be nothing but an intentional mistake for which you are blameworthy or [evidence that] you are extremely stupid and do not deserve to issue opinions relating to religious knowledge?" He said, "What you say must be true, unless there is or could be a proof." I said, "I have seen a woman of whom it was confirmed to me that she always menstruates for a day and no longer; it has been confirmed to me about [a number of] women that they always menstruate for less than three [days] and about [a number of other] women that they always menstruate for fifteen days, and about one or more women that they always menstruate for thirteen. How is it that you claim that what we know to occur does not occur?" Al-Shāfiʿī said: He said, "I only say it because of something I transmit from [the Prophet's Companion] Anas ibn Mālik."[27]

Al-Shāfiʿī proceeds to identify the hadith in question, which posits that a menstrual period lasts no less than three and no more than ten days, and cast doubts on its authenticity.[28]

As we have seen above, al-Shāfiʿī then presents al-Shaybānī's protest against the counterintuitive judgments resulting from the principles of Abū Yūsuf. However, al-Shāfiʿī taxes his anonymous interlocutor (who may represent al-Shaybānī himself, or a follower of al-Shaybānī) with promoting rules that are equally artificial. He declares, "You have found fault with something faulty, but I find that you have entered into something resembling that which you found fault with. You can't find fault with something and then agree with it!"[29] He challenges al-Shaybānī's principle that a period of intermittent bleeding should be treated as one continuous menstrual period as long as the intervals without flow add up to less than the total days of bleeding, asking on what textual or rational authority it is based. His opponent refers it to experience, that is, the fact (in his view) that women's periods are often discontinuous.

In contrast, al-Shāfiʿī insists categorically that a woman is never men-struating when she is not bleeding, even if the flow stops for "an hour." She can assure herself of her purity by inserting a white cloth or piece of cotton and checking it for blood. His opponent asks what happens if the woman confirms her purity in this way, only to find that her bleeding resumes after a day or two. Al-Shāfiʿī responds simply that she is pure when she is not bleeding, and her state of menstrual pollution returns only when the bleeding recommences. God commanded men to refrain from contact with their wives when they were menstruating and approach them again when they were pure, al-Shāfiʿī argues (in a reference to verse 2:222 of the Qurʾan). How can anyone know when a woman is menstruating, except by observing when she is bleeding? In short, he concludes, both rational inference and the Qurʾan indicate that "she is menstruating when she experiences bleeding, and pure when she is not."[30]

On the next page of *Kitāb al-Umm*, however, al-Shāfiʿī is credited with a system almost indistinguishable from that of his Hanafi opponents. Rabīʿ states that his "final" position was that a menstrual period could last no less than a day and a night and no more than fifteen days, and that the minimum length of the period of purity between two menstrual peri-ods was similarly fifteen days. Thus, if a woman were to bleed for a day and then cease for a day, "we would instruct her" (*amarnāhā*) to perform a full ablution (*ghusl*) and pray on the day when she was not bleeding, because it could be the beginning of her period of purity and she should not refrain from prayer without positive knowledge that she is impure. If she were then to bleed on the third day, "we would know" that the previ-ous day (on which she did not bleed) was a day of her menstrual period, because it is impossible to have a one-day period of purity, given that the minimum purity period is fifteen days. Any time that she ceased to bleed, "we would instruct her" (*amarnāhā*) to perform complete ablutions and pray, because she might actually be pure. If the bleeding returns and ulti-mately exceeds fifteen days, "we would know that she was suffering from chronic bleeding, and would say to her, 'repeat [the prayers for] every day when you refrained from prayer except for the first day and night'—because it could be that her menstrual period is only a day and night, and she should not refrain from prayer unless she is certain that she is menstruating."[31] The second opinion outlined by Rabīʿ, in which a set minimum and maximum duration of menstruation potentially generate complex and artificial conclusions about a woman's ritual purity, is the one that became prevalent among later Shāfiʿīs.[32]

The arguments attributed to al-Shāfiʿī in *Kitāb al-Umm* suggest that, far from constituting an interregional squabble over technicalities with no inherent significance beyond their association with crystallizing schools, the debate was centrally concerned with different understandings of the relationship between menstrual purity and actual bleeding. Jurists were keenly aware that the Mālikī system preserved a clear relationship between ritual purity and the woman's observation of blood, while its Hanafī rival disengaged juristic theory from apparent physical reality in potentially surprising and disturbing ways. The statements attributed to al-Shafiʿi do not, it is true, draw any explicit conclusions about the individual woman's resulting ability or inability to make judgments about her own purity status. However, the two models attributed to him in *Kitāb al-Umm* have clear (and divergent) implications in this regard. In the first passage, it is not clear whether the reports he cites about the length of women's menstrual periods are understood as being on the *authority* of women, or simply *about* them; yet surely women must be the ultimate source of the claims. The idea that a woman can easily determine her own purity status by checking with a white cloth certainly seems to put the question in her own hands. In contrast, it is significant that in the discussion attributed to Rabīʿ, which reintroduces the numerical limits rendering the law of menstrual purity so complicated, judgments about the woman's purity status are removed from the woman's domain and issued by a juristic "we." The repeated statements that "we would know" and "we would instruct her" insistently imply that the woman would need to consult a legal scholar in order to reach the subtle and changing judgments about her purity dictated by the system. It is perhaps significant that, of the two views attributed to al-Shāfiʿī in *Kitāb al-Umm*, it is the one that confers more authority on scholars (rather than lay women) that was perpetuated within the school.

Menstruation as a Subject of Litigation: The *ʿIdda*

Scholars who analyzed the parameters of menstruation were not only concerned to undergird their own hermeneutic authority. The observation and definition of menstrual cycles was not merely an abstract interpretive matter, but potentially raised a concrete and pragmatically significant legal issue: the determination of the length of the ʿidda waiting period for a divorced woman, which is based on counting menstrual periods.[33] The length of the ʿidda is of great concern to jurists because it affects not merely the ritual life of the individual woman, but the material interests of her soon-to-be former husband. The potential for a woman to inflict harm on her husband through manipulation of the ʿidda is suggested by the remarks of the Mālikī Qurʾan commentator al-Qurṭubī (d. 671 A.H./1272 C.E.), who notes that the ʿidda also determines the husband's ability to finalize or revoke his divorce: "If a divorced woman says that she has menstruated when she has not, she takes away [her husband's] right to take her back. If she says that she has not menstruated when she has, she obliges him to pay support that is [actually] not obligatory for him, so she harms him."[34] Jurists generally seem to assume that the woman's interest lies in the swift expiration of the ʿidda, which allows her to leave her ex-husband's home and enter into a new marriage. As we will see, the possibility that women might claim the expiration of the ʿidda in an unusually short period of time is one addressed by many scholars. To define a menstrual period completely empirically, without any numerical limits regulating the time elapsed in a normal cycle, opens the possibility that the ʿidda might indeed expire with unseemly haste. Furthermore, it raises the specter of women claiming to have experienced the requisite three menstrual cycles within an extremely brief time, without the possibility of challenging their claims on the basis of any set juristic standard.

In fact, there are documented cases (although from a later historical period) suggesting that women could indeed exploit the unilateral ability to interpret and report their own menstrual cycles to their material advantage. David S. Powers has reconstructed the case of a woman in twelfth-century Morocco whose blatant and repeated misstatements about her menstrual periods (and the consequent expiration of her ʿidda) apparently allowed her financially to exploit two different husbands.[35] Examining the surviving marriage contracts of a much-married former slave woman in fourteenth-century Jerusalem, Yossef Rapoport concludes from the short spaces of time after which she twice swore in court to have completed three menstrual cycles (after one month and two months, respectively) that "[l]ike many other divorcées, she gave a false statement regarding the completion of three menstrual periods in order to shorten the waiting period between the dissolution of one marriage and the conclusion of another."[36] It was thus not completely without reason that jurists were wary of the power associated with women's unfettered ability to monitor and represent their own bodily processes.

The possibility of a woman claiming suspiciously swift expiration of her 'idda was one that was pondered very early in the tradition. The section on menstrual purity in the ṣaḥīḥ of al-Bukhārī (d. 256 A.H./870 C.E.) contains a subsection on the question of a woman who claims to have menstruated three times within one month.[37] As three menstrual cycles (qurū') is the Qur'anic standard for the duration of the 'idda (verse 2:228), it can be assumed that the implicit question is whether this claim can be accepted if it would entail the expiration of her waiting period in one-third of the expected period of time. Al-Bukhārī, whose chapter headings often contain explicit juristic reasoning, includes in the title of this section another passage of the relevant Qur'anic verse: "It is not permissible for them [i.e., women] to conceal what God has created in their wombs" (Qur'an 2:228). In the body of the section, al-Bukhārī supports his implicit Qur'anic argument with a legal precedent: a report that the early jurist Shurayḥ (who died sometime toward the end of the first century of the Islamic era) and the fourth caliph, 'Alī, held that a woman who claimed to have menstruated three times in one month, supporting herself with the testimony of a group of her kinsfolk,[38] should be believed.

Al-Bukhārī then offers three alternate opinions—none of which, interestingly, is traced back to the Prophet. One, attributed to the Meccan jurist 'Aṭā' [ibn abī Rabāḥ, d. 114–115 A.H./732–733 C.E.] and the 'Irāqī Ibrāhīm [al-Nakhaʿī, d. ca. 95 A.H./716 C.E.], states that "her cycles are as they used to be" (aqrā'uhā mā kānat)—that is, presumably, that a woman's 'idda is to be calculated according to her customary cycle in the past, and she thus cannot claim to have had unusually short periods. The next report, again attributed to 'Aṭā', is that a menstrual period (al-ḥayḍ) can last from one to fifteen days. This is clearly an attempt to impose a standard and enforceable (although not very restrictive) juristic limit for the minimum or maximum length of a period. Although al-Bukhārī does not cite one, it would presumably be combined with a minimum length for the period of purity, resulting in a set standard for the minimum length of an entire cycle. In the final report, the 'Irāqī jurist [Muhammad] ibn Sīrīn [d. 110 A.H./728 C.E.], is asked about a woman who bleeds again five days after her last period. Presumably the issue is whether this resumed bleeding can be counted as a new menstrual period. Ibn Sīrīn is reported to have replied, succinctly, "Women known best about such things" (al-nisā' a'lam bi-dhālika).

The scenario presented by al-Bukhārī raises two related questions. One is whether there is an objective standard (one that could be determined and applied by jurists) by which a woman's claim about the short duration and swift succession of her menstrual periods could be declared implausible. This is a question of knowledge. The other is whether, as a matter of law and ethics, women are responsible for the accuracy of their own statements about their menstrual cycles. Al-Bukhārī seems to evoke this issue by citing a Qur'anic statement emphasizing women's obligation to give accurate testimony about matters relating to their "wombs." This is a question of moral and legal capacity.

Mālik is said to have been presented with the same question raised by al-Bukhārī. According to the Mudawwana, "Ibn al-Qāsim said: I asked Mālik, 'If [a woman] says, 'I menstruated three times in one month' [is she to be believed]?' [Mālik] said, 'The women should be consulted about this; if they normally menstruate and become pure in this way, she should be believed.'"[39] It is unclear whether "the women" in question are those of the individual woman's kin group or women (such as midwives) with special expertise. In any case, the arbiters will be of the female sex, and on their authority a woman can sustain what might otherwise appear an unlikely claim about the swiftness of her cycle. Nevertheless, early Mālikīs were not willing to let his naturalistic approach to menstrual purity (or his deference to women's authority in this regard) completely erode the duration of the waiting period. Extremely short bouts of bleeding may count as menstruation for purposes of ritual purity, but they do not count as cycles for the purpose of calculating the 'idda.[40] Al-Shāfi'ī is supposed to have provided a rationale for such a distinction: since the objective of the 'idda, confirmation that the woman is not pregnant, is not established by short, irregular periods of bleeding, a woman experiencing such short bouts of bleeding must consider herself in doubt and refer back to the standard of three lunar months mandated in the Qur'an (verse 65:4) for menopausal women or others without a menstrual cycle.[41]

Perhaps unsurprisingly, the only major jurist willing to draw the empirical approach to its logical conclusion with respect to the *'idda* is the Ẓāhirī maverick Ibn Ḥazm (d. 671 A.H./1272 C.E.). Ẓāhirism ("Literalism") denied any obligation to follow the precedents of the established legal schools in favor of direct application of the revealed texts of Qur'an and hadith; in Ibn Ḥazm's context, it was a discourse that challenged the authority of an entrenched Mālikī establishment in Muslim Andalusia. Thus, its followers' interpretations were not subjected to the social pressures of institutionalized application. Ibn Ḥazm holds a position similar to that attributed to Mālik and to the younger al-Shāfi'ī, that there is no basis for any criterion to determine whether a woman is menstruating or not other than the presence or absence of bleeding. He differs from both, however, in arguing that there is similarly no basis for the claim that periods of purity occurring in quick succession do not count toward the calculation of the waiting period after widowhood or divorce.[42] Ibn Ḥazm's response to possible challengers is straightforward and rigorous: "If they were to say, 'According to your opinion, the *'idda* can expire in a day or two?!' we say, 'Yes! And what of it? Where did God or His Prophet forbid this?'"[43]

Legal scholars also pondered the second issue raised in al-Bukhārī's discussion, namely, the question of women's special moral responsibility and qualification to bear witness to issues relating to their own bodies. The principle that women's statements about their own menstrual cycles were to be legally accepted (at least insofar as they were deemed factually plausible according to the principles of the school in question) was subject to several different interpretations. One was simply that women alone were privy to such intimate facts, and that the difficulty or impropriety of obtaining independent confirmation (particularly from male witnesses) rendered it necessary to accept their testimony on such subjects. In a stronger sense, the principle could be understood as reflecting a sacred trust placed by God in women. Both these ideas are implicit in the statement attributed to Sulaymān ibn Yasār (early Medinian jurist, d. ca. 100 A.H./718–719 C.E.), "We have not been ordered to uncover women and look at their genitals; this has been confided to them, because they hold the trust (mu'tamanāt)."[44] The Mālikī commentator and jurist Ibn al-'Arabī (d. 543 A.H./1148 C.E.) similarly states that verse 2:228 refers to the woman's authority to bear witness with respect to both pregnancy and menstruation, "because God Most High placed her womb in her trust (ja'alahā amīna 'alā raḥmihā), so that her statement on the subject is accepted, because there is no way of knowing about it except by her report."[45] In stating that the woman is the carrier of a trust (that she is mu'tamana or amīna), the commentators obliquely refer to verse 33:72 of the Qur'an, in which God states: "We offered the Trust to the heavens, the earth and the mountains; they refused it, out of fear of it. The human being took it on; indeed, he is inveterately unjust and foolish." The classical exegetical tradition offers many different interpretations of the nature of the Trust, one of which is women's responsibility to bear witness to their own menstruation and pregnancy.[46]

Yet a third interpretation is that, due to their unique degree of experiential exposure and personal concern, women enjoy epistemological privilege with respect to the rules of menstrual purity. This idea was applied by some scholars not merely in the sense that women could provide raw factual testimony as to the length of their menstrual periods, but in the sense that they had an enhanced ability to interpret the relevant legal texts. Women's authority, from this point of view, was not merely experiential but hermeneutical. One textual issue that concerned scholars was the ambiguity of the unique term qar' (pl. qurū') in the Qur'anic verse regulating the waiting period of the divorced woman (2:228). It was clear that the woman was required to wait three menstrual cycles, but it remained to be determined whether the waiting period began and ended with a menstrual period or with a period of purity. The unusual word qar' was variously interpreted to mean either of these two things. The Prophet's widow 'Ā'isha was reported to have expressed the opinion that the term qar' referred to a period of purity, although other early authorities expressed the opposite view.[47] After endorsing 'Ā'isha's opinion on lexical grounds, al-Shāfi'ī is supposed to have declared (echoing the opinion of Ibn Sīrīn on the maximum length of a menstrual period), "Women know best about this" (al-nisā' bi-hādhā a'lam).[48] According to one later Shāfi'ī source, he continued to observe that women know best about this "because this is something that only women experience" (*li'anna hādhā innamā yubtalā bihi al-nisā'*).[49] Interestingly, al-Bayhaqī describes this as a statement dating from al-Shāfi'ī's "old" (i.e., Iraqi) period, before the final revision of his opinions in Egypt.[50] As we have seen, he appears to have made a transition from strong emphasis on the authority of women and the possibility of different menstrual patterns (expressed in his debates with the followers of Abū Ḥanīfa) to a greater assertion of external juristic standards.

The idea that women enjoyed epistemological authority with respect to textual reports on issues of menstrual purity was also applied by some scholars to the issue of the transmission of hadith.[51] This position is described (and refuted) by the eleventh century C.E Mālikī legal theorist al-Bājī. Unlike most specialists in the discipline of hadith, some early Ḥanafīs emphasized the importance of the legal comprehension of the report on the part of the transmitter who reported a given statement or action from the Prophet. They applied this reasoning even (or, indeed, especially) at the level of the initial report by the Companion of the Prophet who functions as an eye- or ear-witness.[52] (By the classical period, this kind of consideration was anathema to hadith scholars, who regarded the Companions as immune to criticism of their qualifications as transmitters due to their unique religious status.)[53] One corollary of this emphasis on personal comprehension of the legal implications of a report, according to al-Bājī, was the idea that transmission by someone to whom the ruling in question personally applied should be given precedence over transmission by someone who was not personally affected. Thus, in dealing with reports about menstruation, transmission by women would be given precedence over transmission by men. (Conversely, in dealing with ritual purity rules regarding the penis, reports from men would be given priority.) This reasoning was based on the idea that someone who was personally subject to a given rule would naturally be more concerned to preserve and master it precisely.

Al-Bājī indignantly rejects this reasoning, arguing that if a transmitter is trustworthy his or her personal involvement with the ruling is irrelevant. Thus, in dealing with reports about the alms tax one does not give priority to transmission by the wealthy, and in dealing with reports about the tax on grain one does not give priority to transmission by farmers. Furthermore, transmitters do not preserve reports exclusively for the sake of applying them in practice; rather, they hope to reap the reward for passing them on to others who will apply them.[54]

Menstrual Purity Revisited: Scholars of the Thirteenth Century C.E. and Beyond

As we have seen, the tension between menstruation as a complex juristic construct accessible only to the learned elite and the obvious claims of women to familiarity with the functions of their own bodies was rooted in debates of the second century of the Islamic calendar (eighth century C.E.). The same issues were once again vigorously debated, sometimes in even more ideologically pointed ways, amidst the flowering of postclassical Islamic legal thought in Mamlūk Syria. Some of the greatest—simultaneously the most innovative and most influential—legal thinkers in Sunni history were active in this period. Perhaps the greatest thinker of the Shāfiʿī school was the Damascene scholar Muḥyī al-Dīn al-Nawawī, who died in 676 A.H./1272 C.E. Interestingly—and perhaps typically of the Shāfiʿī school—his legal opinions reflect both deference to the expertise of women on matters of menstrual purity and commitment to a technical system that must have rendered many legal judgments about menstrual purity alien to any commonsense or observational approach.

One of these fatāwā states, firmly and unconditionally, that women's testimony is to be accepted in matters relating to menstruation, just as it is accepted with respect to childbirth, nursing, and physical defects in private parts of the (female) body. Interestingly, he suggests that this is an issue that has once again been raised by his contemporaries. After citing two authorities on this point, al-Nawawī remarks rather impatiently:

> I have mentioned [this point] here only because it has arisen anew in our time (ḥadathat fī zamāninā); some [scholars] have fallen into confusion because they are unfamiliar with the transmitted [statements] on this subject, and some of them have fancied that it is difficult for [women] to be [fully] cognizant of it (annahunna yaʿṣuru iṭṭilāʿuhunna ʿalayhi). This is an odd [claim] (hādhā ʿajīb)—how can experienced women be

unaware of something that they have dealt with, in themselves and others, for most of their lives?! (*kayfa yakhfā 'alā'l-niswa al-khabīrāt mā hunna mumārisāt lahu fī anfusihinna wa-fī ghayrihinna mu'ẓam a'mārihinna*)[55]

The reason why some jurists might have doubted the ability of even "experienced" women to reach findings about menstruation becomes all too evident, however, when one consults al-Nawawī's other fatāwā relating to menstruation. Sufficiently representative is a fatwa dealing with the options for fasting open to a woman experiencing chronic abnormal bleeding. Al-Nawawī presents several possible solutions to such a woman's need to perform a ritually valid fast for a specific number of days, including one positing a mathematical formula in which the days she must fast to ensure x number of valid days equals 2x+1 (or, possibly, 2x+2). Thus, if she is obligated to fast for two days she must actually fast for five days, specifically, the first, third, seventeenth, and nineteenth days of the month, plus any additional day of her choice in the remaining eleven days of the month.[56] Given that the generation and application of such algorithms requires skills utterly unrelated to the experience or observation of irregular menstrual bleeding, it is no wonder that some of al-Nawawī's contemporaries questioned the competence of individual women or female folk practitioners to reach authoritative findings on the subject in problematic cases.

A radical rejection of the technical purity discourse of the classical schools was framed by Ibn Taymiyya (d. 728 A.H./1328 C.E.), another Damascene scholar who was a much younger contemporary of al-Nawawī. Ibn Taymiyya, although he identified with the Ḥanbalī school of law, also insisted on rigorous and comprehensive adherence to the primary textual sources of Qur'an and hadith; thus, his substantive opinions not infrequently diverge from the received doctrines of his school. Ḥanbalī school tradition held that the eponymous founder, Aḥmad ibn Ḥanbal, had posited that the minimum length of a menstrual period was one day and the maximum was fifteen (or possibly seventeen) days; the minimum length of the intervening period of purity was thirteen days.[57] In contrast, Ibn Taymiyya notes that while God made a number of legal rulings dependent upon menstruation in the Qur'an and the sunna, He did not establish upper or lower limits for its duration or for that of the period of purity between two menstrual periods—despite the general relevance of this question to the religious community and their pressing need to resolve the issue. Anyone who establishes such limits (as have many religious scholars) is thus acting in contravention of the revealed sources. The soundest position is that there is neither an upper nor a lower limit; rather, whatever a given woman experiences as a consistent pattern ('āda mustamirra) is a menstrual cycle, even if her period is unusually short or long. If she bleeds all the time, in contrast, it is not menstruation; it is known from both revelation and lexicography that a woman is sometimes pure and sometimes menstruating (that is, alternation between purity and menstruation is an integral part of ḥayḍ, "menstruation," both linguistically and in the authoritative texts).

In support of the position that there is no upper limit to the length of the period of purity between menstrual periods, he points out that there are women who never menstruate at all. There is also, in his view, no lower limit; a woman may menstruate three times in a single month, and it is possible that she could do so in an even shorter period of time. However, if she claims that her 'idda has expired in less than the customary timespan (al-ʿāda al-maʿrūfa), she must have supporting testimony from members of her family (biṭāna min ahlihā), as is transmitted from 'Alī in a case of this kind. The basic principle is that any blood that comes out of the womb is menstruation unless there is some indication that it is istiḥāḍa. Menstruation is a natural process, while istiḥāḍa is a pathological phenomenon; the default assumption is of health, rather than sickness.

Any time that a woman sees blood flowing from her womb, it is presumptively menstruation, and she ceases to pray because of it. A woman who does develop chronic bleeding should follow her preexisting menstrual cycle, or follow the variation in the quantity and quality of the bleeding if it is discernible. If both of these fail, she should follow the cycle that is most prevalent among "her women" (ghālib ʿādāt nisāʾihā); all of these approaches are documented in the sunna, and the imam Aḥmad followed all of them. There is also no set minimum age at which a girl's bleeding can be deemed to be menstruation, or maximum age at which it ceases to be regarded as such. Menopause, referred to Qurʾanically as the point at which a woman "despairs" of menstruating again (c.f. verse 65:4), is defined by Ibn Taymiyya very literally as the point at which the individual woman comes to the subjective conclusion that her cycle has ceased, even if this occurs as early as forty. If she later becomes convinced that her cycle has returned, she is no longer juristically deemed menopausal (*āyisa*).

Those scholars who attempt to set limits for the duration of menstruation and purity do so, according to Ibn Taymiyya, without any valid textual basis. There is no parameter (*ḍābiṭ*) for what may empirically occur. While one person may know of no menstrual period lasting less than three days, another may know of a case lasting a day and a night, and yet another may know of one even shorter. If we make what we know into a legal limit, then we are engaging in legislation based on a lack of knowledge; and nonexistence of knowledge is not the same as knowledge of nonexistence. If there were an actual legal limit, the Prophet would have been the one to know and communicate it. The fact that he did not do so indicates that he referred it to what is known by women and what is called "*ḥayḍ*" in the Arabic language. For this reason, many of the early authorities of the community (*al-salaf*) used to say when they were asked about menstruation, "Ask women; they know best about that"—that is, they know what occurs with respect to menstruation and what does not.[58]

Ibn Taymiyya's interpretation of the rules of menstrual purity thus places maximal emphasis on the de facto observation of bleeding by the woman in question (and the cumulative knowledge of women as a group), and minimizes the generation and application of abstract standards by legal scholars. Even in case of the suspiciously swift expiration of the *'idda*, the woman's word is decisive as long as it is supported by her kin. He prominently cites the early scholarly dictum acknowledging women's unique expertise on matters of menstruation. Ibn Taymiyya's opinions in this area probably reflect his lack of respect for the authority claims of the classical schools of law as much as his respect for those of women. Dismissing the doctrines and precedents established by the schools as having no basis in revelation, he leaves only two valid sources of knowledge about menstruation: the guidance of the Prophet and the testimony of women.

In Damascus of Ibn Taymiyya's time, women were involved not merely in establishing the empirical parameters of normal menstruation (primarily for themselves, and based on commonsense criteria), but in the hermeneutic process of forming and disseminating scholarly opinions on the subject. Women could be not merely informants but authorities, and make rulings not only for themselves but for others. On occasion, some tension accompanied the assertion of women's hermeneutic authority in this area. Fāṭima bint ʿAbbās ibn Abī'l-Fatḥ (d. 714 A.H./1315 C.E.), whose activities as a religious teacher began in Damascus and continued in Egypt after she moved there sometime after 700 A.H., was particularly known for the fact that "she used to ascend the pulpit and preach to the women." The circumstance of her preaching from the *minbar* was particularly disturbing to Ibn Taymiyya, until he had a dream in which the Prophet Muhammad himself assured him of her virtue.[59] One of her most famed scholarly exploits was a debate on the law of menstruation with the prominent Shāfiʿī jurist and legal theorist Ṣadr al-Dīn ibn al-Wakīl (d. 716 A.H./1317 C.E.). She prevailed over the male scholar and declared, "You know this as a matter of [theoretical] knowledge, while I know it as a matter of both knowledge and practice!" (*anā adrīhi ʿilman wa-ʿamalan*). Indeed, purity of law may have been an area of special interest to women scholars; somewhat later in the Mamlūk period, al-Sakhāwī reports that Khadīja bint ʿAlī al-Anṣārī (d. 873–874 A.H./1469 C.E.) "informed [other] women concerning the chapters [from the law books] on menstruation and like matters."[60]

However, deference to women's commonsense judgments on matters of menstruation did not necessarily entail a similar degree of respect for their arguable epistemological privilege on issues of legal interpretation in this area. Ibn Taymiyya's closest and most prominent disciple, Ibn Qayyim al-Jawzīya (d. 751 A.H./1350 C.E.) argued vehemently against the proposition that ʿĀʾisha's interpretation of the word *qarʾ* (menstruation or purity) should be given priority over those of male authorities. After citing al-Shāfiʿī's argument that ʿĀʾisha's opinion should be preferred because "women know more about this," he retorts:

The response is to say: Who made women more knowledgeable about God's intent in His book, and better in comprehending its meaning than Abū Bakr al-Ṣiddīq, ʿUmar ibn al-Khaṭṭāb, ʿAlī ibn Abī Ṭālib, ʿAbd Allāh ibn Masʿūd, and Abū'l-Dardāʾ, (may God be pleased with them), and the greatest of the Companions of the Messenger of God (God's blessings and peace be upon him!)? The fact that [this verse] was revealed with respect to [women] does not indicate that they know more about it than men. Otherwise, women would know more than men about every verse that was revealed about women, and it would be incumbent upon men to defer to their authority (*taqlīduhunna*) with respect to its meaning and legal significance. Thus, they would know better than men about the verse on breastfeeding, the verse on menstruation, the verse forbidding sexual relations with a menstruating woman, the verse on the waiting period of the woman whose husband has died, the verse on pregnancy and weaning and their duration, the verse forbidding them to display their charms except to those [men] who are mentioned in it, and other verses that relate to [women] and were revealed about them. It would be necessary for men to defer to their authority on the legal rulings and meaning of these verses, and that is absolutely impossible. How could that be, when knowledge about revelation revolves around comprehension, knowledge, and the ampleness of intellect—and men are more entitled to this than women and have a greater share of it? Nay, there is scarcely a case where men and women have differed on an issue but that the truth is on the men's side.[61]

Unsurprisingly, Ibn Taymiyya's arguments against the artificial conventions of the classical legal schools' models of menstrual purity did not prevail; in three out of the four schools, scholars continued to posit numerical parameters whose application could result in extreme divergence between the observation of bleeding and the legal judgment of menstrual pollution. However, there is some reason to think that the complex and abstruse nature of the resulting legal and numerical calculations limited their relevance and appeal. The Ottoman-era Hanafi reformer Muhammad Pīr ʿAlī al-Birgivī (d. 981 A.H./1573 C.E.) attempted to revive a technical discourse on *ḥayḍ* that he clearly believed had fallen into desuetude. He writes that although it is obligatory for women and their husbands and male guardians to know the rules relating to menstrual and nonmenstrual bleeding, "This is abandoned in our time; indeed, it has become as if it had never been mentioned. People do not distinguish among menstruation, postpartum bleeding, and abnormal bleeding, and do not distinguish between bleeding that is [legally] significant and that which is [legally] void." This, he states, is partially because the standard legal manuals (mutūn) omit most of the relevant issues, and few people own or comprehend more advanced and extensive legal texts. Furthermore, the texts in circulation are marred by copyists' errors, because no one has been concerned with this subject for a long time. The issues related to this subject are numerous, difficult, and subject to juristic debate. As for the author himself, he claims to have devoted half his life to mastering this area of the law.

Significantly, the customary embellished invocation of God that opens his discussion emphasizes men's moral authority over women in religious matters: "Praise be to God who has given men stewardship over the affairs of women (ja'ala'l-rijāl 'alā'l-nisā' qawwāmīn, c.f. Qur'an 4:34) and commanded them to admonish them, discipline (ta'dīb) them, and instruct them in religion."[62] Although he does not explicitly raise the issue of women's firsthand expertise in the area of menstruation, he frames his discussion in the context of men's responsibility to determine legal norms and inculcate them in women.

Despite al-Birgivī's concerns, it is clear that even the most technical and abstruse forms of legal discourse about menstrual purity were still popular among some of his contemporaries. Al-Birgivī's enormously influential Shāfi'ī contemporary Ibn Ḥajar al-Haytamī (d. 973 A.H./1566 C.E.), an Egyptian who settled in Mecca, produced a number of fatwas applying complex numerical models to concrete problems of menstrual purity. The texts of the inquiries (istiftā') suggest that, at least in some cases, he was receiving urgent questions about actual women who were waiting for guidance. One, concerning a woman who had experienced eight days of bleeding only eleven days after her normal menstrual period and wanted to know whether it should be treated partially or completely as abnormal bleeding, ends, "Give us a legal opinion with clarification, because it is needed!" (aftūnā bi'l-tawḍīḥ fa'l-ḍarūra dā'iya ilā dhālika). Ibn Ḥajar's answer is thirty lines long, and may or may not have satisfied the questioner's longing for clarity. In another case, Ibn Ḥajar responds to a question about Ramadan fasting by a woman experiencing irregular bleeding with a complicated numerical algorithm, followed by the disarming admission that "there is not enough room on the paper to provide the reasons for that."[63]

Al-Haytamī's manifest interest in the technical ramifications of menstrual purity cannot have been completely idiosyncratic in his time. An unnamed Shāfiʿī scholar from the southern Yemeni region of Ḥaḍramawt sent al-Haytamī an epistle on the law of menstrual purity, seeking corrections and approval. The writing of the essay is represented as being motivated by "the difficulty of the [legal] chapter of menstruation and the numerousness of the errors that the great authorities of our school have committed in it, not to mention other [lesser scholars]."[64]

Conclusion

It was not until the twentieth century that the complex models of menstrual purity developed by the scholars of the classical schools were completely eclipsed (to the point that they could simply be ignored, rather than refuted) in the thinking of many leading legal scholars. In part this reflects the widespread (although certainly not universal) waning of the institutional and epistemological authority of the schools themselves in favor of direct reference to the primary sources of Qur'an and hadith. (The outsized modern influence of Ibn Taymiyya may also have played its part in this respect.) This development also reflects a rise in the influence and prestige of other discourses about the human body, particularly that of biomedicine. Although these changes have deep implications for the ability and authority of women to make judgments about the religiolegal implications of their own bodily functions, they generally have not been promoted (or contested) overtly on the basis of their gendered implications.

Yūsuf al-Qaraḍāwī, a prominent media figure trained at al-Azhar and associated with the Muslim Brotherhood,[65] writes that the Yemeni scholar al-Shawkānī (d. 1255 A.H./1839 C.E.) was correct in stating that there are no transmitted reports about the maximum or minimum length of a menstrual period that are sufficiently trustworthy to form the basis for legal argumentation.[66] The second generation of Muslims (the "Followers" who knew members of the generation contemporary with the Prophet, but were themselves too young to have encountered him) made various, mutually contradictory statements about the minimum and maximum length of a menstrual period. However, al-Qaraḍāwī observes, there is no proof in anyone's statement but the

Prophet's. Some of them even held that a woman could menstruate three times in a single month (his incredulity toward this statement is emphasized by two exclamation points). Al-Qaraḍāwī then cites Ibn Sīrīn's statement that "Women know best about that." He remarks:

> The meaning of this is that in that regard one should have recourse to induction [al-istiqrā', that is, the cumulative collection of empirical data], while making use of what the professors specializing in women's diseases say about that. [God] Most High said, "No one can tell you like one who is well informed (khabīr)" (Qur'an 35:14), and He said, "Ask one who knows about it/Him (khabīran)" (Qur'ān 25:59). This is a science that the fuqahā' (Islamic legal scholars) do not know; only doctors know it, so they are "the ones who know" about it (khubarā'uhu, the plural of the term used in the two Qur'anic verses), the people who have knowledge about it and expertise with respect to it, so one refers to them.[67]

Al-Qaraḍāwī's invocation of Qur'anic proof texts for the authority of medical experts draws skillfully on the shifting meaning of the word khabīr ("one who knows"). The word khabīr in Qur'an 35:14 is traditionally understood to refer to God, the All-Knowing;[68] the reference in Qur'an 25:59 is variously understood to be to God, to the Prophet Muhammad, or even to the Qur'an.[69] In contrast, al-Qaraḍāwī creates a direct linkage between the Qur'anic counsel to question "ones who know" and the professional expertise of medical specialists.

It is certainly striking how swiftly al-Qaraḍāwī segues from Ibn Sīrīn's deference to the knowledge of women into an invocation of the knowledge of doctors. While he advocates an empirical approach to the duration of a menstrual period, it is ambiguous whether this simplification returns authority over problematic cases to the commonsense judgment of women or simply transfers it from one body of predominantly male experts (religious scholars) to another (doctors with biomedical training). While women may be both Islamic legal scholars and medical practitioners, in each case the overall discourse is informed by the perspective of a male majority at the top of the authority structure.

The long-term debate over the authority to define, interpret, and bear witness to a woman's menstrual cycle operated on several levels. It was perhaps the material consequences of judicial claims about the expiration of the 'idda that inspired much of the scholarly debate around the interpretation of irregular bleeding, reflecting male anxieties about women's ability to manipulate the process of divorce and remarriage. However, there were also broader issues of epistemological authority at stake that, while of lesser practical import in individual cases, were perhaps of deeper significance overall. Scholars' promotion of artificial and technical models of menstrual purity not only moved judgments on matters of menstruation out of the primary purview of women, but valorized the specialized knowledge developed and transmitted within the schools of law. In this sense, it favored not simply the authority of men or of scholars in general, but the authority of the schools. It is thus no coincidence that the scholars who most fearlessly asserted a naturalistic model of menstrual purity, Ibn Ḥazm and Ibn Taymiyya, were precisely those who challenged the authority of the schools. Nevertheless, the debate ultimately reflected assertion and contestation of women's unique knowledge of the female body.

NOTES

1. Abū'l-Faraj Jamāl al-Dīn ibn al-Jawzī, *Aḥkām al-nisā'*, ed. Ziyād Ḥamdān (n.p.: Mu'assassat al-Kutub al-Thaqāfīya, 1408 A.H./1988 C.E.), 42.
2. A woman is simply not obligated to perform the five daily prayers while menstruating, and thus need not make them up later; in contrast, if her period interrupts the mandatory fast of Ramadan she must compensate by fasting the requisite number of days at another time.
3. Charlotte Elisheva Fonrobert, *Menstrual Purity: Rabbinic and Christian Reconstructions of Biblical Gender* (Stanford: Stanford University Press, 2000), 103.
4. Ibid., 113.
5. Ibid., 110–113.
6. Mālik ibn Anas, *al-Muwaṭṭa'*, Kitāb al-ṭahāra, Bāb ṭuhr al-ḥā'iḍ.
7. Of course, it is conceivable that concepts or assumptions from the medical tradition had some de facto impact on the discussion of menstruation in Islamic ritual law; however, the focus in this chapter is on modes of authority within this discourse, and to the best of my knowledge figures such as Galen are never invoked in this context as authoritative sources.
8. This report appears in the most authoritative Sunni hadith collection, the *Ṣaḥīḥ* of al-Bukhārī (d. 256/870), Kitāb al-ḥayḍ, Bāb al-istiḥāḍa.
9. For the texts of relevant hadith see, for instance, Abū Isḥāq al-Shīrāzī, *al-Muhadhdhab fī fiqh al-imam al-Shāfiʿī*, ed. Muhammad al-Zuḥaylī (Damascus: Dār al-Qalam, 1992 C.E./1412 A.H.), 1:148, 150; Muwaffaq al-Dīn Ibn Qudāma, *al-Mughnī* (Beirut: Dār al-Kutub al-ʿIlmīya, n.d.), 1:324–338.

10. See, for instance, ʿAbd al-Razzāq ibn Hammām al-Ṣanʿānī, *al-Muṣannaf*, ed. Ḥabīb al-Raḥmān al-Aʿẓamī ([Beirut: al-Maktab al-ʿIlmī, 1983]), 1:299–300; ʿAbd Allāh ibn ʿAbd al-Raḥmān al-Dārimī, *Sunan al-Dārimī*, ed. Muṣṭafā Dīb al-Baghā (Damascus: Dār al-Qalam, 1412/1991), 1:222–223.

11. Ṣanʿānī, *Muṣannaf*, 1:300.

12. Norman Calder has argued that *Kitāb al-Aṣl* is actually a collection of individual monographs which themselves are not authored works but the residue of a long period of legal development represented by successive strata of argumentation within the text. See Norman Calder, *Studies in Early Muslim Jurisprudence* (Oxford: Clarendon Press, 1993), 39–44. While the section on menstruation certainly seems to be a monograph, in form it differs sharply from those analyzed by Calder in that its internal structure is both rigid and consistent. The only major interruption in the monotonous uniformity of the text is represented by a spirited refutation of a principle attributed to Abū Yūsuf following the first hypothetical case. The argumentation is sustained and fairly sophisticated; it includes one reference to a hadith of the Prophet. According to Calder's criteria, it would probably be identified as an interpolation dating from a period later than the body of the text. However, there is little evidence for this view. While there are no other passages displaying similar levels of argumentation, this is quite natural in view of the fact that the remainder of the text consists of mechanical applications of the principles discussed in this passage. There is no further discussion of principles because there are no further principles to discuss.

13. Muhammad ibn al-Ḥasan al-Shaybānī, *Kitāb al-Aṣl al-maʿrūf bi'l-Mabsūṭ*, ed. Abū'l-Wafāʾ al-Afghānī (Beirut: ʿĀlam al-Kutub, 1410/1990), 1:407–408.

14. Ibid., 1:411–412.

15. This pious ejaculation (*subḥān allāh*) is often used in Arabic as an expression of incredulity.

16. Muhammad ibn Idrīs al-Shāfiʿī, *Kitāb al-Umm*, ed. Muhammad Zuhrī al-Najjār (Beirut: Dār al-Maʿrifa, n.d.), 1:65.

17. Shaybānī, *Aṣl*, 1:417.

18. Ibid., 1:419.

19. They examined scenarios such as the following: a woman bleeds for two days, stops for three, bleeds for another two, stops for another three, and then bleeds for one more day. According to al-Shaybānī's rules, one adds up the days of bleeding at either end of the first three-day period without blood; since the total, four days, exceeds the number of days of purity, the woman is (retroactively) considered to have been menstruating for the entire seven-day period. The ambiguity arises when one turns to the second three-day period without bleeding. Does one add up the two days of actual bleeding at the beginning and the one day of bleeding at the end, yielding a total of three? In this case, the days of bleeding do not exceed the days of purity, and the woman is considered

to have been ritually pure for those three days. On the other hand, if one were
to consider not the preceding two days of actual bleeding but the preceding
seven days, which were all (according to the first calculation) technically days
of menstruation, the total would be eight days of menstruation before and after
the three days of bleeding, the days of menstruation would exceed the days of
purity, and the woman would thus be considered to have been ritually impure
for the entire eleven days. While Hanafi jurists apparently preferred the first
interpretation, the ambiguity persisted. Kamāl al-Dīn Muhammad ibn ʿAbd
al-Wāḥid al-Sīwāsī, *Sharḥ fatḥ al-qadīr* (Beirut: Dār al-Fikr, 2nd ed., n.d.), 1:173.

20. Mālik ibn Anas al-Aṣbaḥī, *al-Mudawwana al-kubrā, riwāyat al-imam Saḥnūn ibn
    Saʿīd al-Tanūkhī ʾan al-imam ʿAbd al-Raḥmān ibn Qāsim* (Beirut: Dār al-Kutub
    al-ʿIlmīya, 1426/2005), 1:152.
21. Ibid., 1:153.
22. Deference to the experience and integrity of women was not the only rationale
    adduced for Mālik's position. The Ḥanbalī scholar Ibn Qudāma cites Mālik
    (presumably as a paraphrase or inference of his position, rather than a literal
    quotation) as stating that "There is no defined limit (*ḥadd*) for the minimum
    [length of a menstrual period]; it may be an hour [i.e., a very short time],
    because if there were a defined limit for its minimum length a woman would
    not stop praying until that defined limit had passed." In other words, if bleeding
    did not qualify as menstruation (rather that irregular bleeding) until it exceeded
    a certain minimum duration, up to that point women would always have to
    account for the possibility that they were not in fact menstruating and that they
    were obligated to pray. Since there is no textual or practical precedent for this,
    there must be no lower limit. See Muwaffaq al-Dīn Ibn Qudāma, *al-Mughnī*
    (Beirut: Dār al-Kutub al-ʿIlmīya, n.d.), 1:320.
23. Mālik, *Mudawwana*, 1:153.
24. ʿAbd al-Malik ibn ʿAbd al-ʿAzīz, Mālikī, Medina, d. 214/829.
25. Abūʾl-Walīd Muhammad ibn Aḥmad ibn Rushd, *Kitāb al-Muqaddimāt
    al-mumahhidāt li-bayān mā iqtaḍathu rusūm al-Mudawwana min al-aḥkām
    al-sharʿīyāt waʾl-taḥsīlāt al-muḥkamāt li-ummahāt masāʾilihā al-mushkilāt*, ed.
    Muhammad Ḥujjī (Beirut: Dār al-Gharb al-Islāmī, 1408/1988), 1:129.
26. See E. Chaumont, s.v., "Shāfiʿī," *Encyclopedia of Islam*, 2nd ed. (Leiden: Brill,
    1960–2005).
27. Shāfiʿī, *Kitāb al-Umm*, 1:64.
28. Ibid., 1:64–65.
29. Ibid., 1:66.
30. Ibid., 1:66.
31. Ibid., 1:67.
32. ʿAbd al-Raḥmān al-Jazīrī, *Kitāb al-Fiqh ʿalāʾl-madhāhib al-arbaʿa* ([Beirut]: Dār
    Iḥyāʾ al-Turāth al-ʿArabī, 1406 A.H./1986 C.E.), 1:127–128.
33. Qurʾan 2:228 states that divorced women must wait three menstrual cycles
    (*qurūʾ*, about which term see below) before remarrying.

34. Muhammad ibn Aḥmad al-Anṣārī al-Qurṭubī, *al-Jāmi' li-aḥkām al-qur'ān*, ed. Sālim Muṣṭafā al-Badrī (Beirut: Dār al-Kutub al-'Ilmīya, 1424/2004), 2:79.

35. David S. Powers, "Women and Divorce in the Islamic West: Three Cases," *Hawwa* 1 (2003), 36–39.

36. Yossef Rapoport, *Marriage, Money and Divorce in Medieval Islamic Society* (Cambridge: Cambridge University Press, 2005), 66, 67.

37. Al-Bukhārī, *Ṣaḥīḥ, Kitāb al-ḥayḍ, Bāb Idhā ḥāḍat fī shahr thalāt ḥiyaḍ*.

38. The phrase is *biṭāna min ahlihā mimman yurḍā dīnuhu*, suggesting that at least some (if perhaps not all) of the relatives who vouch for her are male. In a version of the anecdote presented by Wakī' (d. 306/917), 'Alī directs that the verdict be based on the testimony of the woman's female neighbors (*jārāt*). (Muhammad ibn Khalaf Wakī', *Akhbār al-quḍāt*, ed. 'Abd al-'Azīz Muṣṭafā al-Marāghī (Cairo: al-Maktaba al-Tijārīya, 1322/1947), 2:387.

39. Ibn Rajab al-Ḥanbalī, *Fatḥ al-bārī sharḥ ṣaḥīḥ al-Bukhārī*, ed. Maḥmūd ibn Sha'bān ibn 'Abd al-Maqṣūd et al. (Medina: Maktabat al-Ghurabā' al-Atharīya, 1417 A.H./1996 C.E.), 2:146.

40. See Mālik, *Mudawwana*, 1:152, where it is noted that a woman with intermittent bleeding is considered pure on the days when she sees no blood, "but those days do not constitute a period of purity (*ṭuhr*) by which she calculates her waiting period after divorce." According to the classical Mālikī school, each menstrual cycle must include a period of purity lasting at least fifteen days; see, for instance, Khalīl ibn Isḥāq, *Mukhtaṣar sayyidī Khalīl*, printed with Muhammad ibn 'Abd Allāh al-Khurashī al-Mālikī, *ḥāshiyat al-Khurashī*, ed. Zakarīyā 'Umayrāt (Beirut: Dār al-Kutub al-'Ilmīya, 1417/1997), 1:381.

41. Shāfi'ī, *Kitāb al-Umm*, 1:66–67.

42. 'Alī ibn Aḥmad Ibn Ḥazm al-Andalusī, *al-Muḥallā bi'l-āthār*, ed. 'Abd al-Ghaffār Sulaymān al-Bundārī (Beirut: Dār al-Kutub al-'Ilmīya, 1424/2003), 1:405.

43. Ibid., 1:411.

44. Qurṭubī, *Jāmi',* 3:79.

45. Ibn al-'Arabī, *Aḥkām al-qur'ān*, ed. 'Alī Muhammad al-Bijāwī ([Cairo]: 'Īsā al-Bābī al-Ḥalabī wa-Shurakāh, 1387 A.H./1967 C.E.), 1:186.

46. Ibid., 3:1576-1577.

47. See Muhammad ibn Jarīr al-Ṭabarī, *Jāmi' al-bayān 'an ta'wīl āy al-qur'ān* (Beirut: Dār al-Fikr, 1408 /1988), 2:438–445 (the opinion attributed to 'Ā'isha is on p. 442).

48. In al-Muzanī's *Mukhtaṣar,* this statement appears to be the end of a report transmitted from 'Ā'isha (*Mukhtaṣar al-Muzanī*, printed as last volume of Shāfi'ī, *Kitāb al-Umm*, 217); however, other sources make it clear that this was considered to be a statement by al-Shāfi'ī.

49. al-Fakhr al-Rāzī, *al-Tafsīr al-kabīr* (Beirut: Dār Iḥyā' al-Turāth al-'Arabī, n.d.), 6:89.

50. Aḥmad ibn al-Ḥusayn al-Bayhaqī, *Ma'rifat al-sunan wa'l-āthār*, ed. Sayyid Kisrawī Ḥasan (Beirut: Dār al-Kutub al-'Ilmīya, 1412/1991), 6:28–29.

51. The classical discipline of hadith criticism did not distinguish by gender in evaluating the qualifications of a hadith transmitter, but reports reflect early debates over the qualifications of women (particularly as the initial witness on whose authority the statement or action was attributed to the Prophet). See Asma Sayeed, "Gender and Legal Authority: An Examination of Early Juristic Opposition to Women's Ḥadīth Transmission," *Islamic Law and Society* 16 (2009), 115–150.

52. See, for instance, Muhammad ibn Aḥmad al-Sarakhsī, *Uṣūl al-Sarakhsī*, ed. Abū'l-Wafāʾ al-Afghānī (Haydarabad: Lajnat Iḥyāʾ al-Maʿārif al-Nuʿmānīya, n.d.), 1:342.

53. On the evolution of the Sunni stance regarding the probity of the Prophet's Companions, particularly as regards the transmission of hadith, see Scott C. Lucas, *Constructive Critics, ḥadīth Literature, and the Articulation of Sunnī Islam* (Leiden: Brill, 2004), 22–85.

54. Abū'l-Walīd al-Bājī, *Iḥkām al-fuṣūl fī aḥkām al-uṣūl*, ed. ʿAbd al-Majīd Turkī (Beirut: Dār al-Gharb al-Islāmī, 1407/1986), pp. 744–745. See Wael B. Hallaq, *Authority, Continuity, and Change in Islamic Law* (Cambridge: Cambridge University Press, 2001), 130.

55. *Fatāwā al-Imām al-Nawawī*, ed. ʿAlāʾ al-Dīn ʿAlī ibn Ibrāhīm ibn al-ʿAṭṭār al-Dimashqī and Maḥmūd al-Arnāʾūṭ (Damascus: Dār al-Fikr, 1419 A.H./1999 C.E.), 18–19.

56. Ibid., 17–18.

57. Ibn Qudāma, *Mughnī*, 1:322, 324. The thirteen-day lower limit for the duration of purity seems to be based on an inference from the report that Aḥmad considered it possible for a divorced woman's (three-cycle) *ʿidda* to expire in one lunar month, if there was supporting proof (*bayyina*). Assuming three menstrual periods of the minimum length of one day each, this would leave two thirteen-day periods of purity in a twenty-nine-day lunar month.

58. Taqī al-Dīn Ibn Taymiyya, *Majmūʿ al-fatāwā*, ed. Muṣṭafā ʿAbd al-Qādir ʿAṭā (Beirut: Dār al-Kutub al-ʿIlmīya, 1421/2000), 19:113–114.

59. Ṣalāḥ al-Dīn Khalīl ibn Aybak al-Ṣafadī, *Aʿyān al-ʿaṣr wa-aʿwān al-naṣr*, ed ʿAlī Abū Zayd et. al (Beirut: Dār al-Fikr al-Muʿāṣir/Damascus: Dār al-Fikr, 1418 A.H./1998 C.E.), 4:28–29; see also Ibn Ḥajar al-ʿAsqalānī, *al-Durar al-kāmina* (Beirut: Dār al-Kutub al-ʿIlmīya, 1418 A.H./1998 C.E.), 3:136, where she is listed as Fāṭima bint ʿAyyāsh (and alphabetized accordingly). Fāṭima's mosque-based activities were brought to my attention by Irfana Hashmi and by Saadia Yacoob in her paper "Women and Law in the Pre-Modern Middle East: Reconstructing the Lives of Female Jurists (faqihat)," presented at the Middle East Studies Association annual conference in Washington, D.C., November 24, 2008.

60. Jonathan Berkey, *The Transmission of Knowledge in Medieval Cairo* (Princeton, N.J.: Princeton University Press, 1992), 173 (citing al-Sakhāwī, *al-Ḍawʾ al-lāmiʿ*, 12:29).

61. Ibn Qayyim al-Jawzīya, *Zād al-maʿād fī hady khayr al-ʿibād* (Beirut: Muʾassasat al-Risāla, 1399/1979), 5:636.

62. Muhammad Pīr 'Alī al-Birgivī, *Dhukhr al-muta'ahhilīn wa'l-nisā' fī ta'rīf al-athār wa'l-dimā'*, ed. Hidāyat Hārtfūrd and Ashraf Munīb (Damascus: Dār al-Fikr, 1426/2005), 65–66.

63. Ibn Ḥajar al-Haytamī, *al-Fatāwā al-kubrā al-fiqhīya* (Beirut: Dār al-Kutub al-'Ilmīya, 1417/1997), 1:114–116.

64. Ibid., 1:122–123.

65. For a multifaceted examination of the figure of al-Qaraḍāwī, see Bettina Gräf and Jakob Skovgaard-Petersen, eds., *Global Mufti: The Phenomenon of Yusuf al-Qaradawi* (New York: Columbia University Press, 2009).

66. Al-Shawkānī, somewhat like Ibn Taymiyya, emphasized a textual rather than a strictly school-based approach to Islamic law. See Bernard Haykel, *Revival and Reform in Islam: The Legacy of Muhammad al-Shawkani* (Cambridge: Cambridge University Press, 2003).

67. Al-Qaraḍāwī, *Fiqh al-ṭahāra* (Cairo: Maktabat Wahba, 2002), 274.

68. See, for instance, Muhammad ibn Jarīr al-Ṭabarī, *Jāmi' al-bayān 'an ta'wīl āy al-qur'ān* (Beirut: Dār al-Fikr, 1408/1988), 22:126; Muhammad ibn Aḥmad al-Qurṭubī, *al-Jāmi' li-aḥkām al-qur'ān*, ed. Sālim Muṣṭafā al-Badrī (Beirut: Dār al-Kutub al-'Ilmīya, 1424/2004), 14:215.

69. See, for instance, Ṭabarī, *Jāmi' al-bayān*, 19:28; Qurṭubī, *Jāmi'*, 7:43; Ibn Kathīr, *Tafsīr al-qur'ān al-'aẓīm* (Giza: Mu'assasat Qurṭuba, 1421/2000), 10:317.

4

Gender Duality and Its Subversions in Rabbinic Law

CHARLOTTE ELISHEVA FONROBERT

Introduction: The Rabbinic Logic of Gender Duality

In the early, canonized rabbinic legal texts we find an extensive list of individual laws and norms organized explicitly and purposefully according to gender categories. According to the titular paragraph, rabbinic laws and norms can be categorized into four groups designed to underwrite a logic of gender duality. Most basically, norms and laws apply to people as either men or as women, categories that operate as a seemingly referential framework. Further, the text continues, there are laws that apply to people irrespective of whether they are men or women, grouped together as the "ways of both men or women." The referential categories "men" and "women" remain in place. However, at the same time as gender duality is turned into the framework of Jewish law, the logic of gender duality itself is subjected to a test, in that the list is compiled to answer an implicit "what if" question: what if a person is neither man nor woman? What if duality is embodied in one person? What if a person is not one but two, man and woman, ἄνδρας (*andras*, man) and γυνή (*gynae*, woman), an (אנדרוניגוס, *androginos*)?[1]

[As for an] *androginos*
there are ways in which "he"[2] is similar to men
and there are ways in which "he" is similar to women
and there are ways in which "he" is similar to both men and women
and there are ways in which "he" is not similar neither to men nor to women.
   (cited according to ms. Vienna, Tosefta Bikkurim 2:3)

It is the reality of the person who is both man and woman, and therefore something else (and *androginos*) that puts the rabbinic logic of gender duality to a test. To begin with, the masculine pronoun foregrounds the grammatical strictures of language, leaving the *androginos* with the male personal pronoun, a default at best, marked here as "he." Rabbinic Hebrew, like most other languages grammatically organized by a logic of gender duality, allows for a default only, as would English were it not for the neologisms produced during the past two decades of gender queer activism, giving us choices of third person gender-neutral pronouns, most prominently perhaps "ze" and "hir."[3] Moving between reading the ancient texts and writing about them in contemporary English, the tension of thinking about gender in two different temporalities is perhaps best captured—at least for my purposes here—by granting the rabbinic texts their default grammatical gender when citing them, while contemporary English allows me to use third person gender-neutral pronouns in my own voice.

What follows the titular paragraph framing the androginos rhetorically as either-or, both, or neither-nor "as if" man and woman is the list of the individual rabbinic laws and norms illustrating the respective categories. Finally, at the end of what is clearly an early rabbinic effort at a taxonomy of gender and law, the compilers of the list attach an opinion attributed to an individual, named sage that is marked as a contrary opinion with respect to the preceding list: "Rabbi Yossi,[4] however said: The *androginos* is a creature *sui generis*, and the sages could not decide with respect to him/her whether s/he is a man or a woman" (ibid., 2:7).

Thus, this brief outline of a text presents one of the most explicit articulations in the early rabbinic legal compilations on the way in which gender not only underwrites, but also *organizes* the formulation and categorization of law. Although sidelined in earlier feminist scholarship on rabbinic Judaism and gender, this text has received more attention during the last few years in the scholarship on gender in rabbinic Jewish culture,[5] in the Jewish queer, trans, and intersex activist community,[6] and most recently in rabbinic scholarship informed by queer theory.[7] Much of this recent interest has been driven by the figure of the *androginos* and the recognition that the rabbis of old were interested in what has received more public attention only in recent years, especially in the United States, as the phenomenon of intersexuality. Indeed, this text is in the process of becoming as iconic to Jewish queer scholarship and activism as the other and perhaps more infamous map of gender and law in early rabbinic law did in Jewish feminist criticism and scholarship, Mishnah Kiddushin 1:1–7 and its exclusionary politics with regard to women. That text not only spells out one of the conceptual underpinnings for marriage in rabbinic law ("acquisition," mKiddushin 1:1),[8] thereby framing Jewish social life, but it does the same for Jewish religious life by categorizing commandments along the lines of gender:

> All the commandments with respect to the son that are incumbent upon the father—men are obligated, and women are exempt.
>
> All the commandments with respect to the father that are incumbent upon the son, both men and women are one and the same—they are obligated.
>
> All the prescriptive commandments that are time-bound, men are obligated and women are exempt.
>
> And all the prescriptive commandments that are not time-bound, men are obligated and women are exempt.
>
> And all the proscriptive commandments whether they are bound by time or not, both men and women are one and the same—they are obligated.[9]

From the beginnings of second-wave American Jewish feminism this text and its exemption of women from the duties and obligations that define a Jewish man's religious life—observed to this day in various forms by some contemporary Jews—played a galvanizing role.[10] Just as this passage and its categorical statement on the relationship of women (and men) to law cannot be made sense of other than with some kind of feminist theory, the rabbinic investment in the figure of the *androginos* can sensibly be explained only in light of what we have learned from queer theory and from queer identity politics.

Still, I want to start my contribution to this volume by offering another reflection on this rich text, not only because it is a complex and multifaceted text, but also because I want to sideline—heuristically only, not conceptually—the figure of the *androginos* itself, and the issues, problems, and possibilities that the seductiveness of hybridity has to offer.[11] My focus is on the very choice made by the compilers of the *androginos* list to foreground gender as an organizing category of rabbinic law and normativity, and on the accompanying question of what motivated and drove such a choice. Further, my question is not just about the gender theoretical work the list itself does but about the decision by the compilers of the larger anthologies of rabbinic law to preserve this approach to organizing law.

That the list is invested in testing and demonstrating the logic of gender duality that drives much of rabbinic thinking is fairly obvious already from the above. Whether it does so successfully is an important question that allows us to think beyond the logic of gender duality. But a further, critical question to be asked is what might have compelled the compilers of the list to foreground gender as an *organizational* category of the laws and norms they subscribed to, one moreover that underlines in such emphatic terms the logic of gender duality. Further, I am interested in the ways that the body, or rather representations thereof, is both present in and absent from this list; in other words, I want to consider what strategic role representations of the body play in the superimposition of law on gender and gender on law.

As to the first point, it is by now widely recognized that the earliest canonized text of rabbinic Judaism—the Mishnah—and the contemporaneous extracanonical legal material assembled in its compendium volume, the Tosefta—are variously invested in formulating laws and norms regulating gender relations, leaving a lasting imprint on the organization of Jewish social and religious life to this day.[12] In this effort, the assurance of reproduction serves as one of the organizing centers,[13] underwriting a gender economy that can be described as being driven by a logic of gender duality, a duality that is anything but equitable. From early on, the project of Jewish feminist criticism has been to question the hierarchy and the exclusionary mechanisms inherent in the gender duality of rabbinic law. Feminist critics strove to diagnose—and continue to diagnose—the root causes of women's exclusion from the traditional production of rabbinic intellectual culture, the culture of *talmud Torah*, but they did not necessarily attend to its underlying logic. Women were rabbinic Judaism's Other;[14] the rabbis envisioned a patriarchal society, but a "kinder gentler patriarchy,"[15] while the rabbinic intellectual project is based in a profound androcentrism, although arguably one that is by no means stable and is questioned repeatedly.[16] But what Jewish feminist critics have not questioned is the rabbinic commitment to a conceptual gender duality as such. The reasons for this are of course complicated, but surely one reason is that so much work needed to be done (and continues to be done) to render women visible in an intellectual culture from which they had been excluded and in which they have been invisible for so many centuries. Where women had to gain visibility, a voice,[17] a presence, Jewish feminist criticism itself needed to be committed to gender duality.[18] It is queer theory (and practice) that has come to question the very logic of gender duality, and to apply this question to the production of rabbinic normativity as well.

Significantly, the underlying assumptions of Jewish feminist critical work up until very recently, arguably, has been that the logic of gender duality is the product of what is given, the product of social reality, in the sense that the rabbinic intellectual project merely reflected what in social reality is the duality of "women" (*nashim*) and "men" (*anashim*), merely inflecting it with their values. It is the quasi-self-evident metahistorical continuity of gender duality that allows us to read ourselves into those rabbinic texts, with the effect that women and men today self-evidently fill the shoes set out by the categories articulated in the earliest rabbinic laws, in many cases by reflex more than due to reflection. As I write about the above text again, I realize this pattern, in that my immediate hermeneutic reflex is to refer to the *androginos* as a construct, or a "figure"—in the sense of the German *Denkfigur*—whereas the "men" and "women" of the titular paragraph cited above are self-evident categories, referential categories, descriptive categories. But here I am ahead of myself. My point for now is simply to reconsider the nature of the rabbinic logic of gender duality, not merely because this remains a profound question for Jewish feminist criticism and thinking. The rabbis themselves question the logic of gender duality. Here is where the list comes to play a role again: I want to suggest that we read the compiler's choice to foreground gender as an organizational category of rabbinic law and normativity as the product of a need to justify the logic of gender duality, a need that is the product of a cultural and historical moment of uncertainty. That is, we can read the emphatic insistence on gender duality expressed above as calling into question the logic of duality at the very moment of justifying it, following a Shakespearean hermeneutic principle: "The lady doth protest too much, methinks." The more emphatic the justification, the less self-evident is the logic of duality. In the act of justifying the logic of duality, therefore, the text reveals it as a cultural project in need of persuasion and convincing, rather than merely pronouncing (or reorganizing) law. So let us take a look at the list.

Early Rabbinic Taxonomy of Gender and Law

As has been noted in philological scholarship,[19] in its written stage in the manuscripts available to us the list leads a somewhat ambiguous textual life. It appears both as part of the Mishnah,[20] the earliest and most authoritative compilation of rabbinic law, and the Tosefta,[21] the compilation that presents extra-mishnaic legal material, organized in correspondence with the mishnaic system. Between the Mishnah and the Tosefta the lists of individual laws differ, to such a degree that the philological scholar speaks of two different manuscript traditions.[22] The titular paragraph cited above, however, remains more or less stable in the various manuscripts. For our purposes we will sideline the question of what the relationship between the two manuscript traditions might be, which versions and which contexts of transmission might be originary. These are important questions for the historiography of the transmission of early rabbinic traditions, even when in the end they may prove unanswerable.

Minimally, we can assume that the list had a life of its own, in the stage before being subsumed in the larger compilations of the Mishnah and the Tosefta, perhaps even in an oral stage.[23] As a discrete unit, it continues to have a life of its own even within the larger compilations, in that it presents a distinct way of organizing law.[24] Further, under the four groups or categories of laws organized in the titular paragraph, the compilers list a variable number of laws to fit those categories. The variation within the manuscript versions of the list itself underlines its fluid nature as a list within the structure set out in the titular paragraph. The text presented here follows the manuscript version of the text that includes most individual rulings,[25] with no claims that this version is any more original than the shorter versions:

2:4
(A) [THESE ARE] THE WAYS IN WHICH "HE" [I.E., THE *ANDROGINOS*] IS SIMILAR TO MEN:

   i. "he" is rendered impure by a whiteness—like men[26]
   ii. "he" "takes" (a wife) but is not "taken" (as a wife)—like men[27]
   iii. "he" is not allowed to go into seclusion with women[28]—like men
   iv. and "he" does not "receive maintenance" with the daughters—like men[29]
   v. "he" is not dressed [in a feminine way] nor should "he" cut "his" hair [in a feminine style]—like men
   vi. and "he" should not be rendered impure by the dead—like men
   vii. and "he" transgresses on "Do not round the corners of your head, nor should you mar the corner of your beard" [Lev19:27][30]—like men
   viii. and "he" is obligated to all the commandments spelled out in the Torah—like men.[31]

2:5
(B) [THESE ARE] THE WAYS IN WHICH "HE" IS SIMILAR TO WOMEN

   i. "he" is rendered impure by a redness (*'odem*)—like women,[32]
   ii. "he" is *not* allowed to go into seclusion with men—like women
   iii. "he" is *not* obligated for levirate marriage—like women,[33]
   iv. and "he" does *not* share [in the inheritance] with the sons—like women
   v. and "he" does *not* partake of the holiest sacrifices (*kodshe kodashim*)[34]—like women
   vi. and "he" is disqualified from giving testimony in court—like women
   vii. and if "he" had sex in transgression (*niv'al ba-aveirah*) "he" is disqualified from the priesthood—like women.[35]

2:6

(C) [THESE ARE] THE WAYS IN WHICH "HE" IS SIMILAR TO BOTH MEN AND WOMEN

i. people are held responsible for any damage caused to "him," like for man or woman

ii. the one who kills "him" intentionally, gets capital punishment.

iii. if accidentally, "he" flees to the cities of refuge, like for either man or woman

iv. "his" mother continues to count out the days of the blood of purity[36]— like men and women and she brings a sacrifice on "his" behalf like men and women.

v. "he" inherits all inheritance—like men and like women[37]

vi. "he" partakes of all the sacrifices of the outer district [gevul][38]—like men and like women

vii. and if "he" says: behold, I am a *nazir* who is both a man and a woman, "he" is indeed a *nazir*.[39]

2:7

(D) [THESE ARE] THE WAYS IN WHICH "HE" IS NOT SIMILAR NEITHER TO MEN NOR TO WOMEN

i. People do not incur penalty because of "his" sin offering/impurity[40]

ii. and people do not burn the heave-offering [terumah] on account of "his" impurity[41]

iii. and "he" is neither evaluated as man nor as woman[42]

iv. and "he" is not sold as a Hebrew slave neither as man nor as woman

v. and if "he" says: behold, I am a *nazir* who is neither man nor woman, "he" is a *nazir*.[43]

We can easily observe that most of the individual rulings listed here can also be found in different contexts elsewhere in the Mishnah, within their "proper" topical context in the canonized and therefore normative order of the Mishnah, where gender operates in the background or is woven into the general fabric of formulating law. It seems fairly obvious that the list cites rulings from the other contexts and reorganizes them here according to gender categories, in order to move gender into the organizational foreground. However, if we consider the relationship between the list and the rest of the Mishnah, the principle of inclusion or exclusion of items on the list is not easy to determine, if at all. One principle of selection would appear to be rulings from contexts where the Mishnah already entertains—in loco—the question of gender ambiguity arising from the figure of the *androginos*: the mishnaic tractate dealing with the impurity of male genital discharges [*Zavim*] mentions the *androginos* and hir sibling "figure," the *tumtum*, the person whose gender identity is not yet recognizable (2:4 [i] above); the tractate on the laws of levirate marriage mentions hir (2:4 [ii] above); the tractate dealing with menstrual and birth impurity considers the possibility of an *androginos* birth (2:6 [iv]); the tractate that considers the biblically derived evaluation of a person for the purposes of vowing contributions to the Temple [*Arakhin*] mentions the *androginos* in order to exclude hir from these calculations (2:7 [iii]). On the other hand, two further legal discussions of the *androginos* found elsewhere in the Mishnah are left out, namely, the exclusion of the *androginos* from the pilgrimage to the Temple obligatory for men (Mishnah Hagigah 1:1), and the complications arising from an *androginos* baby regarding the question of circumcision (Mishnah Shabbat 19:3).[44] Why these are excluded from the list, we cannot tell. Arguably, the former might easily have fit into the second paragraph, on the "ways in which 'he' is similar to women," while the latter would not have fit easily into the groupings of law here and may therefore have been excluded purposefully. Finally, other items in the lists cite laws where gender is important in various ways, but do not mention the *androginos* explicitly.

This latter observation seems significant when thinking about the list as such, meaning as a text genre. As noted above, lists can be found in various contexts of the Mishnah, and they serve a variety of functions, such as mnemonic devices. A philological scholar might argue, therefore, that the compilers of our text were not considering gender per se, nor that the compilation represents an alternate attempt of thinking and thereby organizing gender within the organization of law and norms in early Judaism, but that the list served as a mere mnemonic device like other lists. However, the emphatic nature of the effort involved here, of citing widely and making direct and indirect reference to various areas of law to my mind indicate otherwise, at the very least that form and contents cannot be separated, at least not in this case.

From Seder Nashim (the Order of "Women") to Seder Androginos

We may, therefore, read the compilation as an emphatic effort to fore-ground gender as an *organizational* category, one that the creators of the larger compilations of the Mishnah and Tosefta chose to preserve. It proposes a different ordering system,[45] albeit not a different legal sys-tem, since the individual laws are by and large citations.

This alternate ordering system insists that the logic of gender duality is comprehensive, omnipresent, and totalizing, even when gender should conceptually not matter. Consider for a moment the last two groups: the *androginos* is "similar to both men and women" and the confusing double negative ze is "not similar neither to men nor to women." Under the first heading we find the laws of capital crimes, where what seems to matter is that the victim is human: "people are held responsible for any damage caused to him," (2:6 [i]), just as when the victim were man or woman.[46] After all, it is not gender that establishes victimhood. But the framing: "like both men and women" does not translate into "gender does not matter." On the contrary, it makes gender duality the referen-tial framework. Similarly, an *androginos* child is a child when there are no siblings (2:6 [v]). Alternately, impurity laws multiply if need be: the miscarried fetus can be considered both male and female (2:6 [iv]). The last heading is equally if not more deceptive. Contrary to the sugges-tive echo of the Pauline formulation in Galatians 3:28 (in Christ there is "neither male not female")—about which more in the conclusion—"neither men nor women" here invokes laws that apply only in the case of supposed gender certainty, significantly related mostly to the Temple and its gender economy. The laws of dedicating the monetary equivalent of a person, derived from the biblical law, do not apply for an *androgi-nos*, because—as the Mishnah formulates in the relevant topical con-text—only a person who is "certainly male or certainly female" (M. Ara-khin 1:1) can be thus evaluated, for the purposes of dedicating money to the Temple. Aside from representing a unique locution in early rabbinic legal rhetoric, "certainly male or certainly female" is almost a climactic and the most emphatic moment implied in the compilation, as it reveals the project of the list: rabbinic law negotiates between two binary oppo-site poles, "men" and "women," "certainly male" and "certainly female."

That is, overtly the list is to uphold what the mishnaic order as a whole integrates within its normative work, namely, gender duality, even as it does so by raising the specter of the "figure" of the *androginos* that would subvert that logic. The very framing of this taxonomy of law and gender seems to undermine and question this apparent gender order that comes to its fullest expression in rabbinic marital law of the Mishnah (Seder Nashim). The overt question that the compilers of what I want to suggest we could think of as the "order of the *androginos*" (*seder androginos*) pose is the question about gender ambiguity, and what it would do to the Mishnah's normative gender order (the "Order of Women") that is ruled by the two binary categories of men and women. What the compilers seem and perhaps even seek to push us into asking is whether that system can or cannot manage ambiguity. By doing so ambiguity is put in relationship to a body of law(s) that is represented as organized around the two seemingly self-evident categories of "men" and "women." On such a backdrop, it is "obviously" the *androginos* who is merely a "figure" (*Denkfigur* or thought experiment) and who appears "artificial," requiring explanation, while the categories "men" and "women" appear seemingly self-explanatory, referential categories, rather than figures just the same way, or at the very least taxonomic categories. Whether or not that is the intention of the compilers of the list, it certainly is the effect of the list. For all intents and purposes we can describe this as a naturalizing effect of gender: third gender as a thought experiment underwriting a logic of gender duality, rather than all gender categories as thought experiments. As I will point out next, the invocation of physicality plays a crucial role in this strategy.

Whiteness Equals Men as Redness Equals Women

One last point bears emphasis here, and that is the choice of introduction to the first two paragraphs of our newly entitled compilation, the *seder androginos*. "Whiteness" (*loven*), a white genital discharge renders a man impure, just like "redness" (*'odem*) renders a woman impure. These idioms are easily glossed over but deserve a closer look. They are at best general or summarizing references to the vast area of early rabbinic purity law, compiled in the mishnaic order of *Tohorot* ("Purities"). As noted above, the Mishnah does explicate in that topical context that "an *androginos* and [his sibling category, the] *tumtum* are rendered impure by blood (*dam*) like a woman, and by a white discharge (*loven*) like a man" (M. *Zavim* 2:1). Bleeding renders one a woman for purposes of the impurity laws, as white genital fluids render one a man. Or differently put, it is the fluids that position a person on the gender map of purity laws. The particular choice of locution in the *seder androginos* is remarkable: "Whiteness" as a term for male genital discharge can be found elsewhere in the Mishnah and Tosefta, as in the passage just cited to which the *seder androginos* seems to bear an intertextual relationship, but "redness" is a unique locution in the mishnaic law of menstrual impurity.[47] We do find the juxtaposition of whiteness as a bodily essence of men and redness as the bodily essence of women in the later talmudic mythical embryology—much discussed—according to which

> there are three partners in the creation of a person (*'adam*): the Holy one of Blessing, and his father and his mother. His father emits whiteness from which evolve bones, sinews, nails, marrow that is in the head, and the whiteness (*loven*) that is in the eye. His mother emits redness (*'odem*) from which evolves skin, flesh, hair, and the black that is in the eye. And the Holy One of Blessing places in him [or her] spirit, soul and facial features. (Babylonian Talmud 31a)[48]

This text appears in the Babylonian Talmud and is not entirely contemporaneous with the compilations I am considering here.[49] It does emerge from the same logic of gender duality, however, now mythologically elevated, and could perhaps be considered a narrative effect of the thinking that underwrites the *seder androginos* as well.

Be that as it may, in the normative and regulatory rhetoric of the earlier compilations the more common terms are *zov* (flow) and *dam* (blood). Again, therefore, the formulation in *seder androginos* that juxtaposes the whiteness that is the lynchpin of men's impurity, and the redness that is women's, seems to be driven by the effort to intensify polarity, and disavow ambiguity in order to underwrite the logic of duality. The juxtaposition of whiteness and redness, therefore, can be read as a strategy of naturalization of this logic. Gender duality is not merely an organizing principle of law and social relations, it is made to reflect the physical, as in visual polarity.

Conclusion

The careful reading of the compendium that in this essay I have suggested we could refer to as the *seder androginos* demonstrates not only
how essential the logic of gender duality is to rabbinic law, but how hard
the rabbis have to work to enable this. The former is not in and of itself
a new insight, since arguably the project of Jewish feminist criticism
in its engagement of rabbinic texts has been to read rabbinic texts in
such a way as to recognize the gender hierarchy and androcentrism that
dominates rabbinic law. But a critical reading of the *seder androginos*
can make a contribution to the ongoing conversations about the future
of Jewish feminism when it considers the compendium as a project of
thinking about gender, and not merely as a mnemonic device. The *seder
androginos* presents an alternate way of mapping law and gender, an
alternate taxonomy of law, one that foregrounds gender as an organizational category of the Mishnah's legal project. As a gender theoretical
project it foregrounds gender duality as the referential framework even
for entertaining the hybrid category of the *androginos*. But by doing so,
as I have argued here, it reveals that very framework as a product of cultural negotiation, rather than one of either biblical law or natural law.

Seder androginos, we may presume, had its historically contemporaneous interlocutors, namely, those who subscribed to a Pauline gender utopianism, according to which gender duality is transcended "in
Christ" (Gal 3:26–28). Indeed, in many ways the *seder androginos* reads
as a direct response to Paul: You say there is "neither male nor female"?
We say law applies to men and women, since there is "certainly male
and certainly female" (Mishnah Arakhin 1:1). You say that "in Christ"
there is no more gender difference for Israel? We say that gender difference, nay gender duality, is the essence of what it is to be Israel.

Arguably, the emphatic insistence is an indicator of how difficult it
is to maintain the logic of gender duality as that which organizes Jewish law and norms, as that which forms its theoretical framework. But
by preserving *seder androginos* these same compilers also point to the
fact that the conversation about the binary gender order was a live conversation within rabbinic circles and not merely between rabbis and
Christians. The binary gender order certainly did not fall into place

easily with the formulation of early rabbinic law. It remained a matter of negotiation as the Mishnah was compiled, and *seder androginos* and *seder nashim* were juxtaposed with each other.

As feminist interlocutors of the *seder androginos*, however, it is our task to keep these negotiations open, to renegotiate Jewish gender, that is, gender theories in conversation with the texts, traditions, and language that we inherit and choose to inherit. The *seder androginos* opens a variety of paths to Jewish feminist and queer futures that range anywhere from a path of choosing hybridity and deconstructing dualities and binary opposites, to a path of expanding gender diversities, a different future, but one with a Jewish past.

NOTES

1. A rabbinic neologism in the Mishnah. I will leave the term untranslated here, which allows me to avoid the pitfalls of rendering the rabbinic term in English, genderwise limited in its own way. On the complicated medical history inherent in the English use of the term "hermaphrodite," now see importantly Max Strassfeld, "Classically Queer: Eunuchs and Androgynes in Rabbinic Literature," Ph.D. dissertation, Stanford University, 2013, 139–140. Both my own previous work (see n. 4) and Max Strassfeld read the rabbinic use of this term in its Greco-Roman cultural context, to which the calque clearly points. Of particular interest is Pliny's slightly contemporaneous reflection on the Latin neologism: "Persons are also born of both sexes combined—what we call *hermaphrodites*, once called androgyny and classed as prodigies *(prodigiis)*, but now as entertainments *(deliciis)*" *(Naturalis Historia* 7.3.34). See my "Regulating the Human Body: Rabbinic Legal Discourse and the Making of Jewish Gender," in *The Cambridge Companion to the Talmud and Rabbinic Literature*, ed. Charlotte Elisheva Fonrobert and Martin Jaffee (Cambridge: Cambridge University Press, 2007), 293 n. 38.

2. In "Classically Queer," Max Strassfeld translates the passage using the third gender pronoun "since the question being raised here is precisely how the *androginos* fits into various gendered laws," p. 140. Even though I find this compelling, I am making a different choice here. Clearly, my choice here—"he" to indicate the default—is not elegant either. Neither of these choices is perfect.

3. See Kate Bornstein, *My Gender Workbook: How to Become a Real Man, a Real Woman, the Real You, or Something Else Entirely* (London: Routledge, 1997).

4. In two of the most important medieval manuscripts of this text, mss Kaufman (Bikkurim 4:5) and Parma (Bikkurim 4:4) of the Mishnah, the scribe put Rabbi Meir, which is important for those who seek the coherence of individual rabbinic opinions, as already the Talmudic discussions do, especially the

Babylonian Talmud. But this is not to my interest here. In any case, there is no Talmudic discussion for this tractate mishnaic tractate.

5. See my own "The Semiotics of the Sexed Body in Early Halachic Discourse," in *How Should Rabbinic Literature Be Read in the Modern World*, ed. Matthew Kraus (Piscataway: Gorgias Press, 2006), 79–105, and "Regulating the Human Body: Rabbinic Legal Discourse and the Making of Jewish Gender," in *The Cambridge Companion to the Talmud and Rabbinic Literature*, ed. Charlotte Elisheva Fonrobert and Martin Jaffee (Cambridge: Cambridge University Press, 2007), 270–295. It was initially Chana Safrai, one of the pioneering women in the scholarship of rabbinic literature in Israel, who had invited me to contribute an entry on "Gender Identity in Halachic Discourse" for the encyclopedia *Jewish Women: A Comprehensive Historical Encyclopedia* (at www.jwa.org/encyclopedia) with the explicit request to discuss the various gender ambiguities in halachic discourse that got me to deal with this text. In none of these did I consider the list as a whole. Accessed 21 October 2013.

6. Anne Fausto-Sterling's *Sexing the Body: Gender Politics and the Construction of Sexuality* (New York: Basic Books, 2000) is one of the earlier texts to lend some prominence to the antique Jewish knowledge of intersexuality as expressed in the figure of the *androginos*, rendered by her as an hermaphrodite and its sibling figure, the *tumtum*, the not yet "clearly" sexed person (p. 33). The rabbinic text has been taught numerously in the Jewish trans- and intersex community, by brilliant young teachers and rabbis such as Elliot Kukla, Reuben Zellman, and others. Some of this teaching has found its way into print in Noach Dzmura's pioneering collection, *Balancing on the Mechitza*, in which see Kukla's and Zellman's contribution "Created by the Hand of Heaven: Making Space for Intersex People" (182–187) and Judith Plaskow's "Dismantling the Gender Binary within Judaism" (187–211). Noach republished part of my essay on "Regulating the Body," (167–179) in order to join an "academic" piece to the collection of reflections assembled in that volume. Looking at that volume I remain almost envious of the joyous creativity of the younger scholars and activists in their use of the rabbinic texts. That work could be done only by Max Strassfeld in "Classically Queer."

7. See Max Strassfeld's "Classically Queer." The scope of Strassfeld's dissertation reaches from the early rabbinic texts to the later Talmudic discourse. In many ways the thoughts presented here are the product of a conversation with Strassfeld's dissertation, who brings queer theory into conversation with the rabbinic texts and demonstrates how deeply relevant the rabbinic texts are to so many recent conversations in gender queer theory and how those conversations help us make sense of the rabbinic texts. My focus here is somewhat different and not focused so much on the question of gender ambiguity, but on its counterpiece, the rabbinic investment in the duality of gender as a cultural project.

8. For a more recent discussion of the tension between the notion of "acquisition" (*kinyan*) and "sanctification" (*kiddushin*) in rabbinic marriage law, see Gail Labovitz, *Marriage and Metaphor: Constructions of Gender in Rabbinic Literature*

(Lanham, Md.: Lexington Books, 2009), especially chapter 1: "A Woman Is Acquired: The Rabbinic Marital Metaphor," 29–63.

9. Following ms. Kaufman.

10. See Rachel Adler's famous essay, "The Jew Who Wasn't There: Halacha and the Jewish Woman," first published in the West Coast magazine *Davka* in 1971 and then anthologized in *The Jewish Woman: An Anthology* (*Response: A Contemporary Jewish Review* 18 [Summer 1973], 77–82), now also exhibited in The Jewish Women's Archive (http://jwa.org/feminism/_html/JWA001.htm). Most recently, Elizabeth Shanks Alexander has devoted an entire monograph to the interpretive history of just one of the statements, the exemption of women from time-bound prescriptive commandments. See her *Gender and Timebound Commandments in Judaism* (Cambridge: Cambridge University Press, 2013). She argues that this exemption was not originally rooted in a supposed rabbinic "ideology of gender," but was a product of a merely "academic" exercise in legal hermeneutics. Her somewhat problematic differentiation between gender ideology as a cause and gender ideology as an accidental product of formalistic hermeneutic exercises aside, to my mind the passage as we have it in the Mishnah now clearly articulates an early rabbinic investment in gender duality. As such, this passage is familiar to the compilers of the *androginos* list, as we shall see.

11. Strassfeld, "Classically Queer," represents a reading informed by queer theory.

12. The Mishnah is organized into six largely topical "orders" (*sedarim*) one of which—under the titular category of "Women" (*Nashim*)—is devoted to the laws of marriage, mishnaic law, and the legal language that it develops, although much commented upon, expanded, and readapted over the centuries—remain normative in many social and religious contexts of Jewish life today.

13. E.g., Mishnah Yevamot 6:7; Tosefta Yevamot 8:4. On the interpretive history of the biblical injunction in rabbinic Judaism, see Jeremy Cohen, *"Be Fertile and Increase, Fill the Earth and Master It": The Ancient and Medieval Career of a Biblical Text* (Ithaca: Cornell University Press, 1989).

14. Paula Hyman, "The Other Half: Women in the Jewish Tradition," in *Response: A Contemporary Jewish Review* 18 (Summer 1973), 67–75. Judith Romney Wegner, *Chattel or Person? The Status of Women in the Mishnah* (Oxford: Oxford University Press, 1988).

15. Daniel Boyarin, *Carnal Israel: Reading Sex in the Talmud* (Berkeley: University of California Press, 1993).

16. Charlotte Fonrobert, *Menstrual Purity: Rabbinic and Christian Reconstructions of Biblical Gender* (Stanford: Stanford University Press, 2000).

17. Judith R. Hauptman, *Rereading the Rabbis: A Woman's Voice* (Boulder, Colo.: Westview Press, 1998).

18. In that regard second-wave Jewish feminist criticism was beholden to the premises of liberal feminism and its focus on gender asymmetry/ies, while arguably the focus of postliberal, third-wave feminism has shifted attention to

the differences amongst women, thereby deconstructing gender duality as a primary conceptual framework.

19. For this text most prominently represented by Saul Lieberman and his critical edition of the Tosefta, including our tractate. Saul Lieberman, *Tosefta Kifshuta: Shvi'it- Bikurim*. [Hebrew] New York: Jewish Theological Seminary of America, [1955] 1992.

20. Mss. Kaufman and Parma, as the fourth chapter of Mishnah Bikkurim, and the first printed edition of Napoli. Clearly, mss. Kaufman and Parma versions are closely related to each other, as will emerge from the notes below, and from what Lieberman considers one tradition in the process of transmission.

21. Mss. Vienna and Erfurt, as part of the second chapter of the same tractate.

22. In his critical edition of the Tosefta, Lieberman therefore presents both the manuscript traditions synoptically, which Max Strassfeld rightly emphasizes is a rare step for Lieberman in his method of producing the critical edition. Strassfeld, "Classically Queer," 159–160.

23. Martin Jaffee, "Writing and Rabbinic Oral Tradition: On Mishnaic Narrative, Lists, and Mnemonics," *Journal of Jewish Philosophy and Thought* 4, 1 (1995), 123–146, has most prominently argued for the imbrication of orality and writing specifically rabbinic textual genres such as lists. By now, there is a significant scholarship on this genre in rabbinic literature, a common form of presenting law in the early rabbinic texts.

24. For a brilliant reading on the ways in which the list got patched into its respective places in the larger compilations, see Strassfeld, "Classically Queer."

25. Ms. Vienna of Tosefta Bikkurim. The numbering per Roman numerals is of course mine.

26. That is, if ze has a white genital discharge, presumably from the male genitalia, the levitical laws of impurity applying to a man would apply to hir. The parallel formulation of this law can be found in Mishnah *Zavim* 2:1: "Regarding a *tumtum* and an *androginos* one imposes upon them the stringencies applying to a man (*homrei ha-ish*) and the stringencies applying to a woman (*homrei ha-ishah*). They are rendered impure by *blood* (*dam*) like a woman, and by a *white discharge* (*loven*) like a man" (ms Kaufman).

27. See M. *Yevamot* 8:6: "An *androginos* 'takes' (a wife) but is not 'taken' (as a wife). Rabbi Eliezer says: Regarding (sex with) an *androginos* one incurs the death penalty by stoning as with a male (*ke-zakhar*)." In the background of Rabbi Eliezer's opinion is M. *Sanhedrin* 7:4, which lists sex with a male among those transgressions that are in the category of death penalty by stoning. For an extensive discussion of M. Yevamot 8:6, see Strassfeld, "Classically Queer," chapter 4.

28. See M. *Kiddushin* 4:12: "A man may not remain alone with two women, but a woman may remain alone with two men. Rabbi Simeon says: Even one man may remain alone with two women when his wife is with him, and he may sleep with them in an inn, because his wife watches over him."

29. This refers to mishnaic inheritance law, which distinguishes between actual inheritance and maintenance. In M. *Ketubbot* 4:6, the Mishnah expounds: "Rabbi Eleazar ben Azariah expounded before the sages in the vineyard at Yavneh: The sons inherit and the daughters receive maintenance." Elsewhere, in M. *Bava Batra* 9:1, the Mishnah rules the following: "If a man died and left sons and daughters, and the property was great, the sons inherit and the daughters receive maintenance. But if the property was small the daughters receive maintenance and the sons go a-begging." On this remarkable text, see Miriam Peskowitz, *Spinning Fantasies: Rabbis, Gender and History* (Berkeley: University of California Press, 1997), 124–128. In M. Bava Batra 9:2, the Mishnah discusses the case of the *tumtum* as one of the offspring.

30. Meaning, those biblical prohibitions apply to him. On these last two laws, compare M. Kiddushin 1:7, where the prohibition to cut either the forelocks or the beard and the prohibition to be rendered impure by the dead are listed as exceptions to the general rule that all biblical prohibitions (as opposed to obligations or "positive laws") are incumbent upon both men and women. It seems clear to me that M. Kiddushin 1:7 serves as an intertext for the pairing of this with the following ruling (viii), hir obligation for all the positive commandments.

31. Ms. Parma and Kaufman of the Mishnah (both as Bikkurim 4:2) list i), v), ii), viii) and add the obligation to levirate marriage as its second rule. Ms Erfurt inserts viii) right after iv) and then repeats viii) without "spelled out in the Torah" at the end. This doubling seems to be the result of a scribal error.

32. See n. 12. The Hebrew here is interesting, however, since the more common referent for women's genital discharge is "blood" (*dam*), rather than redness. So also in the parallel text in M. Zavim 2:1.

33. For the laws of "levirate marriage," see Deuteronomy 25:5–10. Accordingly, a man is required to marry his deceased brother's widow if that couple did not have children. She cannot marry anybody else unless her brother-in-law has explicitly and ritually refused to marry her. The function of a levirate marriage is solely to produce offspring for the deceased brother.

34. Which the priests have to eat in the Temple. Therefore wives of priests did not get a share of this kind of sacrificial food.

35. Ms. Parma and Kaufman of the Mishnah list i), ii) [then vii) from the men's group as not applying as in the case of women, then vi) from the men's group as not applying as is the case for women], vi), vii) (divided into two, transgressive sex and disqualification from the priesthood).

36. Lev 12:1–8 discusses the impurity subsequent to giving birth. It distinguishes between the initial period of impurity (in the case of boys 7 days, in the case of girls 14 days), which is likened to the mother's menstrual impurity. Afterwards, however, she is in a different phase in which she counts out 33 days for boys and 66 days for girls. Bleeding during those days is still attributed to the birth and would not render her impure. The mishnaic tractate devoted to the laws

of menstrual impurity, Tractate Niddah (3:5–6), discusses the case of counting days after the miscarriage of an *androginos* or *tumtum* fetus.

37. The assumption being that there are no brothers.

38. "Outer district" means external to the Temple, and this can refer to either Jerusalem or the rest of the land of Israel. There are types of sacrificial food that the priests can eat with their families outside the Temple.

39. Ms. Parma of the Mishnah (as Bikkurim 4:4) list i), iii) and ii), iv), vi), v), vii). Here ms Kaufman differs slightly and has i), iv), vi), [adds rule about the holiest sacrifices as such], v), vii). Further, the language in i) differs from the version in the Tosefta.

40. Commentators here suggest that the text should be emended from sin-offering to impurity, since the former makes no sense. In the case of the latter, the implication would be that if the *androginos* goes to the Temple while he has a genital discharge others who touch him do not incur a penalty.

41. Normally, the heave-offering is burned once a man or woman in a status of ritual impurity have touched it, since it can no longer be used as sacrificial food.

42. Under certain circumstances the monetary value of a person can be established, such as when a person swears to dedicate the value of his son to the Temple. Leviticus 27 establishes the fixed values of categories of people, which are dependent on age and gender. Obviously, a woman is worth significantly less than a man, and the children and old people are worth less than adult men between the ages of 20 and 60. The Tosefta apparently concludes here that a hermaphrodite cannot be evaluated at all. Compare Mishnah *Tractate Arakhin*, the tractate that deals with "vows of valuations": "Everyone—priests and levites and Israelites, women and slaves—may vow another's Valuation and their Valuation may be vowed by others. . . . The *tumtum* or the *androginos* may vow . . . another's Valuation, but their Valuation cannot be vowed by others, since only their Valuation may be vowed who are *certainly male* or *certainly female*" (M. *Arakhin* 1:1).

43. Both ms. Parma (as Bikkurim 4:4) and ms Kaufman (as Bikkurim 4:5) of the Mishnah list [(i) from the previous section, in total contradiction to that ruling—for damage to him one is *not* responsible], (iii), and (v) (but here he is *not* a *nazir*).

44. Accordingly, the *androginos* baby whose eighth day of life falls on the Sabbath cannot be circumcised on that Sabbath (mShabbat 19:3), while a baby boy who has male genitalia only, can and indeed should be circumcised on the Sabbath if that happens to be his eighth day of life. For the only—albeit very brief—discussion of this fascinating text so far, see my "Regulating the Human Body."

45. For an equivalent effort we may think of the mishnaic tractate that organizes rabbinic knowledge not topically, but "chronologically" by sages to whom the origin of such knowledge is attributed, namely Tractate *Eduyot*, whose place in the Mishnah continues to puzzle scholars. Kenneth Jeremy Wieder, "Mishnah

Eduyot: A Literary History of a Unique Tractate," Ph.D. dissertation, New York University, 2006.

46. On this background it remains instructive to think about the real—and his-torical—alternative offered by the Roman intertext, where Pliny's remark is instructive again, namely, that "persons are also born of both sexes combined—what we call hermaphrodites, once called androgyny and classed as prodigies (*prodigiis*), but now as entertainments (*deliciis*)" (*Naturalis Historia* 7.3.34). This would suggest that in that mentality the *androginos* is considered other than human. As far as the earlier Roman custom of drowning hermaphrodite babies is concerned, see Luc Brisson, *Sexual Ambivalence: Androgyny and Hermaphroditism in Graeco-Roman Antiquity*, trans. by Janet Lloyd (Berkeley: University of California Press, 2002), and the sources cited in his section on "An Ominous Prodigy," 8–31.

47. In fact, in rabbinic conceptualization menstrual blood is precisely not identified by color, at least not exclusively, since it can have a variety of colors, as in M. Niddah 2:5, about which see my *Menstrual Impurity*, 103–128.

48. For a discussion of this passage in the context of rabbinic embryology, see Gwynn Kessler, *Conceiving Israel: The Fetus in Rabbinic Narratives* (Philadelphia: University of Pennsylvania Press, 2009), 133 ff. See also Daniel Boyarin and Lawrence Hoffman, on whether the text implies a gender hierarchy or equiva-lence, as well as Joshua Levinson, all discussed by Kessler. None of them men-tion our compilation.

49. Although the Babylonian Talmud presents this text as an early tradition—a baraita —it is nowhere to be found in the earlier compilations, as Kessler points out. She discusses what she identifies as the "three partners tradition" in rabbinic embryology comprehensively, and considers it to be fairly unique in classic rabbinic literature and its various theories of embryology in that it considers the contribution of the mother to the making of the origin, Kessler, *Conceiving Israel*.

5

Gender and Reproductive Technologies in Shia Iran

SORAYA TREMAYNE

The abundant contemporary Middle East scholarship on Islam and gender has been instrumental in undoing the myth that Islam is a rigid religion not open to change.[1] Over the past three decades, the profusion of information emerging from Muslim countries, especially on women, has thrown light on the dynamics and intricacies involved in the relationship between men and women. Research also has demonstrated the shift in the balance of gender relations as a result of the encounter between the persisting old norms and values with modernity and globalization.[2] In those countries where Islam is taking an increasingly prominent role and religious leaders are getting more involved in the political aspects of governance, gender relations have taken many turns and twists. Modernity and globalization, combined with cultural practices and religious beliefs, have redefined the boundaries of the interaction between men and women in unexpected ways. In what follows, I propose to use the example of the theocratic state of Shia Iran to illustrate the extent to which the involvement of the ruling religious leaders in policies have left a lasting impact on gender relations at all levels in society, both inter- and intragenerationally.

Following the Islamic Revolution of 1979 and the establishment of a theocratic regime in Iran, one of the main aims of the ruling religious authorities became the revival of the old values and norms which had been threatened under the previous regime. Among the priorities was to ensure that Islamic law (sharia) became the basis of the civil code, especially with regard to women's rights and position in society. Under the renewed sharia women were considered mothers and custodians of the family above all and their rights were limited accordingly.[3] At the same time, in the early years after the Revolution the regime was faced with fundamental social and political problems which, if unaddressed, would have threatened its very foundation. These included rapid population growth and an eight-year war with Iraq, which resulted in an economic crisis, testing all the country's resources.[4] The regime found itself in a conundrum. On the one hand, it had to respond to the country's socio-cultural and economic problems by adapting to change and modernity and developing an all-encompassing socioeconomic plan, and on the other it had to do so within a strictly Islamic framework. Some of the policies introduced subsequently concerned women, who the regime had to acknowledge and include in its reforms. The recognition of women's role in development programs had a major impact on gender relations, altering them in unexpected and unintended ways. The outcome of the interaction between Islamic law, the government's modernizing policies, and men and women's responses to them, worked in women's favor in some instances and to their disadvantage in others. However, the dynamics generated by these reforms inadvertently opened the gateway to greater freedom and aspirations for women and proved irreversible. It was a double-edged sword for the authorities. To illustrate these points, I have chosen to examine two examples from the area of reproductive technologies introduced with the approval and full support of senior religious leaders, and to explore their implications for gender relations.

The first example is that of population policies (*barnameyeh tanzim khanevadeh*) and their major and long-term impact on society. The second area is that of assisted reproductive technologies (ARTs), more specifically the third-party gamete donation of sperm and egg for the treatment of infertility. Although the religious leaders' endorsement of the infertility treatment is not official policy, it did require religious approval before the practice was allowed. The latter example is much smaller in scale compared with the population policies, as it only affects the infertile population. Nevertheless, the infertility rate in Iran seems to be higher than the global rate given by the World Health Organization

(WHO), which puts the average infertility rate at around 15 percent. A recent survey of 17,000 households in Iran carried out by the Avicenna Research Centre showed that the infertility rate among the population surveyed was between 20 to 22 percent for urban and rural areas respectively. Therefore, in spite of the difference in scale between the population policies and ARTs, the significance of the latter is clear, as it concerns some of the most important institutions in society, namely, those of reproduction, kinship, and the family. The legitimization of both these reproductive technologies was justified in the interests of the family, which is the most fundamental institution in a Muslim society and which the Islamic regime in Iran is anxious to protect. The legitimization of both reproductive technologies has led to major transformations in the structure of the family and kinship, albeit to different degrees.

Methodology

The data presented in this chapter are drawn from a longitudinal study focusing on the dynamics of reproduction in Iran across three generations. The research started in 1997 and continues to date. It includes several field trips in 2000 in Tehran and Ardebil (northwest Iran) to study the links between gender and development, in 2004 in Yazd (central Iran) to study the impact of education on early marriage, and in Tehran and Yazd on ARTs. The follow-up studies were carried out in 2006, 2008, 2011, and 2012. Since 2003, I have also carried out research among Iranian women refugees in the United Kingdom who had fled from family violence. The main method used throughout has been the anthropological technique of participant observation. In addition, extensive in-depth interviews on early marriage and early pregnancy, and on ARTs, were carried out with medical practitioners and infertile couples at the clinics. The data presented in this chapter are based on 150 cases, and also include the larger network of the kin group of several of the individuals studied.

Iran's Population Policies

The history of Iran's population policies predates the Islamic Revolution and goes back to the creation of the Ministry of Women's Affairs and the inception of a government-sponsored family planning program in 1967. These policies aimed to reduce population growth, which was at 3.8 per annum. But because of their top-down and paternalistic style of implementation that bore little relation to prevailing cultural norms among the target population, they were not as successful as they might have been.[5] However, Iran remained committed to implementing its population policies and participated in the first world population conference in Bucharest in 1974. At that conference, the critical role of women in population policies was acknowledged and links were made between fertility and women's status, associating women's high status with factors such as female education, female literacy, and female labor participation. The assumption was that improving women's conditions would automatically lead to low fertility, smaller families, later age of marriage, and contraceptive use. The literature of the period indicates that women's development was bound up with demographic objectives and was not concerned with the well-being of women as such.[6]

After the Islamic Revolution, the family planning program of the previous regime fell into disarray and the new regime did not formulate an explicit policy, the religious authorities arguing against controlling population growth on religious and political grounds. For example, they claimed inter alia that high population growth was the sign of a strong nation; for this reason the family planning clinics were subsequently dismantled. After the war with Iraq began in 1980, Ayatollah Khomeini encouraged people to have large families and mentioned the need for "the army of 20 millions," referring to the human loss caused by the war. The new regime also lowered the age of marriage from 16 to 9 years for girls, and from 18 to 14 years for boys, following the sharia's instructions.[7] Thus, the population continued to grow and its magnitude raised an alarm when the National Census of 1986 was carried out. It showed that the population had almost doubled in two decades, from 25.7 million to over 50 million. Policy makers realized the enormity of the problem and appealed to the senior religious leaders for their intervention, pointing out that such rapid population growth could pose a major threat to the stability of the regime, which would not be able to fulfill its promises nor meet the demands of the population. Senior politico-religious leaders believed that the population growth had become a strategic challenge and its outcome was too important to be left to individual whim. They showed real commitment and played an active part in the introduction and implementation of new population policies. These well-coordinated policies proved so successful that within a space of ten years the rate of growth dropped from 3.8 in 1986 to below 2 percent in 1996. Iran was awarded the UN Population Award in 1998 for its achievements. World Bank figures show that in 2010 the rate of population growth stood at around 1.5 percent, with variations among rural and urban families. Although many factors were responsible for this success in addition to the support of religious leaders, the role played by the latter proved crucial in the initial stages of implementation. Without their endorsement, the policies would probably have encountered fierce resistance from conservative quarters, as they did under the Pahlavi regime.[8]

The details of the implementation of the family planning policies and the role played by religious leaders have been fully addressed by other scholars and are beyond the remit of this chapter. Here, I want only to mention the effectiveness of the special attention the policies paid to people's sensitivities on matters of procreation. With help from Islamic scholars, the planners presented convincing alternative explanations that questioned the general belief that Islam favors large families and is a pronatalist religion. Religious sermons emphasized that having fewer children and bringing them up as healthy and happy citizens was more in line with what Islam advocates than having too many children who would live in poverty and suffer from ill-health. The history of Islamic family planning was included in the national curricula at schools, in adult literacy classes, and special family planning sessions were organized in mosques and factories. Medieval religious texts by leading Muslim scholars such as al-Ghazali were produced, showing that Islam did not forbid family planning.[9]

One of the key factors in the success of the family planning programs was the realization that women's cooperation and willing participation in birth control were essential if the policies were to succeed. The planners therefore addressed women directly and included them in their programs from the start. Women responded to this invitation with open arms. They welcomed the endorsement of birth control by the religious leaders, and used it to make their own reproductive decisions and counteract resistance from their husbands to the use of contraceptives.

Even several years after the implementation of the family planning measures, many men showed their strong disapproval of birth control. For example, in Yazd and Ardebil, two of the most conservative cities in Iran, I heard women whose husbands objected to their taking the pill, telling them, "*Aqa*—referring to Ayatollah Khomeini—himself has said that we should not have too many children." Health workers, who were responsible for the distribution of contraceptive pills to women in rural areas, also reported encountering male resistance and husbands even inflicting violence on their wives to force them to give up the pill. Many men from more conservative and/or religious groups resorted to coercive measures to prevent their wives from using the contraceptive pill. In Yazd, I came across instances of pregnant women who had come to the maternity clinics asking for an abortion because their husbands had found their pills and forced them to give them up, and/or had raped them to make them pregnant. There were also women who had given up their pills voluntarily and had several children in order to prevent their husbands from marrying a second wife. However, among the more educated and secular groups both men and women were in favor of having fewer children and had either reduced the number of children before the family planning program started or welcomed its introduction and responded positively.

In addition to and in tandem with these policies, an elaborate literacy campaign was also launched. Soon after the establishment of the Islamic regime, coeducation was banned and sex segregation was imposed in keeping with Islamic principles. Contrary to the expectation of a drop in girls' attendance at schools, parents from rural areas and the conservative sectors of society showed great willingness to send their daughters to single-sex schools, and the attendance rate of girls rose considerably. Following such an increase, the need arose for more qualified female teachers and health workers and thousands of new female teachers and health workers had to be trained. However, one of the original reasons for encouraging female education was to educate girls in the Islamic ideals of womanhood. As Golnar Mehran, a professor of education at Al-Zahra University in Tehran, explains:

> One can see a cycle in female education in Iran in which the ruling elite
> seeks to educate the ideal female citizen according to the dictates of an

Islamizing and revolutionary society, thus creating a generation of educated women who, in turn, influence their society and act as role models for young girls, who then seek education as a means of equality and
empowerment.

But the generation of educated young women did not turn out to be the
ideal role model, as anticipated. In Mehran's words:

> The educated women of Iran are pushing the boundaries due to their
> growing tendency to delay marriage and have fewer children, coupled
> with their active search to transform the traditional role of women in the
> family and society, leading to growing female expectations that need to
> be met sooner or later.[10]

Not only did the state policies not succeed in producing the ideal Muslim woman, but their impact on gender relations was profound and
definite. Girls did not stop at secondary education. Instead they went
on to higher education and by 2011 the ratio of female students had
increased to over 60 percent. The result of the rise in female education
has meant the emergence of new aspirations among young women.
They are no longer prepared to fit into the ideal Muslim woman's mold
of being mothers and wives, but demand that they be treated as individuals. Another major impact of education has been a rise in the age of
marriage, although other factors are also responsible for the change in
marriage patterns. Many young educated women who wish to establish
their identity through means other than motherhood do not consider
having children a prerequisite to womanhood. A number of scholarly studies point to an emerging trend among young women not to
marry and/or have a family.[11] So far, this is the case among a minority
of women, but they usually spread out from Tehran or one of the major
cities in Iran to other parts of the country. Although women in smaller
localities are not yet part of this trend, which is often decontextualized
and does not translate into local practice, the issue is deemed serious
enough to have raised an alarm and has provoked a strong reaction
among senior clerics. The ruling clerics are concerned about the social
"side effects" of rising educational standards among women and blame
the declining birth and marriage rates, which in their view leads to the

destruction of the foundation of the family, on women's high level of education. The effect of higher education is viewed as such a threat that in 2011 thirty-six universities across the country decided to ban women from studying seventy-seven subjects due to government pressure. As Shirin Ebadi, the Iranian winner of the Nobel Peace Prize, explains, "The Iranian government is using various initiatives to restrict women's access to education, to stop them being active in society, and to return them to the home."[12] A further recent reaction to both the delay in the age at marriage as well as a drop in the rate of marriage, is reflected in the debates in the Iranian parliament which is proposing to drop the minimum age at marriage from its current limit of 13 for girls back to 9 years, so that it is "fully within Islamic law." Under President Khatami's reformist regime (1997–2005) the minimum age at marriage was increased in 2003 from 9 years for girls to 13.[13] Furthermore, in July 2012 the government announced that it would no longer fund family planning programs and Ayatollah Khamenei, the Supreme Religious Leader, called on women to have more children.[14] However, in spite of new restrictions being reintroduced, Iranian women's increasing awareness of their rights has turned out to be an irreversible process and is acting as a gateway to future choices for women. The process triggered by the government's population and educational policies has fueled women's determination to continue to challenge both the state and their men to expand their freedoms, and goes beyond mere protest.

The advocacy of the family planning program and the campaign for literacy resulted in a shift in reliance on "God's will"[15] and allowed women to make their own reproductive decisions. But as the goals of family planning were being achieved, the initial direct involvement by clerics in population policies gradually diminished and public acknowledgment of women's prominent role as important agents and decision makers moved out of the limelight. Once implementation of the population policies was on track, policy makers turned their attention to maternal and child health, and areas such as the sexual health of young people were limited to basic education and applied within an Islamic framework. A review by the United Nations Population Fund (UNFPA) in 2007 of two decades of government implementation of these policies shows that the only area which has benefited from strong support by the regime has been that of maternal and child health. It became clear that, although women could potentially benefit from the progress made through many reproductive health policies, laws which constrain their rights have not been amended accordingly and have left women in a vulnerable situation vis-à-vis their fathers and husbands.

In spite of their empowerment of women, these policies also proved a double-edged sword in many respects. Women found themselves being able to control their fertility, but at the same time powerless vis-à-vis the Islamic law of marriage, child custody, and other matters. Although women used their newfound ability to make their own reproductive decisions as a bargaining tool to negotiate and gain control in other spheres, this power remained intermittent and lost its effectiveness once they had passed their reproductive years. The areas in which they gained power included the ability to work and become financially independent, and to enforce better conditions for their daughters' educations and future, including the choice of marriage partners.[16] Also, smaller family size combined with rapid urbanization and living away from their hometowns allowed a considerable number of women to reduce the involvement and interference of the larger kin group, especially their in-laws, in family decisions and thus strengthened their position within the household. However, for most women the exercise of power and control remained tentative during the implementation of the population policies. The real impact of these policies was witnessed in the next generation, because their children had become involved in their reproductive decision making. Many women were told by their young children that they should not have more than two children because they (the children) were ashamed to go to school and tell others that there were more than two children in their family. Several women whose case studies I collected recounted their personal experiences of being confronted by their children when they began to expect yet another child. One mother told me that when her teenage daughter heard that she was pregnant again, she said, "You are not a battery hen, why are you having more than two children?" These were not isolated examples. Several of the teachers and rural and urban health workers had similar stories, confirming the role being played by children in preventing their parents from having too many children. The focus of this chapter is therefore on the effect of the population policies on this younger generation who grew to adulthood in the "post-population policy" period.

As I have argued elsewhere, although women gained some powers in specific areas, their empowerment was effectively reduced to a selective reinforcement of capabilities by the regime. For example, the dramatic expansion in women's literacy has been clearly—but not necessarily successfully—used as a tool for inculcating the values and strength of the regime. Yet as Hoodfar has argued, the government failed to introduce any measures to address a key demand of the women's movement: namely, access to employment. Thus, despite the record decline in fertility in Iran and a drastic increase in the literacy rate, women's participation in the labor force, for example, has not followed at the pace women desired, as it has elsewhere in the region.[17] Likewise, on the one hand the government's reproductive health policies paved the way for women to negotiate some form of reproductive autonomy and improved health. On the other hand, the same policies were also used by the theocratic regime to reinforce its Islamic ideology. Thus, although women have remained the focus of government policies throughout, change has occurred within the bounds determined by the sharia and women's role as mothers and custodians of the family. Improvement has therefore been selective, framed by Islamic values, which have at the same time been used to constrain their rights in other spheres such as women's legal rights, women's employment, and their ability to organize politically.

Assisted Reproductive Technologies

The second area where the intervention of religion has played a significant role in gender relations is in the treatment of infertility through the use of modern assisted reproductive technologies (ARTs), especially that of third-party gamete donation of sperm and egg. As the implications of third-party gamete donation for family and kinship have been documented extensively, I shall not elaborate on them in this chapter.[18] As studies have shown, the legitimization of global reproductive technologies and the local responses to them are as varied as the societies themselves. While in many countries where the state is secular the legitimization of ARTs has been the responsibility of legal and ethical committees and religion has played a marginal or even negligible role, in the Muslim Middle East religious leaders have played a prominent role in the legitimization of ARTs to overcome infertility. Their involvement is not surprising, considering that reproduction is one of the most important aspects of an individual's life in Islam, which views it as the duty of every individual to reproduce to ensure the continuity of his or her lineage, kin, and community. Throughout the history of Islam, Muslim scholars and clerics have taken an intense interest in reproduction, especially the female body, as the vehicle for reproduction. Religious scholars' deliberations on the sexual and reproductive life of women are abundant, as Marion Katz's chapter on menstruation in this volume demonstrates. Katz's discussion of the involvement of Muslim scholars in women's menstrual problems testifies that women are not considered fit to pass judgment on their own bodies. But it also shows that reproduction is not a private matter to be decided solely by the individuals involved, but it is also of interest to the larger community. It requires the intervention of people with higher expertise to oversee the proper functioning of reproductive bodies. Muslim scholars, as the custodians of Islamic values, consider it their duty to attend to women's reproductive health and control their sexuality to ensure the sanctity of the family and the purity of the lineage, which they view as paramount for the stability of society.

With the introduction of ARTs in Muslim countries in the Middle East, Sunnis, who constitute the majority of Muslims, allowed the treatment of infertility among married couples. But no form of third-party gamete donation of sperm, egg, embryo, or surrogacy was permitted. As Marcia Inhorn, the leading anthropologist on ARTs in Arab Muslim countries, explains, the main reasons for such a ban is that third-party gamete donation is viewed as equivalent to adultery and as interfering with and confusing lineage and inheritance issues.[19] In his book *Islam and New Kinship*, Morgan Clarke explains the importance of establishing the lineage through procreation as follows:

> According to the vision of the Islamic legal establishment, relations of filiation (*nasab*), are not mutable or fluid, but are given, paradigmatically—but not exclusively—through procreation. Relation through procreation is not, however, a sufficient condition for the establishment of *nasab* in Islamic law. *Nasab* accrues to those conceived within a union of marriage.[20]

Sunnis therefore have consistently argued that no third-party donation is allowed in the treatment of infertility. Senior Shia religious leaders in Iran, on the other hand, have allowed the use of ARTs in all its forms, from the practice of IVF between a married couple, to third-party donation of sperm, egg, and embryo, surrogacy, stem cell research, and sex selection, without breaching any Islamic rules. Soon after IVF became available in the West, Iranian medical practitioners introduced it in Iran. The introduction of IVF between a married couple was considered a medical technology, and Ayatollah Khomeini issued a fatwa allowing masturbation, which is considered *makruh*—that is, disliked or not approved of—in Islam, for the purpose of semen collection. As these reproductive technologies advanced and third-party donation of sperm and egg became available, Iranian jurists were faced with the problem of justifying using a stranger's gamete to treat a married infertile person. The responsibility for allowing or refusing the use of third-party gamete donation fell on the senior clerics, who agreed with their Sunni counterparts that third-party gamete donation was similar to incest or adultery and that donation should take place only between a wife and husband. These clerics, who were sources of emulation (*marja*), resorted to independent reasoning (*ijtihad*) to decide whether to allow or ban third-party gamete donation.[21] Although they have never reached a consensus and they remain divided to date, the approval of *marjas* who were in favor of third-party donation opened the way for the practice. However, the fact that the leading medical practitioners took the initiative of involving clerics in the public debates concerning third-party donation has been widely overlooked.[22]

The deliberations by clerics and Islamic jurists to legitimize third-party donation within the marital union initially led to the use of temporary marriage. Although there is no record of when or how, or even who, first introduced the idea of temporary marriage, the suggestion was welcomed and by the mid-1990s temporary marriage was being extensively practiced at clinics.[23] This practice meant that if a woman was infertile, her husband entered into a temporary marriage—usually for a short time—with the egg donor (Islam permitting polygyny), until the egg was fertilized. Thus the husband received the donor's egg, which was legitimately fertilized with his sperm outside his infertile wife's womb. The fertilized egg was then transferred into the wife's womb. No sexual act took place between the egg donor and the husband at any stage. If the husband was infertile, the process was reversed. The fertile wife divorced her infertile husband, as she could not be married to two men at the same time, and entered into a temporary marriage with the sperm donor to receive his sperm. The practice of sperm and egg donation started in the mid-1990s and in 1999 the supreme religious leader, Ayatollah Khamenei, gave his opinion on third-party gamete donation, endorsing both sperm and egg donation subject to "no touch or gaze taking place." Although third-party donation had been practiced for some years by that time, it was his approval which gave gamete donation "official" legitimacy. Ayatollah Khamenei's fatwa did not even refer to temporary marriage as a condition for donation and only emphasized the avoidance of "touch" and "gaze." To date, it remains unclear as to who should avoid "touch" and "gaze," the donor and recipient or the medical practitioner and the infertile person, and the phrase is interpreted differently depending on who uses it and to what purpose. However, Ayatollah Khamenei's endorsement made it easier for medical practitioners to engage in third-party donation openly. While the approval of egg donation did not cause any problem, that of sperm donation led to a great deal of protest and anger among more conservative segments of society, and there was also strong protest by some conservative clerics and even members of parliament.[24] To this day, religious and conservative medical practitioners do not allow sperm donation. As a result, semi- or fully funded government clinics only practice egg donation, and sperm donation takes place only in select private clinics. The practice of temporary marriage has gradually diminished, and currently (in 2014) most clinics practice third-party donation without going through this ceremony. The third-party donation of sperm and egg was not regulated by any laws and followed Islamic ethics alone. As a result numerous ethical and legal problems have arisen for both medical practitioners and infertile couples, which they resolve as best they can in the absence of a law enforcement body.[25] When embryo donation was introduced in Iran, the clerics could not find any justification in the Qur'an to allow it. A law was passed permitting embryo donation in 2003, but it remains vague in several areas and leaves medical practitioners, donors, and the recipients of embryos in limbo.

The official involvement of the religious authorities aside, religion plays an important role among infertile individuals themselves, especially those from conservative and religious social groups. In seeking fertility treatment, many still refer to their *marja* for his approval, while some refrain from seeking treatment altogether on the grounds that it was God's will that they should be infertile. Interestingly, interviews with infertile couples reveal that they are not always aware of the fatwas and views of the higher religious authorities and act on their own beliefs or follow the opinion of their sources of emulation or *marjas*.[26]

Having discussed the jurisprudential aspects of third-party donation, in what follows I examine some of consequences of third-party donation on gender relations. In discussing the link between infertility and gender, three factors must be taken into consideration. Most infertile couples who seek treatment come from the conservative segments of society and are religious; infertility remains a major stigma; and male infertility is still denied by many men and dismissed as impossible. For many infertile couples, the first step is to satisfy themselves that they are not breaching any religious taboos. As Inhorn puts it, "Muslim couples want to make sure that they are making their babies in an Islamic way."[27] Interestingly, a visit to the website of some fertility clinics in Iran shows that some Shia couples, whether Iranian or Shia from other parts of the world seeking treatment in Iran, emphatically ask for "a Shia egg."[28]

Cases in my study show that most of the infertile individuals had consulted with their *marja* before coming to the clinic. However, some couples mentioned that they had first gone to their own *marja*, who had advised them against the treatment. "But we thought of going to another *marja* and asked around to find out which one approves of ARTs, and went to him and he gave his approval. We now know that we are not breaching any Islamic rules." The importance of religious approval for those seeking fertility treatment is also shown by other studies, such as the following:

Many women in the study considered infertility to be beyond their control—i.e. their "fate" and "the will of God." They argued that if they were not able to "bring children" into the world, this was God's wish, and they referred to Qur'anic verses to support their contention. Accordingly, if God does not will a woman to be fertile, no treatment will ever be able to help her. Nonetheless, God also expects women to seek solutions to their suffering; thus, searching for infertility treatment is meritorious and is conceived of as part of God's test of an infertile woman's patience and endurance.[29]

These beliefs are shared by couples in need of surrogate mothers. A study carried out on 238 women in the infertility clinic in Tabriz (eastern Azerbaijan), shows that 15 percent of the women were against the practice of surrogacy because of their religious beliefs. The study concludes that "in spite of the positive attitude of the women in the study, further efforts are needed to increase the acceptability of surrogacy." A considerable majority also thought that religious matters should be dealt with before legal ones.

Infertility, especially male infertility, remains a major stigma in Iran, as in many other parts of the world, and the blame often falls on women. Even when it is clear that the man is the infertile party, he tries to hide it and asks his wife to pretend to be the one who is infertile. Many women agree willingly. For example, in "The Iranian ART Revolution" by Abbasi-Shavazi, women confided to the researcher that their infertile husbands had threatened them with divorce if they did not agree to take the blame for the couple's infertility.[30] Infertility is thus generally viewed as a woman's failure to reproduce. Although there has been no follow-up research to study the life stories of couples who have conceived and gone home with a baby, the general assumption is that these technologies have made families happy and have improved the status of women within the family and among kin. Pictures of such parents with their children cover the walls of fertility clinics together with thank you notes from the parents.

A further contribution of ARTs has been to allow infertile couples to seek treatment secretly and be spared the stigma of infertility, although this is still difficult to do in practice. In theory an infertile couple can go to the clinic and seek treatment without anybody finding out. However, close contact with one's kin group is often unavoidable in Iranian society, and relatives tend to get involved, especially in matters relating to reproduction. So the couple can only resort to ARTs discreetly if it can get away from the close network of the kin group. Another difficulty is that in cases of third-party donation many infertile parties resort to their siblings or close relatives for gamete donation, which makes it impossible to hide the facts.

In general, sperm and egg donation have resulted in a host of moral, religious, and legal problems, in addition to social and cultural ones. These problems were not foreseen by the religious authorities who approved them. Gender relations are no exception. While in cases of female infertility women have submitted to the treatment willingly, male infertility provokes strong negative reactions in men. When they find out that they are infertile, men's ideas of manhood and masculinity are shattered and, in some extreme but not rare cases they resort to violence to compensate. Among some of the cases in this study, even those infertile men who had initially agreed to resort to donor sperm rejected the child later, either by actually dissociating themselves from him, becoming indifferent toward him, or falling into depression and suffering ill-health themselves. Violence among infertile men is so widespread that the two leading fertility clinics in Iran have launched their own research projects on violence. The Avicenna Research Centre has made a film based on the life story of one of its infertile patients, and the Royan Institute has carried out research on violence among its infertile patients. Women seem to be at the receiving end of violence from their husbands regardless of which party is infertile. The two following cases, which I have discussed at length elsewhere,[31] demonstrate some of the negative aspects of third-party donation and its impact on gender relations. While by citing these stories I do not mean to suggest that all infertile men turn to violence, several cases of male infertility in this study confirm that men had used some form or degree of violence toward their wives.

The first case is that of an infertile couple who sought treatment in the United Kingdom soon after third-party donation became available. The treatment was successful and the wife gave birth to triplet girls, one of whom had green eyes and all three of whom had blonde hair. It became obvious that one of the parents was not the biological parent and that a third-party gamete had been used. On their return to Iran, the husband, who had carried out the negotiations with the clinic but had not revealed that he was the infertile party, lost face in such a way that he blamed his wife, accusing her of having slept with the doctor at the clinic, and subjected his wife and the children to extreme violence for twenty years. The violence ranged from regular severe beatings to asking schools to expel the "bastard," "Christian" children. The wife's father and brothers also sided with her husband, stating that infertility is a female problem and he could not have been infertile. After several years of abuse, she divorced her husband and found a boyfriend. But her ex-husband caught her in bed with her boyfriend and called the police. She was arrested for having a sexual relationship with a man to whom she was not married, raped while in police custody, and sentenced to stoning for adultery. At that point she ran away and sought asylum in the United Kingdom, where I met her. A few years later all three of the husband's brothers found out that they were infertile too and agreed that it must have been their brother who had been the infertile party.

The second case is one of third-party egg donation involving another woman refugee in the United Kingdom. She was married to a violent man and thought that having a child would make him less violent. But she was nearly forty years old and needed fertility treatment to conceive. After consulting with her *marja*, she resorted to a donor egg and conceived twins, one of whom was aborted after her husband beat her, as he regularly did. Soon after the birth of the child, her husband, knowing how attached she was to the child, abducted the child and started blackmailing her for money. When she refused, he reported her to the Revolutionary Courts for having converted to Christianity, an act which is punishable by death in Iran. At this point she ran away and became a refugee. She has not seen her child for several years and even when she found him, he did not want to see her, having lived under his father's influence for years.

Conclusion

In discussing the interaction between religion and gender in Islam, I have chosen two examples from Iran, which is a Shia country and a theocracy. Both examples involve modern reproductive technologies, which have been practiced with the full endorsement of the senior ruling clerics. The clerics fully supported the population policy programs, which aimed at reducing population growth, and approved assisted reproductive technologies (ARTs) for the treatment of infertility.

Although the purposes of these technologies seem to be opposed to one another, both formed part of the same agenda which, it was emphasized, was not just about reducing population growth but also about helping infertile couples receive treatment.[32] In this chapter, I have shown that without the endorsement of the senior clerics these technologies could not have been applied, well received, or even accepted by their users. I have also argued that the successful application of these technologies has had significant unintended and unanticipated consequences, and has led to profound transformations in the structure of the family and in gender relations.

For women, their liberation from uncontrolled and multiple pregnancies and childbirth, combined with better health and greater access to education and employment, opened up new possibilities allowing them to go beyond their traditional female roles and aspire to equality with men, and even break into areas which had been traditional male preserves.[33] Rapid socioeconomic development also resulted in urbanization and mobility, and many families moved away from their hometowns and formed smaller families. This freed women from the relentless interference of their kin group, especially their in-laws, and strengthened their position vis-à-vis their husbands and the family. The overall outcome for women has been an outwardly liberated and "modern" woman, seeking recognition not as a mother or wife, but as a person in her own right. These aspirations are not limited to young women from secular and highly educated backgrounds, but include women from all social groups, including conservative and religious ones.

I have shown that the real impact of these changes became evident among those, especially the women, who were either born or grew up during the implementation of the population policies, between 1986 and 1996. The aspirations of these women had not been anticipated by the Islamic regime, as they went in the opposite direction from its expectation of reproducing the ideal Islamic female role model. However, in spite of such profound changes the Islamic regime has not altered its legal and political structures. In fact, the authorities have taken a retrograde step by trying to restrict women's freedom further to make them fit into the mold of mothers and wives, as opposed to giving them recognition as individuals outside the family. The ongoing struggle between the state attempting to harness women, and women's provocative responses, has become the defining factor in dictating the state's next move toward them. In other words, regardless of the negative or positive actions of the state, young Iranian women are chipping away at the restrictions imposed on them and in so doing evoke the Old Persian saying that "rights are to be taken, they are not given" (*haq gereftanist na dadani*).

As a result of the ongoing tensions between young people and the state, a generation of women has emerged which, in the quest for recognition of their womanhood, seems to have violated many cultural and religious rules from sexual taboos to the sanctity of marriage and family. At the same time, the analysis of the data in this study also points to another reality, which reveals a different perspective on the identity and aspirations of women. While the relationship between the genders and with the state may have changed, when women come face to face with making decisions about some of the most fundamental core cultural values, for example marriage or reproduction, their modernity and individuality can be put to the test and proven skin deep. This is particularly true of a great number of women for whom change is more form than substance. Regardless of their level of education and degree of modernity, for most women being married and having children remains key to their identity, social status, and womanhood. This persistence of cultural values can be observed nowhere better than among cases of infertility, where infertile women comply fully with cultural norms. Even for highly educated and those who might be considered "modern" infertile men and women, the stigma of infertility seems as strong as it is for the older generation or for their less educated and more conservative counterparts. To date, regardless of how successful and independent a young woman may be, her status as a mother prevails over that of the professional in society. While marriage patterns and attitudes toward fertility and childbearing may have changed, the actual values attached to the status they provide for women remain firmly anchored in old norms and values.[34] As research in fertility clinics shows, a considerable number of women seeking fertility treatment are highly educated, professional, have married late, and are past their reproductive age, which is why they are resorting to fertility treatment. There are also older women who have been divorced and have remarried, and need to secure their marriage by having a child.[35]

Finally, the two reproductive technologies discussed in this chapter, which were intended for contrary purposes, have also led to contrary outcomes as far as gender relations are concerned. While population policies empowered the younger generation of women and led to a narrowing of the gender gap, the endorsement of third-party fertility treatment has widened the gap between infertile men and women. In cases of infertility, regardless of who is infertile, women have had to comply with the expectations of their husbands and often those of other close male relatives, to maintain their position in society. Even the scientific proof that men can also be infertile has not changed men's behavior toward their wives. On the positive side, however, ARTs have provided some choices for women, for example by allowing them to delay marriage and childbearing, knowing that they can have a child through the preservation of their eggs. However, this remains more of an ideal than a reality for most women, who are under intense pressure by their husbands and/or kin group and in-laws to reproduce soon after getting married.

As the women of post-population policies strive to establish their identities as women rather than as mothers and wives, and in the process also define the boundaries of gender relations, the question arises as to whether these young women's resistance and new aspirations are a passing "rebellion" or a profound and lasting "revolution."

NOTES

1. See, for example, inter alia, Deniz Kandiyoti, *Gendering the Middle East* (Syracuse, N.Y.: Syracuse University Press, 1996); Camillia El-Solh and Judy Mabro, eds., *Muslim Women's Choices: Religious Belief and Social Reality* (Providence: Berg, 1994); Inger Mari Okkenhaug and Ingvilid Flaskerud, *Gender, Religion and Change in the Middle East: Two Hundred Years of History* (Oxford: Berg, 2005); and Soraya Tremayne, "Not all Muslims Are Luddites," *Anthropology Today* 22, 93 (2006), 1–2.

2. See, for example, Mariz Tadros, ed., "Religion, Rights and Gender at the Crossroads," *Institute for Development Studies Bulletin (IDS)* 42, 1 (December 2010).

3. Firoozeh Kashani-Sabet, *Conceiving Citizens: Women and the Politics of Motherhood in Iran* (New York: Oxford University Press, 2011), 215–217.

4. Homa Hoodfar, "Population Policy and Gender Equity in Post-Revolutionary Iran," in Carla Makhlouf-Olbermeyer, ed., *Family, Gender and Population in the Middle East: Policies in Context* (Cairo: American University in Cairo Press, 1995); and Amir Mehryar et al. *Draft Country Population Assessment Report* (Plan Organization of Iran, 1998), unpublished with limited circulation.

5. Homa Hoodfar, "Bargaining with Fundamentalism: Women and the Politics of Population Control in Iran," *Reproductive Health Matters* 4, 8 (1996), 30–41; and Carla Makhlouf-Obermeyer, "Reproductive Choice in Islam: Gender and State in Iran and Tunisia," *Studies in Family Planning* 25, 1 (1994), 41–51.

6. See Soraya Tremayne, ed., *Managing Reproductive Life: Cross-Cultural Themes in Fertility and Sexuality* (New York: Berghahn Books, 2001).

7. See Soraya Tremayne, "And Never the Twain Shall Meet," in Maya Unnithan-Kumar, ed., *Reproductive Agency, Medicine and the State: Cultural Transformations in Childbearing* (New York: Berghahn Books, 2004).

8. See, for example, Mehryar, *Population Assessment Report*; M. Jalal Abbasi-Shavazi, "La fécondités en Iran: L'autre révolution," *Population et Sociéte* 373 (November 2001), 1–4; Hoodfar, "Population Policy and Gender Equity"; Tremayne, "And Never the Twain Shall Meet"; and Kashani-Sabet, *Conceiving Citizens*.

9. For more on the medieval Islamic debates on family planning, see Carla Makhlouf-Obermeyer, "Women, Islam and Population: Is the Triangle Fateful?" *Working Papers Series* 6 (Harvard: Harvard School for Public Health, Center for Population and Development Studies, 1991), 42–43. As Makhlouf-Obermeyer explains, "A clear consensus exists among schools of Islamic law that family planning is permissible. This is based on the absence of any prohibition against birth control in the Koran and on general statements in the Koran that God does not want to burden man but wishes to improve his life. More specifically, statements in the *Hadith* indicate that withdrawal *(azl)* was practiced in Mohammad's time and that he did not discourage his followers from the practice. " As Makhlouf-Obermeyer points out, the Sunni and Shia positions on birth control are the same in substance. They derive from the work of al-Ghazali, the most celebrated theologian of Islam, who establishes five reasons for which birth control may be allowed.

10. Golnar Mehran, "Gender and Education in Iran." Background paper prepared for the Education for All Monitoring Report 2003/4. *Gender and Education for All: The Leap to Equality*. http://unesdoc.unesco.org/images/0014/001468/146809e.pdf.

11. Interview in September 2012 with Dr. Amir Ebrahimi, an Iranian urban sociologist and geographer working mainly in Tehran on women and the public space. Also see Fatemeh Torabi and Angela Baschieri, "Ethnic Differences in Transition to First Marriage in Iran: The Role of Marriage Market, Women's Socio-Economic Status, and Process of Development," *Demographic Research* 22, article 2 (8 January 2010), 29–62, http://www.demographic-research.org/Volumes/Vol22/2/22-2.pdf. Accessed 24 September 2013.

12. Interview given to BBC on 2 September 2012. I heard the program myself on BBC Radio 4, Today Program between 8 and 9 a.m., but I am not sure that there is a link or whether it is still functioning.

13. Darren Weir, "Iran Moves to Legalize Marriage for Girls under Ten Years Old," *Digital Journal* (25 July 2012), http://digitaljournal.com/article/329317. Accessed

24 September 2013, http://iranian.com/main/news/2012/08/23/iran-moves-legal-ize-marriage-girls-under-10-years-old.html Accessed 29 October 2013.

14. Elizabeth Leahy Madsen, "Iran's Surprising and Shortsighted Shift on Family Planning," *New Security Beat* (8 August 2012), http://www.newsecuritybeat.org/2012/08/irans-surprising-and-shortsighted-shift-on-family-planning/ Accessed 24 September 2013.

15. In 2009 the Iranian president, Ahmadinejad, announced that the number of children in a family is in the hands of God and therefore people must stop family planning and start having more children. As an incentive to do so, he proposed to open bank accounts, depositing a considerable sum of money for each new child being born. However, this was not well received by people. In 2011 the Iranian parliament reversed the decision and put a stop to the payments.

16. See, for example, J. Salehi-Isfahani and G. Taghvatalab, *Marriage Squeeze and the Changing Pattern of Marriage in Iran* (Princeton: Princeton University Press, 2009), Working Papers Series, http://iussp2009.princeton.edu/papers/93356

17. Hoodfar, "Bargaining with Fundamentalism."

18. The following scholars have written extensively about Islam and ARTs: Marcia Inhorn, *Local Babies, Global Science: Gender, Religion and In Vitro Fertilization in Egypt* (New York: Routledge, 2003); Marcia Inhorn, "Making Muslim Babies: IVF and Gamete Donation in Sunni versus Shia Islam," *Culture, Medicine, and Psychiatry* 30, 4 (2006), 427–50; Marcia Inhorn and Soraya Tremayne, eds., *Islam and Assisted Reproductive Technologies: Sunni and Shi'a Perspectives* (New York: Berghahn Books, 2012), 1–24; Soraya Tremayne, "The Moral Ethical and Legal Implications of Egg, Sperm and Embryo Donation in Iran," Paper presented at the International Conference on Reproductive Disruptions: Childlessness, Adoption and other Reproductive Complexities, University of Michigan, Ann Arbor, Mich., 19 May 2005; Tremayne, "Not All Muslims Are Luddites"; Soraya Tremayne, "Law, Ethics and Donor Technologies in Shia Iran," in Daphna Birenbaum-Carmeli and Marcia Inhorn, eds., *Assisting Reproduction Testing Genes: Global Encounters with New Biotechnologies* (New York: Berghahn Books, 2009), 144–164; Soraya Tremayne, "The 'Down Side' of Third Party Donation: The 'Happy Family' Rhetoric in Iran," in Marcia Inhorn and Soraya Tremayne, eds., *Islam and Assisted Reproductive Technologies*, 130–157; Morgan Clarke, *Islam and New Kinship: Reproductive Technologies and the Shariah in Lebanon* (New York: Berghahn Books, 2009), 45–48.

19. Inhorn, "Making Muslim Babies."

20. Clarke, *Islam and New Kinship*. See also Inhorn and Tremayne, eds., *Islam and Assisted Reproductive Technologies*, 6.

21. The nineteenth-century development of the concept of "sources of emulation" (*marja-e taqlid*), or Shia religious scholars who are to be followed for their learnedness, the Shia emphasis on independent reasoning (*ijtihad*) to find new answers to new problems. However, the interpretations of these texts have not been monolithic; differences of opinion have emerged among the four Sunni

legal schools (*madhhab*) and on basic principles, such as what constitutes lineage, or who can be considered the legitimate parent or child in a family. Likewise, Shia leaders are not unanimous in their views and remain divided in their interpretations and verdicts on the extent to which the ARTs can be applied. See Inhorn and Tremayne, eds., *Islam and Assisted Reproductive Technologies*, 6.

22. Two leading institutions have pioneered ARTs in Iran, namely, the Avicenna Research Centre and the Royan Institute. The Avicenna Research Centre, headed by Dr. Akhondi, has pioneered the opening up of debates at conferences and has published extensively on the religious, legal, and social aspects of ARTs. See above references, under Avicenna Research Centre.

23. Temporary marriage is a form of marriage unique to the Shia school, whereby a man and a women agree to get married for a specified length of time, which can be anywhere between one hour and ninety-nine years. See Shahla Haeri, *The Law of Desire: Temporary Marriage in Iran* (London: I. B. Tauris, 1989).

24. For a fuller discussion of the fatwas given for and against third-party gamete donation, see the Avicenna Research Centre's publications: *Essays on Modern Human Reproductive Techniques from the View of Jurisprudence and Law* (2001); *Essays on Gamete and Embryo Donation in Infertility Treatment: From Medical, Theological, Ethical, Psychological and Sociological Approaches* (2007). Both are in Persian. Also for fatwas on surrogacy, see Shirin Garmaroudi-Naef, "Gestational Surrogacy in Iran: Uterine Kinship in Shia Thought and Practice," in Inhorn and Tremayne, eds., *Islam and Assisted Reproductive Technologies,* 157–194.

25. For a discussion of ARTs and Islamic ethics in Iran, see Robert Tappan, "More than Fatwas: Ethical Decision Making in Iranian Fertility Clinics," in Inhorn and Tremayne, eds., *Islam and Assisted Reproductive Technologies*, 103–130.

26. See, for example, Abbasi-Shavazi, "La fécondité en Iran: L'autre révolution," *Population et Société* 373 (November 2001), 1–4; and Garmaroudi-Naef, "Gestational Surrogacy in Iran," in Inhorn and Tremayne, eds., *Islam and Assisted Reproductive Technologies*, 157–194.

27. Inhorn, "Local Babies, Global Science," paper presented at the Embryo and Gamete Donation Conference organized by the Avicenna Research Center, Tehran, 2008.

28. See, for example, "IVF Cost at Dr. Erfanian Clinic, Iran," www.ivfcost.net/ivf-cost/ivf-cost-at-dr-erfanian-ivf-clinic-iran. Accessed 26 September 2013.

29. Abbasi-Shavazi, "La fécondité en Iran."

30. Ibid., 15.

31. See Inhorn and Tremayne, eds., *Islam and Assisted Reproductive Technologies*, 130–157.

32. For more details on this, see Tremayne, "And Never the Twain Shall Meet," 181–203.

33. For further information on links between education and delay in marriage, see the following, inter alia: http://www.brookings.edu/~/media/research/files/

papers/2010/6/iran%20youth%20salehi%20isfahani/06_iran_youth_salehi_isfa-
hani. Accessed 26 September 2013.

The percentage of women married by age twenty has fallen from 60 percent
for the 1964 birth cohort to under 30 percent for the 1984 cohort. Delayed
marriage clearly has some positive effects such as an increased opportunity
for accumulation of human capital, particularly among women. However, in a
culture where it is difficult to socialize and interact with the opposite sex before
marriage and where marriage is typically a prerequisite for being accepted
as an adult, delayed marriage can have deleterious effects (Gregg 2005). The
importance of marriage in the lives of these youth is illustrated by the responses
to a question in the SWTS regarding the most important goal in their lives.
"Having a good family life" was the most popular response among both men
and women. This response was favored over the next most popular one, "being
successful in work," by 50 percent over 14 percent for women and 31 percent
over 28 percent for men (Statistical Center of Iran 2006).

34. The social, political, and individual value of motherhood is also shown by
    Kashani-Sabet in her groundbreaking study of the meaning of motherhood,
    Conceiving Citizens.

35. Clear evidence of the persistence of old cultural norms and values can be found
    in the importance attached to female virginity by both men and women. The
    number of young liberated women secretly seeking hymenoplasty to restore
    their virginity is so high that it has once more engaged the clerics, and one
    of the Grand Ayatollahs, Sadeq Rohani from Qom, among others, has issued
    a fatwa permitting the operation. If a woman loses her virginity, her fear of
    rejection by her future husband, who could be an educated and modern man,
    and the negative reactions of his or even her own family, drives her to have her
    hymen repaired so that she can get married as a respectable girl. On virginity in
    Iran, also see Janet Afary, *Sexual Politics in Modern Iran* (New York: Cambridge
    University Press, 2009), and Janet Afary, "Recreating Virginity in Iran," guard-
    ian.com, 12 May 2009, http://www.guardian.co.uk/commentisfree/2009/may/12/
    virgin-hymen-repair-iran Accessed 26 September 26, 2013. Also see Ahmadi
    Azal's 2011 M.Phil. thesis, "Reconstructing Virginity in Iran: Hymenoplasty
    as a Form of Resistance," submitted to and accepted by *Medical Anthropology
    Quarterly.*

PART III

Crimes of Passion

Formative Texts and Traditions

Religious legal texts could not—and did not—anticipate all the dilemmas and conflicts that would develop in modern society. Jurists and legal scholars in both the Islamic and Jewish traditions have had to rely on legal precedent, customary practices, or reason to address specific aspects of women's position in their respective religious communities or to explain popular customs that have assumed the status of law. In addition to legal documents, literature and literary tropes offer other prisms through which to understand the parameters determining gender interactions in Judaism and Islam.

The three chapters in this section focus on the different ways in which gender roles and representations play out in Islam and Judaism, whether in ancient formulations or modern laws. Lori Lefkovitz begins with an archetypal story central to both Jewish and Islamic traditions—the tale of Joseph (Yosef or Yusuf)—and compares its retelling within both sets of religious texts. She argues that the rendition of Yusuf in the Qur'anic version supports the larger emphasis Islam places on the infallibility of God's messengers, whereas the Jewish stories of Yosef underline the prophet's vulnerabilities and express ambivalence over masculinity. In employing a literary analysis, Lefkovitz follows the evolution of the Joseph stories in both traditions, demonstrating how powerfully these texts and tales have reverberated in subsequent renditions over the years and how they reveal competing notions of gendered ideals.

Catherine Warrick and Lisa Fishbayn Joffe then turn to legal texts and decisions, discussing the complex legal structures that emerged in Jordan and mandatory Palestine, respectively. In both cultures, men and women are subject to multiple, often contradictory, layers of legal control in their lives. The mixture of colonial regulations, the Ottoman legal code, and distinct Muslim or Jewish customs created an intricate set of expectations for both genders. Warrick and Joffe each shows the influence of patriarchal religious structures in negotiating modern interpretations of family law and both draw on legal evidence from civic and religious contexts to do so. Colonial authorities often engaged in dialogue with male elites, who privileged their status in defining family law. In certain instances these decisions favored tribal custom and elevated customary practices to the status of common law.

Warrick offers a perceptive perspective on the subject of honor killings in the Arab world. Given the morally repugnant nature of honor killings, it is understandable that they have received undue attention in the West as a significant social critique of certain Islamic communities. As Warrick argues, honors killings are not authorized in Islamic law, yet they have been practiced in various societies. She begins by discussing the differences between passion and honor in legal contexts. By reviewing the controversy over honor killings in Jordan, which has received popular attention, she discusses the social and cultural framework that allowed honor killings to become customary in parts of the Arab world. Warrick evaluates the precedents for the Jordanian penal code in French and English laws to explain the ways in which such crimes of passion are understood and ultimately practiced.

Joffe considers the impact and influence of rabbinical courts in adjudicating family law in mandatory Palestine and the newly established state of Israel in 1948. She explains the authority of religious courts in determining marriage and divorce and analyzes the ways in which the dominance of rabbinical courts during the mandate period posed an impediment to achieving women's equality in Israel. Joffe's analysis points to the unanticipated consequences of allowing religious law to become civil law, ultimately creating a legal system in Israel that deprives women of equality in matters of marriage and divorce.

Together, the chapters in this section deconstruct portrayals of masculinity, gender, and women in distinct literary, legal, and social frameworks. Women and men respond differently to societal pressures that help to define their gender roles vis-à-vis one another. In both Islamic and Jewish traditions, men and women struggle to meet these expected norms and grapple with the consequences of these legal precedents.

6

Not a Man

Joseph and the Character of Masculinity in Judaism and Islam

LORI LEFKOVITZ

Joseph (favored son of Jacob, the last of the biblical patriarchs) is one of the shared heroes of Judaism and Islam, though he is differently nuanced by those traditions, beginning with the scriptural texts themselves and in centuries of subsequent narrative expansions.[1] Asking what those differences might suggest about variations in masculinity and gender identities, in this essay I carry out a textual twin experiment, treating Yosef (the Hebrew for Joseph) and Yusuf (the Arabic pronunciation) as genetically identical, so to speak, equivalent descendants of patriarchs with similarly split cultural roots, but entirely separate characters—doppelgängers—because raised in disparate (if often contiguous) cultural environments.[2] To the extent that it is possible to generalize about either tradition—to discover a Yosef who steps out of the cacophony of transhistorical Jewish conversation in commentary and art over the generations—and a Yusuf who harmonizes among Islamic characterizations over expanses of time and place, I will suggest that Yosef is positioned ambivalently, a site of projective anxiety about masculinity, while Yusuf, in correcting biblical ambiguities in favor of a more consistently virtuous hero, also embodies a more secure masculinity, a projection of comfort with the compatibility of male chastity and male authority.[3]

The elaborate—and over the millennia, amply elaborated—stories of Joseph enjoy uniquely sustained attention in the sacred scripture of both Judaism and Islam, occupying chapters 37 to 50 of the biblical book of Genesis (dated from the eighth century B.C.E.) and the whole of Sura 12 of the Qur'an (early seventh century), the longest sustained narrative in the Qur'an.[4] It is a beloved story in which the hero repeatedly swings from heights to depths, and back up again, beginning with his privileged boyhood, when as his father's favorite (child of the more beloved wife) he incurs the envy and resentment of his ten older brothers for dreaming grand dreams and flaunting the special coat that was a gift from their father. His brothers sell him into slavery, but he rises to a position of power in the home of Potiphar, whose wife tries unsuccessfully to seduce the beautiful servant. In prison, the dreamer proves himself a gifted reader of dreams, because of which he rises to second in command to Pharaoh, from which position he protects Egypt from famine and restructures the economy. Unrecognized by his brothers when they arrive to secure food, Joseph tests their character, ultimately reconciles with them, and arranges for the family to resettle comfortably in Egypt, thereby setting the stage for the national enslavement and miraculous liberation of the Exodus.

In an episode of the Joseph saga reported in the Qur'an but absent from the Hebrew Bible, Potiphar's wife, who had evidently become subject to court gossip following her failed seduction of the Hebrew slave Joseph, invites these catty women to visit and lays a banquet before them, complete with sharp knives; when Joseph is summoned to their company, they are so enthralled that they unwittingly slice into their fingers and declare (apparently in unison), "Perfect is Allah! This is not a man; this is none but a noble angel" (Qur'an 12:31).[5] Rabbinic Midrash (a genre of Jewish legend) of the same period, which embraces versions of the story related in the Qur'an, also includes stories with a rather different assessment of Joseph's identity as a man.[6] If the Qur'an's "city women" (as they are called) doubt Joseph's identity as a man, supposing hyperbolically that he is instead an angel, the Midrash Genesis Rabbah glosses the failed seduction by imagining a different gap between Joseph's identity and what it means to "be a man." In this story, an anonymous matron approaches Rabbi Yosé and asks what we can only presume to have been a question that the rabbis were asking themselves:

"Is it possible that Joseph, at seventeen years of age, with all the hot blood of youth, could act thus?" While Rabbi Yosé reassures the matron that Joseph must indeed have successfully resisted the boss's wife because scripture does not withhold details of sexual sin (evidenced in the Bible's record of the shameless behaviors of Joseph's elder brothers, Reuben and Judah), Rabbi Samuel ben Nahman suggests another possibility. When the Bible reports that "not a man" was in the house on the day of the attempted seduction (Gen. 39:11), the Rabbi goes afield to interpret the text as slyly indicating *of Joseph* that "on examination he did not find himself a man."[7] The reader of this Midrash must appreciate the euphemism and conclude what one annotator makes explicit: "He actually went in to sin, but found himself impotent."[8] If the Qur'an's Joseph is something more than a man (an angel), this Jewish legend's Joseph is something less than a man.[9]

The Qur'anic story's elevation of Joseph to angelic status inaugurates a relatively consistent Islamic tradition of unqualified admiration for the great prophet Joseph, whose beauty and virtue are synonymous and who models a masculine ideal that combines sexual desirability and self-restraint. An extravagant narrative tradition confers the name Zuleika on Potiphar's wife, reinterprets her designs on Joseph as the adoration due to a perfected man of God, and even weaves magical love stories, some religiously allegorized (as in the celebrated fifteenth-century poet and Sufi sheikh Jami's *Joseph and Zuleika* in which the woman's obsessive love represents that of a Sufi for his Creator). Joseph, as he is represented both in the Hebrew Bible and in the Jewish stories that elaborate on the Bible, is a more mixed character. Although later Jewish sources often do maintain Joseph as a paragon of virtue in stories cognate with popular Islamic romances, there are also Jewish stories that more fully honor the ambiguities implicit in the Bible's characterization. In these commentaries, Joseph's beauty and virtue are both occasionally manqué. From early rabbinic Midrash through "The Amazing Technicolor Dream Coat," Joseph is increasingly bound up in a history of Jewish gender difference that classified Jewish men as anomalous men, making Joseph a complicated role model. Sinned against by his brothers, to be sure, but not altogether innocent himself, Joseph's distinction among men (his beauty, intelligence, chastity, and professional success) became fraught symptoms of Jewish gender difference.

If cultural heroes are sites of projections, then the differences between the Yosef of Jewish lore and the Yusuf of Islamic lore suggest alternative self-conceptions in each communal cultural unconscious. Not only is the Qur'anic representation of Joseph consistent with the Qur'an's generic, theological interest in preserving the infallibility of Allah's prophets (a point I have developed elsewhere), but Yusuf's qualities elaborated over time combine to create the portrait of a self-possessed hero, a position that betrays less authorial anxiety than that which comes to be manifested in successive representations of Yosef.[10] Reading these multiple figures consolidated in matching proper names as cultural projections opens them (or perhaps better, their successive re-creators) to psychoanalytic evaluations, more specifically to an interrogation of the peculiarities of ethnic masculinities as defined relationally, in relation to the women in their stories, to one another, and to the imagined manliness of other men.

Potiphar's Wife (Zuleika)

The varied characterizations of Potiphar's wife well exemplify how Joseph becomes subject to different judgments depending on how his seductress is understood. Potiphar's anonymous wife is relatively undeveloped in the Hebrew Bible, where her purpose is to fill a role: For the beautiful hero to resist sexual temptation, the female must be proffered as temptress. She simply creates the circumstances both for the characterization of Joseph as a paragon of chaste piety and for the next significant plot development, his imprisonment. To the extent that Jewish traditions trouble to develop the lascivious wife's character, it is generally to intensify her vilification. In the Bible, Joseph declines her repeated demands that he "lie with her" with protestations of loyalty to his generous lord, her husband (rabbinic interpreters occasionally suggest that his use of the word "lord" means that he is thinking of God), until the fateful day when Joseph abandons his cloak in flight, enabling her to produce it as false evidence of sexual aggression.

In the Midrash, she is obsessive, sometimes repulsive, and sometimes attractive, but always inexcusable. In one case, she holds onto Joseph's garment, kissing it and fondling it, as it "grows old in her keeping"; she "speaks like an animal," and she goes to great lengths in

Rembrandt depicts a flagrant display of aggressive female sexuality in sharp contrast with other seventeenth-century artists (such as Reni, Cignani, or Guercino) who represent a more appealing wife of Potiphar and a more ambivalent Joseph. Rembrandt Harmensz. van Rijn (1606–1669), *Joseph and Potiphar's Wife*, 1634. Etching. 9.6 x 11.6 cm. Museum of Fine Arts, Boston. Harvey D. Parker Collection. P417. Photograph © 2014 Museum of Fine Arts, Boston.

her seductions, using an iron fork to force Joseph's gaze in her direction.[11] The very many examples of Christian paintings of the seduction of Joseph take advantage of the opportunity of their Old Testament story to represent a flagrant display of female sexuality. On close analysis, Joseph in these paintings is often susceptible to being read as emotionally torn, caught in the tensions between terror, lust, and resistance. His beauty is typically that of a classic youth, while Potiphar's wife is more variously represented; she is sometimes startlingly young and adorable (as in Carlo Cignani's seventeenth-century painting) and other times older and grosser (as in Rembrandt), but always highly sexualized.[12]

Islamic traditions complicate the woman's character, more often than not, generously; her very attraction to the perfected Joseph is, by definition, a redeeming quality. Whereas in the biblical account Potiphar's wife's accusations lead to Joseph being unjustly imprisoned, the Qur'an, ever championing justice, arranges for the woman's manipulations to be discovered by her husband. Because the garment is torn from behind, it is read as a sign of Joseph's having been pursued rather than having been the pursuer. Here, Joseph prefers prison to having to stave off the advances of Egypt's women, specifically because he fears that he might succumb and become "of the ignorant" (Qur'an 12:33). This fear clarifies that he is not without healthy desire, but rather is of strong will. His will and his desires are both so powerful that he is willing to submit to incarceration to keep his urges in check. The men see fit to imprison Joseph for a while, and the wife seems to suffer no particular consequence for her misdeed. This detail, combined with the story of the banqueting women, a blood sisterhood that establishes Joseph's irresistibility, opens the possibility of a sympathetic reading of the desperate woman of the house.

Karen Gayane Merguerian and Afsaneh Najmabadi observe that many religious commentaries on this story overemphasize the "guile" of Potiphar's wife and extrapolate from the behavior of the story's women an essential association of female sexuality and guile. They also celebrate the efforts of women readers "to reappropriate Zulaykha and decenter the notion of guile," opening up "new interpretive possibilities."[13] In the context of Jewish disparagement of Potiphar's grossly sexual wife, I notice the relative benevolence in Islamic treatments of this desiring woman. The increasingly forgiving characterization of Potiphar's wife in Islamic traditions led to an iconography very different from the familiar lascivious images of Potiphar's wife in Christian paintings; in the latter, she is almost always depicted partly naked in her bed, tugging at Joseph's garment. By contrast, Zuleika in Persian art (which favors the Qur'anic scene of Joseph in the assembly of women) is rarely represented grabbing Joseph into her bed but rather, kneels down before him, grasping his robe in supplication. In some versions of the story, such as the sixteenth-century Persian *Joseph and Zuleika*, the couple is liberated to marry after Zuleika—who at first symbolizes the wantonness of paganism—destroys her idols.[14] Just as Joseph is a model of patience and self-discipline, Zuleika is faithful in her love of Joseph through great trials; she is impoverished and repentant; she grows ugly from age and want. In this condition, she encounters Joseph again, and he accepts her love, prays to Allah, and her appearance is restored. In other versions of the story (such as *Joseph and Zuleika*, India, eighteenth century), Zuleika, in a classic punishment for sexual crimes, plucks out her eyes in grief after Joseph's death. In all these variations, she models the virtue of a repentant sinner.

With an investment less in the unqualified heroism of Joseph than in the recuperation of a sexually aggressive heroine, a heroine who permits herself the unprejudiced freedom to desire a foreigner and a servant, Alice Bach and Mieke Bal are among the strong feminist readers of this Bible story who favor the more sympathetic reading of Potiphar's wife made plausible by Islamic traditions. Both read explicitly through (and against) Thomas Mann's novelistic re-creation of the Joseph story. Bal reports that her experience of the Qur'an as an adult happily contributed to her revision of her earlier readings of the wife, readings that had been fostered by a Catholic school childhood education that presumed that a forward, adulterous-designing woman must be bad, bad, bad. Bal's subsequent encounters with the text and later legends made for the possibility of a liberating identification with this foreign, royal, female character—reconfigured by Bal as a heroine—who saw and "fell for," a man, "knew" what she wanted, and then attempted to seize it.[15]

What is significant here is that where Joseph's ambiguities are airbrushed in the Islamic retellings, Potiphar's anonymous wife, who is subsequently humanized with the name Zuleika, acquires complexity and ambiguity. She becomes more interesting, and her interest to readers propels us to imagine a more interested Yusuf. The Bible paints a mirror portrait, with Yosef more complex and morally ambiguous, and his temptress flattened in her role as vixen. Two points: first, our (albeit historically variable) assessment of Joseph as a man is necessarily tied up with the elaborations of the woman (later women) in the stories; second, while the Qur'an flattens Joseph in his goodness, it corrugates the Bible's flat portrait of the wife. In another chiasmus, while Jewish commentaries occasionally develop the negative features of Joseph's character implicit in multiple episodes in the Bible (such as his arrogance and arguably, cruelty to his brothers) and leaves the woman flat, the Qur'an flattens the hero, who is one-dimensional good, and complicates his nemesis, sometimes to the point of reversing our assessment of her.

We will see that a similar dynamic operates with the other characters' variable representations, specifically in this relational assessment of masculinity: in the Hebrew Bible and later Jewish stories, Joseph's brothers, for all their villainy, are developed in ways that allow us to appreciate their dislike of Joseph and provisionally excuse their hatred as a symptom of their natural male competitiveness and need for love and power. If they are worse men of God than Joseph, they may be better men, in a competing sense of the word "men" (idealizations of masculinity). In another mirror narrative move, Islamic traditions weaken the masculinity of Potiphar, who purchases Joseph for his wife at her request, and who is variously uninterested in her, incapable of satisfying her sexually, a eunuch, or simply grossly heathen or ineffectual. He is often Joseph's ally. The point here is that in the Jewish context, Yosef's relative effeminacy (he is sometimes imagined to be primping) is developed in contrast with his more masculinized brothers, while in the Islamic context, Yusuf's manliness is seen in relief against the background of his first employer's contrasting weakness.

A Dreamy Beauty

Yosef's beauty, incidental in the biblical account, becomes his identifying feature in the subsequent Jewish tradition. In his youth he is represented as a dreamer, and in his adulthood, his saving skill is dream interpretation. The combination of beauty and dreaminess after the Middle Ages comes to contrast with the admired qualities of men of action. Moral strength and physical strength increasingly live in uneasy relationship, and in Jewish stories Joseph's fancy coat, his boastfulness, and his resisting Potiphar's wife are all details of an increasingly suspect masculinity. In Islamic contexts, by contrast, Yusuf is elevated to an idealized status. He is analogized to the Prophet Muhammad— who is gifted with the story of Yusuf as a consolation during his year of grief and who, like Yusuf, will be elevated; and in some Shiʻite traditions he is also a partial model for Yusuf-e Zahra (Zahra's Yusuf), the twelfth or hidden Imam, the messianic redeemer who waits, just as Yusuf waited to be restored to Canaan.[16] Yusuf thus embodies enduring values. Whereas the Joseph of the "Amazing Technicolor Dream Coat," the popular twentieth-century English musical, is nothing if not campy, the Joseph depicted in contemporary Iranian television is a teen idol.[17]

Biblical heroes who are characterized with beauty as an apparently unambiguous feature of their heroism have been susceptible to having their beauty compromise their heroism—particularly their masculinity—in subsequent Jewish renderings. Joseph and David, for example, are both explicitly beautiful, but as ideals of masculinity evolved over time and accrued ethnic variations, these icons foregrounded the opposition between strength and intelligence. David is the little guy, the youngest brother who defeats Goliath through cunning rather than might. Uncompromisingly beautiful in the Bible, Joseph in the later tradition is represented as vain and effete. He flaunts his decorated coat and he is boastful. The Midrash, which associates these features with Joseph's being described as "a lad," imagines the boyish Joseph curling his hair, penciling his eyebrows, and parading around in high-heeled shoes.[18] Jews may have associated this unflattering portrait of Joseph with his assimilation into Egypt (he was so transformed that he was unrecognizable to his older, stronger brothers, whereas Joseph knew them immediately), a luxuriant culture in some Western fantasies as early as Philo's *Allegorical Commentary*, in which Egypt stands for Rome, Joseph is a sinner of materialism, and the text functions to warn his first-century readers against the dangers of assimilation. (In writing less directed to his own community, Philo portrays Joseph more kindly, as an example of what the Jews can offer.) In other legends, Joseph is imagined to have been born circumcised—like his father Jacob—a sign of coming into the world already perfected, but susceptible to an unconscious association of these perfect men being like women, who also have no need of circumcision.[19] Thomas Mann's novel makes much of Joseph's resemblance to his mother; in his retelling, the gifted coat had been Rachel's, and wearing it, Joseph looks so like her that Jacob is transported back to his having fallen in love at first sight. Joseph, like Jacob and Isaac before him, and by contrast with their outdoorsy brothers Ishmael, Esau, and Joseph's brothers in the field, becomes the *Jewish* hero, who is typically mama's favorite, comparatively small and domestic. This stereotype of Jewish maleness persists in popular culture, for example in the films of Woody Allen.

Because Sura (chapter) 12, a unique romance, is atypical in the Qur'an, perhaps to justify its placement in the Holy Book, the third ayah (verse) specifies that the Joseph story is the "best" story. Tradition lauds this Sura as having been offered to the Prophet to console him following the deaths of his beloved wife and the uncle who raised him. The story is read as a demonstration that the Almighty lifts the faithful out of despair, creating an analogy between Joseph and the Prophet of Islam, who during a time of relative political weakness is encouraged to identify with Yusuf, who rose from the depths. Fatima Zahra, the Prophet's daughter, mother of the Imams, including her Yusuf, will be avenged for her martyrdom by *her* Yusuf. This promise contributes to the Qur'anic Yusuf's standing as a figure of virtue and power. If the Woody Allen character is a contemporary stereotype of the clever, neurotic, and creative Jewish man, the modern spinner of dreams on the analyst's couch, Yusuf in contemporary Islamic popular culture preserves the connotations of his prototype. I have been directed to an Iranian serial drama "The Life of Prophet Yusuf," an epic of forty-five hour-long episodes directed by Farajollah Salahshoor, available in full on SHIATV, which aims "to promote education and understanding while building a historic archive relating to contemporary Islamic thought."[20] In this popularization, Yusuf is less a dreamer than a dreamboat, an ideal man.

The relatively minor details of Joseph's sexual self-control, his beauty, and his association with dreams become the identifying features of his heroism and that which distinguishes Joseph from other men. Susan Docherty observes that in Jewish Hellenistic texts such as *The Jewish Antiquities* and the romance *Joseph and Asenath* (circa first century), "the frequent emphasis on Joseph's self-control and beauty may be due to the fact that these were characteristics much admired in Hellenistic circles."[21] Indeed, when Joseph is called upon to interpret Pharaoh's dreams, this master of self-control becomes a preacher of self-control, and he interprets Pharaoh's visions as divine messages to avoid over-indulgence. The ruler dreams of fat cows and lean cows, strong wheat and weak wheat, metaphors impenetrable to all Pharaoh's advisers. But Joseph appreciates them as messages about patience and frugality, and accordingly advises Pharaoh to save his surpluses for the days of famine that will come. Joseph, uniquely, is the adviser who can successfully preach discipline, and patience yields abundance as well as political and economic power. Like his father Jacob before him, who made Laban wealthy when managing his estate, Joseph is the economic adviser whose business wisdom enriches the Pharaoh, who feels ever after indebted to Joseph. Later Joseph is thought to embody the qualities that Diaspora Jews most valued: he rises to power because of his intelligence and hard work. He is a thinker. He is fair and loyal, and because his loyalty enriches his master, he is welcomed close to the seat of power, where he deserves trust, and rewards that trust by offering counsel critical to national success. I will suggest that this admiration is equivocal at best, that Joseph becomes a source of self-consciousness and worry, exposing the paradox that Jewish men aspire to being ordinary men, yet feel the need to rise above the ordinary as a survival strategy. Had Joseph not proven himself exceptional as an interpreter and as an economist, he would have languished in prison, the cliché of the foreigner falsely accused of having aggressed against a powerful woman.

Fathers and Brothers and Other Men

Joseph's position in relation to other men, first his father, who favors him, his brothers, who envy him, Potiphar, who elevates and debases him, and then Pharaoh, who depends on him, delimits his masculinity as much as his relationship with the women of the story. The Bible and Qur'an report Jacob's reaction to Joseph's youthful dreams differently. When Yosef dreams that the sun, moon, and stars (understood to mean his family) all prostrate themselves before him, he incurs his father's disapproval and Jacob sends Yosef to follow in the fields after his older brothers without hesitation. Once more, the Qur'an's prophets have more insight. Jacob cautions Yusuf not to share his dreams with his brothers lest he incite their envy. He is reluctant to allow Joseph to join his brothers, fearing that an animal will get him. In the biblical account Jacob is presented with Yosef's torn and bloodied coat as proof that an animal had attacked him. Yusuf's coat, in the Qur'an, is bloodied but not torn, evidence to the prophet that Yusuf is still living. We see that while this garment is torn in the Bible and whole in the Qur'an, the reverse is true of the garment left behind with Potiphar's wife. In the biblical account that coat is whole, false evidence that is believed, and the missing tear from the childhood coat is displaced in the Qur'an's story, the sign that Potiphar's wife lies. The cumulative effect of these differences is that Yosef is punished for a hubris of which even Jacob disapproves, while Yusuf is established immediately as an agent of Divine will, which his brothers try but fail to thwart.

The brothers having invented a murderous animal to cover for their having sold their brother Joseph to a passing caravan engenders midrashic elaborations in the animal code. In the Midrash, Joseph's arrogance is compounded by his having slandered his brothers to their father with claims that they are lustful. This elaboration apparently works to justify Joseph's becoming the victim of a woman's lust, fair punishment for his having conjured lust to defame his brothers. More-over, the rabbis call the woman a bejeweled "she-bear," observing that it is a wise man that sees her fangs and not her jewels. The invention of the crime of slander does more than provide a cosmic justification for Joseph's being tormented by Potiphar's wife; it has the additional effect of exaggerating Joseph's cruelty to his brothers by showing him delib-erately alienating their father's affections to keep the patriarch's love to himself, as if paternal love is a zero sum game. Until this point in Gen-esis, paternal love had been something of a zero sum game as the nar-rative chose between competing brothers in each previous generation. In this generation of tribal leaders, however, Joseph's need for exclu-sive love is no longer appropriate to the narrative logic. (Exodus, which immediately follows, features a triumvirate of sibling leaders in Aaron, Miriam, and Moses, characterized less by competition than by coop-eration.) Combined with the textual detail that Joseph is boastful and a dreamer, Joseph slandering his brothers suggests that the rabbis had a measure of sympathy for the brothers who sold the hero into slavery, wanting to be rid of this irritant in the family.

All of Genesis can be characterized as a series of stories about sibling rivalry, beginning with Cain murdering Abel. Of all the later brothers, it is Joseph whom the Midrash (Genesis Rabbah) will associate with Abel. Abel is characterized by the very description that later attaches to Joseph: "he is penciling his eyes, curling his hair, and lifting his heel." In the rabbinic imagination, Joseph is likened to Abel, the first char-acter to earn his brother's murderous rage. In both cases, the Midrash supplements the textual explanation of favoritism with a description of the favored brother primping. Apparently the rabbis appreciated the unconscious need to dispense with a potentially embarrassing, self-absorbed, competitive, irritating brother.

The Joseph story is the last in a series of narratives of fraternal rivalry. In the earlier stories, Ishmael and Esau are loved by their fathers but not favored by the story. In this final iteration of the pattern of sibling rivalry in Genesis, Joseph's brothers occupy the position of Ishmael and Esau, but this proliferation of brothers resents their father's expression of favoritism for Joseph. In doing so, they give expression to the injustice of the text's earlier rejection of Ishmael and Esau in favor of their younger brothers.

The earlier generations represent maternal favoritism in the matriarchs Sarah (who promotes her son Isaac and banishes Hagar's firstborn Ishmael) and Rebecca (who promotes the younger twin Jacob over Esau), while Abraham and Isaac express paternal ambivalence, as each father seems prepared to remain loyal to his firstborn. Joseph, as the beautiful son, is interpreted variously by the Midrash as having inherited the features of his father and of his mother. These partnered sources of Joseph's beauty, Rachel and Jacob—who are first cousins through the maternal line—are overidentified with one another, and it is Jacob's alignment with the mother that leads to the preferential treatment that creates the circumstances for fraternal vengeance. In effect, Joseph's brothers avenge Ishmael and Esau in the narrative logic, a logic that repeats obsessively and with increasing intensity stories of fraternal rivalry.

If Ishmael, as the child of Hagar, the "stranger," the "other woman," can be understood to alienate Sarah (who banishes him and Hagar for the dubious crime of "playing"), Esau and Jacob are twinned, multiplying the injustice of maternal betrayal. When Rebecca prefers Jacob at Esau's expense, she goes so far as to dress Jacob in the clothes of his brother. These first patriarchs retain at least in part the loyalty of their fathers, who bequeath the patriarchy in each case to the mother's younger son, but not without reluctance. In the Joseph saga, the brothers proliferate. They are up against full paternal absorption into the will of the beloved mother. All are legitimate sons of the father with rights to the narrative future denied Ishmael and Esau, and Joseph's many brothers become proactive in restoring the male order of primogeniture and the rule of men. (Interestingly, the false accusation of Potiphar's wife is expressed as an accusation that Joseph was "playing" her—usually translated as "mocking," but the same verb describes Ishmael's behavior with Isaac.) The rabbis, who are unforgiving of Ishmael and Esau and go out of their way to account for any appearance of injustice in the Bible's rejection of these elder brothers by inventing exaggerated flaws for them, had no similar investment in discrediting Joseph's brothers. Instead, they would have seen themselves as descendants of these tribal leaders. Required by the story to condemn the brothers' cruelty, they nevertheless account for it by appreciating how obnoxious Joseph's arrogance must have been to his brothers.

In her rereading of Thomas Mann's elaboration of Joseph in his novel, Mieke Bal characterizes Mann's "Yusuf" (her nomenclature) as megalomaniacal, a sin worse than sexual transgression. She sees the repeated identification of Yusuf as the "true son" as prefiguring the Christ but also as an indication of his identification with the beautiful and beloved Rachel and of Jacob's obsession with this *one* son. For our purposes, what is important is that Bal reads Mann's Yusuf as "the feminine man of trisexual appeal," that is, a man who is attractive to both men and women (though unable to master himself). Bal argues that Mann, writing in the era of Nazism, is polemicizing, recuperating the effeminate Jew through Yusuf.[22] By calling him Yusuf, however, it seems to me that Bal elides how different Yosef and Yusuf had become. Mann's paradigmatic effeminate Jew is indeed best exemplified in the figure of Yosef who had been so transmogrified in the commentaries as to have earned the hatred of less complicated men. The Qur'an's Yusuf has no such effeminizing textual afterlife.

Instead, the Islamic tradition includes stories in which a pious Zuleika dreams of marrying the beautiful and righteous vizier of Egypt. Her father arranges the match with the vizier—who turns out to be a eunuch delighted at the prospect of such an extraordinary bride. When Zulieka meets her husband she is shocked and distressed that he is the wrong man. Once Joseph appears in her life—the real figure of her dreams and the future vizier—she pursues him relentlessly, arranging ultimately to have him imprisoned so that she may gaze upon him in secret while he prays (another favorite subject of Persian art). In some versions of the romance, Zuleika persuades her husband to outbid all others at auction for the beautiful Hebrew slave, and the husband imagines that the slave will be their adopted son.

In this tradition, Zuleika's designs on Joseph are part of the Divine plan, and her marriage is one in which her virginity had been preserved. If, in some rabbinic stories, Joseph is a weak man by comparison with his older stronger brothers, in the Zuleika stories in which Potiphar is a eunuch (the word *saris*, used to describe him, is susceptible to being translated as either "prince" or "eunuch"), the husband's sexual incapacity functions to heighten Joseph's masculinity and desirability. Potiphar allies with Joseph and loves him, even in the face of his wife's obsession, positioning Joseph less as the trisexual who is loved by man and woman than as the man of God to whom everyone is attracted, including all the women of the court. As details accrue to Yusuf's narrative, he becomes more and more humble, choosing to retreat to prison and prepared to serve when called. In these narratives, sexual energies concentrate in the body of the self-disciplined hero, who is rewarded in the end with a happy marriage, power, and wealth.

Other Women—Asenath; City Women

In the Hebrew Bible, a grateful Pharaoh confers on Joseph the name Zaphenath-paneah; and gives him as a wife Asenath the daughter of Potiphera priest of On (Gen. 41:45). The conferral of an Egyptian name on Joseph contributes to his coming to be seen as a paradigm of the Diaspora Jew in later generations, who like Queen Esther after him, is a magnificent beauty, close to power, and a savior to his people. In both cases, beauty is linked to marriage to someone in power, in Esther's case the king himself, and in Joseph's case the daughter of the priest Potiphera. Like Potiphar's wife, Asenath has no narrative future in the Bible itself but a rich life in later stories. The preeminent commentator Rashi identifies Potiphera with Potiphar, so Joseph marries not the wife but rather the daughter of his former master, a sign of his rise in power. By some accounts Asenath is the adopted daughter of Potiphar, the birth child of Dina, Joseph's sister who had been raped by Shechem. (In this way, the rabbis protect Joseph—or themselves—from intermarriage.) In other stories, Asenath and Zuleika are conflated, reconciling the two marriage traditions.

The Jewish adventure romance *Joseph and Asenath* is the fullest elaboration of Joseph's domestic future.[23] In this romance, which accounts for and explains away Joseph's marriage to an Egyptian (differently than by making her Dina's daughter), Asenath, who is beautiful and rich, falls in love with Joseph, converts to Judaism and marries Joseph, to the pleasure of all concerned. Asenath's interest in Joseph and the court's pleasure in the marriage elevate Joseph's status by making him beloved of Egyptian royalty. As the adventure develops, Pharaoh's son and Joseph's brothers plot to kill Joseph in order to have the beautiful Asenath, a plot that is, of course, foiled. This first-century narrative reinstitutes the murderous fraternal rivalry, adding the Pharaoh's son to their envious fraternal order. A different effect is achieved by stories that multiply the women (adding Zuleika, the court women, and Asenath) from stories that multiply the men. In one set of stories in the Qur'an and Midrashim about the assembly of women, multiplying the women develops a triangle of desire that situates Joseph as a worthy object of romance, a man whom women want and for whom they compete. Competition between women restores virility to the patriarchy: Rachel and Leah compete for Jacob after he flees from his brother Esau's revenge, and weakened by being on the lam and a pawn of his mother, Jacob is ultimately recovered for the patriarchy by the sisters' competition for his seed. This restoration of his masculinity leads to his fathering twelve sons. In the story of Joseph and Asenath, by contrast, the men proliferate and compete over a woman, reversing the triangle of desire. Since Joseph has to defend his wife against the desires of other men, her desirability is magnified at his expense.

The Paranoid Position: Yosef and Melanie Klein

In her study of postbiblical representations of Joseph, Susan Docherty is typical of students of this material in her observation that most Jewish stories render a fully positive Joseph because Joseph is a positive role model of the successful (so-called) Diaspora Jew. She observes the enduring power of Joseph's story in Islamic art and literature and the "obvious appeal of these chapters for later Jews, who took pride in the story of one of their ancestors rising to such an important position in the powerful Gentile land of Egypt. In particular, those Jews who actually lived in Egypt, or other parts of the Diaspora, may have found an important role model in Joseph, who was so successful in his adopted home, but who remained faithful to his Jewish heritage." Emphasizing Joseph's characteristics as a dreamer and interpreter, Leslie Fiedler in his 1967 essay, "Master of Dreams: The Jew in the Gentile World," identifies Joseph as the "archetypal ancestor of all Jewish dreamers," of the "successful poet and the respected shrink, the Jewish artist and the Jewish doctor."[24] Wendy Zierler, who describes how "Fiedler traces a literary line from Joseph all the way to Sigmund Freud and Franz Kafka, noting Freud's worldwide success as a dream interpreter, healer and author," remarks upon Fiedler's heteronormative assumptions in his celebration of a number of "American Jewish male writers as descendants of the biblical Joseph: Nathaniel West, Henry Roth, Delmore Schwartz, J. D. Salinger, Bernard Malamud and Philip Roth." Zierler playfully observes that "Fiedler includes the poet Allen Ginsberg in his list of Joseph's literary descendants, noting Ginsberg's promotion in his poetry of psychedelic drugs ('appropriate to a new sort of Master of Dreams,' p. 188); he even mentions Ginsberg's status as a 'mama's boy,' identified not with his father but with his mother, Naomi (like the biblical Joseph, whom Jacob loves best because he identifies him with his beautiful mother)." But, as Zierler observes, Fiedler makes nothing of Ginsberg's homosexuality.

Fiedler and Docherty exemplify an unself-conscious identification of prominent Diaspora Jews and Diaspora Jewry with the mythic hero, Joseph. Beyond taking pride in Joseph's professional success, Docherty further explains the Joseph story's sustained popularity by adding the literary merits of the story and the fact that Joseph is one of the most "multi-dimensional or ambiguous" figures in the Hebrew scriptures.[25] While she enumerates Joseph's negative characteristics (his boastfulness, arrogance, and his tormenting treatment of his brothers), she elides the possible significance of these negative characteristics for Jewish readers over the generations. Instead, she recognizes that praise for Joseph as the first Diaspora Jew who resists assimilation reverberates through the ages, beginning with Mattathias's speech to his son in the anti-assimilationist polemic of the first Book of Maccabees, and she neglects the thin stream of commentary that distances itself from Joseph as a role model.

By Docherty's reading, Joseph's appeal lies in the special combination of his Jewishness and his political power, evidenced by his closeness to the Pharaoh, a closeness that the biblical text belabors in its representation of Pharaoh's gratitude to Joseph for having saved the Egyptian economy. This gratitude is expressed in the lavish gifts Pharaoh bestows, including the gifts of an Egyptian name and wife, in the honor and elevated status Joseph is afforded, and in Joseph's brothers' observation that Joseph "is like" Pharaoh himself. Later in the Bible, Moses, as the adopted grandson of the Pharaoh of his generation, enjoys similar proximity to power, and like Joseph, in the bookend chapters of the enslavement of the Israelites in Egypt, will claim his Jewish identity with a vengeance to lead the people in the Exodus, the central myth of Judaism. Read structurally in this way, Moses picks up where Joseph left off, writing Joseph's life backwards, undoing his childhood identity, outing himself as a Jew, and then taking his people out. Queen Esther, married to the king, is another court Jew who will also reveal her Jewish identity at a critical moment to save her people from a death decree. These biblical heroes—while often described as unequivocal role models—present psychological difficulties for the people who embrace them as models of the "successful Jew."

The presumption of most reception critics of Jewish Joseph stories that Joseph is a source of Jewish pride because he is a successful Jew (measured in the usual terms of money, power, prestige, and influence) depends on the cultural conviction that power is an all or nothing advantage. I want only to observe that in all the biblical cases, political power for Israelite leaders who have been claimed by their people *as successful Jews*, in the context of their own narratives, represent the promise (or simply the merest hope) of safety in desperately threatening social circumstances. The context of desperation that elevates the "successful Jew" also makes this kind of Jew necessary. Just below the surface lies the message that it would be better were there no need for heroic advocates, leaving Jewish men to aspire to ordinariness. This hero may not be as lucky as he seems.

Joseph, upon revealing himself to his terrified brothers, who fear that he will exact just vengeance for their having sold him into slavery, ejecting him from their family and depriving him and his father of one another (egregious crimes), reassures them that he has forgiven them because he understands his fate to have been God's plan. Joseph, who has experienced the depths and the heights, can afford such magnanimity because of the enormity of the power reversal between himself and his brothers. Recognizing first that Joseph's success was achieved at great personal cost and after immense suffering, none of which is spared the reader, is the first step toward appreciating that Jewish identification with Joseph must be ambivalent. Such cultural identification assimilates a range of characteristics: first Joseph's alienating obnoxiousness and arrogance as well as his interpretive genius (politics needs good readers), personal self-discipline, suffering, and triumph.

Borrowing from Eve Kosofsky Sedgwick's use of Melanie Klein's psychoanalytic object relations theory, I want to offer a corrective to the usual appreciations of Joseph's success. Klein and the systems theory that follows from Klein's thought resist traditional psychoanalytic binaries, the teleological march from immaturity to maturity and the "zero sum games and excluded middle term . . . where one person getting more love means a priori that another person is getting less" (the fear of Joseph and his brothers).[26] Klein's analysis entails a critique of Freud's psychic equation of power and omnipotence. If for Freud omnipotence is the subject's ever-present need, for Klein power is as much a fear as a wish, the product of contradictory desires. The greedy infant's discovery that helplessness or omnipotence are not the only options, that life is not "all or nothing," is a relief rather than a disappointment, the recognition that it is possible to negotiate a win-win.

These middle ranges of agency that Klein describes, in Sedgwick's formulation, "the notion that you can be relatively empowered or disempowered without annihilating someone or being annihilated, or even castrating or being castrated—is a great mitigation of that endogenous anxiety."[27] Joseph is a particular hero for Freud: not only do they share a father named Jakob and not only are both professional dream interpreters, but Joseph's story illustrates the Freudian principle that repression creates the possibility of civilization. In contrast to Freud's stages of infantile development, Klein introduces the concept of positions, naming the paranoid/schizoid position as the state into which we are born. This state cannot tolerate ambivalence and projects the negative parts of the self on to others. Self-loathing leads to the conviction that others loathe you. Ultimately, however, the infant experiences her own negative feelings as threatening to others and to the self. She experiences dread. For Freud, power creates obedience. For Klein, dread replaces Freudian repression, with the recognition that good and bad are inseparable. Depressive anxiety is then a welcome element of mature relationships, a position from which one can repair the parts of the infantile fragmented black and white, good and bad world. I am reading Klein through Sedgwick in part because Sedgwick uses Klein to explain the place of paranoia in queer theory and queer criticism—the paranoid position marked by "insatiability, hatred, envy, and anxiety," a place of projection, and the self-fulfilling expectation that one is disliked. The depressive position is an "anxiety-mitigating achievement" (p. 636). Joseph invites a queer reading.

In the limited way that is possible here, I want only to suggest that Joseph's achievement of omnipotence, his dream reading, his happy love with his father Jacob, his admirable self-control—all together represent a Freudian ideal so culturally familiar that it is easy to accept at face value the claims that Joseph remains the paradigmatic Jewish role model. But the unhappy facts of Joseph's life as well as the less than admirable traits of his character, the queering of his identity in a substream of rabbinic thought (which amounts to a self-queering) suggest the inadequacy of the dominant Freudian reading. Instead, I want to offer that the implied Jewish reader who identifies with Joseph's successful outsider status, occupies positions of paranoia (constantly aware of the bookend threats of enslavements and re-enslavements, the violent extremes of Joseph's life as he goes down and up from heights of adoration to pits of resentment, from the depth of prison to the heights of power) and of depression in the Jewish identification with Joseph's success. Joseph freezes the Jew in the position of infantile dread, less delighted in the omnipotence that comes with political success than wishful for the missing middle term, where it is not all-or-nothing, where one person's loss is not another's gain, where two brothers can both be loved, and one does not have to choose between castrating the other or being castrated oneself. At the intersection of Yosef's gender and ethnicity is contradiction, the site of cultural ambivalence, the embodiment of anxiety with its mixed consequences and impulse to projection.

I am exempting Yusuf from this analysis because Yusuf begins his life in the Qur'an, which makes gentle the seesaw of Joseph's life with an omnipresent Allah, who takes the mystery out of fate. Yusuf is not principally a successful ethnic foreigner but rather an allegorical figure for patience. In Klein's vocabulary, he can be said to occupy a reparative position, integrating oppositional forces. He rides the waves of life confident in his and Allah's purpose, confident that being beloved is not a liability, confident that his self-control defines his manliness and attractiveness (rather than compromising it). Each expansion on the life of Yusuf, from medieval epic poems, to later romances, tapestries, and television contribute to Yusuf's popularity as a dreamboat rather than the "dreamer"—with all the mixed connotations of that word—that he is in the Hebrew Bible. Yusuf's masculinity fits comfortably in a culturally fixed binary. Yosef moves in a wider gender spectrum, and his success compensates for a compromised masculinity within a system that increasingly judged Egypt as a place of effeminate men. Yusuf, by contrast, is fully assimilated into an Egyptian ideal.

Ethnic Masculinity, Stereotypes, and Violence against Women

So-called "crises in masculinity" are proffered as sociological explanations for violence against women. Terror attacks, war, low employment—characterized as situations with the psychological consequence of men feeling helpless when there is a (self-) expectation of efficacious control—all correlate with higher incidences of domestic violence. One corollary of the stereotype of Jewish men as less than full men, a gender somewhere on the spectrum between men and women (evidenced over time, for example, in the European conviction as late as the seventeenth century that Jewish men menstruate,[28] or in Woody Allen's hypochondriac self-presentations) is that "Jewish men do not beat their wives." Neither repressed nor repressing rage, Jewish men are naturally feminine and are therefore more likely to be victimized by their overbearing, overempowered wives than to be overbearing themselves. The history of underreporting of domestic violence in the American Jewish community has been attributed in various ways to this cultural conviction about Jewish men (because of Jewish women's higher likelihood of shame; higher likelihood of being disbelieved; collective communal blindness; the unwitting complicity of rabbinic authorities for whom the possibility of Jewish violence had been unimaginable). The masculinity of the Israeli Jewish man (the "muscular Jew" located in the fields of nature or war) was initially created in deliberate opposition to the studious, gentle Jewish man (of the old European schoolhouse or prayer space), a countertype whose brutality could be entertained as a possibility.[29]

By contrast, Western stereotypes of the oppression of Muslim women—interpretations of the veil as effacement, readings of the Qur'an as encouraging husbands to discipline their wives, the critique of sharia law as permitting wife beating—have led to the opposite (comparably incongruous) conviction that Muslim men beat their wives. Sociology that postulates a contemporary "crisis in Islamic masculinity" enforces this prejudice with the implication of naturally hypermasculine, frustrated men whose concentrated internal rage finds release at home. So, if in the fantasy of the American and European cultural imagination Jewish men never beat their wives, Muslim men do routinely. This contrast highlights how Jewish men's perceived diminished masculinity differs from the way that Muslim and Israeli men are imagined to suffer from "crises in masculinity"; these are "crises" precisely because these men are imagined to have natural qualities of masculinity that are circumstantially "in crisis," while the old-world Jewish man begins from a place of comparatively weak physical urges. Yosef finds himself "not a man"; Yusuf is "not a man" because he is an angel with urges so powerful that he has to lock himself up to control them. To the extent that these prejudices derive in part from the mirror stereotypes of the feminized Jewish man and the masculinized Muslim, they miss the complexity afforded to male sexuality in the unconscious of the respective traditions as revealed in the Yosef/Yusuf narratives, in which sexual self-restraint is an anxiety for Jewish men and a point of pride for Muslim men.

Yosef, the Jewish Joseph, develops from his biblical origins into a hero who is a product of cultural ambivalence. His beauty, piety, intelligence, and closeness to power are at once a source of pride and a source of worry. The particular overriding worry is that Joseph's very qualities explain his suffering: first, his brothers' envy, which in the early part of his life leads to his being sold into slavery, and later to the suspicion that leads to the ruin of his descendants, who prosper in the land of Goshen until there "arises a Pharaoh who knew not Joseph" and enslaves the whole population. These worries persist in Jewish self-perception, the fear that their own best qualities invite envy and murderous reactions. (Kadya Molodowsky's Yiddish poem, "Merciful God," written in the immediate aftermath of the Shoah, begs God to "choose another people" and "take back the divine gift of our genius.") Compromised masculinity correlates with an exaggerated empowerment of Jewish women, an early instance of which is the Midrash that allows that the enslaved Israelite men would have fallen into despair, having refused to procreate under slavery because of the threat to their newborn sons, but Israelite women cajoled and tricked them into sex.

Yusuf is, rather, spared regret. His good behavior earns him only rewards, allowing him to grow ever more confident in the compatibility of desirability and chastity. The fact that women—not only Zuleika but all women everywhere—find him endlessly appealing glorifies this prophet of Allah, who enjoys the rewards of his piety partly in the shape of the devotion of women, a devotion that heightens our apprehension of him as a desirable man. Appreciated alike by the men whom he serves as a reader of dreams and as a manager of affairs of state, Yusuf is comfortable in and rewarded for a life of self-discipline. A preacher of patience, he interprets the parable of the lean cows and the fat cows to teach Pharaoh and the reader the power of planning and self-restraint, with the promise that such restraint will eventually bring exponential reward. While the Jewish narrative, paranoid, predicts that goodness will lead to destruction (jealousy, enslavement, and murderous hatred), the Islamic narrative emphasizes that goodness will be rewarded multifold.

The intersection of gender and ethnicity creates kaleidoscopic effects, exposing the artifice, the constructed nature, of sex and sexuality, the cultural and historical variability of manifestations of so-called "gender," and the extent to which ethnic self-definition and (competing) outside perceptions particularize peculiar idealizations of masculinity and femininity. A comparative analysis of the sort offered in this volume contributes fragments of colorful detail to the kaleidoscope and adds speed to its spin. Judaism and Islam are not ethnicities, however, but rather are (somewhat kindred) religious traditions, each of which has become understood in terms of varieties of ethnic manifestations, and both of which have been subject to varying degrees to the "Orientalizing" impositions of the West. The effort to say anything meaningfully precise or conclusive in such a comparative study only yields absurdity, and it is this absurdity—the hopeless definition of boundaries around identity categories—that must perhaps always be the main and final point. The details of the effort, however, reveal the high stakes for which this game of identity categories is played, with life and death consequences in history and to societies.

NOTES

1. Kate Simpkins, working as a graduate assistant, extensively researched the secondary sources and images across traditions for this essay. Her help was invaluable.

2. I will use Yosef, a transliteration of the Hebrew pronunciation, to refer to Jewish versions of Joseph, and Yusuf, a transliteration of the Arabic, to refer to Islamic representations, and Joseph, generically, to refer to our subject in this English-language essay.

3. I intend the use of the term "position" in the following discussion to evoke Melanie Klein, whose psychological theory replaced Freud's stages of development with descriptions of "positions," configurations of object relations, defenses, and anxieties within a dynamic unconscious. This dynamism of the unconscious is created largely by introjection and projection. I am grateful to my colleague Laura Green, chair of the English department of Northeastern University, who directed me to Eve Kosofsky Sedgwick's use of Klein on paranoia as soon as I described my idea that Yosef is susceptible to being read as a site of projective anxiety.

4. Shalom Goldman, in *The Wiles of Women/The Wiles of Men: Joseph and Potiphar's Wife in Ancient Near Eastern, Jewish, and Islamic Folklore* (Albany: SUNY Press, 1995), 58, suggests that the biblical story develops from still earlier Egyptian stories.

5. Sahih International translation of the Qur'an.

6. Rabbinic Midrash here refers to Jewish exegetical, homiletic, narrative commentaries from the classical period, relatively contemporaneous with the Qur'an. *Midrash Tanchuma* and *Midrash ha-Gadol* both include variations of the tale of the court women cutting themselves, as do later Jewish exegetical texts. The Qur'anic story may derive from one of these sources or from an earlier Jewish pre-text, rather than the other way around. James L. Kugel argues that "the Jewish origin of the story is beyond dispute."See James L. Kugel, *In Potiphar's House: The Interpretive Life of Biblical Texts* (San Francisco: Harper San Francisco, 1990), 55.

7. Midrash Rabbah to Genesis LXXXVII: 6–7. Soncino, Brooklyn, 1983. Using the midrashic technique of punning, Rabbi Samuel suggests that Joseph went in to sin, with his bow ("keshet") drawn, but after seeing a vision of his father, the

bow relaxed ("kasheh"—i.e., lost its hardness). Another Talmudic dispute (in Sotah 36:b) is a dramatic tale of effective repression: Joseph intends to sin, but his "bow" became disarmed, his "arms" strengthened, and as he dug his nails into the ground, his seed was scattered through his fingernails! Prooftext Genesis 49:24; Genesis Rabbah 87:7.

8. Footnote to the Soncino English edition.

9. In response to having heard a version of this essay presented at the University of Otago, my colleague in New Zealand, Najibullah Lafraie, allows my being playful with the language here and grants the significance of the larger argument, but rightly suggests that I clarify two points: first, the Arabic word for "man" in this context, "*bashar*" is without gender connotations, and might be better translated as "mortal"; and second, while "the Egyptian women in the story do seem to consider angels above humans," a belief of many Muslims, "neither in the Quran nor in Muslim tradition are women seen as a different order of being"; similarly, "the Quran itself does not consider angels an order higher than humans." Email correspondence, August 8, 2012. The caution here is against artificially imposing the concept of a great chain of being, with women subordinate to men and men subordinate to angels, all different orders of being, on the Qur'an. I am grateful to Dr. Lafraie for noticing this unintended implication of my word play.

10. See Lori Lefkovitz, *In Scripture: The First Stories of Jewish Sexual Identities* (Lanham, N.C.: Rowman and Littlefield, 2010); and Lori Lefkovitz, "Coats and Tales: Joseph Stories and Myths of Masculinity," in Harry Brod, ed., *A Mensch among Men* (Freedom, Calif.: Crossing Press, 1988), 19–29.

11. Genesis Rabbah to 39:10 and 39:16.

12. For the Church Fathers, Joseph is without ambivalence, a type of Christ: especially beloved of the Father (emblematized in the beautiful coat), whose flight to Egypt saves him, and who is persecuted by his brothers (the Jews).

13. Karen Gayane Merguerian and Afsaneh Najmabadi, "Zulaykha and Yusuf: Whose 'Best Story'?" *Journal of Middle East Studies* 29, 4 (November 1997), 488.

14. Masoud Ghorbaninejad, who is a Northeastern University graduate student in English and who comes from Iran, expresses his sense of the sequel to Sura 12 of the Qur'an in the popular imagination. In an email, he generalizes that: "The Islamic tradition has it that the Potiphar's wife, during the time of the famine, had been reduced to a blind beggar. She and Joseph meet on the streets, and Potiphar's wife tells him how she's repentant but still loves him. Then Joseph sends for her and, to her surprise (because she had done him so much wrong, was no more beautiful, &c &c), asks for her hand in marriage. When she accepts, Joseph prays to God, and youth, sight, and beauty (and even virginity as it seems) are all restored to her. So at the end they become lawfully married." Email correspondence, 17 January 2012.

15. See especially the first chapters of Mieke Bal, *Loving Yusuf: Conceptual Travels from Present to Past* (Chicago: University of Chicago Press, 2008). On page 9, in

a chapter called "First Memories, Second Thoughts," Bal describes her Catholic school as party to making our "cultural memory" of this story. She writes that this education "worked": "As far as I can remember, I have tended to associate falling in love with guilt and being in love with the need to lie."

16. The Jewish tradition also speaks of a "Messiah son of Yosef" as well as a "Messiah son of David."

17. Again, I am grateful to Masoud Ghorbaninejad for the reference and the information that the Joseph of this soap opera is a teen idol. The show can be watched on the Internet: http://www.shiatv.net/plist.php?plist=536 [Episodes 1–25]; http://www.shiatv.net/plist.php?plist=547 [Episodes 26–45] Both Accessed September 17, 2013.

18. Genesis Rabbah to 37:2, glossing "Joseph was a boy."

19. Genesis Rabbah 84:6. See also Wendy Zierler, in "Joseph(ine), the Singer: The Queer Joseph and Modern Jewish Writers," *Nashim* 24 (Spring 2013), 97–119, who sees in the midrash that the brothers cast Joseph into a pit of snakes as yet another encoding of Joseph as a sexually vulnerable woman. Zierler directs our attention too to Avivah Zornberg's observation that Joseph's name—"Yosef," the added son, derives from the Hebrew word for additional—bespeaks "excess," which Zierler suggests is well understood as the excess of queer "campiness."

20. Referenced above, note 14.

21. Susan Docherty, "Joseph the Patriarch: Representations of Joseph in Early Post-Biblical Literature," in Martin O'Kane, ed., *Borders, Boundaries and the Bible* (New York: Sheffield Academic Press, 2002), 201.

22. Bal, *Loving Yusuf*, 59–60.

23. The date, authorship, and provenance of this romance of twenty-nine chapters are disputed. Anonymous, and originally composed in Greek, with early versions in several other languages, scholars debate whether this pseudepigraphic text is Christian or Jewish; most date it to the first or second century C.E., though some have suggested a century earlier or as many as four centuries later. The oldest extant version is in Syriac from the sixth century.

24. Leslie Fiedler, *The Collected Essays of Leslie Fiedler* (New York: Stein and Day, 1971), II, 178.

25. Docherty, "Joseph the Patriarch," 195.

26. Eve Kosofsky Sedgwick, "Melanie Klein and the Difference that Affect Makes," *South Atlantic Quarterly* 106, 3 (Summer 2007), 631.

27. Ibid., 632.

28. John L. Beusterien, "Jewish Male Menstruation in Seventeenth-Century Spain," *Bulletin of the History of Medicine* 73, 3 (Fall 1999), 447–456.

29. Max Nordau coined the phrase "Muscle Jew" in 1898 in a speech he delivered at the Second Zionist Congress in Basel, Switzerland, on August 28; he would later advocate for a "muscular Judaism." See Todd Samuel Presner, *Muscular Judaism: The Jewish Body and the Politics of Regeneration* (New York: Routledge, 2007).

7

Dishonorable Passions

Law and Virtue in Muslim Communities

CATHERINE WARRICK

As the problem of honor killings has become more widely reported in the West, the popular perception is that such killings are a specific attribute of Islamic society or particularly Islamic law. This is perhaps understandable, as honor crimes are usually depicted as a type of gender violence unique to Muslim countries or Muslim communities in Western countries. In fact, honor killings are neither mandated nor explicitly tolerated by Islamic law, and a growing chorus of legal and religious scholars decries this common misunderstanding. However, while honor killings are not part of Islamic legal principles or jurisprudence, the practice is often informed (or misinformed) by popular attitudes about Islamic law.

Untangling the relationship between honor killings, Islamic law, and Muslim societies is a complex and politically charged task. Honor killings are used to enforce traditional social norms, and thus they are linked (among other things) to the politics of community identity and cohesion: this is why both traditionalist apologists for the practice and anti-Muslim critics of Islam both point to honor killings as essentially and indelibly Islamic. From another point on the political spectrum, some feminist commentators who oppose both honor killings and anti-Muslim rhetoric wonder if we should even continue to use the term "honor killing." As violence against transgressive women, and indeed even explicit justification of such violence as a defense of male honor, are hardly unique to Muslim societies, the exclusive use of the term "honor killings" to describe killings in Muslim communities may, some argue, do more to obscure accurate understanding than to enlighten.

Understanding the legal treatment of honor killings requires that we pay careful attention not only to statutes and judicial practices, but to these questions of community identity, gender norms, power, and terminology that form the social context for both the practice of honor killings and the criticisms of that practice.

This chapter examines two law-related aspects of honor killings, focusing primarily on the Arab Muslim world. First, in the texts and applications of Arab criminal codes, there is an interesting apparent legal conflation of honor and passion that serves to mitigate criminal responsibility for violence against women. This constructs a legal arena in which women's sexual passions are the offense and men's violent passions are the (partially tolerated) remedy. Second, the social context of this legal construction is informed in part by competing claims about Islamic legal requirements regarding the treatment of transgressive women: some authorities condemn honor killings as murder, while others suggest that such killings serve as a necessary social control over female morality in the absence of fully shariʿa-based, or Islamic, legal systems.

The first part of this chapter explains the conflation of honor and passion in law. In honor killings, the female victim's alleged sexual misconduct, which contravenes community norms of virtuous behavior, is the provocation for the killer's violent response which is (partially) excused because it was provoked by and directed toward her. This understanding of passion and provocation is not unique to Muslim (or Arab) societies; rather, it is common across legal systems and has applications outside the honor context. Provoked passion rules, when applied to domestic and family violence, attribute diminished criminal responsibility to the male killer, and attribute blame for the killing to the woman who is the victim of the crime. The examination of honor killings can provide a useful illumination of this interaction of law and society, not because such killings are unique to Muslim communities, but because they are both linked to claims of community identity and morality *and* comparable to similar sociolegal phenomena elsewhere.

In part two, I argue that the social context of this legal construction is, among many Muslim communities, informed in part by competing claims about Islamic law. Honor killings are popularly linked to Islam in the views of some Muslims (and many if not most Western observers), but Islamic and other authorities generally acknowledge that the link is more imagined than real, as a matter of both shari'a and state statutory law. However, there are competing claims about the acceptability of honor killings as they relate to shari'a. Some authorities, particularly those who are employed in official religious positions within state bureaucracies, condemn honor killings as a violation of the Islamic rules and norms about homicide. Others, notably leaders of Islamist parties with wide appeal among social conservatives, have argued that honor killings, while perhaps undesirable, are understandable, excusable, and perhaps even necessary as a tool for controlling women's morality in the absence of fully shari'a-based legal systems. These competing claims are not only differences of opinion about shari'a and its role in society, but also a way to advance political claims about authority and tradition that, for Islamists, are a chief means of challenging the legitimacy of ruling regimes in the Arab world.

Honor crimes provisions in modern Arab legal codes are not an enforcement of religious dictate itself, but of traditional social norms about female sexuality and collective honor. Interestingly, these gender norms are acknowledged and partly protected in the law even where those norms, or the methods of enforcing them, conflict with other legal norms. Thus, a legal code that purports to regulate violence makes exceptions for a particular kind of violence that has a special traditional standing. The law serves many purposes, and public order is only one of them: another is bolstering the legitimacy of the state by acknowledging and incorporating, where possible, "authentic" traditional practices.[1]

Laws that regulate honor killings rely on constructions of passion that treat collective norms as explicative of individual behavior. Thus, when collectively held honor is affronted (by the woman's alleged misconduct), this would and even should, in some views, provoke a rage in certain privileged individuals (male relative killers). The individual is then judged not really criminally responsible for his actions because they arise not from his individual choice but from the need to enforce social order and shared moral norms, the pursuit not of individual interests but of the common good. This is readily seen in honor killers' claims that they "had to" kill, and in the frequent treatment of such killers as defenders of morality, or even heroes, in their own local communities. As Egyptian novelist Salwa Bakr put it, "these crimes are committed under the pretext that these men are defending not only their honor, but society's morality."[2]

In the Arab world as in the West, state criminal law is, in its texts and practices, usually nonreligious and individualist, but is also a tool readily used to serve religious, traditional, and collective purposes. Honor killings are not mandated or endorsed by shari'a, and criminal codes in the Arab world are not generally based on shari'a.[3] Yet the inclusion of honor-related provisions is widely perceived as a nod to deeply entrenched conservative norms often closely allied with, and even mistaken for, religion. The persistence of honor-killing provisions is not anomalous or accidental in modern criminal codes; rather, their function as tools of collective and traditional norms is useful to modern regimes' claims of legitimacy and authenticity with certain audiences. It is because these provisions have conservative traditional appeal that they are retained even though they violate other constitutional and legal norms of equality, regulation of violence, and the rule of law.

I. The Conflation of Honor and Passion

Honor killings and similar practices are known in many societies, although popular attention has focused on their prevalence in the Muslim and Arab worlds. Western commentary on honor killings often treats the practice as completely foreign to Western conceptions of rights, law, and gender equality, but in fact there are striking similarities, both in principles and in law, between honor killings and the more familiar Western phenomenon of "crimes of passion"[4] in which a wife or girlfriend is killed. By comparing the two phenomena, I hope to illuminate some of the fundamental social forces at work in the law, as well as to dispel exceptionalist notions of honor killings that treat this type of violence as unique to Muslim societies.

An honor killing, as practiced in Arab societies,[5] involves the murder of a girl or woman by a male relative, usually her brother or father, for a perceived affront to norms of sexual virtue. The Western pattern, by comparison, is likelier to involve the killing by a husband or lover of a wife or girlfriend who has been unfaithful or who seeks to leave a relationship. Although honor and passion are conceptually distinct elements of such crimes, they are closely related in law and in social understanding, as I will demonstrate below.

In both honor killings and crimes of passion, legal systems make special provisions treating a particular kind of homicide more leniently than other murders. These special provisions apply almost exclusively in cases in which the victim is female, the killer male, and the relationship between them either sexual or familial. The leniency of the law may be textual, as when codes specify reduced penalties for such crimes, or a matter of practice, as when judges or juries prescribe light sentences out of sympathy with the killers.

The legal treatment of this type of homicide fosters the maintenance of a particular moral and social order by social rather than state actors, but with the cooperation and partial imprimatur of the state. By privileging a particular set of homicides—those committed against sexually transgressing women—these laws serve moral and social purposes that undermine not only the equal protection of men and women under the law, but also the restriction of the authority to use violence to public actors who are defined and constrained by law—in other words, the limitation of violence to state actors rather than private ones.[6] The problem is a clash between a political rule-of-law norm and a moral norm embodied in honor-killing laws and legal practices. Where the moral norm, as defined by the endorsers of honor killings, is established as an accepted basis for deviation from the public legal norms and rules, the law itself is weakened, violence is linked to virtue, and the consequences for individuals are potentially lethal.

Crimes of Passion

A crime of passion is a killing that takes place when the killer is in a furious rage with the victim, as opposed to a premeditated or an accidental killing. The killer's fury is considered to hamper his ability to behave reasonably, and thus he is not deemed fully responsible for his actions.[7] Acting in the heat of passion does not erase criminal responsibility, but it does potentially limit it. Such homicides are usually treated as a lesser degree of crime than other murders, with correspondingly lower criminal penalties. For example, in Jordan, a finding that a violent crime was committed in a "fit of fury" rather than premeditated can reduce the penalty by up to one half;[8] in most U.S. states, such homicides are treated as manslaughter rather than murder and thus carry lower penalties.[9]

An interesting element of the crime of passion is the assessment of the victim's role in the crime. The passion that reduces criminal responsibility is not simply any fit of fury; it must be the consequence of some provocation by the victim. "The typical victim in a heat of passion case is someone who has 'asked for it.'"[10] Thus a man's discovery of his wife's adultery could be regarded as a provocation causing him to lose his reason and act in the heat of passion. Crimes of passion are not necessarily about adultery, however; a terrible insult in a quarrel, for example, might be considered to inflame the passion of one party, causing him to react violently.[11] In any case, it is not fury alone that attracts the partial sympathy of the law but *provoked* fury, where that fury is then directed at the party responsible for causing it.

It is important to note that the concept of a crime of passion need not be gendered. Nonsexual and non–gender role-related provocations can be considered sufficiently provocative of passion to mitigate criminal responsibility. Also, women as well as men could theoretically benefit from crime of passion provisions. However, crime of passion defenses are commonly used in cases in which gender is an issue, such as wife murder, and they have overwhelmingly tended to benefit male killers of female victims.

Thus, a theoretically neutral principle, inscribed in facially neutral statutory language, produces a strongly gendered effect. This reflects the social understanding of what constitutes provocation, and how much provocation the "reasonable man" (or, in recent years, the "reasonable person" or "reasonable woman") can withstand before reacting violently.[12]

Crime of passion provisions are not always gender neutral even on their face, however. Among civil law systems such as those of continental Europe, the French code provided a well-known example of a specifically gendered provision for homicide based on passion. The French

Penal Code of 1816 commuted the punishment of a man who killed his wife or her partner upon catching her in the act of adultery.[13] This provision was removed from French law in the mid-1970s. The law did not require that the killer actually have acted in a fit of fury; rather, it treated the circumstance of discovered adultery as one in which a man would naturally lose his temper.

This begins to conflate the individual's passionate fury with social norms of gender roles and honor. The understanding of crimes of passion in most Western countries has been the provocation-leading-to-rage-leading-to-homicide model—again, gender neutral in theory, but distinctly disadvantageous to women in practice.[14] But assessments of provocation are necessary to evaluate furious passion as the basis for a homicide, so codes and courts alike have elaborated on the circumstances that would produce such rage. Blackstone, the venerable scholar of the English common law, drew a distinction between systems that treated wife murder as justifiable (excused) homicide and those, such as the English one, that treated it as punishable voluntary manslaughter, but he added that such killings were the "lowest degree" of manslaughter because "there could not be a greater provocation" than a husband's betrayal by his wife.[15] Thus we see how the law binds together social norms, specifically those about gender roles, and its treatment of individual behavior assessed through the lens of those roles.

"Honor Crimes"

"Honor crimes" (now often written with quotation marks to indicate dispute over the claim of honor) have received most attention in the Arab and Muslim world, particularly in Jordan and Pakistan.[16] Honor crimes, or honor killings, are homicides carried out by family members against girls and women[17] who are believed to have harmed the family's honor through misbehavior; this misbehavior is usually sex-related but need not be adultery. Thus women and girls have been killed for marrying against their families' wishes, dating, talking to boys on the phone, causing gossip about their dress and behavior, and the like. Honor killings take place among both Muslim and Christian communities in the Middle East and Asia.[18] The usual pattern is for a girl or woman to be killed by her brother, father, or uncle rather than a husband or lover.

This type of killing is in some respects very similar to crimes of passion, in particular the elements of victim blaming and the perpetrator's fury. "Honor killers" frequently claim in court that their criminal responsibility should be regarded as limited owing to the rage they felt toward the victim's "bad behavior." However, the social understanding of the justifiability of honor killings (often also reflected in court proceedings) is not that the perpetrator's rage caused him to lose control, but that the victim's behavior caused a type of social harm and loss of honor that would (naturally, appropriately) provoke such a response from the killer. The crime-of-passion claim would in nearly all cases seem to be invalid on its face anyway, as victims are usually killed not in the first heat of passion but days or weeks after their "bad act" has come to light.

These killings are partially accommodated in the criminal codes of a number of Arab and Muslim-majority countries. For example, Article 340 of the Jordanian Penal Code (amended 2001), Article 237 of the Egyptian Penal Code, Article 548 of the Syrian code (amended 2009), and Article 562 of the Lebanese code (amended 1999) all make some provision for honor-based killings. These provisions have become controversial in recent years and some attempts at reform have been made. However, these have so far led only to occasional minor changes in the codes, with little evidence that these revisions have had any effect in practice.

A good example is the Jordanian provision which has been the subject of much commentary, political activism, and scholarship. Until 2001, Article 340 read:

i. He benefits from an exculpatory excuse who surprises his wife or one of his female unlawfuls [*muharim*, a woman related to him by a close enough degree to preclude marriage between them] in the act of adultery with another man and kills, wounds, or injures one or both of them.

ii. The perpetrator of a killing, wounding or injury benefits from a mitigating excuse if he surprises his wife or one of his female ascendants or siblings with another in an unlawful bed.[19]

After several years of activism, efforts by the royal family to change the law, and resistance in the parliament to enacting any changes, the law was amended slightly.[20] The element of exculpation, which would relieve the killer of any penalty, was removed, and the element of mitigation, which would result in lighter sentencing, was retained and extended to women killers in some circumstances. An additional paragraph was added to try to separate honor-related defenses from self-defense or crime-of-passion claims. It seems widely accepted that these reforms will change nothing in practice in either the rate of honor killings or the prosecutorial outcomes of such crimes. One activist called the changes "merely symbolic,"[21] and indeed the honor-killing rate in Jordan has remained relatively stable before and after the amendment.[22] More thorough reforms to the law have so far proved impossible due to substantial opposition from Islamists and other social conservatives.

Another approach to legal reform has focused not on the honor-specific statutes but rather on other provisions that in practice have more effect on the penalties for honor killings. In the Syrian case, recent efforts have targeted Article 192, which reduces the penalties for those who commit crimes out of an "honorable motive."[23] The definition of "honorable motive" is not specified in the law, which has allowed judges a great deal of discretion in applying the provision to honor killers. The amendment of Article 192 appears to be politically unpopular, particularly with conservatives, following on an earlier amendment to Article 548, which was accomplished through presidential decree rather than legislation. The changes to Article 548 mandate a minimum two-year sentence in honor-related killings,[24] but it is not clear what effect, if any, Article 192 will continue to have on sentencing.

Convergence of Passion and Honor

Passion and honor are conceptually different justifications for femicide, and they tend to find legal accommodation in different legal systems, but as the descriptions above suggest, there are some notable similarities. In crimes of passion, particularly the "model" passion killing involving a husband and an adulterous wife, the fury is often described as arising from an assault on a man's honor or status. The wife's adultery is an insult to his masculine honor; his fury at such a grievous insult is thus regarded as understandable and even proper, as we see in court documents and other sources. Essentially, the furious passion is partially justified because it arises from an insult to honor, or something very like it.

Honor crimes seem to involve the same human emotions and social understandings of gender roles and norms, approached from the other direction. In these cases the insult to honor is itself accommodated in law, but in a manner which, both in text and in practice, ties this honor-harm to the fury that it would "naturally" provoke. Again, the violent response to provocation is treated as worthy of some degree of toleration. In fact, the much-discussed Article 340 of the Jordanian penal code described above has only rarely been used in court; it is far more common for killers to rely on a different article for their defense:[25] Article 98 provides a reduced sentence for someone who commits a homicide in a "fit of fury" caused by a "bad act" on the part of his victim.[26] This provision is very similar to the provoked-passion rule in common law systems (and to other such provisions in Arab laws, such as Article 242 of the Syrian criminal code). The element of honor is still socially and legally important as the circumstance in which the passion is justifiable, but it is the fury itself that legally qualifies the killer for a light penalty.[27]

Indeed, actual fury need not even be demonstrated; such killers are presumed to have been enraged, and the provoked-passion defense is successful even in cases where the homicide took place long after the provocation and was clearly premeditated. It is the social understanding of the justifiability of the killer's rage and its violent result that is important rather than the individual's literal loss of self-control during a fit of fury.

In short, both crimes of passion and honor crimes seem to recognize the same social reality: insults to masculine honor and authority make men furious.[28] They also accommodate and perpetuate a clear moral norm: not only do such insults provoke fury; this fury is to some degree proper, even virtuous, and therefore deserving of special leniency in the law.

Perhaps it should not be surprising that the law and practice surrounding the two forms of femicide are similar. We have seen that both French and English law, in accommodating particular forms of crimes of passion, specified circumstances where the passionate fury was understood as a partially or completely acceptable response to an insult to masculine pride or honor; the French law was the direct progenitor of the Arab and some Western laws, where it became more explicitly about honor while still being connected to the furious response to provocation.

The Implications for Rights

These legal phenomena have several damaging results. By sanctioning the killing of allegedly transgressive women, the state puts actual lives directly at risk. Indirectly, but importantly, an entire segment of society is disadvantaged; among other things, the legal codes and practices described here disadvantage women by treating femicides more leniently than other homicides, and by making available to men criminal defenses that are not equally available to women. Formal legal inequalities like this essentially create a republican rather than democratic type of citizenship, in which laws are created in representative bodies, but not all citizens have equal standing in creating them nor are they subjects of those laws in the same way. These disparities are justified (by some) in the context of honor killings on the basis of purportedly nonpolitical norms—tradition, religion, and the like—or on the basis that the rules themselves have widespread popular support.

In the longer term, legal accommodation of such allegedly virtuous violence perpetuates a type of social order that subordinates the freedom, moral autonomy, and actual lives of some individuals to the moral judgment and physical coercion of others. This reinforces disparities in power and access to public life that inevitably marginalize and silence a significant proportion of the population. So long as the state finds its interests well served by those traditional power structures that it effectively preserves here, this will likely continue. However, this long-standing arrangement is increasingly coming at a cost for states, due to challenges from both human rights advocates and religious authorities.

A Clash of Norms

Laws that accommodate, fully or partially, the types of femicide described above are recognizing and giving legal force to social norms. This is, after all, what laws typically do, and it is even necessary for the legitimacy of the laws that they reflect the values of their societies. The effect works in the other direction as well, however, since laws do not simply reflect society but also shape it.

The social norms reflected in these laws and legal practices are generally traditional understandings of gender roles, masculine authority, and public morality that treat men and women quite differently. The norm of masculine honor (and rage) in regard to the behavior of a wife, daughter, or sister is a problem for both gender equality and the rule of law (both religious and secular) when it is given legal force. A possible counterargument to this position, however, is that this is not inequality, but something like separate-but-equal treatment. Let's take the example of adultery-related spousal murder. As spouses are (or were) in different legal and social positions in a marriage depending upon their genders, the law might properly recognize the effect that these roles and social expectations have on the behavior of the actors. However, in partially tolerating honor killings, such laws perpetuate the unequal (not simply different) legal status of men and women, husbands and wives, sisters and brothers, and so on, and they subject some members of society to less protection of the laws than others. Not only are standards of virtue different for men and women, but their conduct and the social evaluation of it are treated as moral questions belonging to the private sphere and thus not fully protected by public legal norms that would otherwise regulate the violence that is used to enforce these standards of virtuous behavior.[29]

As an example of the linking of morality with femicide law, in the debate over the legal treatment of honor killings conservative parliamentarians have argued that changing the law would destroy society by introducing moral corruption.[30] In this view, these laws simply serve a social good—public morality—by perpetuating traditional social norms about women's behavior. The more serious argument, however, is that these laws are apolitical, dealing with culture or families or something else outside the public and political realm. However, as the laws define the state's treatment of individuals and have an effect on the differential legal standing of citizens on the basis not of their actions but of their genders, they are as political as any other area of state-created law. They not only reflect but also shape and enforce shared understandings of rights, virtue, and punishment.

II. Religious Contexts for Secular Laws: Claims about Shariʿa and Honor Killings

I have asserted above that the laws regulating honor killings in the Arab world are secular in origin and operate as part of secular, rather than shariʿa-based, criminal codes. I do not mean to imply, however, that the social meaning of honor killings, and even support for existing legal accommodations of the practice, is unrelated to religion. Both in the West and in the Arab world, there is a widespread perception that honor killings are an aspect of shariʿa, specifically the rules for punishing adultery. This is incorrect as a matter of both law and practice. Islamic law in its various schools has never permitted killings of this type, and the current statutes regulating honor killings do not originate in shariʿa or other Islamic sources.

While the "death penalty for adultery" is a widely recognized feature of shariʿa criminal law, honor killings do not meet any of the rules. First, adultery or fornication (both encompassed by the term *zina*) must be proven by the testimony of four witnesses to the actual physical act of sexual congress. Indeed, according to Hallaq, the witnesses must describe the act in detail, confirming that they saw complete penetration take place, and the testimony of each witness must be identical to the others, or they all face punishment for false accusation.[31] An accuser who cannot bring four trustworthy witnesses likewise stands to be punished for false accusation: eighty lashes.

If there are four witnesses to the sexual act, they provide this testimony to a court, not to a family. The court then rules on the crime and if the parties are found guilty, they are punished by the public authorities, not by private actors. The punishment for *zina* is severe: extramarital sex with or by a married woman is a capital crime, for which the punishment is stoning. If the woman is unmarried, however, the punishment for both parties is one hundred lashes.

The evidentiary standards for *zina* convictions are remarkably strict. Even confession by one adulterous partner is insufficient to convict the other; in the absence of eyewitness testimony, if an individual confesses to *zina* and names a partner, the other person's sworn denial means that the confessor will be punished for two crimes: his/her own confessed *zina*, and falsely accusing the other person.[32] These standards make it impossible to convict anyone of *zina* based on rumor or unsupported accusation.

Honor killings, which are most often committed on the basis of gossip or opinion, do not meet the standards of evidence; indeed, two of the four Sunni schools of jurisprudence reject even extramarital pregnancy as evidence of *zina*, as it could be the consequence of rape.[33] Honor killers often do not even claim that the victim had engaged in extramarital sex; more commonly, a young woman or girl is accused simply of inappropriate behavior. Even when accusations of extramarital sex are the justification offered for an honor killing, they are often false. According to a Jordanian medical examiner, girls killed for alleged premarital sex almost always prove upon autopsy to have been virgins.[34]

Furthermore, as honor killings are undertaken by private actors, with no public finding of guilt or assignment of punishment, they also violate the standards of judicial and executive authority whereby only the proper authorities may mete out judicial punishments.

It is on this latter basis, of judicial and executive authority, that many Islamic religious leaders condemn honor killings. The Grand Mufti of Syria has rejected both honor killings and the Syrian law that has accommodated them,[35] as have scholars from al-Azhar in Egypt[36] and the Jordanian monarch's advisor on Islamic affairs.[37] These rulings are sometimes perceived as a function of the scholars' relationship to the current ruling regimes, but there are historical precedents as well; Judith Tucker cites 'Abd al-Fattah al-Tamimi, an eighteenth-century mufti, as ruling that brothers have no special role in the "chastisement" of their sisters suspected of sexual misconduct.[38] Perhaps more notably, in late 2007 Sheikh Muhammad Hussein Fadlallah, chief cleric of Hizbollah, issued a fatwa forbidding honor killings and calling them "repulsive acts."

Honor killings are a popular topic on websites that provide online fatwas and answers to questions about Islamic law. Islamonline.net provided several scholarly statements on the subject in a 2002 article. Scholars from North America and the Middle East were cited to demonstrate the unacceptability, in Islamic terms, of honor killings. Sheikh Ahmad Kutty of the Islamic Institute of Toronto focused on the danger honor killings pose to the rule of law, arguing that Islam "does not allow people to take the law into their own hands and administer justice, because doing so will be leading to chaos and lawlessness."[39] While also pointing out that Islam values every soul, he stressed the threat of the "law of the jungle" if individuals took it upon themselves to pass judgment and mete out punishment. The former head of al-Azhar's Fatwa Committee, Sheikh 'Atiyya Saqr, argues similarly that "people are not entitled to take the law into their own hands, for it's the responsibility of the Muslim State . . . to maintain peace, security, etc., and to prevent chaos and disorder from creeping into the Muslim society." Another scholar, Sheikh Muhammad al-Hanooti of the North American Fiqh

Council, likewise stresses that "only the government can apply the law through the judicial procedures." He adds, however, that honor killings are "unjust and inhumane action. The murderer of that type deserves punishment."

The Defenders of Honor Killings—Sort Of

Leaders who defend honor killings, or at least resist efforts to increase legal penalties for them, often walk a fine line, claiming that such crimes are not acceptable as a matter of shariʿa, but resisting calls for changes to the law on the grounds that the tradition serves a virtuous purpose by maintaining female morality, and that assaults on the tradition are the work of foreign enemies. Sheikh Hamza Mansour, a former Secretary-General of the Islamic Action Front party in Jordan and currently a member of parliament, has said that "It's as if the government is giving up our personality to turn us into a Westernised society. . . . But we believe there are political forces which stand behind this issue, and they are trying to destroy the family."[40] Ten years earlier, the then Secretary-General of the same party, Dr. Abdul Latif Arabiyyat, objected to characterizations of honor killings in the foreign press as an element of Islamic law, but simultaneously argued that in the absence of the full adoption of a shariʿa-based legal order, the tradition serves to enforce religious guidelines for moral behavior.[41] In the Jordanian debate on the honor killings law, the efforts to toughen penalties for these crimes have occasionally been described as a "Zionist plot." A female Islamist member of parliament, Dr. Hayat al-Museimi, voted against the amendment on the grounds that it "encouraged family disintegration."[42]

The two strands of argument, about public morality and cultural preservation, are closely related. It is a long-recognized tactic, this argument that culture rests with women and that safeguarding "our women" against foreign influence is the best way to preserve a group's identity and cohesion. Furthermore, the belief that honor killings are somehow connected to shariʿa is also linked to cultural preservation. Hélie-Lucas has called Islamic family law "the preferential symbol of Islamic identity,"[43] and in this light we can see an obvious conflation at work in the justifications for honor killings: many people who endorse the practice regard it as both a family matter and related to (or literally a part of)

Islamic law. Since Islamic family law is a powerful identity symbol as well as "the last fortress of the shari'a to survive the ravages of modernization,"[44] the religious justifications for honor killings are also about cultural (or identity group) preservation. These ideas may be historically inaccurate and religiously misinformed, but technical incorrectness is no barrier to their social power.

As described above, the entanglement of honor killing with shari'a is perpetuated by the statements of leaders who use their religious credentials to endorse what they know to be a traditional, rather than religiously mandated, practice, as in the examples above. This is a likely factor in shaping public opinion on the issue; if leaders continue to conflate religious and traditional claims, it is hardly surprising that the public does as well. Furthermore, while many leaders point out that honor killings are traditional rather than religious practices, they do not actually condemn the tradition. At most, they may describe it as unfortunate and wish for its mitigation; the sheikh of a Yazidi community in northern Iraq said, in response to the stoning of a teenaged girl (who had been under his protection at the time), "Honour [sic] is a big thing here and each one deals with it differently. It was down to her family to cleanse her shame. Maybe kill her with one bullet, electrocution, any manner but not through this awful stoning."[45]

A reporter who did an unscientific but illuminating survey of a Syrian working-class neighborhood's attitudes toward a well-publicized local honor killing found that "more than half of them [the people she spoke to] believed that the practice of honor killing is protected—or outright required—by Islamic law."[46] However, findings in other contexts have sometimes differed; another news report cited a Jordanian study that found that "nearly all the perpetrators [of honor killings] questioned were aware that what they had done was a breach of Islamic as well as state law."[47] Public opinion generally seems to follow a pattern: opponents of honor killings describe it as a cultural and not a religious practice and argue for its eradication on grounds of rights or correct understandings of Islam, or both. Advocates and apologists for honor killings either claim Islamic endorsement for the practice, or acknowledge that shari'a does not permit such killings, but endorse it instead on the basis of the preservation of traditions and/or its function in controlling public morality.

One of the most effective counterarguments against honor killing opponents is that by seeking to dismantle local traditions they are
undermining their own culture, probably at the behest of foreign enemies. Thus the Islamic arguments against honor killings have taken on
greater importance not only for religious leaders but also for women's
rights activists, as these are harder to dismiss as foreign conspiracy.
Whether this approach is likely to alter the opinions of those who support honor killings is as yet an unanswered question.

Virtuous Violence or Evidence of Depravity? The Risks of Linking Honor to Community Identity

Within Muslim communities, both in the Arab world and in the West,
the practice of honor killing has its advocates and its opponents. The
difference between them is not religiosity; religious leaders and devout
believers can be found on both sides of the issue. The notion that
Islamic law permits, let alone requires, honor killings is however clearly
not a mainstream view among religious scholars, as we have seen above.

In fact, religious advocates and apologists for honor killings have
a view of Muslim society more in common with that of anti-Muslim
commentators than with those Muslims who oppose honor killings.
Defenders of honor killings generally make one of two claims: that the
practice enforces shari'a-mandated norms of sexual chastity, and/or
that the notion of honor is so essential to traditional culture that those
who violate it are a danger to society and public morals. These claims
place the enforcement of female sexual chastity, within or without the
law itself, at the center of the definition of the community by representing it as religiously or culturally mandatory, or both. This view treats
the "corrective" violence of honor killings as virtuous because it remedies a problem of public sexual immorality and simultaneously reinforces the social power attached to masculine honor.

Anti-Muslim sentiment in the West is often informed by this same
essentializing view of punitive violence, particularly its use against
women. There is a widespread belief that Islam is uniquely oppressive
of women on a range of issues, from inheritance to clothing to freedom of movement. This view of Muslim women's oppression, combined
with the perception of shari'a as a legal code that advocates stonings

198 << CATHERINE WARRICK

and amputations, has permeated public debates on religious accommodation and, more recently, the potential role of Islamic law in Western
countries. Nick Griffin, the leader of the far-right British National Party,
has cited honor killings specifically as evidence that Islam is incompati-
ble with European societies, describing them as an epidemic in Western
Europe and as "what you get when you have an Islamic state."[48]

Thus, defenders of honor killings in the Arab world, for example,
advocate legal tolerance of the practice on the basis that (among other
things) it helps to preserve Muslim society in the face of immorality and
foreign influence. Those in the West who seek to exclude Muslims from
their societies by targeting immigration or the extension of religious
accommodation, likewise argue that this practice typifies something
essential to Muslim communities—but of course in their view, such
communities are not worth preserving and certainly are not compatible
with the societies of the West. The view that honor killings are somehow connected to the essence of Muslim community order therefore
has two different potential sociolegal effects, in two different political
contexts. In the Arab world, this view supports efforts to preserve the
legal accommodation of honor killings, effectively granting impunity to
men who murder female relatives. In the West, this view contributes
to the opposition to religious accommodation for Muslim minorities,
whether in dress, schooling, or the use of shariʿa-based dispute resolution. The former tends to undermine the rights and status of women
by (allegedly) valuing the community's interests over the individual's,
while the latter tends to undermine the status of minority communities
on the basis of (alleged) concern for the rights of women.

Conclusion

Honor killings are an important example of what happens when the
legal system preserves traditional gender norms through a connection
to both public morality and social identity. That honor killings still find
some accommodation in Arab legal systems is evidence not of the fundamental "Islamicness" of these systems, but of the power of cultural
claims; where cultural authenticity is at issue, as in postcolonial states,
then the state has a tactical interest in making use of cultural elements
to bolster its own legitimacy. In such cases, the operation of the law

becomes highly dependent on whoever has the authority to proclaim what is "authentic." This is how honor killings, as a traditional practice, become linked to claims not only about public morality and traditional gender norms, but also about the preservation of Islamic society. Criticisms of honor killings on grounds of women's rights are rather easily recharacterized by traditionalists as assaults on morality and thereby on both religion and social cohesion.

So far, efforts to reform the legal treatment of honor killings have been limited in their successes; a few changes to statutory language, but little more than that. If the law is to be effectively reformed, not only in its texts but in its operation, opponents of honor killing must both strip the practice of its falsely Islamic garb and challenge its accommodation in states' legal systems.

NOTES

1. A more extensive treatment of the issue of gender, law, and state legitimacy can be found in Catherine Warrick, *Law in the Service of Legitimacy* (Aldershot, U.K.: Ashgate Publishing, 2009).
2. Quoted in Douglas Jehl, "For Shame: Special Report: Arab Honor's Price: A Woman's Blood," *New York Times*, 20 June 1999.
3. Nearly all Arab criminal codes are modeled upon European codes, and they are created and amended by legislatures; they are not religious in either form or substance. Saudi Arabia is one of the only exceptions to this rule.
4. Crimes of passion are those in which an act of violence was committed by a person who was provoked past the point of reason by the offensive actions of the victim; that is, the passion is the furious passion that precipitated the violent act, not sexual passion. Crimes of passion are not necessarily related to sex or gender, but I am focusing here on a particularly common category of such crimes, those in which the victim is female and whose relationship with the male killer was an element related to the crime.
5. My research on honor killings and law focuses on the Arab countries; descriptions here may not reflect practices everywhere in the Muslim world.
6. The use of punitive violence by private actors is also one of the most common bases for condemnation of honor killings by Islamic religious authorities (see below).
7. Gender-neutral language would be misleading here, as the model crime of passion in common law has long involved a male killer, often provoked by a female victim, and I am focusing here on cases of femicide that are almost exclusively perpetrated by male killers.
8. Article 98 of the Jordanian Penal Code.
9. The state of Washington treats crimes of passion as second-degree murder; all other states treat them as manslaughter. Joshua Dressler, "Rethinking the Heat

of Passion: A Defense in Search of a Rationale," *Journal of Criminal Law and Criminology* 73, 2 (1982), 421–470, n.10.

10. Ibid., 439–440.

11. In Blackstone's *Commentaries on the Laws of England*, he gives the example of a man who has had his nose violently pulled by another man. Apparently eighteenth-century bar fights were funnier than modern ones.

12. The "reasonable woman" standard has itself been the subject of criticism from feminists and others on various grounds, most commonly that it "impos[es] a single, uniform standard on a group . . . whose subordination has been made possible by the attribution to it of uniform, usually condescending, attributes." Katharine T. Bartlett, *Gender and Law: Theory, Doctrine, Commentary* (Boston: Little, Brown and Co., 1993), 485.

13. Article 324, "Dans le cas d'adultère, le meurtre commis par l'époux sur l'épouse, ainsi que sur le complice, à l'instant où il la surprend en flagrant délit dans la maison conjugale est excusable." The reverse case, of a wife killing an adulterous husband, was not excusable.

14. In recognition of the gender disparities in the effect of provoked-passion rules, the Australian state of Victoria amended its criminal code in 2005 to remove provocation as a defense to homicide. See Tanya Giles, "Murder Excuse Killed; Provocation Out as Defence," *Herald Sun* (Melbourne, Australia), 5 October 2005.

15. Blackstone, *Commentaries on the Law of England* [1765], Book 4, ch. 14.

16. For a more extensive treatment of the law and politics of honor killings in the Jordanian case, see Warrick, *Law in the Service of Legitimacy*.

17. The vast majority of victims of honor killings are female, but there is one country, Pakistan, where significant numbers of men are also killed in honor killings. In the province of Sindh in 2002, 36 percent of the 382 honor killing victims were men. See "Nexus of Illiteracy and Honour Killing," Sindh Education Department, www.sindhedu.gov.pk/Links/karokari%20new.htm.

18. According to one report, in Upper Egypt Coptic families and Muslim families are statistically equally likely to commit honor killings. See Katherine Zoepf, "A Dishonorable Affair," *New York Times*, 23 September 2007.

19. Article 340, Jordanian Penal Code (my translation). Section entitled "Excuse in Homicide."

20. Human Rights Watch, "Honoring the Killers: Justice Denied for 'Honor' Crimes in Jordan," 16, 1(E) (April 2004). www.hrw.org. The text of the amended law is:

1. There shall benefit from the mitigating excuse (*Uthur Mukhafif*) whosoever surprises his wife or one of his ascendants or descendants in the crime of adultery or in an unlawful bed, and kills her immediately or kills the person fornicating with her or kills both of them or attacks her or both of them in an assault that leads to death or wounding or injury or permanent disability.

2. Shall benefit from the same excuse the wife who surprises her husband in the crime of adultery or in an unlawful bed in the marital home and kills him

immediately or kills the woman with whom he is fornicating or kills both of them or attacks him or both of them in an assault that leads to death or wounding or injury or permanent disability.

3. The right of lawful defence shall not be permitted in regard to the person who benefits from this excuse nor shall the provisions of "aggravated circumstances" apply.

21. Emily Nafaa, quoted in Rana Husseini, "Women Activists Set Their Eyes on 2002 Polls after Positive Legislative Changes," *Jordan Times*, 3 January 2002.

22. Jordan's rate of honor killings has remained at about 20 to 25 per year, based on official accounts, but there is general agreement that this figure is much lower than the actual number of such crimes, as many are disguised as accidents or suicides. The rate of honor killings in Palestinian society was reported to be on the increase in both 2006 and 2007, with around 60 or more such crimes by one account. Some estimates of honor killings in Syria claim an annual number between 200 and 300, while others give numbers as low as 30 or 40. "2006 Bloodiest Year for Honour Killings," Ma'an News Agency (Palestine), 5 December 2006; "Increase of Killing under Pretext of Honor Crimes in Gaza," *al-Quds al-Arabi*, 2 August 2007; "300 Honor Crimes Per Year and Reduced Sentences to Perpetrators," al-Arabiya.net, 1 August 2007, all via Mideastwire.com; Saad Jarous, "Syria Increases Penalty for Honour Killings," *Asharq al-Awsat*, 8 July 2009.

23. "Syria: Inclination to Annul Law Alleviating Sanctions in Honor Crimes," *al-Quds al-Arabi* (via Mideastwire), 1 December 2009.

24. Jarous, "Syria Increases Penalty for Honour Killings..

25. Lama Abu Odeh, "Crimes of Honour and the Construction of Gender in Arab Societies," in *Feminism and Islam: Legal and Literary Perspectives*, ed. Mai Yamani (New York: NYU Press, 1996).

26. Warrick, "The Vanishing Victim," 29–34.

27. The penalty for murder is death; most "honor killers" in Jordan serve something like six months in prison, and even less elsewhere.

28. Support for honor killings is not limited to men, however; polls demonstrate approximately equal levels of support among men and women. The law posits a male killer's fury, but that fury is often shared by other family members affected by the perceived loss of honor.

29. There is a bit of an inconsistency here as regards public and private norms. Defenders of honor killings generally claim that the issue should not fall within the scope of (public) criminal law, because the regulation of behavior and sexual morality within the family is a private matter. However, the perceived need for an honor killing hinges upon the public shame borne by the family of a transgressing woman. It is only because the matter is public that the killing is allegedly necessary in the first place.

30. Deputy Usama Malkawi, an attorney from Irbid, Jordan, quoted in Rana Husseini, "Opposition to Article 340 Driven by 'Zionists, Western Interests,' Says Oweideh," *Jordan Times*, 25 February 2000.

31. Wael B. Hallaq, *Shariʿa: Theory, Practice, Transformations* (Cambridge: Cambridge University Press, 2009), 311–314.

32. Ibid., 314.

33. The Hanafi and Shafiʿi schools hold that even in the case of an extramarital pregnancy, the usual standards of evidence for *zina* are still necessary for a conviction; if a pregnant unmarried woman claims she was raped, that claim is sufficient. The Ḥanbalī and Maliki schools treat the pregnancy as proof of zina, but they permit the woman to defend herself against the charge by offering evidence that she was raped. This evidence does not have to meet the normal standards of evidence for other rape charges; the woman can rely on circumstantial evidence and need not provide eyewitnesses. (Hallaq, *Shariʿa* 314.)

34. Dr. H. Jahshan, interview, 1999, Amman, Jordan.

35. Zoepf, "A Dishonorable Affair."

36. Rana Husseini, "Al Sabeel Survey Weighs In against Amending Article 340," *Jordan Times*, 23 February 2000.

37. Rana Husseini, "Sabeel to Publish Survey on 'Crimes of Honour,'" *Jordan Times*, 22 February 2000.

38. Judith Tucker, *In the House of the Law: Gender and Islamic Law in Ottoman Syria and Palestine* (Berkeley: University of California Press, 1998), 166.

39. Islamonline.net fatwa collection, 17 June 2002. All quotes in this paragraph are taken from an answer to a question about the legal standing of honor killings in Islam.

40. Quoted in Richard Spencer, "A Question of Honor," *Sunday Telegraph* (London), 6 December 2009.

41. Interview, April 2000, cited in Warrick, *Law in the Service of Legitimacy.*

42. Quoted in Jamal Halaby, "Women's Rights Plan Rejected in Jordan," *Associated Press*, 5 August 2003.

43. Marie-Aimée Hélie-Lucas, "The Preferential Symbol for Islamic Identity: Women in Muslim Personal Laws," in Valentine M. Moghadam, ed., *Identity Politics and Women: Cultural Reassertions and Feminisms in International Perspective* (Boulder: Westview, 1994).

44. Hallaq, *Shariʿa*, 446. The only remaining elements of shariʿa in most Arab legal systems are in the area of family or "personal status" law.

45. Hala Jaber, "'Honour' Killings Grow as Girl, 17, Stoned to Death," *Sunday Times* (London), 4 November 2007.

46. Zoepf, "A Dishonorable Affair."

47. Spencer, "A Question of Honor." Unfortunately he does not provide information about the study or its authors.

48. Nick Griffin, "The Islamization of Europe," speech at Clemson University, 24 October 2007, http://www.youtube.com/watch?v=Cf8UwD-AXE0, at 3:38 and following. He goes on to claim that Islamic countries cut off the hands of small children who steal bread when starving. Accessed 23 September 2013.

8

Legislating the Family

Gender, Jewish Law, and Rabbinical Courts in Mandate Palestine

LISA FISHBAYN JOFFE

Introduction

Theorists of gender and multiculturalism often focus on the role institutions play in shaping conflicts over women's rights. Institutional
arrangements that distribute the power to regulate areas of social life
and to review actions of courts and government can be designed to
enable, encourage, or impede a dialogue between state institutions
and religious or cultural minorities over how discriminatory practices
can be brought in line with human rights norms.[1] These practices are
often embodied in codes of personal religious law, regulating marriage,
divorce, sexual propriety, child welfare, and inheritance. Religious citizens may be subject to regulation not only by the laws of the state, but
also by the laws of the religious tradition to which they adhere.

The coexistence of multiple, overlapping, and possibly conflicting
regimes of legal regulation within a single state is described as legal pluralism. Under conditions of legal pluralism, a situation which pertains
in every complex modern state:

Law and legal institutions are not all subsumable within one "system" but
have their sources in the self-regulatory activities which may support,

complement, ignore or frustrate one another, so that the "law" which is actually effective on the "ground floor" of society is the result of enormously complex and usually in practice unpredictable patterns of competition, interaction, negotiation, isolationism and the like.[2]

By the end of the Ottoman Empire during World War I, the diverse inhabitants of Palestine were governed by a number of intersecting and overlapping legal regimes. While matters of civil, criminal, corporate, and public law were dealt with by state courts applying European style legal codes, for most citizens family law matters lay in the hands of shariʿa courts for Muslims.[3] Special dispensation was made to allow the family disputes of religious minorities, such as Jews and Christians, to be dealt with by their own religious courts.[4] A similar policy of split jurisdiction based on religious affiliation was adopted during the period of the British Mandate for Palestine from 1920 to 1947.

When the modern state of Israel was created in 1948, a compact was struck between Zionist leaders and representatives of the ultra Orthodox community.[5] In exchange for public expressions of support from the Orthodox organization, Agudath Israel (Union of Israel), for the creation of the Jewish state in testimony before the UN body considering the bid for statehood, the Jewish Agency for Israel made four key promises: to accept the Jewish Sabbath as a national day of rest; to provide for the observance of kosher dietary laws in public institutions; to provide public funding for Jewish religious education; and to confer exclusive jurisdiction over family law cases involving Jews upon state-supported rabbinical courts.[6] While the vague nature of these commitments and the political power of the ultra-Orthodox at that time could not enforce them, dominant political interests in supporting the notion of Israel as a Jewish state resulted in laws being passed in the first decade of the state's existence that made good on some version of these undertakings.[7]

This arrangement has been called the "status quo" agreement because it retained in place the power distribution over family law enforced by the British authorities during the Mandate period. The decision has had dramatic and long-lasting impact on the content of Jewish and Islamic family law and the rights of women in Palestine and the modern state of Israel. However, contemporary Israeli legal historians argue that rather than being an uncontroversial continuation of Jewish legal practices from time immemorial, Orthodox religious authorities used legal reforms instituted under British Mandate rule as an occasion to "fix and impose—by statist means—their version of tradition, their version of Jewish law and their ideas concerning the desired composition of Jewish tribunals."[8]

There is no option to enter into a civil marriage in the state of Israel. Every citizen, however irreligious or disaffected with her religious tradition, must take family law disputes to religious courts. By giving the religious courts a monopoly over performing marriages and granting divorces, this agreement has created an institutional form that makes egalitarian transformation of religious law very difficult. Because couples seeking divorce have no choice but to subject themselves to the jurisdiction of religious courts, they cannot refuse to appear before them even when they object to the discriminatory legal provisions being applied. Because the state is committed to supporting the jurisdiction of rabbinical courts, demands made upon the rabbinate to make its law and procedure more fair to women are met with obdurate refusal.[9]

This chapter will consider the role played by the creation of state-sanctioned rabbinical courts during the British Mandate period in creating this status quo. I argue for reading this development in light not only of the political tensions being negotiated between Orthodox and secular factions in the period leading up to the founding of the state of Israel, but also in light of the British colonial policy of indirect rule as a method of governance for multicultural states. The role of British legal policy in the constitution of the legal institutions of the state is a neglected area in Israeli legal history.[10] This chapter draws on new historical work that explores the negotiations over power, law, and legitimacy between colonizer and colonized during the Mandate period. It also seeks to expand on this work by drawing out its implications for the regulation of family law and the rights of women and children that are so centrally implicated by this area of the law. While incremental improvements to women's status under some specific religious laws were made under British rule during the Mandate period, the consolidation of a structure of split jurisdiction over family law that it oversaw renders the achievement of pervasive gender equality a difficult and complex task.

In part II, the lessons learned by the British about governing ethnically, religiously, and legally plural dominions through policies of indirect rule will be described. The negative impact of indirect rule policies for the development of family law and the rights of women subject to it will be detailed. The section concludes by showing the ways in which an atypical form of indirect rule was applied in Mandate Palestine.

Part III will describe the Mandate government's role in perpetuating and enhancing Ottoman policies that gave power over family law to indigenous religious leaders. In particular, it shows how rabbinical authorities' interests in consolidating a role for themselves as central to the public life of the new national home were served by the Mandate program to recognize and streamline the operation of religious courts.

Finally, part IV analyzes the impact of this patriarchal compromise over family law in the development of religious family law in Palestine during the Mandate period. On key issues such as the rights of women to inherit and the abolition of child marriage, British policies of deference to indigenous authorities on family law matters undermined the effectiveness of egalitarian law reform efforts in Palestine.

The Lessons of Indirect Rule

In order to understand how the British approached the challenge of governing an ethnically and religiously diverse Palestine, it is useful to consider the strategies for efficient colonial administration they had developed in other jurisdictions. The British mapped the lessons learned elsewhere on to the interpretation and elaboration of the plural Ottoman regime they found in Mandate Palestine. Unlike the conquest of North America, where small indigenous populations spread over a wide territory were neutralized by treaty and subdued by force, the question faced by British colonists during the scramble for Africa in the mid-nineteenth century was how a small group of colonists could govern a colonized population that vastly outnumbered them.[11] They addressed this challenge with the development of a policy of "indirect rule" whereby local government should, wherever possible, be carried out through the cooptation of indigenous political institutions.[12] With regard to African law, British banned some indigenous practices as repugnant to British morality, but the bulk of customary law, dealing with petty crimes and the civil law matters of family, inheritance, and land tenure were to be left intact to evolve naturally along with the worldview of its adherents. Indirect rule had three key features: the distribution of jurisdiction between colonial and indigenous law along subject matter lines, negotiation about this distribution between colonial authorities and patriarchal tribal leaders in the indigenous community, and the subjection of indigenous norms to extinguishment if they were deemed repugnant to British moral norms.

Under indirect rule in Africa, the parameters of the indigenous legal realm were established in a way that disadvantaged women.[13] By the early twentieth century, official customary law throughout southern Africa had taken on a particularly authoritative and patriarchal cast. In part this occurred because the legal codes were the product of negotiation between colonial and customary elites at a time of dramatic social and political change. Official accounts of customary law were produced through consultation with men in positions of patriarchal authority and through observation of the workings of traditional courts. Where they acted as informants, it was in the interests of senior men such as hereditary chiefs and communal elders to present a version of customary law which was relatively stable and which privileged their interests.[14]

Women were also disadvantaged by the translation of African customary norms into rules enforceable in British courts. The imposition of colonial adjudication entailed the creation and application of clear rules in areas that had previously been regulated through the application of flexible, nontechnical standards.[15] This rendered invisible the complex, negotiated quality of African adjudication.[16] In particular, it gave prominence to the claims of certain dominant groups, primarily older married men, by characterizing these claims as enforceable legal rights. Conversely, the claims of other members of society, such as women and young men, were framed as purely moral ones, enforced through communal pressure alone, if at all.[17] This is most apparent in the context of property law. Official customary law was drafted to protect the formal rights of senior male family members to inherit a male relative's estate under the doctrine of primogeniture, but the traditional rights of women, dependents, and younger male family members to live upon the land and be supported out of its proceeds were rendered inchoate and unenforceable against these newly empowered heirs. Having reduced these complex and fluid legal relations to rules subject to the doctrine of precedent, colonial adjudication also impaired the capacity of African law to grow and change in response to changing social conditions and internal political demands, including those for greater gender equality.[18]

Colonial and apartheid governments may have had their own reasons for cooperating in the reinvigoration of indigenous law. The most significant threat to white rule in the twentieth century came from educated, organized, and urban Africans rather than from traditional leaders and their constituencies. The British came to regret the erosion of what they saw as tribal discipline and the decay of customs that formerly kept young people in check.[19] The reification of traditions of gender inequality in the African family legitimized and naturalized notions of obedience to one's natural superiors that also served to legitimate white supremacy.

The exercise of power by indigenous authorities in many areas of Africa was subject to a "repugnancy proviso" whereby the colonial authorities could invalidate legal norms viewed as repugnant to morality. These clauses were often used to deter those practices viewed as simply intolerable, such as the infanticide of twins, trial by ordeal, and slavery.[20] Sometimes it was used to achieve advances for women, for example in banning child betrothal, forced marriage, levirate marriages (of a widow to her husband's kinsman) and seed-raiser unions (in which a woman is compelled to marry the widower of another woman in her family as her replacement).[21] These advances reinforced an understanding of African traditional norms as intrinsically backward and patriarchal. While many of these practices could have been abolished through the progressive interpretation of customary law,[22] the agency for achieving gender equality was routinely credited to the civilizing intervention of British colonial judges bearing British colonial morality. Such decisions suggested a stronger contrast between attitudes toward women's rights in these legal regimes than existed in reality. In the early twentieth century, the Transvaal Supreme Court rendered a series of decisions declaring that all customary law marriages based on the payment of *lobola* (brideprice) should be denied legal recognition as repugnant to British morality because they amounted to the uncivilized purchase of a wife.[23] This was contrasted to the supposed legal equality enjoyed by men and women under British "civilized customs."[24] At the time, however, these civilized customs made a wife subject to the "marital power" of her husband such that she was effectively a legal minor under his guardianship unable to manage her property or enter into contracts without his permission.[25]

At least formally, the British governance enterprise in Palestine differed from that in Africa. It was shaped both by different attitudes toward the local population and a shift in the understanding of the rights to self-determination of subject peoples. As distinct from colonial rule, the Mandate system was developed in the period after World War I to deal with governance of colonial territories that had belonged to defeated powers.

While the British and other triumphant colonial powers might have been inclined to divide these territories amongst themselves through annexation, the Mandate system was developed to offer the inhabitants of these territories the possibility of eventual self-determination. The Mandatory States were entrusted with tutelage over these peoples exercised on behalf of the League. The Mandatory thus had a duty to avoid annexation of the subject territory and to support the well-being and development of the people.[26]

Some scholars of international law question whether the Mandate system was designed to transcend colonialism or simply re-create it in a different form.[27] One of the early proponents of the League of Nations was South African Prime Minister Jan Smuts who argued for a coalition of civilized nations while laying the groundwork for formal apartheid in South Africa. He believed in the essential inferiority of black Africans and that the role of white government was to exercise beneficent but undemocratic rule over them.[28] The framework of the Mandate system is based on a similar notion of beneficent tutelage by civilized nations over formerly colonized peoples who were "incapable of or deficient in the power of self-government."[29]

The Mandate system was applied to the former territories of both the German and Ottoman regimes.[30] The character of the Mandate differed depending upon "the stage of development of the people, the geographical situations of the territory, its economic conditions and other similar circumstances."[31] The Covenant stated that:

> Certain communities formerly belonging to the Turkish Empire have reached a stage of development where their existence as independent nations can be provisionally recognized subject to the rendering of

administrative advice and assistance by a Mandatory until such time as
they are able to stand alone. The wishes of these communities must be a
principal consideration in the selection of the Mandatory.

The three-tiered system of Mandatory powers reflects this racial hierarchy, with opportunities for self-governance linked to the level of civilization of the subject people. The Mandates for Palestine (including
Transjordan, Syria, and Lebanon) and Iraq were "A" mandates, which
meant that the mandatory authority was to be only a nominal governance force, largely focused on supporting the process of transition to
self government.[32] Conversely, African and Pacific territories subject to
"B" and "C" mandates were subject to much greater administrative control by the mandatories.

   However, in Palestine, the creation of transitional bodies that represented the entire indigenous population proved difficult. Leaders of the
Palestinian Arab community did not want to legitimate a Jewish presence and the objective of creating a Jewish homeland by serving alongside Jewish representatives in a legislative or advisory council, or to form
an Arab Agency to parallel the Jewish Agency for Palestine. Accordingly, the Mandatory government in Palestine was unique among the
League "A" mandate countries in exercising pervasive administrative
and legislative authority, "a Crown Colony in all but name."[33]

   Imperial policy was committed from an early stage to facilitating
Jewish settlement and supporting the creation of an effective sovereign
government.[34] The terms of the Mandate for Palestine also required that
the authorities safeguard the religious rights of all inhabitants, Jewish
and Muslim alike.[35] This entailed respecting their personal status and
religious interests,[36] providing for freedom of conscience and free exercise of worship,[37] and being responsible for such supervision of religious
bodies as might be required for public order and good government.[38]

   Mandate authorities deployed the technologies of colonialism in setting policy for the governance of these territories, including the perpet-
uation of policies of indirect rule.[39] In Palestine, the British did not create a system for distributing power between local elites and the central
colonial authorities. The existing Ottoman imperial legal system already
divided power between the imperial authority and indigenous groups
along subject matter lines, placing family law under the jurisdiction of

minority religious communities.[40] As in indirect rule, the Ottoman state coped with the challenge of governing a diverse population by retaining direct control over matters of national importance such as security and taxation, and by granting jurisdiction over other legal issues to religious millets.[41] Initially, this dispensation extended only to Christians, and to a lesser extent to Jews as fellow "people of the book," but this tolerance was eventually extended to other groups as well.[42]

The extent of the powers delegated also did not remain static. Over time, many of these were transferred over to the Ottoman state, leaving religious groups with power only over family law and charitable trusts.[43] As in Africa, negotiation among patriarchal governments was at the expense of women's rights under family law. While western powers pressured the Ottoman Empire to adopt western commercial law to facilitate trade, there was little interest internally or externally in modernizing family law.[44] Governments fighting reformist battles against Islamists on other fronts were willing to accede to their demands in the context of family law, "using women as exchange money in order to pacify their fundamentalist opponents."[45]

British Mandate authorities mapped their governance strategy on to this existing legal form. The repugnancy proviso played a very limited role in the administration of family law in Mandate Palestine. As the discussion of levirate marriage under Jewish law in the following section will show, this had the perverse result that practices that had been outlawed as repugnant in southern Africa were allowed to stand in Palestine. Courts created for the Bedouin in the Beersheba district in 1918[46] were formally empowered to apply tribal custom, insofar as it was not "repugnant to natural justice or morality."[47] However, British authorities preferred to attempt to negotiate with Bedouin leaders to bring an end to practices such as trial by ordeal or child slavery rather than to extinguish these practices through application of the repugnancy clause.[48]

The repugnancy proviso did not apply even nominally to the laws of the Jewish, Islamic, and Christian communities of Mandate Palestine. Palestine's shari'a-based family law regime, codified in the Ottoman Law of Family Rights passed in 1917,[49] was admired as "a form of modern scientific legislation."[50] The British continued to apply it in Palestine even after it had been repealed in Turkey and replaced with secular legislation based on European civil codes.[51] Similarly, the British saw Jewish law as a complex and highly developed legal code, the emanation of a complex and highly developed culture. Like Roman Dutch law in southern Africa, Jewish law in Palestine was seen as derived from canonical sources similar to those that underpin English law. In the standard telling of this legal story, English law merely operated to refine procedures and fill the lacunae in an otherwise developed set of civilized indigenous legal arrangements.[52]

Consolidation of Rabbinical Court Hegemony during the Mandate Period

In the ferment of the British Mandate period, rabbinical courts seized the opportunity to have their powers enhanced and altered. The history of Israeli family law since that time has been a struggle to wrest authority over various aspects of family law from the rabbinical courts. The scope of their exclusive jurisdiction has been narrowed from the full range of family law matters to the solemnization of marriage and divorce. The rabbinical courts and civil courts now enjoy parallel jurisdiction over most matters ancillary to divorce. The question of which court will be seized of the case is often determined by a race to the courthouse. Wives usually find it advantageous to initiate proceedings in civil courts while husbands may seek to have the case dealt with under Jewish law alone in rabbinical courts. Rabbinical courts do not, for example, award alimony payments after divorce, do a poor job of evaluating the best interests of children in custody cases, and may turn a blind eye to attempts by men to use their power to withhold divorce as a bargaining chip in settlement negotiations.[53]

In addition to the parties, the judiciary in both systems has an interest in acquiring and holding jurisdiction. Jewish law has long been concerned about the possibility that parties living in legally plural multicultural states will take their disputes to Gentile courts. Jewish law requires that, where possible, Jews take disputes with other Jews to Jewish courts.[54] The elaboration of these rules reflects the context of their development. For centuries, Jewish law was the subject of fragile toleration by dominant legal authorities who might persecute Jewish leaders or prohibit Jewish practices. Jewish legal sources thus developed extensive and detailed rules regarding the relationship between

Jewish courts and civil courts which were aimed at preserving Jewish legal autonomy.[55]

The prohibition against using Gentile courts was first pronounced soon after the destruction of the Second Temple in 70 C.E. when Jews had the option of using the courts of the Roman Empire.[56] Where both parties are Jewish, it is forbidden to litigate before non-Jewish judges or in their courts. This prohibition applies even if both litigants have agreed to the court's jurisdiction and even if these courts rule in accordance with Jewish law.[57]

The reasons given for supporting the maintenance of this prohibition are both principled and pragmatic. On principle, the prohibition is understood to derive from a divine command contained in the Torah. Compliance with it is, therefore, compulsory. It is a *chillul hashem* (a scandal which brings the community into disrepute) to reject courts applying the laws handed down from G-d. The *Schechina*, the presence of G-d, is said to dwell on earth when a *beit din* (Jewish court) rules justly.[58] Use of Gentile courts thus constitutes a lost opportunity to find holiness and to fulfill the commandment to study and follow the laws of the Torah. Ottoman Jews were also advised against using non-Jewish courts for prudential reasons. Gentile courts may not be fair to Jews because they may be staffed by anti-Semites. Even well-meaning judges may apply the laws of a community permeated by anti-Semitism.[59] Failure to understand the nuances of Jewish society may lead non-Jewish courts to be too harsh or too easy on a Jewish party.[60] Use of Gentile courts was said to engender enmity within the Jewish community and toward it.[61] Finally, the interests of the rabbinical courts and the Jewish law they championed were clearly threatened by routine resort to Gentile courts. Even where these courts decided in ways consistent with the principles of Jewish law, reliance upon them would undermine the authority of Jewish courts and render them irrelevant.[62] The veracity of these rabbinical claims about the corruption and unfairness of shari'a courts is called into question by the widespread willingness of Jews to use them for the resolution of intercommunal and intracommunal disputes. Why would Jewish parties turn to them, against the tenets of their religion and the exhortations of their clergy, if they did not expect based on experience to be treated fairly or to gain advantages that were not otherwise available to them?[63]

This challenge was particularly pressing during the period before and after the creation of the state of Israel. Faced with the creation of a state in which courts would be staffed by Jewish judges and the law might be assumed to reflect Jewish legal norms and cultural values, the rabbinate had to consider whether resort to these courts would also be prohibited by Jewish law. The Talmud recognizes the legitimacy of a category of inferior courts described as "the courts of Syria" which had been chosen in ancient times by the local communities to resolve disputes in the absence of qualified judges with expertise in Jewish law. These judges relied on commonsense notions of justice, fairness, and equity rather than *halacha* (Jewish law). The prevailing opinion in Jewish law is that such courts are only acceptable in the absence of qualified rabbinical judges. Moreover, newly created Israeli civil courts would not merely rely on common sense, but would create an elaborate and alternate system of legal norms and precedents. Resort to such courts would therefore also amount to rejection of the supremacy of Torah law:

> The essence of . . . the prohibition of resorting to a secular judicial system, is the deinstitutionalization of Torah law and its subsequent nullification by atrophy and neglect, through the conscious choice of criteria other than Torah law. That this "other law" is made by Jews in the Knesset and interpreted by Jews in the Israeli judicial system does not alter the fact that a conscious choice was made to forego Torah law for other law.[64]

Despite stern cautions from rabbinical authorities, many Palestinian Jews in fact used Ottoman shari'a courts to deal with family law issues when it suited them.[65] Islamic doctrine mandates toleration for Jews, Christians, and other adherents to monotheistic religions on the basis that these faiths constitute imperfect precursors to Islam.[66] Jews might take their cases to Ottoman courts in order to make use of their more extensive enforcement powers or to shop for a forum whose doctrines might offer a more advantageous result.[67] After passage of the Tanzimat reforms in the nineteenth century, Jews enjoyed greater personal freedom and community autonomy but remained a tolerated minority subject to some degree of legal and social discrimination.[68] Still, non-Muslim women, both Jewish and Christian, sought divorce in Ottoman courts under shari'a law because the opportunity to initiate divorce was denied them under their own religious laws.[69] The *qadi* might grant the divorce directly under shari'a law or refer the matter back to the Jewish court with an order that the *dayan* rule in accordance with the *qadi's* judgment.[70] Jewish widows in Ottoman Palestine preferred to have their spouses' estates administered by Ottoman courts because they awarded women a greater share of the estate than did rabbinical courts.[71] The emphatic exhortations against use of Gentile courts in some of the Jewish law literature, in the pre-state period and in the present, may thus reflect a reactionary struggle by rabbinic authorities against the clear willingness of Jewish plaintiffs to use them.

Family law has been a key site for this struggle over jurisdiction. Under Jewish law, a divorce is effected through the delivery of a bill of divorcement (a *get*) from the husband to the wife before a *beit din* (rabbinical court). The wife does not have the power to issue a divorce herself but can request that her husband divorce her and ask a *beit din* to consider whether there are grounds under Jewish law for a *beit din* to request or instruct her husband to grant her a divorce. A woman who lacks such grounds or whose husband chooses not to comply with rabbinical advice that he ought to grant a divorce may become an *agunah*, a woman chained to a dead marriage. A woman who refused sexual relations and sought to divorce her husband simply because she disliked him did not have grounds for divorce and was characterized as a rebellious wife. In order to pressure her to return to her husband, she was denied both a divorce and financial support from her husband for one year. Some desperate women turned to Gentile courts seeking their help in ordering their husbands to divorce them, even though such coerced divorces are not considered valid under Jewish law.[72]

The Talmud itself deals with the propensity of women to turn to non-Jewish courts to protest the discriminatory practices of Jewish law courts.[73] The Talmud includes statements by rabbis of the Amoraic period (200–500 C.E.), explaining that they declare divorces resulting from orders of Gentile courts invalid in order "to stop each and every Jewish woman from seeking the assistance of a non-Jewish court to [compel a *get*] and thus release herself from the control of her husband."[74]

Conversely, talmudic commentators of the Gaonic period (700–1000 C.E.) dealt with the women's use of Gentile courts by making the law more accommodating to women.[75] The Geonim instituted wide-ranging reforms to stop this practice by calling upon the husband to release the wife and empowering the *beit din* to coerce him into doing so when necessary. Unfortunately, this sympathetic approach to the captive wife has since fallen into disuse.[76] By the mid-twentieth century, demands for women's rights under Jewish family law were once again conceived as a challenge to rabbinical authority.

While Mandate authorities initiated some improvements to women's rights under religious law, the grant of jurisdiction over family law to religious courts made the path to gender equality under Jewish family law a more arduous one. By the end of the Ottoman era, religious courts in Palestine, including that of the Jewish millet, had lost much of their legal authority. By 1914, shari'a and rabbinical courts had exclusive jurisdiction only over family law.[77] However, rabbinical authorities could not for the most part rely on the courts of the realm to enforce rabbinical court judgments. "[Ottoman] courts accepted the ruling of the Jewish courts if they matched Muslim rulings and in such cases served as a punitive instrument for the Jews. The Jewish courts had no power of coercion in other cases, but were dependent upon the willingness of those who turned to them to accept their rulings."[78]

In the new Jewish state under creation, the rabbinical courts faced the risk of losing the few enforcement powers they had if Jews had the option to turn to civil courts to resolve their family law disputes. Orthodox nationalists were strategic in urging the creation of state-sponsored rabbinic courts during the Mandate period because they suspected, correctly, that they would have de facto control over them. Secular Jews would lack the expertise in Jewish law and desire to run these courts, while the ultra-Orthodox would continue to maintain their own courts independent of the state.[79] The insertion of rabbinical courts into the civil justice regime created under the Mandate meant that rabbinical authorities could avoid competition for legitimacy and deploy the force of the new state to enforce their judgments. The entrenchment and administrative reorganization of rabbinical courts enhanced their power to enforce rigid and conservative conceptions of Jewish law by removing the option for adherents to adopt alternative interpretations of Jewish law or to exit from the jurisdiction of Jewish law altogether to a civil marriage regime.

Under the Palestine Order in Council of 1922, jurisdiction over matters of personal status was vested in the existing courts of the religious communities.[80] Rabbinical courts were conferred exclusive jurisdiction over cases involving marriage or divorce, alimony, and confirmation of wills,[81] and could acquire jurisdiction over other aspects of personal status with the consent of the parties. Their jurisdiction extended over all Jews who were registered as members of the Knesset Israel (Hebrew People Living in the land of Israel), but Mandate regulations allowed individuals to opt out of their jurisdiction.[82] One might opt out to reject religious authority or because one viewed state courts as having an insufficiently orthodox conception of Jewish law.

The Mandate authorities put great effort into reforming the procedure and administration of these religious courts. After all, indirect rule was predicated on the existence of organized, effective, and cooperative indigenous collaborators. If these did not exist or their authority was in doubt, the British would often create or support them. In the Jewish community, the British reorganized institutional forms that had been fragmented by ethnic and political dissension. Ottoman rulers recognized a chief rabbinate in Constantinople/Istanbul as far back as the fifteenth century, but this role was short-lived and its incumbents' authority was quite limited as compared to that of the Patriarch leading the Orthodox Christian millet.[83] By the end of the sixteenth century, the position of chief rabbi of Istanbul went unfilled, but the taxes payable to the state for the privilege of having an independent administration with a rabbi as its head continued unabated.[84] Positions of leadership in the community were shared and contested amongst influential religious and secular leaders who emerged from the community itself.[85] Unlike the Christian community, "the Jews had no traditional centers or established hierarchy on which the Ottomans could rely as a basis for an administrative system, or on which the subjects could rely as a basis for countering and resisting the Ottoman regime."[86] The Ottomans re-created the office of chief rabbi (*Haham Bashi*) in Istanbul in 1835.[87] The indigenous Palestinian Jewish community also had a chief rabbinate appointed by Ottoman authorities. Through the office of *Haham Bashi*, the Jewish community was subject to corporate regulation and taxation. At some points, there were two recognized chief rabbis, one for the Sephardi community and another for the Ashkenazi.[88] By the early twentieth century, the Palestinian Jewish community still lacked a unified comprehensive organization. There was dissension among the Sephardic community subject to the authority of the *Haham Bashi*, while many Ashkenazim chose to remain outside the authority of the chief rabbinate altogether.[89] In the eyes of the British, this arrangement was read as an absence of "recognized ecclesiastical organization" to which they could effectively delegate power.[90] The Jewish community was, therefore, "invited" to redress this lack by adopting the model of an elected Rabbinical Council under the control of a joint chief rabbinate in 1921.[91]

The Muslim community had been governed by Ottoman law and central legal institutions. The Ottoman system of religious courts was preserved, but their authority over non-Muslims was extinguished.[92] Under the Mandate, a framework for Islamic law adjudication within the borders of the Mandate territory was created. Alongside the chief rabbinate, in 1921 the British established a Supreme Muslim Council to deal with matters of personal law, religious appointments, and *waqf* (charitable trusts for private or public purposes). This included the power to appoint *qadis* (judges) in shari'a courts.[93] Article 51 of the Palestine Order in Council granted shari'a courts exclusive jurisdiction over matters of personal status and *waqfs*.[94]

British authorities were aware that there were conflicting views in the Jewish community about both the source and content of Jewish legal norms that would govern their new society. They had conducted two inquiries into how to structure authority over religious law. One looked at all communities while the other focused on the Jewish community specifically. Members of the Jewish community proposed various options, including civil courts, a Jewish secular court, plural Jewish religious courts, or a centralized religious system of law.[95] Most favored a centralized rabbinical authority but urged that its jurisdiction be confined to religious matters alone.[96] The British chose the latter model as the path of least resistance.

This option enjoyed support from the right and the left within the Jewish community. While the ultra-Orthodox favored recognition of multiple Jewish courts without a supreme authority, they were in agreement that family law matters should be governed by religious law alone.[97] While secular lawyers attempted to articulate a modern conception of Jewish law to be enforced by civil courts in other areas of law, they raised no objection to allowing religious courts to maintain sole jurisdiction over family law.[98]

While it is not surprising that ultra-Orthodox authorities supported rabbinical control of family law, the reasons for the abandonment of the family law realm by advocates for a progressive "Hebrew law" (mishpat ivri) are less clear. The latter supported a new model of jurisprudence, legitimated by its relationship to the Jewish legal tradition developed during centuries of exile but also superseding the sacred texts in which they were elaborated. Proponents argued that while Jews lived in exile in other nations, it had been appropriate that Jewish legal norms were developed through the rubric of religion. However, now that Jews were to hold the instrumentalities of the state in their hands, Jewish values could also be expressed though secular law making.[99] The religious aspect of Jewish law was viewed as "a matter of form, an outer layer enclosing a cultural core" which could be stripped away to reveal essential values to be translated into new forms.[100] However, in spite of the fact that in many jurisdictions, including Mandate Palestine, the primary jurisdiction of rabbinical courts was in the resolution of family law disputes, this grand project of reformation did not include family law and the rights of women and children subjected to it. The symbolic confinement of religious law to the field of family law while modernizing other areas of law was apparently acceptable to most secular Palestinian Jews during this period.

This was all the more curious given that debate over the future of Jewish personal law, and the position of women in it, was rife elsewhere in the Jewish world at this time. The Conservative/Masorti movement in particular sought to implement a dynamic conception of halacha.[101] Indeed, one of the central issues through which the Conservative movement in America defined itself against Orthodoxy was the development of remedies for agunot, women unable to remarry because their husbands refuse to grant them a divorce.[102] Indeed, some looked to the creation of a Jewish state as a development that would create conditions under which the vestiges of gender inequality under Jewish law would be stripped away. Justifications for this legal innovation invoked

a familiar trope, ascribing inequality under minority law to the deform-
ing effects of colonialism. The current state of Jewish law, some argued,
was not an accurate reflection of Jewish legal sources and moral norms
because it had failed to develop properly during centuries of exile and
colonization:

> The social conscience of the modern world insists on the recognition
> of the equal spiritual status of men and women. There is ground to
> believe that, had the autonomy of Jewish communal life and the conti-
> nuity of Jewish legal development been undisturbed, such equalization
> would by now be an accomplished fact well on its way to accomplish-
> ment. But with the arrest in the development of Jewish law, not only
> has progress in this direction been arrested, but the impotence of Jew-
> ish communal agencies to enforce Jewish law has deprived women in
> many instances even of such protection of their legal rights as they
> could claim in past ages.[103]

This rosy view was apparently shared by Norman Bentwich, a British
Jewish civil servant who served as attorney-general of Mandate Palestine from 1920 to 1931 and later became professor of international law
at the newly founded Hebrew University in Jerusalem. In defending the
granting of exclusive authority to make and enforce personal status law
in Palestine on the rabbinate—that has proved so damaging to the pros-
pects for women's rights—he argued that this decision would inspire
the development of more progressive rules:

> There is reason to expect that in the free atmosphere of Palestine, Jew-
> ish law will be systematically developed to accord with the liberal views
> of our time as to the relations of men and women. The development
> has been impaired by the abnormal conditions of the Jewish commu-
> nities in Eastern Europe since the Middle Ages. As soon as a Jewish
> religious centre is established in the national home, the authority of
> the rabbinical body to change the law would be recognized through-
> out the diaspora and Jewish law on matters of family right could be
> modified, as it was modified in the happier days of the great jurists of
> Babylon, Persia, Egypt and Spain during what are known as the Dark
> Ages of Europe.[104]

Patriarchal Compromise in Mandate Family Law

British colonial policies regarding the effective management of religiously and culturally diverse colonies laid the groundwork for the reconfiguration of legal authority over family law during Mandate Palestine. British interests in the efficient administration of indigenous affairs led to the strengthening of rabbinical courts. British interests in the pacification of ethnic strife may have led them to take a deferential approach to intervention in practices that discriminated against women under the family laws of Palestine. While Mandate authorities initiated some positive innovations in family law, their attitudes of deference made successful enforcement of these advances difficult. The impact of this ambivalence can be seen in the way the Mandate authorities dealt with demands for succession law reform and the establishment of a minimum age of marriage.

Jewish women's inheritance rights improved during the Ottoman period, but the invigoration of rabbinical authorities undermined the effectiveness of succession law reform during the Mandate period. According to *halacha*, in the absence of a will to the contrary a man's property descends to his male heir. The wife is entitled to the return of her marriage portion as set out in the *ketubah* (marriage contract). If she chooses not to enforce this claim immediately, she is entitled to housing and maintenance from the estate by the heirs.[105] If provision is not made by the heirs, she is entitled to sell estate assets in order to meet her immediate needs.[106] The entitlement to maintenance terminates should she remarry.[107] Often the value of the *ketubah* was negligible and was insufficient to be a source of ongoing support to the widow.[108] In practice, even these rights might prove difficult to enforce. A widow could be left with little more than a fraction of her *ketubah* money upon the death of her husband. The rights of creditors, which might have included the institutions of the Jewish community itself, sometimes took precedence over the rights and needs of the widow to be maintained out of the estate.[109]

Under the Ottoman system, members of minority communities such as the Jewish community had had the option of using Ottoman courts to deal with succession issues. When they abolished the supervisory role of Islamic courts under the Mandate, the British did not want to leave members of the Jewish community without alternate recourse. Attorney General Bentwich commented:

> It would have been regarded as a grave hardship to many Jews if they had been placed under the exclusive jurisdiction of the rabbinical Court and of the Jewish law in matters of succession and guardianship. The Jewish law has remained in those subjects unprogressive since the Middle Ages, with the result that women have inferior rights as compared with men. The Muslim law, paradoxically, approximated more closely to modern ideas with regard to equality of treatment of men and women in these family rights. There was not, indeed, complete equality, but there was less rightlessness of women than in the Jewish system.[110]

A Succession Ordinance was brought in by Mandate authorities in 1923 to ensure that Jewish women had access to a more advantageous inheritance regime. However, parties could still consent to have their inheritance disputes dealt with under *halacha* before a rabbinical court.[111] Most women would simply refuse this unappealing alternative. However, it posed a particular problem for widows who needed to perform *halitza*, the ceremony that dissolves the obligation to engage in levirate marriage with their deceased husband's brother.

While the African customary law duty to enter into a levirate marriage with the brother of one's deceased husband was extinguished as repugnant in South Africa, it remains valid in Jewish law. A childless widow must either marry her brother-in-law or go through a ritual where he renounces his claim over her. Unless and until he frees her, she is unable to remarry. As in the case of Jewish divorce law, placing this veto power over a woman's marital future in the hands of another sometimes results in refusal to free the widow out of spite or until she hands over payments or property demanded by the brother-in-law. Rabbinical legislation in Israel passed in 1944 imposed a disincentive on such delays by placing the husband's brother under an obligation to provide financial support for the widow until he had freed her to remarry. However, Mandate authorities extinguished neither the underlying requirement to enter into a levirate marriage nor the duty to participate in a ritual to be released from the obligation, thus placing no barriers before this form of extortion.[112]

In Mandate Palestine, the award a widow received under secular inheritance law often exceeded what she would be entitled to under Jewish law. Where the widow required release from the levirate bond, the brother-in-law could insist on making release conditional on her agreement to accept division of the estate in accordance with *halachic* norms. Indeed, in 1945 the Great Rabbinical Court became complicit in such extortion when it affirmed a widow's obligation to surrender her rights under civil law before the court would obligate her brother-in-law to perform *halitza*.[113] Where the brother-in-law was willing to go through with the levirate marriage but the widow refused, she might be subject to further financial loss. If a rabbinical court declared her a "rebellious woman" for refusing to go through with the marriage, she could lose her right to *ketubah* money and support out of the estate as well.[114] While the creation of a civil inheritance statute offered relief to many widows, maintenance of parallel jurisdiction over succession by rabbinical courts allowed this form of gender inequality to be perpetuated. *Halitza*-based extortion continues to be a problem among ultra Orthodox communities in Israel.[115]

Since the passage of the Women's Equal Rights Law of 1951, women in Israel are to be treated as the equals of men even when this conflicts with their rights under religious law. However, at the behest of the Muslim community, section 7 of the legislation allows the parties to opt out of civil law and agree to be subject only to religious law. Muslim women could choose to have their claims dealt with under civil law rather than shari'a law, because it grants them enhanced entitlements.[116] Attempts in 1952 to grant the civil courts exclusive jurisdiction over inheritance were met with a strong backlash from the Muslim public and Jewish religious parties.[117] Since 2001 civil courts and shari'a courts have shared concurrent jurisdiction over most matters except marriage and divorce.[118] However, many Muslim women do not choose to have their cases dealt with under Israeli succession law. This may be because women are unaware that they have this option, or because the courts themselves prefer to follow shari'a.[119] Others suggest that women engage with Islamic law strategically, declining to enforce their formal rights in situations where they estimate that their long-term interests will best be served by preserving family relationships.[120] A recent American State Department report finds that Palestinian Muslim women rarely use civil courts because of social pressures arrayed against having their disputes heard before a Jewish judge in Hebrew.[121] Like rabbinical courts, shari'a courts are also engaged in a struggle for jurisdiction with state courts. This struggle is complicated by a need to assert their legitimacy and independence from Israeli judicial authority. They seek to enhance their legitimacy by suggesting that their authority flows from their reliance on shari'a and not from their appointment by the Israeli government.[122] In contrast to rabbinical courts which have become more reactionary in response to threats to their legitimacy from civil authorities, the Supreme Shari'a Appeals Court has actually become more accommodating to women's rights. While justifying its actions in terms of adherence to Islamic doctrine, it has interpreted this doctrine to include those most favorable to women's claims for divorce, child custody, and choice of arbitrator.[123] Under this progressive interpretation of Islamic law, a woman may be permitted to divorce her husband by *khul* without his consent.[124]

Collusion between Mandate authorities and religious elites also diminished the effectiveness of attempts to bring the international struggle to prohibit the practice of child marriage to Palestine.[125] While a minimum age of marriage for girls was eventually imposed, it was drafted in such a way that it contained loopholes that permitted child marriage to continue largely unimpeded.[126] Indeed, one commentator suggests that British intervention in this area may have been more effective at confirming notions of the backwardness of Middle Eastern cultures relative to progressive British norms than at achieving change on behalf of women.[127]

Until 1917 child marriage was permissible in Palestine. Under Islamic law, the minimum age of marriage for girls was 9.[128] With parental consent, a girl who had undergone puberty could be married even earlier.[129] Between the onset of puberty and reaching full majority at 17, (18 for boys) children could be married with authorization from a *qadi*.[130] Under classical Jewish law, a girl was considered marriageable from the notional onset of puberty at the age of 12. Early marriage was thought to maximize the period of potential procreation while also increasing the likelihood that the bride would be a virgin at the time of marriage.[131] As the Mandate proceeded, the chief rabbinate raised the *halachic* minimum age to 16 "for reasons of health," but exceptions could still be made in appropriate cases.[132] Child marriage was also permissible under Christian law.[133]

Attempts by the Palestine Jewish Women's Equal Rights Association to have the League of Nations intervene to support raising the minimum age in Mandate Palestine in the early 1920s were unsuccessful. Herbert Samuel, the Commissioner for Palestine, urged restraint "in deference to Muslim opinion."[134] Indeed, a British organization defended child marriages, warning that opposition to it was part of a Zionist conspiracy to impose Jewish moral norms on Muslim Palestinians.[135]

However, Palestine had soon fallen behind the United Kingdom, other British colonies, and other nations in the Middle East on this issue.[136] Prior to 1929, the common law age of consent to marriage in the United Kingdom was 14 for boys and 12 for girls. In 1929 it was raised to 16 for both.[137] The House of Lords Select Committee stated expressly that raising the minimum age within mainland Britain was meant to support efforts by the League of Nations to stop child marriage in other countries where it remained a common practice:

> It may be difficult to prove that, in Great Britain, the disparity between the legal age of marriage and the facts of national life impede the progress of morality. But there is evidence that it does impair the influence of Great Britain in co-operating in the work of the League of Nations for the protection and welfare of children and young people and does prejudice the nation's effort to grapple with the social problems arising from the early age at which marriages are contracted in India.[138]

With the support of both Jewish and Islamic feminists but in the face of resistance from religious authorities in both communities, the Mandate government introduced draft legislation in 1933. Unfortunately, it would only have raised the minimum age of marriage for girls to 13, with exemptions permitted if the girl had reached puberty, her guardian had consented, and "no physical ill effects would follow from consummation" of the marriage.[139] This inadequate proposal was met with protests from women's rights activists in Palestine and critical and embarrassing questions of the Colonial Office in the British Parliament.[140] The Colonial Office, arguing that the terms of the Mandate guaranteed freedom of conscience, stressed that any amendments to religious family law required the consent of the groups in question.[141] The final legislation, passed in 1936, raised the age to 15 but retained the proviso that allowed religious courts to approve marriages of underage girls under specified circumstances.[142] The age of marriage for girls was raised to 17 by the state of Israel in 1950 and equalized for boys and girls in 1998.[143] However, the district court was empowered to make exemptions in some circumstances and it remained solely in the remit of the religious courts whether or not to void the marriage.[144] However, little attempt was made to ensure enforcement of these rules[145] and the persistence of child marriage in the Bedouin community in contemporary Israel suggests there is a legacy of apathy and neglect with regard to this issue.[146] According to historian Aharon Layish, the Mandate authorities "scrupulously preserved the status quo as to the material law relating to Muslims; when introducing reforms by means of criminal legislation, such as the ban on marriage of minor girls and on polygamy, he provided a good defense to Muslims and exempted them from penal sanctions."[147]

On succession and on child marriage, the impact of the cooptation of indigenous family law as a mode of governance is made clear. Deference to Jewish and Muslim religious courts allowed discriminatory practices against women to continue through the Mandate period. The Mandate government balanced a desire to offer the women of Palestine the benefits of legal equality against the administrative need to pacify religious authorities.

Admirable as these incremental advances might be, they pale when compared to the impact of turning over exclusive jurisdiction over family law to religious courts. Jews who had once had the option of resorting to state-run family law courts where they treated women more fairly were now coerced into accepting the authority of rabbinical courts. This allowed the realm of family law to become a practical and symbolic outlet for the exercise of power by religious Orthodoxy. The law has been amended to grant all religious courts exclusive jurisidiction only over marriage and divorce. Ancillary matters like maintainence, custody, and property division can now also be dealt with by civil courts. Jewish, Muslim, Christian, and Druze couples may all enter into a race to the courthouse, with men trying to launch proceedings in religious courts that give them preferential treatment while women seek to have the matters heard before civil courts that will treat them more fairly.[148]

It was this new "status quo" that shaped the distribution of power over family law in the nascent state of Israel. The grant of exclusive authority over family law to rabbinical courts has served to immunize them from review, critique, and progressive transformation. The opportunity to reject the jurisdiction of religious family courts that fail to give justice to women has shaped the development of Jewish law in the past and it continues to do so in jurisdictions outside Israel.[149] The removal of this option in Mandate Palestine continues to impede the path to gender equality for Israeli women. Women in Israel, both Jewish and Muslim, continue to struggle to wrest power over family law from religious courts.[150]

NOTES

1. See, for example, Ayelet Shachar, *Multicultural Jurisdictions: Cultural Differences and Women's Rights* (Cambridge: Cambridge University Press, 2001); Monique Deveaux, *Gender and Justice in Multicultural Liberal States* (Oxford: Oxford University Press, 2006).
2. John Griffiths, "What Is Legal Pluralism?" *Journal of Legal Pluralism* 24 (1986), 1, 3.
3. Iris Agmon, *Family and Court: Legal Culture and Modernity in Late Ottoman Palestine* (Syracuse: Syracuse University Press, 2006), 6.
4. Will Kymlicka, *Multicultural Citizenship* (Oxford: Oxford University Press, 1995), 156.
5. Martin Edelman, "A Portion of Animosity: The Politics of the Disestablishment of Religion in Israel," *Israel Studies* 5, 1 (2000), 204, 224.
6. The letter confirming this agreement, signed by David Ben-Gurion, Rabbi Y. L. Fishman, and Y. Greenbaum on behalf of the Jewish Agency Executive, is reproduced in Martin Friedman, "The Structural Foundation for Religio-Political Accommodation in Israel: Fallacy and Reality," in *Israel: The First Decade of Independence*, eds. S. Ilan Troen and Noah Lucas (Albany: SUNY Press, 1995), 51, 52. While this document is not the only source of the status quo regime, it is a good representation of its parameters. Daphne Barak-Erez, "Law and Religion under the Status Quo Model: Between Past Compromises and Constant Change," *Cardozo Law Review* 30, 6 (June 2009), 2495–2507, 2496.
7. Yuksel Sezgin, "The Israeli *Millet* System: Examining Legal Pluralism Through the Lenses of Nation-Building and Human Rights," *Israel Law Review* 43, 3 (2010), 631–654, 638. The *Hours of Work and Rest Law* of 1950 recognized the sabbath as the official day of rest in the country; the *Kosher Food for Soldiers Ordinance* of 1948 provided kosher food in the army; the *Rabbinical Courts Jurisdiction (Marriage and Divorce) Law* of 1953 conferred exclusive jurisdiction on rabbinical courts, and the *State Education Law* of 1953 provided for support for

religious private schools. See Barak-Erez, "Law and Religion under the Status Quo Model," 2497.

8. Ronen Shamir, *Colonies of Law: Colonialism, Zionism and Law in Early Mandate Palestine* (Cambridge: Cambridge University Press, 2000), 66.

9. Ruth Halperin-Kaddari, *Women in Israel: A State of Their Own* (Philadelphia: University of Pennsylvania Press, 2004), 40–65.

10. Ron Harris, Alexandre Kedar, Pnina Lahav, and Asaf Likhovski, "Israeli Legal History: Past and Present," in *A History of Law in a Multicultural Society*, ed. Ron Harris (London: Ashgate, 2002), 7.

11. Colonial officers who had developed their expertise serving in other colonial outposts staffed the British Mandate authority. Shamir, *Colonies of Law,* 9. Colonial authorities had extensive experience applying Ottoman civil law in Cyprus. Norman Bentwich, "The Legal Administration of Palestine under the British Military Occupation," *British Yearbook of International Law,* Issue 1 (1920–21), 139, 140.

12. The innovation was the work of Theophilus Shepstone, the first Secretary of Native Affairs for Natal, but it is often attributed to Sir Frederick Lugard, first governor of British Nigeria. Sally Falk Moore, *Anthropology and Africa: Changing Perspectives on a Changing Scene* (Charlottesville: University of Virginia Press, 1994), 18.

13. Cheryl Walker, *Women and Resistance in South Africa* (London: Onyx Press, 1982), 7.

14. "It is not simply that customary law has changed in both content and form during the colonial period. It is that the circumstances of its development made it a part of an idealization of the past developed as an attempt to cope with social dislocation. It was defensive in spirit, defense not only against British rules but against those Africans whose growing involvement in wage labour and market agriculture was leading them towards different interpretations of obligations and priorities." Martin Chanock, *Law, Custom and Social Order* (Cambridge: Cambridge University Press, 1985), 4.

15. See Duncan Kennedy, "Form and Substance in Private Law Adjudication," *Harvard Law Review* 89, 8 (June 1976), 1685.

16. Martin Chanock, "Making Customary Law: Men, Women and Court in Colonial Northern Rhodesia," in *African Women and the Law: Historical Perspectives*, eds. Margaret Jean Hay and Marcia Wright (Boston: Boston University African Studies Center, 1982), 59.

17. Gordon Woodman, "How State Courts Create Customary Law in Ghana and Nigeria," in *Indigenous Law and the State,* eds. Bradford Morse and Gordon Woodman (Dordrecht: Foris Publications, 1988), 181, 190–191.

18. Amira Sonbol makes a similar point about the impact of the adoption of modern codes of Islamic law. She argues that examination of precodification case reports in Egypt suggest that shari'a courts were far more flexible in their interpretation of Islamic law and more accommodating to women's claims.

Amira Sonbol, "Women in Sharia'ah Courts: A Historical and Methodological Discussion," *Fordham International Law Journal* 27, 1 (December 2003), 225–253.

19. Harold Jack Simons, *African Women: Their Legal Status in South Africa* (Evanston: Northwestern University Press, 1968), 43.

20. T. W. Bennett, "Conflict of Laws—The Application of Customary Law and the Common Law in Zimbabwe," *International And Comparative Law Quarterly* 30, 1 (January 1981), 59, 83; Felicity Kaganas and Christina Murray, "Law, Women and the Family: The Question of Polygyny in a New South Africa," *Acta Juridica* (1991), 116, 120.

21. Nicola S. Peart, "Section 11(1) of the Black Administration Act No 38 of 1927: The Application of the Repugnancy Clause," *Acta Juridica* (1982), 99, 111.

22. Woodman, "How State Courts Create Customary Law in Ghana and Nigeria," 195, 197.

23. *Kaba v. Ntela* 1920 TPD 964, 969. The decisions were later overturned by legislation.

24. *Messdadoosa v. Links* 1915 TPD 357.

25. The marital power for non-Africans was only abolished by the *Matrimonial Property Act* of 1984.

26. Nele Matz, "Civilization and the Mandate System under the League of Nations as Origin of Trusteeship," *Max Planck Yearbook of United Nations Law* 9, 1 (2005), 47–95, 70–71.

27. See Antony Anghie, "Colonialism and the Birth of International Institutions: Sovereignty, Economy and the Mandate System of the League of Nations," *New York University Journal of International Law and Politics* 34, 3 (Spring 2002), 513.

28. Jan Smuts, "The White Man's Task," speech, May 22, 1917 via South Africa History Online, http://www.sahistory.org.za/archive/white-mans-task. Accessed August 16, 2013.

29. Jan C. Smuts, *The League of Nations: A Practical Suggestion* (New York: Hodder and Stoughton, 1918),11.

30. Matz, "Civilization and the Mandate System," 54.

31. League of Nations, *Pacte de la Societe des Nations/ Covenant of the League of Nations* (including amendments adopted in 1924), avalon.law.yale.edu/20th_century/leagcov.asp

32. Matz, "Civilization and the Mandate System," 72.

33. Howard M. Sachar, *The History of Israel: From the Rise of Zionism to Our Times* (New York: Alfred A. Knopf, 1996),129–134. Until 1920, the British held power as military occupier. Under the usages of war, the occupier is prohibited from changing the laws of the occupied territory until peace is made and sovereignty determined. Bentwich, "The Legal Administration of Palestine under the British Military Occupation," 139. From July 1920, with the appointment of the High Commissioner for Palestine, they enjoyed the powers of a civil government and were able to introduce legal innovations. Norman Bentwich, "The Legislation of

Palestine, 1918–1925," *Journal of Comparative Legislation and International Law*, Third Series, 8, 1 (1926), 9.

34. Geremy Forman and Alexandre Kadar, "Colonialism, Colonization, and Land Law in Mandate Palestine: The Zor al-Zarqa and Barrat Qisarya Land Disputes in Historical Perspective," *Theoretical Inquiries in Law* 4, 2 (July 2003), 491, 497.

35. *Mandate for Palestine*, article 2, reproduced at 164, *Annals of the American Academy of Political Science; Palestine. A Decade of Development* 198 (1932).

36. Ibid., article 9.

37. Ibid., article 15.

38. Ibid., article 16.

39. Anghie, "Colonialism and the Birth of International Institutions," 28 (describing the reliance of the League of Nations's Permanent Mandates Commission on Lugard's doctrine of indirect rule).

40. Lynn Welchman, *Beyond the Code: Muslim Family Law and the Shar'i Judiciary in the Palestinian West Bank* (Boston: Kluwer Law International, 2000), 44.

41. Ibid. at 43.

42. See Benjamin Braude, "Foundation Myths of the Millet System," in *Christians and Jews in the Ottoman Empire: The Functioning of a Plural Society*, eds. Benjamin Braude and Bernard Lewis (New York and London: Holmes and Meier, 1992), 72.

43. Uri Kupferschmidt, *The Supreme Muslim Council: Islam under the British Mandate for Palestine* (Leiden: Brill, 1987), 14. Kupferschmidt provides an interesting discussion of the ways in which British policy in Palestine reflects lessons learned from governing other Islamic colonies. Ibid. at 6–13.

44. Annelies Moors, "Debating Islamic Family Law: Legal Texts and Social Practices," in *Social History of Women and Gender in the Modern Middle East*, eds. Margaret L. Meriwether and Judith E. Tucker (Boulder: Westview Press, 1999), 150.

45. Ibid., 150.

46. Asaf Likhovski, *Law and Identity in Mandate Palestine* (Chapel Hill: University of North Carolina Press, 2006), 33.

47. The Palestine Order in Council, 10 August 1922 (League of Nations), article 45.

48. Likhovski, *Law and Identity in Mandate Palestine,* 92–93.

49. It contained provisions dealing with other communities, but only the Muslim sections were continued by the British through the *Muslim Family Law (Application) Ordinance* of 1919. Welchman, *Beyond the Code*, 38–43.

50. Bentwich, "The Legislation of Palestine," 11. The law was subject to heavy criticism from those subject to it. Jews and Christians objected to being subjected to Islamic law. Islamists objected to the law's reliance on non-Hanafi interpretations. The law was abolished for Palestine by the Ottomans in 1919. Moussa Abou Ramadan, "The Shari'a in Israel: Islamization, Israelization and the Invented Islamic Law," *UCLA Journal of Islamic and Near Eastern Law* 5 (2005/6), 81–129, 97-98. In Turkey, the OLFR was abolished in 1923 and replaced with a secular civil code based on the law of Switzerland. Moors, *Debating Islamic*

Family Law, 152. When the West Bank came under Jordanian control in 1951, it enacted the *Jordanian Law of Family Rights*, later replaced by the *Jordanian Law of Personal Status* in 1976. This law continues to be applied by shariʿa courts in the West Bank. Moors, *Debating Islamic Family Law*, 155.

51. Alisa Rubin Peled, "Shariʿa under Challenge: The Political History of Islamic Legal Institutions in Israel," *Middle East Journal* 63, 2 (Spring 2009), 242.

52. U. Yadin, "Reception and Rejection of English Law in Israel," *International and Comparative Law Quarterly* 11, 1 (1962), 59–60.

53. See Lisa Fishbayn, "Gender, Multiculturalism, and Dialogue: The Case of Jewish Divorce," *Canadian Journal of Law and Jurisprudence* 21, 1 (2008), 71.

54. Yaacov Feit, "The Prohibition against Going to Secular Courts," *Journal of the Beth Din of America* 1, 1 (Spring 2012), 30–47.

55. Izhak Englard, "Law and Religion in Israel," *American Journal of Comparative Law* 35, 1 (1987), 185, 187. Conversely, Jewish law offered little guidance on how to respond to conflicts between Jewish religious norms and the civil enactments of a Jewish-dominated secular state.

56. Menachem Elon, "Mishpat Ivrit," in *Encyclopaedia Judaica*, 2nd ed., vol. 14, eds. Michael Berenbaum and Fred Skolnik (Detroit: Macmillan Reference USA, 2007), 342.

57. Menachem Elon, *Jewish Law: History, Sources, Principles* (Philadelphia: Jewish Publication Society, 1988), 15.

58. Simcha Krauss, "Litigation in Secular Courts," *Journal of Halacha and Contemporary Society* 2, 1 (Spring 1982), 35, 48.

59. Jacob Hacker, "Jewish Courts from the Sixteenth to the Eighteenth Centuries," in *The Jews of the Ottoman Empire*, ed. Avigdor Levy (Princeton: Darwin Press, 1994), 153, 156.

60. Ibid.

61. Ibid.

62. Kraus, "Litigation in Secular Courts," 35.

63. Najwa al-Qattan, "Dhimmis in the Muslim Court: Legal Autonomy and Religious Discrimination," *International Journal of Middle East Studies* 31, 3 (August 1999), 431–438.

64. Ibid.

65. Amnon Cohen, "On the Realities of the Millet System: Jerusalem in the Sixteenth Century," in *Christians and Jews in the Ottoman Empire*, vol. 2, eds. Braude and Lewis, 15.

66. Benjamin Braude and Bernard Lewis, "Introduction," in *Christians and Jews in the Ottoman Empire*, vol. 1, 5. This toleration was regulated by a pact called *dhimma*, and those benefiting from it were characterized as "people of the pact" or *dhimmis*.

67. Ibid., 182.

68. Amnon Cohen, "The Jews under Islam: c. 1500–Today," section XVIII, 10, in *Studies on Ottoman Palestine*, ed. Amnon Cohen (Burlington: Ashgate, 2011).

69. Al-Qattan, "Dhimmis in the Muslim Court," 434.

70. Ibid., 431–435.

71. Elimelech Westreich, "Levirate Marriage in the State of Israel: Ethnic Encounter and the Challenge of a Jewish State," *Israel Law Review* 37 (2003–04), 426, 437.

72. Ibid., 499.

73. Judith Hauptman, *Rereading the Rabbis: A Woman's Voice* (Boulder: Westview Press, 1998), 118.

74. Babylonian Talmud, Gittin 88b, as translated by Hauptman. The tractate goes on to state that the latter statement "was fabricated," but Hauptman argues that it is the disclaimer itself that is fabricated, at 111–118.

75. Shlomo Riskin, *Women and Jewish Divorce* (Hoboken: Ktav Publishing House, 1989), 135.

76. Tzvi Gartner, "The Problem of a Forced Get," *Journal of Halacha and Contemporary Society* 9 (1985), 118, 136–137.

77. Peled, "Shari'a under Challenge," 242.

78. Hacker, "Jewish Courts from the Sixteenth to the Eighteenth Centuries," 166.

79. Shamir, *Colonies of Law*, 65.

80. Palestine Order in Council 1922, articles 47 and 51.

81. Ibid., article 51. Since the creation of the state of Israel, some of these powers have been removed by legislation. Succession and wills are now regulated by the *Succession Law of 1965* and finance and property issues ancillary to divorce now fall under the *Spouses (Property Relations) Law of 1973*. Ruth Halperin-Kaddari, "Family Law and Jurisdiction in Israel and the *Bavli* Case," *Justice* 2 (Summer 1994), 37, 37–38.

82. *Knesset Israel Regulation*, Mandate High Commission 1927, section 17(3). Susan M. Weiss and Netty C. Gross-Horowitz, *Marriage and Divorce in the Jewish State: Israel's Civil War* (Waltham: Brandeis University Press, 2013), 10.

83. Braude, "Foundation Myths," 79–81.

84. Mark A. Epstein, "The Leadership of the Ottoman Jews in the Fifteenth and Sixteenth Centuries," in *Christians and Jews in the Ottoman Empire*, eds. Braude and Lewis, 107.

85. Ibid., 108.

86. Ibid., 113.

87. This role was largely ceremonial until 1860, when the incumbents of the office began to be leading rabbis, *dayanim*, and *rosh yeshivot*. Avigdor Levy, "Millet Politics: The Appointment of a Chief Rabbi in 1835," in *The Jews of the Ottoman Empire*, 432.

88. Amnon Cohen, "Ottoman Sources for the History of Ottoman Jews," section XV, in Cohen, *Studies on Ottoman Palestine*, 693.

89. Israel Kolatt, "Religion, Society and State during the Period of the National Home," in *Zionism and Religion*, eds. Shmuel Almog , Jehuda Reinharz, and Anita Shapira (Waltham: Brandeis University Press, 1998), 273, 279.

90. Herbert Samuel, High Commissioner and Commander-in-Chief, *An Interim Report on the Civil Administration of Palestine during the Period 1st July 1920 to 30th June 1921.*

91. Kolatt, "Religion, Society and State during the Period of the National Home," 283.

92. George Emile Bisharat, *Palestinian Lawyers and Israeli Rule* (Austin: University of Texas Press, 1989), 22.

93. Moussa Abou Ramadan, "Judicial Activism of the Shariʿah Appeals Court in Israel (1994–2001): Rise and Crisis," *Fordham International Law Journal* 27, 1 (December 2003), 257. Upon the creation of the state of Israel, almost all qualified Islamic law judges fled the country and there were no schools to train replacements within the state. Islamic law in Israel remained in crisis, interpreted by judges appointed by the state who lacked authority and legitimacy in the eyes of the community. After 1967, judges residing in the newly occupied territories took on the task of restoring the place of Islamic personal law. Abou Ramadan, "Judicial Activism," 258.

94. Since the creation of the state of Israel, shariʿa judges have been appointed by the state. The Greek Orthodox Christian and Druze communities retained and retain their power to choose their own judges to administer their religious laws. Moussa Abou Ramadan, "Notes on the Anomaly of the Shariʿa Field in Israel," *Islamic Law and Society* 15, 1 (2008), 89–90. The Greek Orthodox Church appoints judges from outside the country who do not speak fluent Arabic and who apply a legal code compiled during the Byzantine Empire. A woman may be divorced, for example, for sleeping away from home without her husband's permission, but cannot be granted a divorce even if she proves her husband has whipped her with a lash or beaten her with a stick. Michael M. Karayanni, "The Separate Nature of the Religious Accommodations for the Palestinian-Arab Minority in Israel," *Northwestern University Journal of International Human Rights* 5, 1 (2007), 65.

95. Karayanni, "The Separate Nature of the Religious Accommodations." Such a plural personal law system was also supported by authorities in the Muslim and Christian communities.

96. Ibid.

97. Ibid.

98. Likhovski, *Law and Identity in Mandate Palestine*, 36.

99. Shamir, *Colonies of Law*, 34–35.

100. England, "Law and Religion in Israel," 204.

101. Louis Jacobs, "Conserving Judaism: How the Middle Became a Movement," in *Jewish Religion: A Companion* (Oxford: Oxford University Press, 1995).

102. Max Routenberg, "The Rabbinical Assembly of America: An Evaluation," in David Golkin ed., *Proceedings of the Committee on Jewish Law and Standards of the Conservative Movement 1927–1970, vol. 1: The Agunah Problem* (New York: Rabbinical Assembly, Committee on Jewish Law and Standards, 1997), 898. The document cited is dated 1960.

103. E. Kohn, "President's Message" (1936) in Golinkin, *The Agunah Problem.* The movement's leaders were inspired by an optimistic reading of developments in Mandate Palestine: "Another remote hope lies in the development of Jewish life in Palestine. Already progressive measures in the law have been forced upon the Rabbinate in Palestine by the action and agitation of the Women's Organization for Equal Rights. This organization is now engaged in the Agunah problem and is steadily gaining sympathizers among influential laymen." Louis Epstein, Chair of the Committee on Jewish Law, "Rabbinic Attitude to the Agunah Problem," BRA 2/3 (March 1939). Ibid., 694.

104. Norman Bentwich, "The Application of Jewish Law in Palestine," *Journal of Comparative Legislation and International Law* 9, 1 (1927), 59, 65.

105. Uri Yadin, "The Proposed Law of Succession for Israel," *American Journal of Comparative Law* 2, 2 (Spring 1953), 159.

106. Judith Romney Wegner, *Chattel or Person? The Status of Women in the Mishnah* (Oxford: Oxford University Press, 1988), 139.

107. Avraham Grossman, *Pious and Rebellious, Jewish Women in Medieval Europe* (Waltham: Brandeis University Press, 2004), 127.

108. Westreich, "Levirate Marriage in the State of Israel," 439.

109. Margalit Shilo, *Princess or Prisoner? Jewish Women in Jerusalem, 1840–1914* (Waltham: Brandeis University Press, 2005), 189.

110. Bentwich, "The Application of Jewish Law in Palestine," 62–63.

111. Westreich, "Levirate Marriage in the State of Israel," 439.

112. The requirement to marry the brother-in-law was abolished by rabbinical courts in 1950. This amounted to a "most modest change in the existing rules of *halacha*" that did not express a preference for *halitza* (renunciation) over levirate marriage. It had the effect of offering greater protection for women who were rendered *agunot* by their brother-in-law's refusal to release them. Ibid. However, rabbinical courts still require the widow to go through the ritual of release in order to be eligible to remarry. Israeli rabbinical courts now have the power to order a man to release his brother's widow on pain of imprisonment or loss of civil privileges, but they are loathe to use it. Menachem Elon et al., "Levirate Marriage and Halizah," 725, 728–729, in *Encyclopaedia Judaica*, vol. 12.

113. Westreich, "Levirate Marriage in the State of Israel," 440–441.

114. Ibid., 433. See also Riskin, *Women and Jewish Divorce*, 27–28.

115. See, for example, Elimelech Westreich, "Family Law and the Challenge of Modernity: Debate about Levirate Marriage among Moroccan Sages," *Tel Aviv University Law Faculty Papers*, Paper 121 (2010).

116. Aharon Layish, *Women and Islamic Law in a Non-Muslim State* (Jerusalem: Israel Universities Press, 1975), 287.

117. Ibid., 310–311.

118. *Family Courts Law (Amendment No. 5)*, 2001.

119. Layish, *Women and Islamic Law in a Non-Muslim State*, 288.

120. Moors, "Debating Islamic Family Law," 168.

121. U.S. Bureau of Democracy, Human Rights and Labor, *International Religious Freedom Report for 2011: Israel and the Occupied Territories* (2012), 5.
122. Abou Ramadan, "Judicial Activism of the Shari'ah Appeals Court in Israel," 276.
123. Peled, "Shari'a under Challenge," 258, describing the productive dialogue between the Supreme Shari'a Court and the Israeli Supreme Court, which is also concerned to root its ruling in previous shari'a decisions when possible. On this process of "Islamicization" of secular law norms, see Moussa Abou Ramadan, "Divorce Reform in the Shari'a Court of Appeals in Israel (1992–2003)" *Islamic Law and Society* 13, 2 (2006), 242–274.
124. Ibid., 253.
125. Likhovski, *Law and Identity in Mandate Palestine*, 96–97.
126. Ibid.
127. Zeina B. Ghandour, "Review of *Law and Identity in Mandate Palestine* by Assaf Likhovski," *Modern Law Review* 70, 2 (March 2007), 345, 347.
128. Layish, *Women and Islamic Law in a Non-Muslim State*, 14.
129. Likhovski, *Law and Identity in Mandate Palestine*, 93.
130. Welchman, *Beyond the Code*, 1, 10.
131. Tirza Meacham (leBeit Yoreh), "Marriage of Minor Girls in Jewish Law: A Legal and Historical Overview," in *Jewish Legal Writings by Women*, eds. Micah D. Halpern and Chanah Safrai (Jerusalem: Urim Publishers, 1998), 24–25.
132. Likhovski, *Law and Identity in Mandate Palestine*, 93–94.
133. In 1931, the Palestinian census showed that 12 Christian girls had married while under the age of 15. There were 10 Jewish girls in this category and 200 Muslim girls. Ibid. at 94. The minimum age for women was raised to 17 by the *Marriage Age Law 1950* S. H. 286. The minimum age was extended to men by the *Marriage Age Law (Amendment) Act* n. 4, 1998, S. H. 318.
134. Likhovski, *Law and Identity in Mandate Palestine*, 94.
135. Tom Segev, *One Palestine, Complete: Jews and Arabs under the Mandate*, Haim Watzman, trans. (London: Abacus, 2000), 168.
136. Transjordan raised the minimum age to 16 in 1927, while India raised the age to 14 in 1929. Likhovski, *Law and Identity in Mandate Palestine*, 237 n. 62. Egypt imposed a minimum age of 16 for girls and 18 for boys in 1923. John Esposito with Natana Delong-Bas, *Women in Muslim Family Law*, 2nd ed. (Syracuse: Syracuse University Press, 2001), 50.
137. *Age of Marriage Act* 1929, s. 1 (now reenacted in the *Marriage Act*, 1949, s. 2); Carolyn Hamilton, *Family, Law and Religion* (London: Sweet and Maxwell, 1995), 46. The United Kingdom recognized marriages contracted by minors domiciled in jurisdictions that permit this. Until 2003, such children were not viewed as victims of child abuse simply by virtue of the fact that they were "performing their wifely duties" in having intercourse with their spouse. *Ahaji Mohamed v. Knott* [1969] 1 Q.B. 1968, 2 All E R. 563. This defense of child abuse was repealed by the *Sexual Offences Act of 2003*. Section 23 provides that

a husband will not commit an offence if he can prove that, at the time of the sexual activity, the wife was aged 16 or over. The minimum age was not in the original draft of the bill but was added during parliamentary debate. See *Sexual Offences Bill*, [HL] s. 31(2).

138. 74 H.L. Official Report, 5th Series, Col. 259.
139. Likhovski, *Law and Identity in Mandate Palestine*, 95.
140. Ibid., 96.
141. Ibid.
142. Ibid.
143. *Law of Age of Marriage*, S. H. 1950 at 286, S. H. 1963 at 318.
144. Layish, *Women and Islamic Law in a Non-Muslim State*, 2–3.
145. Welchman, *Beyond the Code*, 44.
146. Halperin-Kaddari, *Women in Israel*, 243–244. For a detailed discussion of the position of Bedouin women under current Israeli law, see Rawia Abu Rabia, "Redefining Polygamy among the Palestinian Bedouins in Israel: Colonialism, Patriarchy and Resistance," *American University Journal of Gender, Social Policy and Law* 19, 2 (2011), 459–493.
147. Layish, *Women and Islamic Law in a Non-Muslim State*, 3.
148. Michael Karayanni, "Living in a Group of One's Own: Normative Implications Related to the Private Religious Nature of the Religious Accommodations for the Palestinian-Arab Minority in Israel," *UCLA Journal of Islamic and Near Eastern Law* 6 (2006/7), 39–43. This law was proposed by a coalition of Jewish and Palestinian feminists and met with opposition from religious and national leaders in the Palestinian community and some Palestinian feminists who felt that it was inappropriate to undermine the authority of a major institution over which Palestinian Muslims and Christians were able to exercise autonomy. Gila Stopler, "Countenancing the Oppression of Women: How Liberals Tolerate Religious and Cultural Practices That Discriminate against Women," *Columbia Journal of Gender and Law* 12 (2003), 154–221, 199–201.
149. See Shachar, *Multicultural Jurisdictions*; Fishbayn, *Gender, Multiculturalism and Dialogue*.
150. Abou Ramadan, "Judicial Activism," 286.

PART IV

Cultural Depictions of Jewish and Muslim Women

The experiences of Jewish and Muslim women in Middle Eastern communities have varied depending on the country in which they have lived, and each state has interacted differently with its minority communities. In addition, the experiences of Jewish and Muslim women have diverged based on their status either as a minority or as a dominant member of society. Through personal memoirs, novels, and film, the authors in this section explore women's complicated relationships with the political structures of the societies they inhabited.

Andrea Siegel discusses the ways in which the "woman question" and the "Arab question" appeared side by side in early Zionist texts. As Siegel points out, many of the authors who wrote on the subject of domesticity and the role of Jewish women in Zionism also commented on Arab-Jewish relations. By explicating several seminal stories from early Zionist literature, Siegel explores the theme of domestic violence among Jewish families and the calls for reform of Jewish domestic life. She also shows the ways in which the "Arab Question" permeated discourses of gender and family life among Zionists. Jewish women, like many Muslim women, were viewed by some writers as potential agents of change and betterment in their communities. At the same time, they treaded a fine line between moral and immoral; dependent and independent; political or apolitical. In addition, Jewish women faced the complexities of coexisting with their Arab counterparts. As Zionist families tried to address the social challenges facing them, they fell victim to domestic violence at times. In those instances, the gendered discourse of Zionist literature often portrayed abusive Jewish men as savages not dissimilar from the depiction of "Arabs." Overall, these stories reveal the internal turmoil of the burgeoning Zionist society in mandatory Palestine and the role of gender relations in those early struggles.

Orit Bashkin describes the lives of Iraqi Jewish women in both Iraq and Israel through a study of their writings. Iraq offers an interesting case study of gender in Arab-Jewish relations since Jews in Iraq had a long-standing presence in the region that became known as modern Iraq. Unlike Zionists, Iraqi Jewish intellectuals often invoked the phrase "Arab Jew" to refer to their identities. However, in the interwar era,

many Iraqi Jewish writers adopted notions of a specific Iraqi nationalism rather than a broader Arab nationalism. As a result the "woman
question," as debated among Iraqi Jews, engaged with similar discourses
elsewhere in the Middle East. With the creation of the state of Israel and
the immigration of Iraqi Jewish women to the newly established nation,
questions of gender relations and patriarchy assumed new significance.
Principally, through an analysis of the autobiography of Shoshanna
Levy, a Jewish woman who attended Iraqi schools in her youth and then
moved to Israel, Bashkin unveils the complex layers of Levy's life and
multiple identities as Iraqi, Israeli, and Mizrahi. As she enters Israeli
society, Levy experiences both assimilation and subtle forms of "other-
ness." Bashkin contextualizes Levy's personal conflicts against the backdrop of Iraqi, Arab, and Israeli politics and culture.

In a similar vein, Hamid Dabashi grapples with the impact of politics
and art on Iranian women before and after the 1979 revolution. Focusing on the works of the Iranian filmmaker Bahram Beizai, Dabashi
explores the dominant female characters in Beizai's seminal films. As
Dabashi argues, Beizai frequently centers his plot on a powerful woman
whose industriousness and hard work bring her dignity. Moreover,
Dabashi explains the importance of mythmaking in the artistic performance of Beizai's cinema. Women's roles become complicated and
reinvented through the juxtaposition of myth and reality. Mythmaking
thus becomes an act of self-assertion for the women in Beizai's films.
As such, his female protagonists at times defy dominant stereotypes of
weakness and male dependence.

The art and literature of Israel, Iraq, and Iran have become key
sources of historical recovery, particularly for understanding gender
in these societies. Artists and writers—both women and men—often
addressed their daily struggles through creative self-expression. While
monumental political events unfolded in these disparate—and often
antagonistic—countries, the authors in this section explore the effects
of politics on the ordinary lives and struggles of Jewish and Muslim
women and their families.

9

A Literary Perspective

*Domestic Violence, the "Woman Question," and
the "Arab Question" in Early Zionism*

ANDREA SIEGEL

[Jewish] national renewal can only originate with the Jewish
woman. . . . The Jewish woman will once more turn home
and family life into what it once was—a center of life, a place
of recovery, a source of evernew strength. Imagine this new
house—Jewish art on the walls, Jewish books on the table,
the practices of meaningful Jewish customs. Then the family will once more collect the quiet strength that easily overcomes everything threatening.[1]

In 1901 Martin Buber authored this picture of a revitalized Jewish nation
in his article, "The Jewish Woman's Zion," for *Die Welt*, the most prominent German-language Zionist newspaper of the era. Buber had recently
taken over editorship of the paper at the invitation of Theodor Herzl and
took the opportunity to put his unique stamp on the fledgling Zionist
movement. Whereas Herzl—the charismatic "founding father" of Zionism—was focused on infusing Western European political savvy into
what had been a rather loose-knit web of local, largely Eastern European

groups, Buber insisted that there was a crucial idea Herzl had missed: it was incumbent upon Jews, Buber argues in articles such as "The Jewish Woman's Zion," to push back against the self-negating assimilatory pressures that had come with emancipation in Europe. He contends that Jewish women adapt themselves to that which is foreign with greater felicity than do their male counterparts;[2] only when women curb this tendency and once again imbue the home with Jewish "customs," "loyalty," and "love" as their distant foremothers did will "the tight family organization in which the life force of our people rested" renew itself.

Despite the many differences between the Zionisms of Herzl and Buber (for instance, Herzl called for the national language of the future state of the Jews to be German, whereas Buber was invested in the birth of modern Hebrew culture), the two leaders indeed shared a common conviction: a family characterized by good domesticity is indicative of a healthy national relation to that which is foreign. In other words, to borrow a notion developed by Amy Kaplan in her essay on nineteenth-century American literature, "Manifest Domesticity," good "domestic policy," so to speak, is a marker of good "foreign policy." Kaplan explains,

> *domestic* has a double meaning that not only links the familial household to the nation but also imagines both in opposition to everything outside the geographic and conceptual border of the home. . . . The idea of foreign policy depends on the sense of the nation as a domestic space imbued with a sense of at-homeness, *in contrast to an external world perceived as alien and threatening.* Reciprocally, a sense of the foreign is necessary to erect the boundaries that enclose the nation as home.[3]

Accordingly, it is no accident that Herzl's utopian novel *Altneuland* (*Old New Land*, 1902) features Sarah and David, a Jewish couple living in marital bliss, their home in Palestine filled with joyful childrearing. Moreover, the couple enjoys a friendship with Reschid and Fatma, Arab Muslims who similarly have "a very happy marriage" with "charming children."[4] All is well, with everyone properly contained and at peace. Buber, for his part, envisions that "the family will once more collect the quiet strength that easily overcomes anything threatening." Although "The Jewish Woman's Zion" does not deal with Arab-Jewish relations and in fact concerns diaspora Zionism (Buber would later become one of the chief philosophers of Arab-Jewish binationalist Zionism), what is of interest to the present study is his belief that "getting the home right" is the foundation for dealing with any external challenges to the realization of the Jewish national future.

Both Herzl and Buber at the dawn of Zionism have tremendous confidence in the potential of the Jewish family to coalesce vis-à-vis an external "other." But what about the Zionists living in Palestine? (Herzl never settled in Palestine, and Buber would not arrive until 1938.) In fact, it was not uncommon for Hebrew authors to illustrate the birth pangs of Jewish nationalist activities in Palestine as fraught with difficulties, disillusionment, and despair. And whereas the revolutionary, socialist, single (usually male) pioneers who came to Palestine in the years immediately preceding and following World War I tended to capture the imaginations of the Hebrew cultural elite,[5] the family as barometer of the nation's success was never completely swept aside. William Handley's study of the American western frontier is instructive: he writes that despite the enduring icon of the single cowboy, "the individual, of course, has never stood alone." In narratives of the American frontier, he writes, marriage and the family serve as a kind of laboratory for the incubation of national affairs: democracy, hope, ownership, and brutality.[6] Yet, whereas Handley argues that family violence plots characterize American frontier literature only *after* the "romanticized and violent encounter with Indians-as-Other" has been largely put to rest, Jewish writing of the Palestine frontier knows no such luxury. In fact, Jewish authors utilize family violence as a springboard for thinking through the romanticized and violent encounter itself.

The "Woman Question" and the "Arab Question" did not develop in isolation from one another in early Zionism. Jewish intellectuals who contributed to the transnational Hebrew literary culture of the late nineteenth and early twentieth centuries authored texts in which the narrative functions of women and Arabs were interwoven. These writers (the vast majority of whom were men) commented upon Jewish-Arab relations while voicing regnant Jewish anxieties about male-female partnerships, familial domesticity, and sexual vitality that had begun to emerge with the Jewish Enlightenment (*Haskalah*) and had continued to evolve thereafter.[7] It is not yet common practice among scholars of Hebrew literature to juggle analyses of *both* race and gender (masculinity *and* femininity) when reading a given text; doing so, however, not only calls attention to less commonly read works, but also highlights deep-set psychological components of the Zionist-Arab conflict alongside more conventionally studied flashpoints such as land acquisition or immigration policies.

There is no reason to assume that domestic violence was any more or less of a problem in Jewish families of the era as compared with those of any other ethnic or religious group. What is of interest is the narrative *function* of domestic violence in the Zionists' quest to establish themselves in the old-new homeland. In this study, I shall review two early short stories on the Arab Question that appeared in Hebrew journals and incorporate domestic violence plots: L. A. Arieli's "Crossing the Styx" (1914) and Zalmen Brokhes's "In the Shadow of the Hermon" (1919). I will then demonstrate the import of domestic violence in Yehuda Burla's novel *Bat Tsiyon* (*Daughter of Zion*, 1930–1931), the Hebrew novel of Mandate Palestine that most clearly enacts Jewish self-separation from the Arabs. In essence, whereas the families featured in the stories by Arieli and Brokhes fail to coalesce as they attempt to gain a foothold in the frontier, the heroine of Burla's story emerges out of domestic violence and into a productive romantic partnership indicative of the author's confidence in the Zionist enterprise.

The authors discussed in this chapter have diverse cultural backgrounds, political affiliations, and agendas. Their narrative uses of violence against women are variegated. Yet amidst the differences, these stories demonstrate a fundamental "gendering" of the Arab Question and "Arabing" (!) of the Woman Question in Zionist culture as tensions were building in Palestine: the interweaving of politics, power, self-control, transgression, and calls for reform of the Jewish family. Moreover, whereas it has become commonplace in Hebrew literary scholarship to argue that Zionism was rather singularly invested in the Jewish male, my analysis of the domestic violence motif will show that authors were concerned about well-directed Jewish manhood *and* womanhood.

Overview: The Arab Question

Joan Wallach Scott in her seminal essay, "Gender: A Useful Category for Historical Analysis," highlights the need for "contextually specific" inquiries into the reciprocalities of gender and politics.[8] One particularly rich area in which to explore such reciprocalities in Mandate Palestine is the Arab Question. A central moral and social issue for modern Jews, dating as far back as Ahad Ha-am's essay "Truth from the Land of Israel" (1891) and continuing to this very day, is what has become known as the "Arab Question" (*ha-she'ela ha-'aravit*); put succinctly by Zionist educator Yitzhak Epstein in a 1905 soul-searching account of Arab peasants being driven from land purchased by Jewish institutions:

> Among the difficult questions connected to the renaissance of our people on its soil there is one which is equal to all others: the question of our relations with the Arabs. . . . We have forgotten one small matter: There is in our beloved land an entire nation, which has occupied it for hundreds of years and has never thought to leave it.[9]

As the initial Jewish immigration waves ('*aliya*, pl. '*aliyot*) to Palestine got under way (1881–1903, 1904–1914, 1918–1923, 1924–1926, 1932–1936, each wave with its own distinct features), Zionists debated Arab-Jewish relations on various fronts—including economics, labor, natural resources, demographics, immigration, and the associated impacts on government structure, language, land acquisition, urban and rural planning, and security. With so many different types of Zionism, the debates were heated: from Vladimir Jabotinsky's revisionist Zionism to Ahad Ha-am's cultural Zionism, from Abraham Isaac Kook's religious Zionism to Ber Borochov's socialist/Marxist Zionism and Judah Magnes's binationalist Zionism.

At first, many Zionist leaders and artists, often quite critical of the West, attempted to infuse what they considered to be Eastern elements into Palestinian Jewish culture: paintings of lush biblical scenes with Jews in oriental dress, short stories that incorporate Palestinian Muslim oral legends, and Jewish defense groups clad in *keffiyehs*. In one of the most extreme expressions of this Palestinian Jewish Orientalism, Joshua Radler-Feldman wrote in a major Hebrew journal of 1907 using high biblical Hebrew:

> There is no distinction or division between a Hebrew and an Arab. . . . / You shall give your sons to him and you shall take unto yourself his sons: / And the blood of his heroes shall enter your blood and you will grow and gain strength: / And each shall find its kind and become of one kind.[10]

A motivating factor for this Palestinian Jewish orientalism was the Zionist romantic search for a plausible ancestry group. Anthony Smith explains that nationalist intellectuals search for a folk culture as the authenticating source for their ethnohistory. One constraint on this search is the plausibility factor: nationalists must choose a folk culture that they can plausibly "rediscover" as their own.[11]

Where to find the mystery, romance, and inner fire of the Hebrew past? For the bulk of Zionists, the Jewish masses who earned their daily bread as rural shopkeepers, itinerant tradesmen, displaced yeshiva students, urban craftspeople, and members of the learned professions failed to fit the bill. Zionist intellectuals looked elsewhere. By the end of the nineteenth century the idea of "the Semite" had taken root in Western thought in works such as George Eliot's proto-Zionist *Daniel Deronda* (1876). According to this English nationalist writer and others who shared her views, Jews were essentially aliens in the West who truly belonged in the East, dwelling side by side with their Semitic brothers and sisters. Jewish Zionists, in turn, further speculated about the Arab and Muslim residents of Palestine as a plausible ancestry group, with David Ben-Gurion early in his career going so far as to write that the Muslim peasants of Palestine were in fact Jewish by blood and the original ancient Zionists.[12] Other Zionists were quite skeptical of supposed shared origins or Orientalist cultural trends. Yosef Klausner, for instance, raised an early protest in 1907: "With what weird joy do these writers depict every *Erets-Israeli* Jew who speaks Arabic and looks like an Arab! . . . [I do] not at all want Jews to mimic the Arabs and the Bedouin."[13] Needless to say, rising tensions with the Arabs dramatically strained orientalist intoxication: from early clashes such as those between residents of Rehovot and Zarnuka in 1913 to the Arab riots of 1920–1921 and again in August 1929, Zionists not only had to reassess their expectations for coexistence but also had to ask themselves whether they were prepared for war.

Overview: The Woman Question

Readers of the late nineteenth- and early twentieth-century transnational publications that linked far-flung Jewish communities to one another would have been familiar with the charge that Jewish *women* were to blame for the community's abandonment of religion.[14] Many writers of the *Haskalah* came from homes of the religious intellectual elite, in which it was expected that the man would aspire to study full-time as a Torah scholar with his fellow men in the yeshiva, while his wife would work in a small business to support the family. *Haskalah* writers mounted a critique of this system for the limits it placed on men, women, and children: for instance, they charged that women were blocked from any serious access to the Hebrew language and suffered from restrictive divorce laws, men were closed off from Western thought and economic self-sufficiency, and boys in the all-male schools were subject to physical abuse by teachers still mired in antiquated disciplinary practices.[15] Yet even as the *maskilim* advocated change, they were often quite nervous about new roles for Jewish women.

If a woman became fluent in foreign literatures, or had occupational aspirations that led her away from home to the cosmopolitan centers of higher education, or wore daring fashions and flirted with strange men, she was often the target of literary derision. Some *maskilim* viewed Jewish women's comparatively frequent exposure to modern foreign literatures as a potential boon to Jewish culture, for women could be change agents who would infuse Jewish life with fresh, positive elements that Jewish men would not so readily encounter;[16] yet the pace of such change could make the *maskilim* shudder when Jewish women's embrace of foreign mores appeared to be too drastic. "Possibly there is no feature of the age more dangerous or more distressing than the growing irreligion of women," warned one writer in London's *Jewish Chronicle* in 1875.[17] The famous East European poet Y. L. Peretz lamented in an 1887 poem "alas, Jewish maiden, to us you are a stranger!" establishing a sharp dichotomy between the acculturating Jewish New Woman and the collective of religiously learned Jewish men. Only the *man*, writes Peretz, currently "is not alien to his people" and "feels their sorrow."[18] Such concerns made their way into early Zionism, as we have already seen in the case of Martin Buber's "The Jewish Woman's Zion."

Moreover, Jewish authors fretted over Jewish women who were intimately involved with non-Jewish men. In the late eighteenth century, for instance, Prussian-born Aaron Halle-Wolfssohn's 1795 *Haskalah* milestone "Hypocrisy and Light Mindedness" featured Yetkhen, whose romantic trysts with Gentile suitors lead her to a brothel. Sholem

Aleichem's unforgettable "Chava" (1905) is the Yiddish tale of a beloved
daughter who runs off with a Russian Christian writer. One of the most
prominent authors of early Zionism, Yosef Ḥayim Brenner, makes the
point in a particularly succinct manner in a 1913 "Notebook" piece
from Palestine: "It is not alien to the nature of a Daughter of Israel to
be attracted to a son of a foreign nation."[19] Women too easily occupied
liminal intercommunal space and had the propensity to leave the Jewish fold. Such panic migrated to Palestine with the new Zionist immigrants, alongside the introduction of egalitarian socialist and communist ideals into Zionism.

The Problem of Liminal Jewish Females "Migrates" to Palestine: Two Short Stories of the Pre-1929 Era

Let us begin with L. A. Arieli's "Crossing the Styx."[20] The Palestine
Hebrew press prior to World War I reported that Jewish girls exceeded
the population of Jewish boys attending local missionary schools, which
offered cheaper and more rigorous educations than the Jewish schools.[21]
Moreover, almost one-quarter of Jewish girls in attendance at these
mission schools at the turn of the century converted to Christianity.[22] It
is thus no surprise that when L. A. Arieli, who was Ukrainian-born and
had moved to Palestine in 1909, pens a story about the lure of conversion, his principal focus is on an adolescent girl in a missionary school.
Her name: Freydl. The story: "Crossing the Styx," set in Palestine during the First Aliya. Arieli writes that Freydl's brother, who engages in
daily Jewish prayer and is also a student at the school, "was not interested in the holy [Christian] studies and his heart was not captivated by
the [Christian] prayers and praises sung by the choir as was his sister's
heart." Freydl, in contrast, excels as she secretly rehearses the role of
Mary for her school's Easter drama.[23]

   The missionary school is Freydl's only place of respite away from
her abusive home. She is accustomed to recognizing the signs of an
impending explosion between her father, Yona Papirshnayder (the
name means "paper cutter" in Yiddish), and her mother, Alte-Leah. The
father's name is apt. When he gets angry, he slices through his wife and
children with emotionally abusive words, including the constant threat
to leave his wife an *agunah* (a woman ineligible for marriage because

she has not obtained from her husband a proper divorce according to Jewish law). Once, Yona "was almost ready to slap [Alte-Leah] across her cheek but he restrained himself . . . and instead with a burst of anger threw a dirty dish . . . and broke it."[24] Freydl's greatest wish is to take her mother and siblings away from the dread of their home and into the welcoming arms of her schoolteacher, a nun.

Yona Papirshnayder is a Russian-Jewish immigrant shopkeeper in Palestine just as Zionism is in its very infancy. His store is on the main street of an unnamed Arab town in which he and his family are the only Jews. He is forced to sell to the local Arabs on credit because they threaten him if he refuses. He has to be careful about where and when he walks outside, for at any time there may be a dead body in the street:

> If the corpse is an Arab the mob would cast an evil eye toward the Hebrew settlement . . . and the danger of being mortally beaten hovers over his head, whereas if the murdered person is a Jew, [Yona] could not stand to witness with his own eyes how the young Arabs would torture the corpse.[25]

Arieli's choice to set a lone Jewish family in the middle of an Arab village indicates the extent to which he projects onto the Palestinian landscape the dynamics of Ashkenazi Eastern Europe with its pogrom threats. In contrast, for instance, to Sholem Aleichem's Yiddish stories of Tevye the Dairyman (who had to trek into town to find a prayer quorum), in Palestine it was largely unheard of for a Jewish family to live alone amidst non-Jews.[26]

Yona's aggression against his family seems moderate only when put into perspective against the violence of the surrounding Arabs. Among the unsavory images in Arieli's story: Arab mothers abandon their babies to the mercy of swarming flies, Arab children hit each other as they run around naked, Arab boys lust after the one Jewish girl in the town, the Arab guard expects a bribe to carry out his responsibilities, the Arab neighbors watch with pleasure as Yona beats Freydl, and the Arabs who own a cart demand an exorbitant price when Yona at the end of the story needs to rent it for a funeral.[27] One night on the way home from her missionary school, Freydl's Arab classmate Khalil stalks her on the roadside and grabs her. When she resists his gropes, barely escaping rape, he screams, "Take this, Jewess!" and delivers mortal blows to the baby sibling she carries in her hands.[28] Yona in turn blames Freydl for being out so late at night. He loses all self-control as he whips his daughter mercilessly, the text itself indicating a domestic breakdown (and perhaps the jarring slap-sound of a whip) through a series of ellipses that interrupt the dialogue:

> He began to bring the belt down with a tense hand, hard as iron, onto Freydl's sleeping body, whipping her with a terrible cruelty. [Her brother] and Alte-Leah awoke from their sleep at the sound of her screams . . . — but after a moment the [mother] wept bitterly [to her husband]:
> —Hangman! Thief! Devour my flesh . . . drink my blood . . . ay ay ay . . . (The girl screamed)—Father . . . dear . . . no more . . . not again . . . I will not go again . . . here, I brought . . . a red ribbon . . . a gift . . .[29]

Freydl tries to pacify her father the only way she knows how, by appealing to the only thing he cares about: material gain. She offers him the sole gift she can, a red ribbon meant to be tied into a cross, given to her by the nun. Arieli here paints a terrible condemnation of the Jewish man who cannot control his anger, and a pitiful picture of a young girl who has gone astray.

A young pioneer enters the narrative and the focus on the story shifts to him. He represents those Jewish idealists for whom "the Land of Israel is beautiful and wondrous," who believe Arab customs to be heroic and "knightly," who try to find hope amidst the daily despairs of Jewish immigrant life in Palestine.[30] He comes upon this household and ultimately he must give up his idealism. The baby dies. Arieli, who often wrote about the faults of the modern Jewish man,[31] paints a pessimistic picture of the ability of Zionist immigration to engender any serious change in the Jewish family. This family is a far cry from Buber's aforementioned early Zionist vision about the restoration of Jewish womanhood, the restoration of the Jewish home, and the restoration of the Jewish nation: "the family will once more collect the quiet strength that easily overcomes anything threatening," Buber had written. In contrast, violence here reigns from without and from within.

Like L. A. Arieli's "Crossing the Styx," Zalmen Brokhes's "In the Shadow of the Hermon" (1919) includes a concern about conversion—but adds to it the problem of Jewish women's attraction to non-Jewish men. Brokhes moved to Palestine in 1903 from Belorussia. He worked in construction and camped with the Bedouin. He wrote "In the Shadow of the Hermon" in Yiddish and gave it to Simkha Ben-Tsiyon, one of the most established Jewish literary figures of the time, to translate into Hebrew. The story appeared prominently in the inaugural year of Ben-Tsiyon's Jaffa-based Zionist journal, Ha-'ezraḥ (The Citizen), in 1919.[32]

To review the plot: a young Ashkenazi Jewish woman, Rachel, lives in a small Jewish village near the Hermon mountain in northern Palestine. Her family is originally from Safed in the Old Yishuv. The Jewish men in her new village are close friends with the Arab men who live nearby. In the opening scene, the Arab and Jewish men sit amicably around a campfire, listening to a tale about a sheikh who killed his wife when he discovered that another man had stolen into her tent. In the following scene, Rachel's father hires Salim to help with agricultural work. Salim is a gallant, "ancient-blood[ed]" local Arab with essentialized wild eyes and boundless passion—in other words, the Zionists' romantic Arab ideal.[33] During the course of the story, Rachel and Salim fall in love and have sex. Rachel's father responds by savagely beating her, pulling a gun on her, raising his staff to her, kicking her and dragging her by the hair.[34] She runs off with Salim, pregnant with his child, and announces her intention to convert to Islam, saying, "I wish to become an Arab woman!"[35] The Jews are ashamed, and the bonds of friendship between the local Jews and Arabs are no more.

Significantly, Brokhes does not paint Rachel in a condemnatory fashion. She is caught in a web of men's designs on her femininity. Her own father, Jacob, fantasizes about being an Arab head of household and jokingly raises the possibility of a Rachel-Salim union by referring to Salim as his son-in-law. Unlike the classical biblical tale in which the patriarch Jacob labors to secure his beloved Rachel, it is Salim the Arab who "works at Jacob's for Rachel."[36] Early in the story, Jacob comments to Salim, "You're the lucky ones, you Arabs. You marry two, three women. Take the example of Abdul Hafez, he took three wives and does not do anything. All the work is on his women."[37] Thus, although Jacob never *actually* gives his blessing for a Salim-Rachel union, at some level he may nevertheless wish to increase his exposure to "Arabness" by bringing Salim into his family line: let Salim substitute as the laborer who pursues Rachel, and Jacob could enjoy the fantasy-life of leisure.

The dynamic of the gaze is a major theme in the story. Avimelekh, Salim's antisocial Jewish rival, aggressively stares at Rachel, and Salim too, for all his good intentions, watches her incessantly. Rachel develops an anxiety about being looked at by the men around her. Even the land itself has become threatening to her. One night, she looks toward the Ḥermon mountain and has a vision "of a man's eye known to her, calling, beseeching, winking at her."[38] For Rachel, in this omnipresent "shadow of the Ḥermon" (from which the story takes its title) the masculine gaze of her village life has become so acute that she projects the dangerous social relations around her onto the landscape. The Land of Israel, contrary to Zionist ideals, is *not* a place of refuge for Rachel.

Of interest in this story is not merely that the Jews and Arabs live so closely together. Rather, it is the psychological and cultural norms of *how* the Jews respond to and cultivate this closeness as they expand their settlement efforts in Palestine. While the Jews, in an effort to put down roots, emulate their Arab neighbors, the Arabs notably do not seek to mimic the habits of the Jews. Brokhes tells us that Rachel's Ashkenazi family builds its house according to the style of the local Arabs, sings Arabic songs, eats Arab food, dresses like Arabs, and speaks the Arabic language.[39] Thus the only framework through which Rachel could reasonably be expected to interpret the value of Salim's presence in her household would be the constantly reinforced assumption of her Jewish settlement that bringing "Arabness" into the Ashkenazi Jewish cultural environment is the highest and most natural expression for the revitalized Jewish family experience in Palestine. Yet the endeavor of entering into the Arab world ends at the Jewish woman's body. Among the six Jewish families in the story, there is a taboo against women fully adopting Arabic dress. Brokhes writes that the Jewish *men* dress as Arabs, whereas the Jewish women dress "half Arab and half European."[40] Jewish women must maintain exterior signs that signify the presence of (albeit ill-defined) limits on the ways in which Jews perform themselves to themselves and to their Arab neighbors.

One marginal character in Brokhes's tale arguably provides Rachel with a model and a means of escape from her precarious situation. In the neighboring Arab village Rachel attends a celebration in which an

Arab woman, "wrapped in black," is engaged in a ritualized Arab sword dance. The dance is a just-barely controlled celebration of sexual attraction. The woman "bring[s] the men . . . to madness [of] desire" while eluding their attempts to catch her. The dance cycle concludes "in peace and quiet" as all "start the merrymaking over again."[41] At the end of the story after Rachel's father has severely beaten her, Rachel appears "wrapped in a black outer garment," an all-black covering reminiscent of the Arab female dancer.[42] When she announces her plan to leave with Salim, she declares in this garb, "I wish to become an Arab woman!"[43] It is a radical act in which following her heart gives her the added benefit of veiling herself from head to toe. She may not be able to avoid being the object of men's gazes completely, but like the female dancer she now takes an active role in her fate. She refuses to be hunted powerlessly. She demonstrates that the regnant notion of the Jewish Woman's Body as *limit site* for proper Arab-Jewish relations in fact backfires, for it offers a signifying exit point for a Jewish woman when her community does not satisfy her ethical, personal, or physical needs. At the end of the story, Rachel leaves the village and heads to an undetermined destination with Salim.[44]

Brokhes (who left Palestine in 1913, came back briefly with a British-Jewish army unit during World War I, and then proceeded to wander to Paris, Argentina, and the United States),[45] thus offers a critique in two spheres. In the sphere of intra-Jewish relations, the beating and aggressive staring by the men in Rachel's life force her to flee. In the sphere of inter-Arab/Jewish relations, Brokhes posits that the Jewish cultural trend of emulating the Arabs as a means to new cultural authenticity can only end in failure. Rachel's father tries to kill Salim, but unlike the more powerful Arabs in the surrounding area with their clearly delineated violent codes of conduct for restoring male honor as narrated in the story's opening campfire scene, Jacob cannot even take revenge successfully. His inability to wield violence "productively" and in a communally agreed-upon manner utterly destabilizes both him and his community. The Arabs merely laugh at Jacob and go back to their village. The Jews are ashamed when their mimicry fantasy crumbles and the two communities go their separate ways. Rachel's father abandons his land, returning with his wife and younger daughter to their old lifestyle in Safed.

In sum, these stories by Arieli and Brokhes exemplify the turbulent, hesitant beginnings of Zionism.[46] They use domestic violence scenarios to vent anxieties about how Jewish men can and should respond to the era's destabilizing Jewish maidens, all the while expressing sympathy for the women's desires to escape patriarchal confines of preceding generations. Meanwhile, authors also refract concerns about Jewish powerlessness in an Arab-majority environment through instances of Jew-on-Jew domestic violence, using the often-essentialized Arabs as a measuring stick for Jewish men's failures of self-control.

Whether the Arabs possess no enviable traits or whether they are gallant and "ancient-blooded," whether they are totally foreign to the Jewish writer or whether they share common experiences, these two stories by Arieli and Brokhes wrap an internal critique of Jewish life within a premise that the passionate, volcanic character of the Arab male is a given. As the eruption of Jewish fathers in episodes of graphic domestic violence are contingent upon the actions of trapped transgressive daughters, the authorial reform-minded chastising voice offers both a condemnation of Jewish fathers' failures to mount a proper response *and* a concern for Jewish women's yearnings. Domestic violence reveals the Jewish men to be dangerously similar to the essentialized, zealous Arab characters who are supposed to be the ultimate "other," the ultimate savage—the predator Khalil in "Crossing the Styx" or the jealous sheikh in the campfire tale of "In the Shadow of the Ḥermon." Ahad Ha-am would write just a few years later, in protest of news that Jews in Palestine had killed an innocent Arab boy in revenge for Arab-perpetrated murders of the early 1920s:

> [In the Diaspora we] always remembered that the great ethical teachings that our ancestors bequeathed us were the teachings of the future that we were obliged to follow even at the risk of our lives until they became the possession of the whole human race; until the animal within us ceased to rule the lives of the individual and society. . . . [Have we returned] only in order to add another small nation of new "Levantines" in one corner of the Orient, who will compete with the Levantines already there in all those corrupted qualities—lust for blood, vengeance, competition, etc.—that are the content of their lives?. . . If that's the messiah, may he not come in my time![47]

The stories by Arieli and Brokhes raise the specter of a "dirty little secret" within the fictional realm of the Jewish home: would efforts to build up the homeland cause the animal within to rule the Jewish soul? Or perhaps the animal, in fact, had never ceased doing so?

Yehuda Burla's *Bat Tsiyon* (1930–1931)

1929 was the rift-year, a kind of existential and political crossroad. One may say that from here began the real,
cultural self-separation of the Jewish community from the
Arab-Palestinian community.
—Yigal Zalmona[48]

While instances of limited violence against Jews had occurred in Mandate Palestine prior to 1929, particularly drawing attention in 1920–1921, the 1929 "events" (*ha-me'ora'ot*, as they came to be known in Hebrew), were significantly more widespread in scope compared to previous flare-ups. Damage was especially shocking in the ethnically/religiously mixed Old Yishuv cities of Hebron/El Khalil and Safed. Mobs murdered 130 Jews (66 in Hebron/El Khalil alone) and inflicted serious injuries on others. Most of the victims were unarmed and of religious households, including families that had been residents of Palestine for generations.

In the wake of 1929, the mainstream Zionist leadership in Palestine articulated a recognition that its work was under unprecedented threat. While many in the dominant socialist Zionist parties had, for years, maintained faith that the Palestinian Arab opposition to Zionism would dissipate, after the bloodshed of 1929 Meir Ya'ari asked the Union of Trade Workers in Palestine (the Jewish *Histadrut*): "A hundred and fifty thousand Jews on a volcano. What will come of this?"[49] Of all Zionist novels written prior to 1948, Burla's novel *Bat Tsiyon* (*Daughter of Zion*) most clearly enacts the Jews' cultural self-separation from the Arab Palestinians.

Burla, who published the novel in the wake of the 1929 Arab riots, envisions this separation through the fate of a Jewish-Arab couple, the Jewish woman Rosa and her Arab husband Tawfiq, both native to Jerusalem. Over the course of *Daughter of Zion*, what starts as an innocent love affair full of hope about the potential of universalism to overcome ethnic and religious divides turns sour. The couple spends the years of the World War I in Europe, and it is in Europe that the incompatibilities between the two become apparent. The two then return to Palestine and attempt to create a life together among the urban Arab elite, ultimately gravitating toward their respective nationalist movements and abandoning their marriage.[50]

It is rare for a woman to drive the plot of a Hebrew novel during the pre-state period, as Rosa does. Yet an analysis of how the Woman Question and the Arab Question function together in the novel reveals how Burla's particular diagnosis of Palestinian Jewish-Arab relations in the 1929 era *depends* on the fact that his central character is a dynamic heroine, and not a hero. Burla's heroine follows in the wake of females such as Sara of Aaron Abraham Kabak's Hebrew *Levada* (*Alone*, 1905) and Tamara of Sholem Aleichem's Yiddish *Der Mabl* (*The Flood*, 1907). These women represent the small but significant contingent of New Women in modern Jewish literature who make choices that serve to model for the men around them a deeply felt connection to the nation.

Burla, a native Sephardi Jerusalemite who would eventually become president of the Hebrew Writers' Association in Israel, attempts in this novel to deal simultaneously with two spheres of discord in Zionist Palestine: Jewish-Muslim and Ashkenazi-Sephardi. The fact that the heroine of *Daughter of Zion* is a survivor of childhood family violence not only allows Burla to posit an idealized women's liberation agenda as a key legitimizing element of secularist Jewish Zionism, but also to position himself as a Sephardi writer who refuses to shrink into a corner as the largely Ashkenazi-led Zionist debates about the future of Palestine swirl around him.

Burla, born in 1886 to a family that had immigrated to Palestine from Ottoman Izmir in the seventeenth century, initially gravitated toward Zionism in the belief that its Hebraist cultural aims were compatible with Ottoman patriotism.[51] Burla's contributions to Hebrew periodicals, like those of his friend and fellow Sephardi pedagogue Yitzhak Shami, frequently called for the reform of Sephardi educational systems and cultural norms in light of Zionist achievements in Jewish education. Yet the difficulty of being a Sephardi writer in a literary culture dominated by Ashkenazi voices was never far from Burla's mind. As he noted in 1930: "The Sephardi feels that he is edged out, that people 'cancel him out.' . . . It is admittedly not obvious or conspicuous—but it is felt between the fingers, and a grudge gains strength in one's heart."[52] In *Daughter of Zion* Burla takes the opportunity to push back against those who would "cancel him out" because he is Sephardi.

Rosa's story in *Daughter of Zion* begins in a patriarchal Jerusalem Old Yishuv home wrecked by domestic violence. Her Ashkenazi father lords over her Sephardi mother:

—Woe is scum like you! How many times have I blackened your flesh, and you have run away—and returned again, come back like a pathetic dog . . .

—Do I come back of my own volition?—she hastened to respond, bitterly—If it were not for my care for your father . . . if he did not come to me always and appease me, begging—would I come back to see you, would I be able to look at your face?

He pounced from his place like a wild animal upon prey, grabbed her throat and bent over her back. She screamed:

—Help! Anyone! . . .

How can a man detest his wife, mother of his children, as a man detests a loathsome bug? . . . [Many times Rosa] watched when her father's face twisted as he looked into her mother's face, how his face was full of ugliness and baseness as he glared at her with glares of a cruel murderer.[53]

Rosa's childhood home is one in which Ashkenazi men, whether from malevolence (Rosa's father) or even mere ignorance (Rosa's grandfather), trap women into positions of powerlessness. It is from such subjugation of women that Rosa, acutely aware of the horrors of violence, must flee.

It is here in this early part of the novel with its focus on domestic violence in the Old Yishuv that readers first encounter the image of a mask or veil. Rosa "is ashamed and embarrassed to mention anything about her home life. . . . [In] front of her friends she is always joyous and serene, happy and light; she must always put a mask on her face."[54] Donna, Rosa's uneducated Sephardi mother (who covers her hair as is conventional for a pious Jewish woman of the Old Yishuv), relies upon a Jewish folk mystical dichotomy of external/internal as a coping mechanism for living with daily abuse. She explains to Rosa: "Every *mitzvah* (sacred commandment) has a body and an essence . . . exterior and interior. . . . When we perform the *mitsvot* with intention . . . [and] in this way we repair essences, worlds, damaged souls."[55] According to Donna the abuse is external, whereas the work of repairing damaged souls such as her own primarily takes place in a realm that is covered and hidden away from the reach of the abuser. Although this line of thought gives Donna peace, it is not a solution for the precocious Rosa, who recoils from the religious hypocrisy she witnesses all around her community.

The veil/mask image, thus anchored in a critique of Jewish life of the Old Yishuv, reappears throughout the novel. Burla follows his contemporary reform-minded writers in the Arab world such as Abd al-Hamid Hamdi, editor of the Egyptian newspaper *al-Sufur* (*Unveiling*, founded in 1915), who argued that the veil is much more than just a veil. It is a symbol through which to offer a larger cultural critique.[56]

When Rosa and Tawfiq take up residence in Switzerland during World War I, Tawfiq feels lost despite the basic French education he had acquired previously in Beirut. In contrast, Rosa, with her background in Western aesthetics (from her Jerusalem missionary school and autodidactic efforts) befriends others interested in philosophical discussions. She thrives as the debates include questions about what roles women should play in society. He, meanwhile, cannot shake off the "many generations of Eastern tradition and education," in which "woman is a creature who must be subordinate to the man." It is "an integral part of his blood," Burla writes.[57] Tawfiq develops an incongruous self-image: a veiled Arab man whose wife is bare faced. "He, the man, must walk around hidden and quiet, put a mask on his face, peer out but hold himself back," Tawfiq thinks to himself, "while she, the wife, makes her way openly and smoothly, lightly and simply."[58]

When Rosa and Tawfiq return to postwar Palestine and she dons the veil per his request, she finds it stifling and cannot thrive despite the domestic opulence of her Muslim surroundings.[59] Burla's most damning reference to the veil comes during the scene in the novel in which Tawfiq makes plans to attend a theater performance at the local Arab Club. At the Club, no actresses are allowed to appear onstage. Men play all the female roles. Burla's position is unmistakable: how can the Palestinian Arab nationalists suggest that they are offering a positive vision for the Land when they cut women out as actors? When love onstage is so full of artifice? Furthermore, the play at the Club is about Samuel ibn Adiya, the most famous Jewish Arabic-language poet-hero of the pre-Islamic *jahiliyya* era. Samuel ibn Adiya, when forced to choose between his promises of hospitality to the Arabian poet Imru al-Qais and the life of his own son, opted to sacrifice his kin for the sake of his non-Jewish guest—a decision which gained him respect and fame for generations thereafter.[60] Yet if Samuel ibn Adiya is "the good Jew" of the Palestinian Arab narrative, it is a narrative in which women cannot represent themselves. Tawfiq's invitation to Rosa to accompany him to the theater comes with a single stipulation: she must be veiled. Rosa rejects the invitation.

For Rosa, trapped in a marriage in which male and female have yet to find a productive balance, the discovery of the Zionist pioneer ethos with its proud, industrious, plainly dressed, and bare-faced women is the culmination of the novel's episodic unfolding.[61] She writes to her husband,

> Now I can express myself clearly and openly. Now the covering, which clouded my face my entire life from the beginning until now, has fallen. . . . I feel as though I have been reborn. . . . Now I have found my path and myself. My path is the path of a human being, . . . a *"bat horin"* ("free woman") like every other human being. In addition to this, I have found that I am a Jewish woman. You know that all my life I have been an opponent of religion, of that which divides and estranges, which eats away at humanity. I have found that the path via which the Jewish nation is marching today is a path of humanity.[62]

Whereas Burla positions Rosa's Zionism as "a path of humanity," a peace-seeking path for "a free woman," he paints Palestinian Arab nationalism as retrograde. Tawfiq, whose fellow activists make fun of him for being married to a Jewish woman, cannot bring himself to warn the Jews of an impending Arab attack being planned in conjunction with the Muslim/nationalist Nebi Musa procession. His father believes that Tawfiq has a "human obligation" to warn the Jews; "but," Tawfiq counters, "there is also an Arab obligation" to the Arab cause that prevents him from fulfilling such a "human obligation."[63]

Crucially, as a female from an observant Old Yishuv Jewish home who witnessed her father's cruelty to her mother, Rosa can make the case that Tawfiq's Arab nationalism is not about freedom, it is not "a path of humanity" with its mob brutality and restrictions on women. Rosa accuses Tawfiq:

> In your desire to be an Arab, you have ceased to be a human being! . . . If this is your nationalism, it is extreme, radical, and seventy times darker than religion! I ran away . . . from similar qualities of religion, and do you think I would bow down my head now before the "glory" of such a nationalism?[64]

Toward the close of the novel, Tawfiq is so heartbroken and confused that he even tries to kill Rosa.

Burla's formulation, then, merges a secularized fealty to the Jewish nation with a women's rights-oriented universalism that supposedly appeals to "humanity" beyond the confines of any particular race. His claim for the justness of Zionism derives neither from, say, the call to provide diaspora Jews with a refuge from anti-Semitism nor from the contention that Jews all over the world look to the Land of Israel as their homeland. These two themes, popular in Zionist rhetoric at the time, do not receive much attention in the narrative. Instead, via the story of a Jewish woman native to Palestine, he outlines his case clearly: the Jews have a right to conduct their efforts in Palestine because they are at the vanguard of a new, progressive social structure.

Rosa and Tawfiq divorce. In the tradition of Ibsen's Nora, Rosa leaves her family in the pursuit of self-discovery and liberty. She begins a new partnership with the Ashkenazi Zionist pioneer immigrant ʿAtsmon, to whom she preaches a philosophy of love reminiscent of August Bebel's German socialist writings on women. Earlier in the European segment of the novel, Burla had discussed how literature must "peer out to tomorrow," it must "be an art of prophecy, which declares that which is coming."[65] Literature in its current state "is afraid of itself":

> Authors are afraid of their heroes. . . . When the hero gets to the climax of his actions, the author hastens . . . to remove him from the stage. . . . Faust, Raskolnikov, Anna Karenina, . . . all of them, all of them, either

they take their own lives, or are handed over to the authorities, or completely repent of their ways. . . . Literature is proceeding hand in hand . . . with the ruling order.[66]

Through this comment, Burla demonstrates a consciousness about the pitfalls of writing a story that hails revolutionary love but brings a taboo couple to a tragic end: to deny a future to a mixed-race (Jewish/Arab) and interfaith (Jewish/Muslim) pairing leaves Burla open to the charge of being afraid of his protagonists. Yet Burla ultimately attempts to sidestep such an accusation by painting Rosa's commitment to progress and social change as able to find expression *only* in her relationship with the Jewish pioneer ʿAtsmon, not in her relationship with the effendi Tawfiq. The love offered by ʿAtsmon, the representative of Zionist socialist pioneers, under Burla's pen is the *true* challenge to "the ruling order" in Palestine.[67]

At the end of the novel, Rosa and ʿAtsmon settle in Motsa. For Burla to invoke Motsa in the wake of 1929 is a clear refusal to surrender in the face of Arab attacks, since Motsa was a flashpoint of anti-Jewish attacks in the 1929 riots and had to be evacuated. Moreover, "Motsa" means "origin." Rosa, an Ashkenazi-Sephardi Jewish woman native to Palestine is of hardy local physical constitution, giving her biological immunity to regional diseases; this local origin allows her to remain healthier than her immigrant Ashkenazi comrades in the malaria-plagued landscape.[68] Rosa may have needed the European socialist revolutionary immigrants to expose her to the values and ideals of diaspora-developed Zionist ideology, but once she is on board her origins in the land position her to lead the Ashkenazi newcomers.

Burla has one-upped his immigrant (mostly Ashkenazi) intellectual peers who would "cancel him out" because he is Sephardi. He offers a nationalist narrative—a *woman's* nationalist narrative—to claim local "dibs" on the question of whose stories, outlooks, and experiences should "count" in the increasingly rancorous debates about the future of Zionism. By choosing to center his story on a *heroine*, Burla, one may suspect, capitalizes upon the expectation that it is usually the male protagonist in modern Hebrew letters whose success or failure over the course of the nationalist narrative is measured according to the extent to which he is able to build himself anew, to change, to experience a *shinui 'arakhin* (a transvaluation of values).[69] Against this literary convention, Burla's wager—that the local child of a Sephardi mother can lead the immigrant Ashkenazi hero any day—is a jockeying-for-position in the Zionist intelligentsia, a move he needs to make while delivering up his Jewish-Arab divorce. Rosa's return to the fold after experimenting with attraction to a non-Jewish man is a return to her native territory, a return to the traits and values which characterized her as an inquisitive child and which now find full expression through the socialist, seemingly secular Zionism that she adopts in her adult life. Her symbolic journey from domestic violence to an emancipatory "at homeness" in the Land of Israel is the narrative mechanism through which Burla offers his rallying cry to his fellow Zionists in the wake of 1929, critiquing *both* the Judaism of the Old Yishuv and Palestinian Arab nationalism. Buber's words could very well apply to the harmony of Rosa's relationship with the Jewish pioneer 'Atzmon: "the family will once more collect the quiet strength that easily overcomes everything threatening."

In sum, Nira Yuval-Davis in *Gender and Nation* emphasizes that culture is "not a reified fixed 'thing' but rather . . . [a] dynamic process, continuously changing, full of internal contradictions." She encourages scholars to track developments that contribute to "defining who/what is a 'proper man' and a 'proper woman'" for the nation, since "the (re) construction of men's—and often more importantly women's—roles in the processes of resistance and liberation" is a central facet of social change among peoples who are in the midst of challenging their historically subjugated status.[70] An investigation into how *both* male and female Jewish characters channel themselves anchors the high stakes, anxiety-ridden fictional scenarios via which contributors to early Zionist literary fora "feel out" the dynamics of Jewish-Arab encounters with an eye toward the Jewish future in Palestine. The domestic violence plots in the works of Arieli, Brokhes, and Burla highlight what has been largely overlooked in Hebrew cultural studies: the domestic sphere with its prominent roles for Jewish women was an integral narrative sieve through which authors probed, blurred, distilled, and created boundaries between Arab and Jew, contributing to the Jewish self-separation process from the Palestinian Arabs that arguably continues to this very day.

NOTES

1. Martin Buber, "The Jewish Woman's Zion," in *The First Buber: Youthful Zionist Writings of Martin Buber*, ed. and trans. Galya D. Schmidt (Syracuse: Syracuse University Press, 1999), 114–116. Brackets in the original translation.

2. It is Jewish *women*, writes Buber, who have "adapted themselves most easily to their environment and adapted its ways" and who have "participated in a most lively manner in the evolving fanaticism of assimilation." Ibid., 114.

3. Amy Kaplan, "Manifest Domesticity," *American Literature* 70 (September 1998), 581–582. Italics added for emphasis.

4. Theodore Herzl, *Old New Land*, 2nd edition. Trans. and with revised notes by Lotta Levensohn, (New York: Bloch Publishing and Herzl Press, 1960), 97. Originally published in 1902. "Reschid" is the spelling used in the translation.

5. See, for instance, a discussion of the visual iconography of the Zionist pioneers in Rona Sela, "Women Photographers in the Private Arena, Women Photographers in the Public Arena, " in *Women Artists in Israel, 1920–1970*, ed. Ruth Markus (Tel Aviv: Hakibutz Hameuchad Publishing House and Tel Aviv University Publishing House, 2008), 99–138. [Heb.]

6. William Handley, *Marriage, Violence, and the Nation in the American Literary West* (New York: Cambridge University Press, 2002), 16.

7. The Jewish Enlightenment, known as the *Haskalah*, spanned the eighteenth and nineteenth centuries, starting among German Jews and expanding throughout Europe. The *Haskalah* preceded the advent of modern Zionism. Its adherents, called *maskilim*, exposed themselves to Western philosophy and secular knowledge, often in conjunction with Jewish emancipation efforts within emerging modern European political systems. Many *maskilim* also explored the biblical text anew and experimented with Hebrew as a language of modern *belles lettres*. There are certain parallels between the *Haskalah* and the Arab *Nahda*; see Sa'ad Albazei, "Enlightened Tensions: Jewish Haskalah and Arab-Muslim Nahda," *Jahrbuch des Simon-Dubnow-Instituts—Simon Dubnow Institute Yearbook* 7 (2008). Moreover, Lital Levy has called for a reorientation of scholarship on the *Haskalah* as "an interregional (global) movement with channels of transmission (e.g. the Hebrew press, literary translations) that crisscrossed Europe, Asia, and Africa." See Lital Levy, "Reorienting Hebrew Literary History: A View from the East," *Prooftexts* 29, 2 (April 2009), 143.

8. Joan W. Scott, "Gender: A Useful Category of Historical Analysis," *American Historical Review* 91, 5 (1986), 1070.

9. Quoted in Benny Morris, *Righteous Victims: A History of the Zionist-Arab Conflict, 1881–2001* (New York: Vintage Books, 2001), 57.

10. Joshua Radler-Feldman [pseud. Rabbi Benyamin], "Vision of Arabia," *Ha-me'orer* 2, 7 (July 1907), 271–273 [Heb.].

11. Anthony D. Smith, *Nationalism and Modernism: A Critical Survey of Recent Theories of Nations and Nationalism* (London: Routledge, 1998), 44–45.

12. See David Ben-Gurion's comments from 1917 in his "On the Origins of the Fellahin," *We and Our Neighbors* (Tel Aviv: Davar, 1931), 25 [Heb.]. The racial composition of Palestine's Arabs was a topic also taken up to refute Zionist claims to the land; see George Antonius, *The Arab Awakening: The Story of the Arab National Movement* (London: Hamish Hamilton, 1938), 17 fn. 1: "nearly two-thirds of the settled Moslem population of Palestine is of original Arab stock."

13. Yosef Klausner [pseud. "Ish Ivri"], "Foreboding," *Hashiloah* 17 (July–December 1907), 574–576. [Heb.].

14. In fact, subsequent research has shown that it was men who tended to leave the community more often, and in more radical ways. Paula Hyman, *Gender and Assimilation in Modern Jewish History: The Roles and Representations of Women* (Seattle: University of Washington Press, 1995), 22 and 48; Todd M. Endelman, "Gender and Conversion Revisited," in *Gender and Jewish History*, eds. Marion A. Kaplan and Deborah Dash Moore (Bloomington: Indiana University Press, 2011), 184.

15. A prime example of *Haskalah* protest over women's lot is Y. L. Gordon's poem, "The Tip of the Yod" [Heb.]. *Haskalah* autobiographies abound with critiques of the high expectations of men of the intellectual elite (see, for instance, Moshe Leib Lilienblum's 1873 *The Sins of Youth* [Heb.]). On physical abuse of boys in the schools, see Simkha Ben-Tsiyon's 1902 "Broken Soul" [Heb.] and Iris Parush, "The Benefit of Marginality: Reading Women in Nineteenth Century Eastern European Jewish Society," in *Studies in East European Jewish History and Culture in Honor of Professor Shmuel Werses*, eds. David Assaf et al. (Jerusalem: Hebrew University Magnes Press, 2002), 134 fn. 32 [Heb.]. On suspicions about the New Woman, see Shmuel Feiner, "The Modern Jewish Woman: A Test-Case in the Relationship between Haskalah and Modernity," in *Sexuality and the Family in History*, eds. I. Bartal and I. Gafni (Jerusalem: Zalman Shazar Center, 1998), 253–304 [Heb.].

16. Iris Parush, "Women Readers as Agents of Social Change among Eastern European Jews of the Late Nineteenth Century," *Gender and History* 9, 1 (April 1997), 66 and 70.

17. Quoted in Hyman, *Gender and Assimilation*, 46.

18. Y. L. (Isaac Leib) Peretz. *Writings of Y. L. Peretz*, 2nd corrected ed. (Tel Aviv: Dvir, 1928), 2:122–123 [Heb.].

19. Quoted in Ehud Ben-Ezer, *Brenner and the Arabs* (Astrolog: Israel, 2001), 70 [Heb.].

20. "Crossing the Styx" was originally published in *Ha-toren*, January–June 1914, 158–171 [Heb.]. All citations in this essay are to L. A. (Levi Aryeh) Arieli (Orlof), "Troubles," in *Collected Works of L. A. Arieli: Stories, Plays, Legends, Essays, Letters,* ed. Milton Arfa (New York: Keren Yisra'el, 1999), 1:197–208 [Heb.]. (In the *Collected Works*, the story "Crossing the Styx" is titled "Troubles," "*Tsarot.*") Arieli reworked "Crossing the Styx" into another story that he published in 1916, "In the Days of the Rains." However, the latter story falls outside the scope

of this essay. Arieli left Palestine and moved to the United States in 1923 due to family and economic troubles.

21. Margalit Shilo, *Princess or Prisoner? Jewish Women in Jerusalem, 1840–1914*, trans. David Louvish (Waltham, Hanover and London: Brandeis University Press and University Press of New England, 2005), 207.

22. Aviva Argov, "Yehuda Burla 1886–1969: Poetics of an Individual and an Epoch," Ph.D. dissertation, Bar Ilan University, 2006, 191 [Heb.].

23. Arieli, *Collected Works*, 1:198–199.

24. Ibid., 201.

25. Ibid., 198.

26. I thank Dan Miron for this note.

27. See Arieli, *Collected Works*, 1:197–206.

28. Ibid., 201.

29. Ibid., 202–203. Ellipses in the original.

30. Ibid., 205–206, 208.

31. See Philip Hollander, "Between Decadence and Rebirth: The Fiction of Levi Aryeh Arieli," Ph.D. dissertation, Columbia University, 2004.

32. In Hebrew, Brokhes's name was written "Brakhot." However, I refer to him as "Brokhes" in accordance with Yael Chaver, *What Must Be Forgotten: Yiddish in the New Yishuv* (Jerusalem: Yad Ben-Zvi Press, 2005) [Heb.].

33. Zalmen Brokhes, "In the Shadow of the Hermon," ed. and trans. Simkha Ben-Tsiyon, *Ha-ʿezrah*, no. 1 (1919), 193. The "Old Yishuv" refers to the Sephardi and Ashkenazi Jews who lived in Ottoman Palestine prior to Zionist immigration waves, primarily in the four holy Jewish towns of Hebron, Safed, Tiberias, and Jerusalem. Many Old Yishuv families depended on financial contributions from Diaspora Jews and prioritized the vocation of Torah study.

34. See Brokhes, "In the Shadow," 283, 287, and 289.

35. Ibid., 290.

36. Ibid., 187.

37. Ibid., 189.

38. Ibid., 198.

39. Ibid., 190, 192, 198, and 199.

40. Ibid., 190. For another picture of a Jewish woman in partial Arab dress, see Israel Eitan, "Galilia," *Ha-meʿorer* 2, 7 (July 1907), 273–275.

41. Brokhes, "In the Shadow," 193. For a visual example contemporary to Brokhes's time, see the photo "Bedouin woman holding sword for sword dance" in the Library of Congress's G. Eric Matson Collection of the American Colony Hotel. For another interpretation of gender and power in a woman's sword ritual, see Hamid Dabashi's discussion of the climactic scene of Bahram Beizai's film "The Balad of Tara," *Close Up: Iranian Cinema Past, Present and Future* (New York: Verso 1994), 94–98.

42. Brokhes, "In the Shadow," 289.

43. Ibid., 290.

44. On the problem of the ending in interracial stories, see Werner Sollors, *Neither Black Nor White Yet Both: Thematic Explorations of Interracial Literature* (New York: Oxford University Press, 1997).

45. Chaver, *What Must Be Forgotten*, 52. In the 1970s Brokhes finally returned to Israel for good.

46. Of the estimated 60,000 immigrants of the First Aliyah, at least half subsequently left Palestine. Of the estimated 40,000 immigrants of the Second Aliyah, at least 60 percent subsequently left Palestine. Data quoted in Anita Shapira, *Israel: A History* (Lebanon, N.H.: University Press of New England, 2012), 33.

47. Quoted in Steven Zipperstein, *Elusive Prophet: Ahad Ha'am and the Origins of Zionism* (London: Peter Halban, 1993), 319–320. Originally published in the *Ha'aretz* newspaper on August 29, 1922.

48. Yigal Zalmona, "Eastward! Eastward?" in *To the East: Orientalism in the Arts in Israel,* eds. Yigal Zalmona and Tamar Manor-Fridman (Jerusalem: Israel Museum, 1998), 63 [Heb.].

49. Quoted in Anita Shapira, *Land and Power: The Zionist Resort to Force, 1881–1948* (New York: Oxford University Press, 1992), 174. David Ben-Gurion at the founding conference of the Mapai Party in 1930 characterized the situation starkly, arguing that "after the 'events' the situation changed. The idea [among the Arabs] of annihilating the local Jewish community has become widely held." See Ben-Gurion, "Our Political Path after the 'Events,'" *Neighbors*, 213 [Heb.].

50. Aviva Argov notes evidence that Burla occasionally referred to his heroine Rosa Rodovits as "Yehuda Rodovits," invoking his own name. See Argov, "Yehuda Burla," 199. Thus, readers can track Rosa's journey from the Old Yishuv to Europe to Arab Palestine to Zionist Palestine as a journey that highlights numerous intellectual influences on Burla's own worldview.

51. Michelle U. Campos, "Between 'Beloved Ottomania' and 'The Land of Israel': The Struggle over Ottomanism and Zionism among Palestine's Sephardi Jews, 1908–13," *International Journal of Middle East Studies* 37, 4 (November 2005), 472.

52. Quoted in Tsafira Ogen, "Yitzhak Shami: The Man and His Work." *Bikoret u-farshanut* [Criticism and Interpretation], 21 (December 1985): 52.

53. Yehuda Burla, *Daughter of Zion* (Tel Aviv: Mitspeh, 1930), Book 1, 31–32 [Heb.]. *Daughter of Zion* consists of three parts: *Ba-metsar* (*In the Narrows*), *Kishalon* (*Failure*), and *Ha-tehiya* (*The Renaissance*). The third part is subdivided into Part A and Part B. Hence *Daughter of Zion* is spread over four separate books, marked accordingly on the title page of each. I cite with the page numbers according to Books 1–4. The first three ellipses in this quotation are in the original.

54. Burla, *Daughter* (Book 1), 35.

55. Ibid., 37.

56. "Women are not the only ones who are veiled in Egypt," wrote Hamdi. "We are a veiled nation." Quoted in Beth Baron, *Egypt as a Woman: Nationalism, Gender,*

and Politics (Berkeley: University of California Press, 2005), 36. The veiling issue was a prism through which the Palestinian Arab press of the 1920s crafted narratives of 'tradition' and 'modernity.' See Ellen Fleishmann, *The Nation and Its "New" Women: The Palestinian Women's Movement, 1920–1948* (Berkeley: University of California Press, 2003), 78. As an Arabic speaker and as a recognized Arab affairs expert for the *Histadrut*, Burla would have been intimately familiar with this press coverage.

57. Burla, *Daughter* (Book 3), 6.

58. Ibid., 6.

59. Ibid., 128. This part of the novel is a critique of Herzl's depiction of the Muslim woman Fatma in *Altneuland*. See also Burla, *Daughter* (Book 2), 122.

60. The play to which Burla refers is most probably Antun al-Jumayyil's "Samuel, or, Allegiance to the Arabs" (*al-Samawal, aw, wafa al-Arab*), published in Cairo in 1909. The "Arab Club" in this scene most likely refers to *al-Nadi al-Arabi*, associated with Hajj Amin al-Husseini (Grand Mufti of Jerusalem and a leader of anti-Zionist activities among the Palestinian Arabs).

61. Burla's depiction of the Ashkenazi pioneers is not one of singular approbation. He attempts to assert his credibility as a nuanced critic of Palestinian Arabs by undercutting the one-dimensionality with which the immigrant Ashkenazi pioneers in the novel speculate about Muslim womanhood. See Burla, *Daughter* (Book 3), 153. Burla's idealization of labor Zionism as egalitarian fails to reflect the deep frustrations felt by the women pioneers, who in fact faced significant discrimination in access to jobs and equal pay. On these frustrations, see Bat-Shava Margalit Stern, *Redemption in Bondage: The Women Workers' Movement in Eretz Yisrael, 1920–1939* (Jerusalem: Yad Ben Zvi and Schechter Institute, 2006) [Heb.].

62. Burla, *Daughter* (Book 4), 226–227.

63. Ibid., 256.

64. Ibid., 264.

65. Burla, *Daughter* (Book 3), 29.

66. Ibid., 29.

67. For comparative studies on the political import of a female character's choice between two lovers who represent competing ideologies, see Michael Clark Troy, "Courting Clio: Allegorical Love Narrative and the Novels of Turgenev," Ph.D. dissertation, Columbia University, 1999. See also Doris Sommer, *Foundational Fictions: The National Romances of Latin America* (Berkeley: University of California Press, 1991).

68. Burla, *Daughter* (Book 4), 400.

69. The famous phrase was coined by the Jewish philosopher and Hebrew writer, Mikhah Yosef Berdyczewski. On the Jewish male protagonist's national narrative in Hebrew literature, see Dan Miron, *Founding Mothers, Stepsisters* (Tel Aviv: Hakibbutz Hameuchad, 1991), 67–68 [Heb.].

70. Nira Yuval-Davis, *Gender and Nation* (London: Sage Publications, 1997; reprint, 2004), 67.

10

An Autobiographical Perspective

Schools, Jails, and Cemeteries in Shoshanna Levy's Life Story

ORIT BASHKIN

Gender relations in modern Muslim and Jewish contexts or, more precisely, the ways in which gender relations in Muslim and Jewish communities changed following the encounter of both religions with European modernity, were a key element in Middle Eastern discourses concerning nationalism, colonialism, and discipline. Conversations about gender relations within Jewish communities in Muslim lands were intertwined into Islamic and Arab discourses about gender, as Jewish women were imagined simultaneously as Eastern, Arab, and Jewish. The migration of many women from Middle Eastern Jewish communities to Israel, a state whose European elites had certain assumptions about gender roles in Arab and Muslim societies, further complicated the self-perceptions of these women and gendered identity politics in Israel more broadly.

As other essays in this book illustrate, when Jewish and Muslim women write about themselves in the modern age, it is very difficult to find a particular text that isolates their gendered concerns from the other topics that occupied women, and men, during this period: nationalism, colonialism, modernity, militarism, migration, class, labor, and freedom. Ella Shohat, in fact, has cautioned against "the dangers of studying women and gender in isolation," within ghettoized and geographically defined spaces, such as area studies, offering in its stead "a relational understanding of feminism," or a definition of feminism as a site of contradictory positions. Critiquing "Eurocentric versions of global feminism which assume a telos of evolution toward a reductive identity practice," Shohat's multicultural approach took into account the global traveling of images, sounds, goods, and populations, while paying heed to specific contexts and locations, and to the sets of questions women in the Middle East have encountered.[1] Nonetheless, as women in the Middle East wrote about themselves, they also integrated, whether critically or uncritically, the writings of Western women and men into their texts. In the second half of the twentieth century, Middle Eastern women wrote as nationalists, communists, feminists, Easterners, Westernizing elite members, religious intellectuals, and modern subjects. While it is indeed impossible to distill a purely gendered voice in their writings, it is also vital to try to reconstruct the ways in which gender interacts with these categories, and what this interaction does to notions of subjectivity and modernity amongst women. In this essay, therefore, I wish to underline the ways in which the category of gender relates to the categories of nation, religion, and region and how they affect Jewish notions of the self.

Iraq is a useful case study through which to consider such gendered identities within an Arab Jewish context. Iraq's urban Jewish community (numbering around 150,000 in 1951) figured prominently in that nation's culture, literature, and economy, and did much to shape Iraq's Arab culture. Iraqi Jewish intellectuals frequently wrote about Jewish and Iraqi identities and their relation to the women's question. These intellectuals often evoked the term "Arab Jew" to signify their identity as individuals whose religion was Jewish, but whose culture (language, literature consumption, and social practices) was that of their Arab Iraqi compatriots.[2] In postcolonial theory, both Ella Shohat and Yehouda Shenhav have discussed the concept as a critical way to consider the ideological and cultural implications of Jewish identification with Arab culture not only in Iraq, but also in Israel.[3] In the interwar period, however, many Iraqi Jews embraced a local form of Iraqi, rather than Arab, nationalism which meant seeing the Kurds and the Turkmans, as well as the Arabic-speaking Shi'is, Sunnis, and Christians, as citizens on an equal footing in the same state, and acknowledging the validity and contributions of Turkish, Persian, and Kurdish cultures to Iraqi society. Furthermore, Iraqi Jews maintained strong transregional connections with Jewish communities whose members did not speak Arabic, especially the Iranian and the Indian. Kurdish Jews, who lived in northern Iraq and spoke a local dialect of Aramaic, maintained economic links with Kurdish Jews in Iran and Azerbaijan, well after the establishment of the Iraqi state in 1921. Consequently, Jewish Iraqi discourses about the meaning of being an Arab, Iraqi, Eastern, and Jewish woman reflected ideas and practices current in various Middle Eastern contexts. The migration of Iraqi Jews to Israel meant that Hebrew was adopted as their writing and speaking language, and that Jews from diverse Middle Eastern states, such as Iraq, Yemen, Turkey, Iran, and Morocco, were labeled broadly by the state (as Shohat has shown) as Mizrahi (Eastern) Jews, although they came from very different sociocultural and sociopolitical backgrounds.[4]

The ability of Iraqi Jewish girls to attend school and later on to enter the Iraqi labor force cemented their affiliation with the larger Iraqi and Arab community. These girls studied Arabic in school and read children's books, newspapers, and magazines in Arabic. Moreover, Iraqi Jewish women lived in a society in which the rights of all women—be they Muslim, Jewish, or Christian—were expanding, and women's emancipation was often discussed in the print media.[5] These realities affected Jewish men and Jewish women and the modes with which they conceived of gender relations within their own community. In Israel, however, Iraqi Jewish women faced harsh realities as poor migrants in a state that identified Arab culture with that of the racially inferior enemy. The dominant assumption by Israeli Ashkenazi intellectuals and bureaucrats was that the state had rescued Middle Eastern Jewish women from patriarchal societies by exposing them to secular—and often socialist—Zionism. Zionist discourse thus presupposed that these Middle Eastern women were not only to be liberated from their Arab surroundings but also from their Jewish fathers and brothers.[6]

In what follows, I examine how the category of gender complicates our understanding of Arab Jewish identities in Iraq and in Israel. I explore the role gender played in constructing national discourses and identity politics, and study the relationships between Jewish Iraqi gendered identities and national (Arab and Zionist) discourses that Iraqi

Jews adopted, molded, and subverted. I do so by analyzing and contextualizing one case study, the life story of an Iraqi Jewish woman, Shoshanna Levy, written in the form of an autobiography.

Texts about the lives of Iraqi Jewish women are diverse and include short stories, poems, novels, and newspaper articles written by and about Iraqi Jewish women. They appeared in Hebrew, Arabic, French, and English; some were written during the 1940s and 1950s in Iraq and in Israel, while others were composed in the 1990s and 2000s. Iraqi Jews from different backgrounds have written autobiographies, including intellectuals, political figures, and ordinary Israeli citizens of Iraqi descent (at times assisted by family members) over the last thirty years.[7] The ability to do so, in tandem with funding by Jewish Iraqi organizations, has resulted in the appearance of several autobiographies written by Iraqi Jewish women in recent years. These autobiographies are written in Hebrew by women who had mastered Hebrew later in their lives, and address an Israeli audience. Some of their authors were members of the Zionist underground and some, despite having been highly critical of Zionism before they arrived in Israel, came to identify with the state and its goals.[8] And yet, even these ostensibly Zionist narratives tell us much about gender relations in Iraq and the creation of a gendered Mizrahi identity in Israel. Moreover, most of these women were at the margins of Israeli society; they were poor and faced discrimination because of their Iraqi origins. What happened, then, to these marginal, often subaltern, voices, when they finally spoke and wrote to an Israeli audience? In my reading of the autobiography of Shoshanna Levy, 'Al Em Ha-Derech (In the Middle of the Road), which was published in Israel in 2001,[9] I consider the Iraqi, Israeli, and Mizrahi components of Shoshanna's identity as constructed in the autobiography, and demonstrate what historians and literary critics might learn from its deconstruction, especially concerning the ways the autobiography subverts national narratives.

Being Jewish, Arab, and Baghdadi: Iraq

Shoshanna Levy was born in Baghdad in 1938. In her autobiography, she provides ample information about the women in her family. Most of the women worked: her grandmothers worked in various jobs that had to do with knitting and tailoring. A seamstress, Shoshanna's grandmother, Simha, asked her client, the wife of the Ottoman governor (*vali/wali*) to find a job for her husband, and so he did. Simha's son, Iliya, traveled to Australia in the 1910s, where he married a Jewish woman called Hanna, who, upon arriving in Iraq, refused to veil herself when she went out of the house, as did Jewish women in the neighborhood. Though she did not speak Arabic well, she found a position as a nurse in the Ottoman hospital in the city, the Majidiyya, and convinced other women in the family to become nurses, including Nazima, Shoshanna's mother (b. 1914), and her sisters Farha and Gurgia. Farha worked in the Majidiyya and later assisted doctors treating eye diseases. When she quit her job following the birth of her oldest son, her sister Nazima took over her position. Nazima and Gurgia both quit their jobs after marrying. The women of Shoshanna's family were not unique; other women in the neighborhood gradually joined the labor force. The Ezer family, who were neighbors, owed their fortune to their insightful grandmother, Khatun, who was a businesswoman with a textile shop. In 1900 Khatun had traveled to India to purchase merchandise not found in Iraq and was able to have her products sold in the Hijaz. Though disabled, Khatun dealt with popular medicine and supported her husband, a rabbi. She likewise paid for her family's education.

The autobiography underscores the powerful women in the family and in the neighborhood. Texts produced by Iraqi intellectuals in the interwar period that deliberated questions relating to women's rights centered on the themes of labor, education, and marriage. The autobiography, however, presents neither the ideal westernized Iraqi women who remained loyal to the tradition of the East while selectively adopting aspects of European education (an oft-discussed image in Iraqi newspapers) nor the abused and secluded Eastern girl (an image that appeared in both British colonial and Iraqi nationalist sources). Rather, the text presents a group of Jewish women who tried to support themselves and their families by entering the labor force during the years 1900 to 1938. In the 1900s, the grandmother's generation found employment in the textile industry, typically working in their homes or in the workshops in their neighborhoods. The gendered nature of this work was reflected in the fact that it attracted widows and other women without other means of support. The women of Shoshanna's mother's generation worked because new opportunities opened up as Baghdad modernized under Ottoman, British, and later Iraqi rule; they benefited from new institutions opening in the city, such as the various hospitals. This reality contrasted sharply with the image presented by the interwar Jewish press in Baghdad of women in seclusion, supported by the labor of their husbands and fathers, who were rescued from a life of servitude and ignorance thanks to the modern intervention of the Iraqi state and Western education. While we cannot corroborate historically some of the details provided in the autobiography, we can at least say that in the 1940s stories about these independent women circulated in Shoshanna's family and inspired other female members. Finally, the arrival of a Western woman to the family, reflecting the transregional connections Iraqi Jews maintained with Jews in India, Australia, and England (Shoshanna had relatives in Calcutta and London) changed the dynamic in the family. This transregionality is reflected in names of the women: some are Arabic (Nazima), some are Hebrew Jewish (Simha, Shoshanna), some Persian (Khatun), and others Western (Gurgia, i.e., Georgia).

An important feature of the depictions of the Baghdadi women surrounding Shoshanna is the tension between their agency and activism, and Shoshanna's perceptions of their lives. About her aunt Farha (d. 1948), a nurse, widow, and mother of two who remarried, she writes: "[W]hen I reconstruct the life-story of my aunt Farha, I cannot see in it even one ray of light. She seems to have been born into a sea of suffering, and forced to swim in it without ever reaching a safe shore."[10] These tensions become even more apparent when Shoshanna depicts her own mother:

> When I reconstruct the life of the woman in Baghdad, or, more accurately, the life of the housewife in this city, I wonder: what aim did she find in her lifestyle? She did not work outdoors; she woke up every day at dawn and started her house chores: cooking, cleaning, and taking care of the children; some went shopping instead of their husbands. A daily routine; only in the Sabbath does she rest. I asked my mother to compare her life in Israel today, when the house is smaller and she has all sorts of appliances to ease the house chores, and her life in Iraq, when the house was big, and most of these appliances were not available. Her reply astonished me. She replied with no hesitation that she felt happiness

in faraway Baghdad in comparison to Israel, and that she truly missed those days. I asked her why? How could that be? She answered simply: "Then we had a joy of life, a joy of creation. We were less dependent on machines, and everything we had, we felt by hand; we sensed the food, we almost talked to it until it was cooked. What do we have here? Everything is prepared, in boxes and in bags; all is frozen, dead, and nothing is fresh, alive. The entire order of things, the cycle of life, went wrong, and was shortened. There is no joy of living and creation."[11]

Shoshanna's assumptions derive from her place of dwelling (Israel) and from her generation (Iraqi women who were schooled in the 1940s). She thus believes that the state of Israel, with its modern technology, has improved women's lives, and she accepts the national Iraqi and Israeli narrative that women in the previous generation (who were uneducated) were doomed to a life of boredom and drudgery. However, the information that she provides sheds a different light on this narrative; women assumed agency and were instrumental in shaping their own lives and those of their children. As we shall later see, Shoshanna's mother lost her social and economic standing when she moved from Iraq to Israel. Her nostalgia for Iraq, which she constructs as a longing for an uncomplicated way of life, makes perfect sense in these circumstances. Like her daughter, she accepts the fact that life in Iraq was simpler, yet she longs for this simplicity which she identifies with a world she can no longer access.

The first half of the autobiography, although written in Hebrew, reflects how Shoshanna comes to feel that she was an Iraqi Jew. Her father, Hesqel, attended Jewish schools, including Shammash high school, where the instruction was in English. After graduating, he worked as a clerk in an export-import company owned by a Jewish businessman. The family lived in a Jewish alley and belonged to the Jewish middle classes. Shoshanna's feeling that she belonged to a modern secularized society was informed by her schooling. At first, she attended a Jewish religious kindergarten called *ustaz*. The *khilfa*, a name given to the man who used to accompany her to the kindergarten, "was the epitome of ugliness and filth; his sight was extremely revolting."[12] Shoshana strongly disliked her teachers and "could not remember learning a single character [of the Hebrew alphabet] in my first class, which was more like a jail to me."[13] The Alliance school for girls, which she began attending in 1945, was a different experience altogether. She was thrilled about the new school uniform, the well-lit classrooms, and the Arabic and French classes offered by the school.[14] Shoshanna recalls in particular three teachers: Madame Cohen, her first-grade teacher; her French teacher; and the Muslim teacher who taught her Arab history. She also points out that her schooling affected her position in the family; she would recite poems she learned at school to her parents, who took pleasure in listening to them.

The notion that secular education was central to social mobility comes up in many autobiographies written by Iraqi Jews, in which they express their disapproval of the religious instruction of their youth. Like Shoshanna's critique of the *ustaz*, many Iraqi Jewish students (men and women alike) depict the transition from a religious school to a modern and Western one as a journey from dark and oppressive surroundings to an illuminated, tolerant, and pluralistic space. The Jewish author Gurji Barshan (b. 1918) remarks that the filthy classroom of his Baghdadi *ustaz* reminded him of a donkey stable. Gurji was troubled by the education he received: "In the first class, the teacher taught us about the Torah. [He continued doing so] in the next classes. . . . I thought to myself: Learning Torah all day? What about the other professions about which I heard from the children of the neighborhood, like math, geography, Bible and history?"[15]

Like Shoshanna's experiences in the Alliance, everything changed for Gurji once he moved to the secular Jewish elementary school al-Wataniyya.[16] The wooden building of the school was clean and tidy, and its teachers, dressed in Western outfits, possessed no sticks with which to discipline insubordinate students.[17] As an adult reflecting on his experiences, Barshan captures the idea articulated in Shoshanna's account, namely, that learning the Torah in Iraq was not of much use. Math, history, and modern instruction were essential for his rise in society. Similarly, Shoshanna's school provided her with the tools vital to her social mobility: knowledge of a foreign language (French) and familiarity with Arab and Islamic history. The state insisted that private Jewish schools, such as the Alliance, teach Arab and Islamic history, as well as Arabic language and literature, and sent Muslim instructors to do so. We note that Shoshanna, years later in Israel, still remembers her Muslim teacher. The school she attended was Jewish, yet its major achievements had more to do with the fact that it was a westernized institution in dialogue with the state than with it being a site of Jewish religious education. In fact, as Shoshanna tells it, it was the Jewish school that contributed to her secularization and integration into Arab society.

Shoshanna's experiences in her school reflect the changes in female Jewish education in Iraq, as well as the changes in the Iraqi education system more generally. The first Jewish primary school for girls, a branch of the French Jewish educational network, the Alliance Israélite Universelle (Hebrew: כל ישראל חברים) named for Laura Kedourie, opened its doors in 1893, largely due to the efforts of young Francophile Jewish men who had graduated from the Alliance. In the years 1900 to 1919 the number of girls attending the school tripled. During the monarchical period, the number of schools for Jewish girls increased, both in the Jewish and the Iraqi sphere, and their opportunities for going on to higher education outside the boundaries of the community expanded. A primary school for girls, named after No'am and Tova Nur'el, was founded in 1927 and the Ministry of Education established a school for girls named after Menashe Salih in 1930. A public middle school for girls was built in 1941–1942 and a middle school was built in 1950 to absorb the graduates of the elementary schools in the Jewish community. Very few schools, however, were coed beyond the third grade. The Shammash Jewish high school was an exception because it offered mixed classes. Beginning in 1927 concern for the occupational options of poor Jewish girls led to the establishment of vocational schools, which instructed girls in sewing, knitting, and other gendered professions. Some limited academic instruction was offered, as volunteers among the community took to heart the sentiment current in the public sphere during this period concerning the need to combat illiteracy. Accordingly, girls in these schools were taught to read and write. In Baghdad, but more so in the south and the north, Jewish girls also attended public schools in which Jewish students were the minority. In both the private Jewish schools and the public schools, Arabic education, namely, an emphasis on Arabic literature, the Arabic language, and Arab culture, played a key role in making girls aware of the fact that they belonged to the greater Iraqi nation. Shoshanna's activities in her household (reading Arabic texts to her parents) mark the great success of this national project.[18]

Although Shoshanna resides in a strictly Jewish alley, she comes to appreciate the larger space in which she lives, namely, Baghdad. Baghdad was indeed the city in which most Jews resided. Jewish writers who identified with Arab culture and contributed to Arabic literature and journalism lived and worked in Baghdad, as did Jewish officials, politicians, and clerks who held key positions in Iraq's economy and the state bureaucracy. The city grew considerably in the first half of the twentieth century, partly because of the waves of migration to the city from the north and the south, and partly because of the activities of Iraq's expanding middle classes. Walking the streets of Baghdad, inhabiting its public places, and attending its cafés, bookstores, libraries, and cinemas, became a constant motif in accounts of the time. Here is how Shoshanna depicts the relationship between herself, her father, and her city:

My father had a weekly practice: to go on a tour, by foot, every Sabbath, in the afternoon. I, and my brother Ephraim, accompanied him. With time, my other brother, Joseph, born in 1945, joined as well. . . . Along the way we would pass different stores whose owners knew my father from his workplace; my father would greet them *al-Salam 'Alaykum*, Peace be upon you, and, as they exchanged greetings, the owners would give us, the little ones, ice cream and candies. On al-Rashid street there was a big and luxurious hotel. We used to enter it, and gaze at a small artificial pond with fish and a fountain located in the hotel's foyer. These were colorful golden fish and we, the children, loved to watch them. Our final station was Ghazi cinema, to watch a movie. . . . Since my father was religious, he did not carry money in his pocket on the Sabbath, and therefore, when leaving the cinema, he would go to a liquor store owned by a Jew . . . borrow money from him for the bus fare back home.[19] In the summers, the tours would continue on the banks of the Tigris. This was truly a wonderful journey. Along the banks were fishermen who lit fires. . . . It was a splendid sight: the maddening smells were in the air; in the background the quiet sound of the wide river was heard, and the lights of the fires and the lamps of the coffeehouses were seen in its waters. When I learned to read Arabic, my father would stop by the signs and ask me to read them: this way my reading of Arabic improved.[20]

This depiction brings to mind Walter Benjamin's account of the *flâneur*, a bourgeois man of leisure who moves along the city streets and interacts with the city crowd. Writing on the spatial aspects of the *flâneur*, Walter Benjamin remarked that the *flâneur* sees the city as his home:

> The street becomes a dwelling for the *flâneur*. . . . To him, the shiny signs of business are at least as good a wall ornament as an oil painting to a bourgeois in the salon. The walls are the desk, against which he presses his notebooks. Newsstands are his libraries, and the terraces of cafés are the balconies from which he looks down on his household after the work is done.[21]

Shoshanna's father is a little different from the *flâneur* as depicted by Benjamin. He is not as secular and keeps the Sabbath laws according to his own understanding (although not to the degree that allows him to miss a film in Ghazi cinema). He does not walk around the city by himself but rather with his family, and his city is less modern than Paris; it has traditional fishermen and its people greet each other, in contrast to the anonymity of the modern metropolis. Noticeably, though, the religiosity of the family is never translated into a strict patriarchal order; while women in the family stopped working as they got married, it was highly important for the father to have his daughter educated and make her an active participant in the city's life. Shoshanna's own movement in the city is determined by her gender, age, and her father's supervision. And yet Baghdad is also a very modern city. The family enjoys what a modern city has to offer: grand hotels built because of tourism and the British colonial presence in the city during the 1920s, the modern cinema, the street signs, and the new cafés, all of which make the streets their home.[22] These notions turn walking in Baghdad into a very modern experience. But perhaps what is unique about walking the streets of Baghdad is how the modern is intertwined with the traditional; the golden fish in the artificial pond appear together with the "real" fish that are turned into delicious *masguf* and the lights of fishermen's fires blend into the modern street lamps, all flickering in the waters of the river. Finally, the fact that Shoshanna knows how to read and write in Arabic, a skill she has acquired in her Jewish school, is integrated into the ways in which she relates to the city; her new knowledge from the school, in other words, allows her to feel at home in the city.

The connections made by growing up in an Arab city and knowledge of Arabic were acknowledged by Jewish men as well. In his autobiography, David Naggar, who lived in the neighborhood of Bab al-Sheikh, depicts the relationship between his neighborhood and identification with Arab culture: "I greatly loved the Arabic language, which is the language of the Qur'an. . . . My love for the Arabic language probably originated from the fact that I was born and raised in a mixed neighborhood of Jews and Muslims [in Baghdad] and I used to hear the mu'azzin's call for the prayer several times a day."[23] Love of the Qur'an, then, is structured on life in a Baghdadi neighborhood that arouses curiosity about the state's religion. Both Shoshanna and David leave the realm of the Jewish neighborhood, interact with their fellow citizens, and become curious about the larger community to which they belong. In fact, in the twentieth century many Jews who became part of the middle classes left their Jewish neighborhoods and moved into mixed neighborhoods. Moreover, this intimate relationship with the city and its association with Arab and Islamic culture became routine through daily walks to Jewish schools from various Jewish and non-Jewish neighborhoods. Shoshanna never calls herself an Arab Jew. She was much younger than some of the prominent Baghdadi Jewish writers who adopted Arabic as their writing language (after being accustomed to writing in Judeo-Arabic[24] during the nineteenth century) and used the term "Arab-Jew" frequently in their writings. And yet she does evoke what made her feel as if she was part of an Iraqi community: knowledge of Arabic and her love of Baghdad.

Shoshanna's experiences, and that of her mother and her aunts, relate to greater changes in the Jewish and the Iraqi public sphere, in which men, and to a lesser degree women, wrote about the "woman question." Jewish, Christian, and Muslim intellectuals, Muslim reformers, and communist thinkers all raised concerns about the need to grant women more liberties and to reform certain social practices relating to education, propriety, domesticity, women's involvement in the labor market, and social mobility. At the beginning of the twentieth century, Iraqi men and women underlined the need to educate the mothers in the nation and enable women to be productive members of the nation-state, while also expressing their anxieties about the westernized behavior of women and their eager imitation of European women. When Shoshanna entered school during the late 1940s, matters had changed.

The years 1945–1958 were an important time for Iraqi feminists in general. After the end of World War II, Iraqi intellectuals from both the left (social democrats and communists) and from the ultranationalist camp demanded women's suffrage as part of their critique of Iraq's electoral and judicial systems. Women's organizations (especially those supported by the state) came to play a vital role in postwar Iraq. Educated Jewish women turned to the outlawed communist and Zionist undergrounds, attracted by their advocacy of women's rights. Female communists, Jewish, Muslim, and Christian alike, distributed pamphlets, campaigned for suffrage, democracy, and welfare rights, and organized demonstrations and public meetings. These changes were most noticeable amongst the Baghdadi middle and upper classes. This was the milieu that Shoshanna and her other family members (the autobiography mentions a Zionist female cousin, for example) were part of, and their lives, as Jews and as Iraqis, reflect the dynamism of this historical context.[25]

Shoshanna is aware of politics and the changing political realities around her. As a ten-year-old child, she recalls the demonstrations that started in 1947 against Zionism and how the men in the family listened to the radio to get more information about the situation in Palestine. In 1948, a wave of demonstrations protesting the state's pro-British policies and the lack of social justice in Iraqi society erupted in Baghdad. They were termed the *Wathba*, "the leap"; through them the various leftist organizations in the city, especially the illegal communist party, declared their resistance to the state. Shoshanna writes that she heard from her parents about these demonstrations and about the politicians whose names were called at protests, but did not understand what they meant.[26] The protests impacted the social order in the neighborhood. A neighbor, a Jewish communist, explains to her about the battle between the people and the reactionary government: "I noted that the communist neighbor began visiting our home often, and became a main source of information about what happened in the city. In general, I felt that there was a harmony and intimate solidarity between the houses and the families populating our neighborhood."[27]

Although Shoshanna notes the factors that separated her from the Iraqi community, such as the *Farhud*, the anti-Jewish riots in Baghdad in 1941, during which over 170 Jews were killed, and the state's fear that every Jew was a Zionist, she likewise recalls the things that brought the people of her neighborhood, and more importantly the people of Baghdad, together. The *Wathba*, she argues, created a feeling of intercommunal solidarity. The sentiments of the little Jewish girl who grows to appreciate her communist neighbor, Eliyahu Ezer, and through him, Jewish-Muslim solidarity, were shared by many. In fact, during the *Wathba*, Jewish intellectuals visited the families of those killed in the protests, and marched hand in hand with other religious officials from the Muslim and Christian communities. The speeches that Jewish intellectuals and officials delivered in public commemorations of the *Wathba*'s martyrs accentuated their loyalty to their Iraqi community.[28] The role of the Jewish communist as a mediator between the Jewish neighbors and the protesters should be seen in a context when many young Jews joined the illegal Iraqi communist party (especially in the years 1941–1947), which allowed them to critique the state yet remain loyal to their notions of Iraqi patriotism and their struggle to end sectarianism in Iraq. Shoshanna also remarks that the communist Ezer family leaned toward Muslim-Jewish cooperation because Eliyahu's father worked with Muslims and his home was constantly open to both Jews and Muslims. The *Wathba* was a major event in Iraqi history. Here the autobiography records the effects of this event on a Jewish neighborhood. While Shoshanna did not take part in the protests, she depicts how the topic that initially occupied only the men in the family became the business of the entire middle-class Jewish neighborhood, and how, although she did not know very many Muslims, she came to identify this struggle as her own. Again, these sentiments are depicted in many texts written by Iraqi Jews during the *Wathba* and many years after it ended.[29]

The sense of intercommunal solidarity did not last for long. The war in Palestine changed everything. Her paternal uncle Ezra, who was one of the most prominent believers in Jewish integration into Iraqi society, and her uncle Rahamim, unwittingly set in motion the chain of events that led to the family's departure from Iraq. Ezra worked for a construction company in Baghdad. In 1936, Iraq experienced a military coup. During this time, Ezra joined an officers' course in Baghdad, changed his family name to the Arab-sounding Murad, and took great pride in strolling through the neighborhood in his officer's uniform. After the coup was crushed, however, he was discharged. He was unable to finish the officers' course, and later moved to Iran and from there to

Israel, where he lived on a kibbutz. Rahamim moved to Israel as well. Shoshanna's father was then arrested for receiving a letter from his brothers in Israel in 1949. He had to pay a huge sum of money to be released from jail and the family was forced to leave for Israel in 1951. A law was passed in 1950 that allowed them to migrate to Israel legally provided they renounced their Iraqi citizenship. In 1951 another law was passed freezing the property of Iraqi Jewish migrants to Israel. This left them poor and they arrived in Israel with no property or money.

Shoshanna's family, like many other Iraqi Jews, suffered because of the war in Palestine. During the years 1947–1951 the Iraqi state increasingly lumped together Zionism, Judaism, and communism, especially during and after the 1948 War in Palestine and the subsequent dislocation and exile of the native Palestinian population. Iraq's leaders wished to uproot Zionism from their midst and therefore embarked on a campaign of collective punishment, during which many Jews were arrested on the basis of false claims that they were either Zionists or communists (although most Jews had nothing to do with either). Although no specific laws were enacted against Jews, their employment rights were severely curtailed, especially in relation to government service, as was their ability to travel abroad and to conduct business outside Iraq. The activities of Iraqi ultranationalist groups, and especially the daily attacks in the right-wing press that accused every Jew of being a Zionist, considerably worsened the position of Iraqi Jews. The assumption that Iraqi Jews were pro-Zionist, moreover, was at odds with the pro-Palestine publications by Iraqi Jews that had appeared in the Iraqi public sphere in the interwar period and in the 1940s. Concurrently, the state of Israel began to negotiate with the Iraqi government about the fate of Iraqi Jews, whose property and place of residence suddenly became a part of the Arab-Israeli conflict. Israel also used Iraq's anti-Zionist campaigns in its propaganda campaign, highlighting the suffering of Iraqi Jews in order to justify the Israeli mistreatment of the Palestinians. In this situation, Arab-Jewish coexistence stood no chance.[30] Shoshanna's family thus left for Israel.

Becoming Poor and Mizrahi: Israel

Despite the Arab and Iraqi nature of Iraq's Jewish elites, Iraq did have an illegal Zionist underground. This became an important factor in

Iraqi Jewish life after 1948, as the state increasingly adopted anti-Jewish measures. It numbered about 2,000 members in 1950. One of the tenets of Zionist ideology was the liberation of Jewish women. In the land of Israel, so it was argued, Jewish girls would find liberty and equality, and reach their full potential, which was curtailed in the conservative diasporic milieu.[31] Iraqi Jewish Zionists articulated these ideas in their speeches and essays.[32] Shoshana's autobiography challenges these nationalist narratives by exploring the hopes of Iraqi Jewish women for secular modernity in the state of Israel in light of what happened to them once they arrived there.

Shoshanna's family arrived in Israel in 1951 virtually penniless, part of a massive wave of newcomers. Holocaust survivors, Jews from Arab lands, and other migrants all flocked to the Israeli state, which had no financial means to absorb them.[33] The family arrived at the *Sha'ar ha-'Aliya*, the main transit camp to which most migrants were directed at the time, where they were photographed for a local newspaper which documented their arrival. Shoshanna depicts the miserable breakfasts they were given in the camp, their suffering from the cold during the winter, and her disappointment at the gloomy reality they encountered in Israel. As it was winter, they did not wash during their stay at the camp, because there was no hot water and because of their disgust with the poor sanitary conditions.

Sha'ar ha-'Aliya was a former British military camp near Haifa, surrounded by barbed wire. Most Iraqi Jews arrived there on crowded trucks after a ten-hour ride. In the camp, most newcomers went through the bureaucratic procedures needed to become Israeli citizens. These included a series of medical examinations and vaccinations; the migrants were given state IDs as well as memberships in the state's health system (Kupat Holim) and the state-controlled Labor Union (the Histadrut). The expectation was that people would stay in the camp for five days, but most stayed for ten. Riots broke out in 1949 when a newcomer was beaten to death by a local policeman. Two years later, in August 1951 riots flared up again as Iraqi Jews resisted being moved to other transit camps. The camp was closed down in 1962. The arrangements for sanitation and hygiene were horrendous, and people had to wait in line for many hours for basic services. Complaints about the lack of the most basic services were reported in the press and discussed in official state circles.[34]

As in Iraq, the resourcefulness of the family's women serves to help the family in times of need. The father, who is initially unable to find a position, becomes dependent on his brothers who had come to Israel before him and who live on a kibbutz called Mishmar ha-ʿEmek, one of the well-known kibbutzim in Israel. Located in the Valley of Jezreel, it had been established in 1922 by a group of Polish Zionists. The kibbutz was known for the battle fought by its members in the 1948 War, when they managed to hold the kibbutz in the face of recurring attacks, and for the casualties it suffered following an Iraqi aerial bombardment during which a few children were killed. Among the denizens of the kibbutz were Knesset members, journalists, and novelists. The uncles suggest that Shoshanna come to live there. The father hesitates, as does Shoshanna, but the mother, who is fearful about her daughter's chances for an education, is the first to agree.

Shoshanna has no idea what a collective community might be and she finds the first weeks in the kibbutz insufferable. Although she has relatives in the kibbutz, she cannot talk to her uncle's wife or the children of the kibbutz, because she does not speak Hebrew. Shoshanna recounts how she arrived at the kibbutz wearing a dress and a plaid shirt that was made in England. She is told to shower by her uncle's wife, a Romanian woman, whose Hebrew Shoshanna does not understand. In the kibbutz, the showers are public and Shoshanna is embarrassed to bathe in the presence of other naked women, since she had never before been naked in public.[35] While the autobiography makes no mention of the DDT[36] with which the new migrants were sprayed upon their arrival to Israel, Shoshanna's symbolic baptism in the kibbutz is seen through the imperative to expose her body to a group of anonymous women whose language she does not understand. Her clothes, which symbolize to her mother the family's westernized Baghdadi practices, are now transformed into a symbol of her Levantine culture, which the kibbutz seeks to uproot.

Nevertheless, Baghdad is still with her in the kibbutz. When she is impressed with the trees and gardens in Mishmar ha-ʿEmek, she is reminded of the Saʿdun park in Baghdad. She sees her uncle, wearing simple work clothes and working with the cows, and both are profoundly ashamed as they recall his flamboyant wardrobe in Baghdad. She writes:

What future awaits us here? Everything is strange and peculiar. I dreamt of coming to Israel, where the family would get a house and I would continue immediately with my studies. And what happened? The parents are dumped in a camp of *muhajirin*, migrants, their pride and honor are crushed to dust, with no privacy, getting their food like the beggars who used to beg at the doors of our home in Baghdad. I am separated from my parents and being kept here, in a sterile paradise, in a place whose customs are strange; I eat and I sleep, without schooling and friends. Occasionally I would cry at night out of a feeling of disappointment and neglect.[37]

The Zionist sense of Israel as a promised land is contested in this account. At this stage in her life, Baghdad is home; the kibbutz, on the other hand, is a sterile paradise. Interestingly, even the Hebrew text evokes the memory of the Arabic, using the Arabic word signifying "migrants," *muhajirin*, rather than the Hebrew word *'olim*. The kibbutzim were the elite of Israel during the 1950s. Their socialist education and the fact that they raised new generations of Sabras (Jews born in Israel) who worked the land and joined the IDF (and whose sons had fought in the 1948 War) symbolized, in national narratives, the success of labor Zionism in producing a new Jew who was entirely different from the feeble Jew in exile.[38] The education of Iraqi Jewish youth in the kibbutzim was seen by the state as an appropriate remaking of the new generation of young migrants educated in Arab lands. There was a strong ideological component attached to this effort, because it was believed that the kibbutzim would rescue the young Middle Eastern Jews from their Levantine diasporic existence, marked by defenselessness, a lack of productivity, and patriarchal oppression. The kibbutzim indeed rescued many Iraqi Jewish teens from surroundings of poverty and neglect in the transit camps, and opened channels for them to integrate into Israeli society. In Shoshanna's account, however, different feelings come to the surface when she depicts her experiences, especially her pain, the way she missed her parents, and her longing for companionship.

Shoshanna finds it difficult to adjust to the new practices of the kibbutz; while she came from a westernized Iraqi society, she does not understand the secularism of the kibbutz. The Shabbat dinner has changed: as she puts it, in Baghdad such dinners were typified by the gathering of a small family and the enjoyment of a fabulous dinner, but on the kibbutz "the family" becomes much larger and the dinner much smaller. The festive nature of Friday nights was therefore gone. Furthermore, the holidays which Iraqi Jews had considered less important now became more significant, yet with their meanings secularized and altered. In Baghdad, Hanukkah was associated with the lighting of candles and the family, whereas in the kibbutz it became a festival marking the revival of the nation of Israel; Passover no longer commemorated the exodus, being transformed into a holiday of liberty and spring; and worse yet, the members of the kibbutz served bread—the eating of which is forbidden during Passover—along with the Matza.[39]

The Israeli state had indeed secularized and nationalized the Jewish past. Jewish holidays were taken out of the realm of the family and celebrated in the public realm, while biblical heroes such as Joshua or the Judges, as well as the protagonists of Jewish holidays such as Judah Maccabee and Moses, were cast as proto-Zionists fighting mighty nations for the independence of the Jewish people.[40] For Shoshanna, the encounter between the two types of Judaism, hers and that of the kibbutz, seems confrontational. It is not necessarily a meeting between East and West, but rather one between different kinds of westernized Judaism; one which was constructed in Baghdad, in an Iraqi context, and the other produced in socialist Israel.

Her lot changes when more Iraqi teenagers come to the kibbutz as members of a group of teens (*hervrot no'ar*). The experiences of Shoshanna's particular youth group have been discussed in various essays and have been immortalized in the novel of Israeli writer Elie Amir, who was one of them.[41] Yet this autobiography offers a different analysis of Iraqi life in the kibbutz because of its unique gendered vantage point. The teenagers, forty in number, speak Arabic and are guided by two instructors from the kibbutz. However, Shoshanna feels that the kibbutz assigned the Iraqis in particular more hours of work at the expense of their schooling. The work in a kibbutz is also depicted in terms of culture shock: her first assignment is to work in the kitchen, where she is told to take some herring out of a barrel. She is so disgusted that she throws up: "On that day I was ashamed to look at the eyes of the workers in the kitchen, and when our eyes crossed I felt the looks of contempt directed at me; how could I dislike the herring, which is considered a delicacy in the cuisine of Ashkenazi Jewry; the Jews from there [i.e., Europe] did not know the meaning of fresh fish."[42] The teen-agers are exposed to socialist indoctrination: they join a socialist youth movement, yet they see the gaps between themselves and those who were born in the kibbutz: "[A]t every step of the way we were let to feel that we did not belong, that we were nothing but a youth group that came from the primitive Islamic lands."[43] Shoshanna is assigned various chores: she cleans houses (which she likes since the women to whose houses she is sent befriend her); she works with the sheep, and she and the other Iraqi girls have to delouse each other, removing the parasites that they pick up from the sheep; and she picks fruits and vegetables in the gardens of the kibbutz. She is academically successful and is greatly encouraged when her instructor, Rivka, tells her she could become a teacher. Eventually, she develops conflicting feelings toward the kib-butz: on the one hand she is committed to it, but on the other hand she senses that the Iraqi youth were discriminated against because they were not born in the kibbutz and because they were Mizrahi.[44] None-theless, she concludes the section dealing with her youth in the kibbutz by saying that "the three years in kibbutz Mishmar ha-'Emek were the most beautiful and happiest in my life. And now, forty years after, I feel the need to express my thanks to all those members who helped shape my personality."[45]

The accounts from the kibbutz shift between national Israeli nar-ratives and personal accounts. Shoshanna's narrative exposes how the kibbutz, a place that was intended to erase differences between Jews of different backgrounds by molding them into a socialist community, actually accentuated the distinctions between the Iraqis and the native Israelis. Their foods make Shoshanna sick, and the Iraqis are made to feel that they are outsiders who need to be transformed in order to fit in. The first time the words "Mizrahi" and "Jews of Muslim lands" appear in the text is in the context of the kibbutz, not when she writes about Iraq. Likewise, she seems unaware of the fact that the kibbutz failed to erase gender differences, continuing to assign women distinct gendered jobs in many cases. On the other hand, she recognizes that Ashkenazi kibbutz members work the very same jobs; she feels grateful for the education she receives, for the Hebrew she is taught, and for her friends; and she recognizes the importance of the contacts she makes, which pave the way for her successful integration into Israeli society. The significance of the autobiography is precisely in this mixture. Shoshanna does not construct binaries of either heroic kibbutz feminist members vis-à-vis the weak oriental newcomers, or Ashkenazi oppressors vis-à-vis oppressed Mizrahim, but rather notes the challenges she met and the varied people who either assisted her or stood in her way.

Iraqi Jews were active in the kibbutzim movement beginning in 1944.[46] The Iraqi youth who came to the kibbutzim faced many challenges related to secular kibbutz society, their education, and their relationships with their parents whom they had left behind. In her insightful study of the Iraqi migration to Israel, Esther Meir points out that the many diaries and letters left by Iraqi Jews who resided in the kibbutzim do not testify to a uniform pattern of integration; some Iraqi Jews admired the kibbutzim while others faced discrimination and complained about it, and they differed in the degree to which they adopted secularism and perceptions of westernization as understood and practiced in the kibbutzim with respect to a wide array of domains, from diet to dress codes to sexual practices.[47] It is clear from the letters written by these Iraqi teens that they internalized secular Zionist ideology, felt they were Jews connected them to Ashkenazi Jews, and sensed that life in Iraq, and indeed anywhere outside Israel, was hopeless and doomed to fail. In a letter addressed to her parents in 1949, Margalit, an Iraqi girl who lived on a kibbutz, wrote:

> I was surprised when I found out you wish to go to America. Do you think Jews are better off there? If you think so, you are certainly in the wrong: although it is quiet there now, Anti-Semitism is rooted deep in the hearts. Wherever a Jew goes he is a Jew. . . . Who knows when will riots against the Jews of America begin? . . . There are all sorts of phenomena [in America] that we, Jews of Iraq, are familiar with and lived through. Why would the Americans and the English not go after the Jews? Is it because they are people of culture and learning? The Germans were men of culture as well.[48]

For Margalit, the lot of Jews in America, Iraq, England, and Germany is the same. The lesson of the Holocaust is that life in Iraq, and indeed life in America, is dangerous for Jews. Even if anti-Semitism does not seem like an immediate danger, it is bound to appear.

However, other Iraqi teenagers expressed different feelings, which are also expressed by Shoshanna, concerning discrimination and racism. A young Iraqi man wrote about the ways in which he was treated in kibbutz Ma'oz Haim:

"Arabs," "ignorant," "blacks," "Did you ever see a movie? " "Do you eat with a fork?" And other such expressions Jews from the lands of the East hear from the members in the kibbutz and its children. I do not think that such an attitude is natural and instinctive. A child in the kibbutz, who says "an Arab" to this man, and a "black" to another, must have heard it from his parents or his teachers. Every kibbutz member should know that such expressions are being rooted in the heart of the newcomer and might besmear the image of the kibbutz and harm its ability to absorb [the newcomers]. In addition, this generates a feeling of inferiority in the newcomer's heart, a factor that might decrease his ideological and pioneering potential.[49]

The letter underlines the feelings of discrimination experienced by the Iraqi newcomers, male and female alike, and the sense that kibbutz members connected Iraqi Jews to other groups marked as non-white. However, it also shows a new recognition that while some Jews in Iraq called themselves "Arab Jews," or identified with Arab culture, for a new Iraqi Jewish migrant now living in a kibbutz, being identified with the Arabs signifies inferiority. Moreover, he sees integration into Israeli society as the supreme goal. The characterization of Iraqi Jews, and indeed all Mizrahi Jews, as blacks, as opposed to the Ashkenazim as white, was documented in accounts of Iraqi young men and women, not necessarily those who lived in kibbutzim. Furthermore, a famous 1949 article published in the daily newspaper *Haaretz* characterized Jews from Muslim lands as people "whose level of knowledge is one of virtually absolute ignorance and, worse, who have little talent for understanding anything intellectual," and thus are "only slightly better than the general level of the Arabs, Negroes, and Berbers in the same regions."[50] The autobiography, in this sense, is in conversation with many other publications at the time, a conversation that reveals that it was in the Jewish state that the differences between various kinds of Jewish communities came into being.

Although Shoshanna devotes much space to her life in the kibbutz, she does not neglect the story of her parents in Israel. After Sha'ar ha-'Aliya, they move to Mansi, a ruined Arab village in the Galilee turned into a transit camp for newcomers. Transit camps (Ma'abarot) were established by the state of Israel all over the country beginning in 1949. Most of the confiscated houses from the Palestinian community were given away to newcomers who came in the years 1948–1949, and therefore most Iraqi Jews who arrived in Israel in the years 1950–1951 found themselves in these camps, alongside migrants from Poland, Iran, Romania, and Yemen. In 1951, a hundred camps absorbed 212,000 people, 80,000 of whom were Iraqis.[51] There were clashes and demonstrations in the camps arising from the migrants' demands for basic citizenship rights such as labor and housing, and in protest of the state's indifference to their sufferings. As Esther Meir has shown, many Iraqi Jews eventually managed to move from the camps to major cities in central Israel because of their resistance to being transferred to remote places in the north and south.[52] Shoshanna's parents "progress" in the transit camp, much as did dozens of Iraqi Jews: first they live in tents, with no furniture; then they find a better tent (badon); and finally they move into a small wooden shack. In addition to the horrendous poverty and the loss of social status, the family cannot communicate well with the denizens of the camp, who are mostly Jews from Iraqi Kurdistan and therefore do not speak Arabic well, and are less westernized than the Baghdadi family.

Family members who live in the kibbutz bring to the camp certain organs of animals that the kibbutz members refuse to eat (such as brains and intestines). The family members in Mansi eat them but also sell them to earn some money (in addition to the meager rations given to them by the state). While these actions save the family, they are depicted as humiliating for both parents and children. When Shoshanna's baby brother is born, there is no ambulance in Mansi and the mother has to have a truck driver take her to the hospital. In 1950s, a polio epidemic hits Israel, and Shoshanna's younger brother David is struck with the disease and is hospitalized in Haifa:

In this hour of trial, my mother appeared to be a true woman of valor (*eshet hayyil*).[53] Every day she traveled between Megiddo and Haifa to visit my brother David and follow his recovery. In these days, with the narrow and unfit roads and the few buses, and with no direct bus line between Megiddo and Haifa, the travel was indeed a nightmare. Moreover, when we note that mother did not master Hebrew and did not know the roads well, we understand what huge mental powers were required from a woman, who only a short while ago lived in comfort and ease, and everything she desired was brought to her. When she could not travel by bus, because she missed it, or had no money, she hitchhiked to travel with any passing car. One time a driver tried to rape her, and she miraculously escaped.[54]

The entire autobiography is very much Shoshanna's travel narrative: from Baghdad to Israel, and from the lower social strata of Israeli society to the Israeli middle classes. Yet out of all that Shoshanna experienced in her life, she chose to single out her mother's actions as the most heroic. Nazima's actions appear courageous and laudable to Shoshanna because of their ordinary nature, namely, her daily endeavors to survive in such harsh conditions and her ability to care for a sick child and ensure that her daughter receives an education. Neither Shoshanna's own journeys in Israel nor the socialist women in the kibbutz are portrayed as models for heroism in Israeli society. Rather, it is the daily battle of one woman, Nazima, that is idealized and commemorated in the text.

This depiction of life in the transit camp as a heroic tale of survival is radically different from depictions of Kurdish and Iraqi Jews in the transit camps of the Galilee that appeared in the mainstream Hebrew press. These stories often focused on the most shocking incidents and emphasized cases of illiteracy and criminality. For example, the mass fighting in the transit camp of Tiberias between Kurdish and Iraqi Jews was widely covered in the press.[55] The official newspaper *Davar* deplored the unnecessary hatred and the exilic practices of the people in the camp, and noted sadly that the newcomers to Israel had done nothing to uproot the "medieval" practices of these "sectarian ghettos."[56] Jacob Aviel wrote in *Haaretz* about the Kurdish and Arab communities in the Tiberias camp:

> Sun, noon, everybody is resting. Only the café "The Star of the East," a shabby cabin, the social center of the people of the transit camp that numbers 4000 people, operates relentlessly. In one corner, around a deck of cards, sits a group of long-mustached, husky young men, whose hair is gelled and whose shirts are colorful, à la Chicago. Everybody, despite the sweat dripping from them, is immersed in a tense game of poker. . . . Others simply gather above cups of coffee, *arak*, and smoky cigarettes, and talk loudly. And above all this commotion and the clouds of smoke filling the cabin rises the shrilling voice of the Damascene singer, Fayruz.

Soon a battle erupts between two men: one from Mosul and another from Kurdistan. The camp's women join the skirmishing: "Women with wild hair stuck their heads through the windows to the place of the fight and started howling, in an oriental fashion, calling their husbands and brothers to help their slaughtered brethren."[57] The space of the transit camp is constructed in the story as a site taken from the Orient; everything about it, from the café named the Star of the East to the voice of Fayruz (who was actually from Lebanon), represents the Orient. Women in particular are reduced to speechless subjects (they howl rather than speak) whose existence is limited to their crumbling shacks and tents and whose only movement is connected to the acts committed by their husbands, brothers, and sons. The dichotomy between passive women and violent men complements the Orientalist stereotypes associated with the East which characterize the report: violence, criminality, wildness, and disorder. On the other hand, the reporter uses metaphors and images associated with Westerners and Hollywood films about mobsters and gang violence to describe the men. The Chicago-style colorful shirts, the game of poker, the tense atmosphere in the middle of the card game at high noon, bring to mind other images of disorder associated with the Wild West and the mafia.

The combination of the various images, however, generates an image of a no-man's-land in which the state has no say and in which violence erupts for the pettiest of reasons. The danger is that this medieval tradition will spill over into normative Israel. These descriptions, not uncommon in the mainstream Israeli press during the 1950s, persisted over time. The power of Shoshanna's personal account in this context is that it turns the story of the migrants in the camp into an epic struggle for survival and highlights the efforts of individuals and their pain and suffering. The state is indeed absent from Shoshanna's accounts, yet its absence in terms of health, welfare, and educational services emphasizes the great courage of the camp's dwellers, especially its women, and their resourcefulness in persevering despite these excruciating conditions.

Shoshanna's decision to leave the kibbutz in 1954 has to do with her desire to become a teacher, a career option that was impossible in the kibbutz because its members expected the youth (those born in the kibbutz and the Iraqi group) to stay in the kibbutzim and work the land. Shoshanna's parents, in the meantime, leave the transit camp and move to the neighborhood of ha-Tivka in Tel Aviv, and from there to Azur, a small town south of Tel Aviv built on the ruins of an Arab village, Yazur. To support herself, Shoshanna works as a cook in a restaurant in Tel Aviv and later in a factory in a town nearby. To earn a permanent salary, she turns to the field in which her mother had worked in Iraq: nursing. With no training, she manages to obtain a position in a psychiatric hospital and depicts, quite vividly, typical events in the hospital, such as force-feeding. Her parents' neighbors in Azur change: their Ashkenazi neighbors leave when they receive compensation from Germany, and Moroccan Jews move in. Shoshanna characterizes her Moroccan neighbors as "noisy," yet she and her family befriend them. The father travels to kibbutz Hazor and spends most of his time there working to support his family; he returns home only on the Sabbath. Eventually, Shoshanna manages to earn enough money to pay for tuition at Seminar ha-kibbutzim, a teaching seminary in Tel Aviv belonging to the kibbutzim movement. It was a prestigious institution established in 1939 by a group from the kibbutzim to train teachers and kindergarten teachers. In 1954, Shoshanna is the only Iraqi among its female students:

> I felt myself like Daniel in the lion's den. In the classroom, I tried not to talk so that my accent, which was not of the native Israelis, would not embarrass me. When I spoke, and my accent gave away the fact that I was a newcomer from Iraq, I felt ashamed and inferior, to a degree, in comparison to the other girls in the seminary. But what wouldn't you do for the cause? My dedication to study in the seminary and to graduate was indeed great.[58]

Shoshanna does not feel she belongs to the seminary's milieu and considers her classmates to be spoiled and superficial. Studying in a house with no electricity and working in the psychiatric hospital, Shoshanna finds some comfort when she tutors an orphan whose father was killed during the 1956 war. One of her greatest joys is when (as part of her training) she teaches at her former kibbutz, whose members had looked unfavorably at her career choices. She regards it as an enormous victory.

Shoshanna's ability to study, like her mother's ability to care for her children, seems heroic. Significantly, although she had been educated in Israel since the age of 11, her accent still marks her as different and Oriental. The same feelings of estrangement she had sensed during her first days in the kibbutz recur in the city. The family's decision to live by a big city is typical of many Iraqi families who resisted the state's attempts to settle them in the Galilee or the Negev. Coming from a middle-class background in Iraq, they realized the importance of living close to the big metropolitan areas and settled in middle and large cities. In Shoshanna's case, the relative proximity to the seminary in Tel Aviv enabled her to receive an education, while her proximity to state institutions, restaurants, and cafés allowed her to support herself. A poor Mizrahi woman at the margins of Israeli society, she manages to find other spaces on the margins of Israeli society—in this case, the psychological hospital—in order to make her way into the labor force.

Finally, Azur, just like the transit camp Mansi, reveals the tensions within different Mizrahi communities. Akin to the tensions between the Iraqi Arabized family and the Kurdish Jews in the transit camp, the Moroccan community is seen as different from the Iraqi one. Both live in the same vicinity because they are not Ashkenazi and are treated as the same by the state, and yet Shoshanna underlines the cultural distinctions of each community.

One of the most traumatic experiences in Shoshanna's life occurs when she is about to graduate from the seminary. She is drafted to the IDF in 1958, and is not given time to take the last two exams needed for the completion of her degree. "I guess I became, for a moment, an important and symbolic figure for the IDF!"[59] she comments cynically. During the course of her military service, she meets different kinds of Israeli women. At basic training, she works as a guard in the military base together with a woman she describes as a "sex bomb," and thus wins some time off because the officers who wish to spend private time with the beautiful girl allow her to leave her shift early. She attempts to save money for her family but in general finds her service torturous: "My service at the IDF contributed almost nothing to me. On the contrary, during the service I endured unpleasant experiences that scared me for life."[60] She is shocked by the sexual openness of some of her fellow female soldiers and is ridiculed and humiliated by them because she is a virgin. When she falls ill, the officer in charge refuses to release her from her shift. She forgets to send a telegram during this shift, and is subsequently sentenced to a month in jail. Her encounter with the prisoners, women from a social stratum even lower than her own, shocks her once more:

> All their conversations were about their sexual experiences, and were accompanied by foul language, and juicy curses, especially against those men who did not get them satisfied. They compared sizes of penises, positions, and performances. Learning from my experience during basic training, I regularly hid my disgust and put a forced smile on my face. I had nothing to tell in this domain, but I pretended to be one of them, and learned from them a few songs in the special dialect of the prisoners.[61]

Shoshanna, however, wins a special position in the jail because of her education, and moderates between the girls and the military commander of the prison. For example, when the prisoners suspect that one of them is pregnant, it is Shoshanna who reports about her, in consultation with the other girls, to the prison authorities. The prisoner is then taken to Haifa where an abortion is performed.

The state represented the service of women in the IDF as proof that its feminist agenda did not distinguish between male and female soldiers. Israel's first prime minister, David Ben Gurion, considered the IDF an ideal melting pot, as did many other officials. For Shoshanna, military service is a maze through which she is forced to navigate, in which officers treat women as sexual objects and which curtails her academic career. She does meet women from other backgrounds in Israeli society, but these encounters mostly accentuate her strangeness rather than result in new social bonds.

During her military service Shoshanna meets Mishal, a soldier of Yemenite origin: "[H]e was dark, and in my eyes handsome, and with a naughty smile."[62] They begin dating as soldiers, much to the displeasure of both families. His Yemenite family seems too religious to Shoshanna, too cold and unwelcoming. When they marry, both families resent the marriage. "Inter-communal marriages" [ben 'adati], Shoshanna writes, namely, the marriages of individuals from different Jewish communities, were uncommon at the time. Nonetheless, both families rejoice at the wedding. After her wedding, Shoshanna makes a living as a teacher of children with special needs. Her schoolmistress is a communist, and therefore an outcast, and treats Shoshanna very kindly. Later, Shoshanna moves to the city of Bat Yam, where she lives with her husband and where her two daughters are born. She now works under a much stricter Ashkenazi schoolmaster, Mr. Mendleson, who is unfair to her because of her Mizrahi origin. Luckily (for Shoshanna at least) he is fired. Her appearance, which was not as "dark" as Ashkenazi Israelis imagined an Iraqi woman to be, helps her succeed in the school, although she adds that it hurt her when people were shocked to hear she was not an Ashkenazi and when she was told that she did not look Iraqi at all.

In June, the 1967 War erupts and Mishal is drafted. Unlike her Ashkenazi neighbors, she listens to the Egyptian broadcast station, *Sawt al-'Arab*, and knows what the Arabs expect of the war. Her sense of stability and happiness changes when at night "the angels of doom" come:

A doctor, a nurse, a rabbi, and another man let me know that Mishal was killed in the war. At this second, I felt that the world stopped. . . . A total silence took over me, my body was paralyzed, and in a look of a lamb going to the slaughter, I tried to get a certain "discount"; let them tell me, at least, that he is badly wounded. But no. They came to me and tore my clothes.[63]

The state is overtaken by a wave of euphoria following Israel's victory in the 1967 War, but Shoshanna is incapable of relating to the general sense of happiness.

Both the Yemenite and the Iraqi communities in Israel were categorized as Mizrahi by the state. At times they were associated with different sets of stereotypes: the Yemenite were seen as naïve, simple-minded, and hardworking, whereas concerns about the inability of bourgeois Iraqi Jews to adapt to a productive socialist lifestyle are voiced in Zionist accounts. Nonetheless, in state discourses about the fate of Jews from Muslim lands the Iraqi, Yemenite, and for that matter the Moroccan and the Egyptian, were all labeled Mizrahi. The autobiography brings a different perspective to our discussion; both Mishal and Shoshanna are from Arabic-speaking communities, but the latter's Iraqi family is more Western and less religious than the former's Yemenite one. In this case, the autobiography once again exposes the tensions between different groups of Jews that came from Muslim lands. These tensions were based on language (differences in the Arabic dialects of various Arabic-speaking Jewish communities; differences between Jews who spoke various dialects of Persian and Kurdish, Jews who spoke Turkish, and those who spoke Arabic), on class affiliations in their states of origins (urban versus rural in particular; in this sense, for example, a Jewish Iranian family from Tehran and a Baghdadi Jewish family might have more in common with one another since members of each family attended the Alliance Francaise schooling system), on their religiosity (with Jews from poorer backgrounds typically depicted as more religious, like the Yemenite Jewish community), and their gender. In Shoshanna's opinion, her marriage to a Yemenite seems to be an intercommunal affair, an expression usually evoked in the context of Ashkenazi-Mizrahi marriages. The account therefore emphasizes the Iraqi, rather than the Arab, component of Shoshanna's Jewish family.

The unique challenge that the autobiography, and the feminine voice it evokes, poses to national narratives is further accentuated when Shoshanna discusses the fate of her husband. Even before the war starts, the fact that she is able to listen to Arab radio broadcasts gives her a different perspective. In Israel, 1967 was indeed a moment of national euphoria, as the state was able to occupy the Golan Heights from Syria, the Sinai Desert from Egypt, and the West Bank from Jordan, all within six days. Moreover, the capture of the eastern part of Jerusalem, including the Temple Mount and the Wailing Wall, as well as many sites mentioned in the Bible, further inflamed Jewish religious and nationalist messianism. It was a period after which glorification of the IDF, right-wing nationalism (especially the settlement

movement), and a general sense that Israel was an invincible regional
power (a notion not shattered until 1973) took hold of the Israeli public.[64] The story of a widow who is unable to identify with the great victory gives a different perspective to this narrative. It illustrates that the
victory in the 1967 war was not divine, as argued by the religious right,
but rather a war fought by ordinary people who paid an unbearable
price. Shoshanna uses a metaphor commonly evoked in the context
of the Sho'ah, "being led as lambs to the slaughter,"[65] which was used
to describe the manner in which the Jews were led to their deaths in
order to underscore the fact that what was a triumph to some was
the gravest disaster to others. Being led as lambs to the slaughter was
often an accusation voiced against Holocaust survivors for not resisting extermination. Here it is the soldiers who are being led by the state
as lambs to be slaughtered on the battlefield. The text, then, shifts the
readers' attention away from the heroic combat of the soldiers (the
way in which Mishal was killed is not described in great detail) to
the women at the home front who had to raise children after their
husbands fell in battle. In an era that glorified the achievements of the
soldiers as part of a masculine national discourse, Shoshanna yet again
brings to the fore those whose voices were less often discussed in the
public space: widowed women and their children.

After 1967, Shoshanna continues working as a teacher to support
her family. More importantly, in 1968 she becomes involved in widows'
organizations which are supported by the state and the IDF and whose
members set about improving their social conditions and demanding
the compensation from the state to which they were entitled, at times
by challenging the state's decisions.[66] As part of her public activity,
Shoshanna arrives at the Knesset. She describes her frustrations when
she and her fellow widows are not allowed to attend a debate regarding
their rights, because the members of the Knesset's labor committee are
taking their lunch break instead. The widows break into the committee's room, and Shoshana addresses the members:

> I told the members of the committee: I left at home my daughter with a
> 40 degree temperature, and lost a whole day of work in school, and you,
> the members of the labor committee deny [our] delegation and prefer
> your stomachs over us? . . . You are all ungrateful. You always tell us, "in

their death they ordered life to us," and indeed, the elite of our people, the members of the Knesset, are having a good time at the expense of the fallen soldiers, whereas the children of the fallen soldiers and their widows should beg at your doors asking for charity.[67]

A Jewish Iraqi parliament member, Shoshanna Arbeli (Irbili) Almozslino, hears her outcry and promises to help. Shoshanna also describes how she befriends fellow widows who come to visit their husbands' graves when she visits the cemetery where her husband is buried. Another avenue that she finds to help ameliorate the difficult conditions she faces as a single mother is to assist Iraqis in various organizations under the umbrella of the Labor Party. She depicts her great joy at hearing the Arabic poetry that she used to listen to in her parents' home as a child, and in particular her sense of empowerment when she helps Iraqi students get stipends to support their education. When she represents the Labor Party in Western Germany in 1985, one of her German hosts tells her that the education system in Israel is inhumane and racist because of the ways in which the Palestinians are treated. She replies:

You, the son of the German people, speak of humane education? What kind of humane education did your people, the people that did the most atrocious, horrendous, and cruelest crimes against humanity, get? By what right do you preach [to] the Jewish people?[68]

Two other avenues that help her cope with her life as a widow and a single mother are mysticism and companionship. She identifies the stories she heard in Baghdad about the powers of rabbis with new trends in Israeli society that focus on numerology, parapsychology, healing, crystals, and visits to shrines of Jewish saints in the Galilee. The autobiography, very interestingly, connects Jewish Iraqi religious narratives about miracles and saints to the new age, globalized forms of mysticism that arrived in Israel in the 1990s. She also finds an Iraqi companion, the Iraqi Jewish historian Yosef Me'ir, who has written extensively about Jewish education, processes of secularization, and communist and Zionist activities in Iraq. He becomes her partner and assists her in writing her life story.

The final section of the autobiography references the means by which Shoshanna cements her position as an Israeli citizen. The first is her activity in widows' organizations. The price she pays allows her to enter the Knesset and confront the Knesset members. When she defies their authority, she evokes her motherhood and her widowhood. The verse, "in their death they ordered life to us," taken from a poem written by Israel's national poet Haim Nachman Bi'alik (1873–1934), is usually read at Israeli funerals of fallen soldiers and in commemoration ceremonies to link the sacrifice of the soldiers to the need to continue life in the land of Israel.[69] Here, Shoshanna makes an ironic use of this verse, arguing that that those who continued to live a joyous life are the members of the Israeli elite. Shoshanna had used the image of a beggar asking for charity when she depicted her parents' situation as poor migrants in a transit camp. Now she evokes the same image to depict her own situation as a widow who is forced to ask the state for the social and economic benefits she deserves. This image of the beggar is thus connected to two traumas: the arrival in Israel and the loss of her husband.

Shoshanna also benefits from her affiliation with other Iraqi Jews. Organizations of Iraqi Jews were set up prior to the establishment of the state by Iraqi Jews who came to Mandatory Palestine. After the mass migration of Iraqi Jews, such organizations became crucial mediators between the state and the new Iraqi migrants. Unlike radical groups such as the Israeli communist party, the organizations of Iraqi Jews never critiqued the foundational narratives of the state. Its members looked at migration to Israel as salvation, referred to Iraq as an exile, and emphasized that Iraqi Jews could contribute much to Israel.[70] Nevertheless, these organizations also voiced criticism regarding discrimination in Israeli society, and thus mediated between the demands of the newcomers and those of the state. These groups also organized learning groups, night classes, teach-ins, Hebrew lessons, and instruction in sewing and knitting for women in transit camps and cities such as Petach Tikva and Ramat Gan, where many Iraqi Jews resided.[71] These organizations strove to have written publications and radio broadcasting hours in Arabic, so the Iraqi community could understand them.[72] In the 1970s and 1980s the Iraqi Jewish organizations give Shoshanna a sense of power because she is able to assist those who were in the situation she had been in when she arrived in

Israel (although by this point the situation of most Iraqi Jews, now living in cities, had improved dramatically and should not be compared
to the conditions in the transit camps). This public activity joins her
again to her Iraqi identity just as cultural nights for Iraqi Jews remind
her of the music she loved as a child. They also link her, as they did
many other Iraqi Jews, to the state, which funds some of its activities
and sends Shoshanna abroad as its representative.

It is in the meeting in Germany that her adoption of an Israeli identity appears most strikingly. Asked how she feels, as a teacher, about the
discrimination of the Palestinians, who speak her mother tongue, Arabic, and who suffered much in the same years that Shoshanna struggled
to gain a livelihood and an education, and on whose destroyed villages
some of the camps and cities Shoshanna's family moved into were established, she can find no way of identifying with them. On the contrary,
she identifies with the Holocaust survivors and reminds her German
hosts that her group represents all Jews, Ashkenazi and Mizrahi alike.
Notably, although the trip was supported by the Labor Party, it takes
place in the 1980s when a right-wing Israeli government underlined
the experience of the Holocaust as a key component of Israeli identity.[73]
Interestingly, in this moment, when she is outside Israel, Shoshanna
becomes a full member of the Israeli community.

Conclusions: A New Agenda?

This very specific reading of a very particular text might suggest a few
ways to think about writing about gendered Jewish identities and their
links to the Arab and Muslim milieu. I have highlighted here the power
of the autobiography to challenge certain national narratives, especially
in Israel, such as the power of state institutions like the IDF to function
as a melting pot for various immigrant Jewish communities. The autobiography also casts in an ironic light the notion that Israel served as a
haven for Mizrahi women by saving them from a patriarchal Eastern
order and offering them more educational opportunities. True, the state
improved the conditions of women from the lower middle classes, and
the urban poor and Iraqi women were given the right to vote in Israel
(a right not granted to them in Iraq until 1958).[74] However, for female
teenagers like Shoshanna who belonged to the Jewish Iraqi middle and

upper classes, there were more educational opportunities for them in their land of origin, which had seen various processes of secularization and the expansion of educational networks. Conversely, in Israel such young women often had to abandon the pursuit of an education in order to assist their families financially. Because of her determination and strength, and because of the initial help given to her by the kibbutz, Shoshanna was able to get an education, but she encountered herculean challenges every step of the way.

The text is an important avenue through which to think about Arab Jewish identities. The autobiography exposes a few circles of identity: the Jewish, a minority group in Iraq which was forced to migrate to Israel; the Iraqi, an identity formed in Baghdad, its schools, and its politics, and preserved in Israel; the Mizrahi; and the Israeli. The Iraqi component of Shoshanna's identity becomes especially salient in Israel as it separates her family from Kurdish and Moroccan Jews, and distinguishes her from the Yemenite family of her husband. At times the Iraqi circle plays a more vital role than her gender. Shoshanna finds little in common with Ashkenazi women in the kibbutz such as her uncle's wife; in the IDF she feels isolated from the women who serve with her because they are more liberal than she is with respect to sex, or come from a lower social stratum, like the women she meets in jail. As for the Ashkenazi women at the seminary, she finds them boring and spoiled. On the other hand, other networks of gendered support, friendship, and companionship, like her shared destiny with fellow widows, her relationship with her mother, and her friendships with Iraqi female teenagers in the kibbutz help her during her life. When characterizing her identity, she never uses the phrase "Arab Jewish"; the word "Arab" is used to depict the Muslim and Christian inhabitants of Iraq. In Iraq, religious identity—that is, being Jewish—is of paramount importance, whereas in Israel, the word Mizrahi is utilized in a binary with Ashkenazi, native Israeli, while the concept "Iraqi" accentuates the group of Jews with whom she identifies most.

This reading might call for a new research agenda within Mizrahi studies which looks at the particular contexts of Mizrahi communities in Yemen, Iraq, Iran, Turkey, and elsewhere in the Middle East and examines the local languages in which Jews wrote and expressed themselves, as well as the varied local and transregional networks to which they belonged. Without considering the specific background of these communities and without understanding the discourses about gender among Muslims and Christians in Iraq, Iran, Syria, Egypt, Yemen, and Turkey, our understanding of gender relations in Israel will always rely on Israeli archives, and hence on a particular set of official discourses, as well as on the self-representations of Jews in Israel after the fact. In my reading of the autobiography, I have tried not only to compare it to accounts in Arabic written in Iraq, but also to Hebrew accounts written in the 1950s in Israel, in order to reconstruct a particular Jewish Iraqi context. Such a reading yields a different periodization of Israeli history: for Shoshanna, the moment of arrival to Israel does not change everything at once as far as her Iraqi identity is concerned. She and her family members continued speaking in Arabic. Indeed, it took a long time to separate Jews from their Iraqi culture. Even after years of assimilation in Israel, this process is only partially successful.

The autobiography unpacks different approaches to religiosity and Judaism. In Iraq, Judaism was used to signal the identity of a minority religious community; in Israel, however, different groups had different perceptions of westernization and its relation to Judaism. In the kibbutz the nationalized versions of Jewish holidays, colored by socialist and Zionist ideology, distinguished Shoshanna's understanding of Judaism from that of the kibbutz members. The same Shoshanna, who depicts her entrance into the Alliance school as a great secularizing moment, also celebrates her new belief in saints and new age mysticism in Israel, which in her mind is connected to the Baghdad she knew as a child and the stories she heard. It suggests that in the Jewish state, the practice of Judaism was determined not only by the sacred Jewish traditions passed from generation to generation in different Jewish communities, but also by the practices of these communities prior to their arrival to Israel, as well as their social status, the languages they spoke, their understanding of secularism, and their ideology.

The autobiography highlights the ways in which the subaltern can and cannot speak, and what happens to her when she speaks, or rather writes, after some years of silence and silencing. At the beginning of her life in Israel, it was impossible for Shoshanna to speak; as a speaker of Arabic she had no language with which to communicate with the hegemonic Israeli, Hebrew-speaking elites, and she was therefore dependent on others to speak for her. As she struggled she earned the power to speak, but that came at a certain price; her voice, as an adult writing in the 2000s, reflects certain national Israeli narratives of which she might have been critical as a teenager and a young woman. More precisely, the text exposes tensions between various voices: that of the state, that of the widow who is expected to behave in a certain way, that of a student in different schools in Iraq and in Israel, and that of a rebel. Through her mediation we also hear the voices of her aunts, her mother, and her grandmothers—the women who were Shoshanna's mentors and role models.

The text is constructed as a travel narrative or a series of travel narratives, tracing the arc of her life from Baghdad to Israel, from the transit camps to the kibbutz, from jails to schools. Readers of the autobiography are reminded of the biblical story of Joseph, which is structured as a tale of rise and decline, as Joseph falls from various peaks in his life only to improve to a better place, fall again, and then rise anew. Shoshanna's autobiographical account is similar, being constructed as a tale of continual rise and fall. While scholars of Mizrahi identity have tended to focus on great moments of rebellion, such as the Mizrahi Black Panthers movement in Jerusalem during the 1970s, or the wave of urban riots in Haifa known as the Wadi Salib riots in 1959, Adriana Kemp reminds us that the actions of individuals are no less important. Resistance to state settlement policies and fighting for access to higher education were also important struggles.[75] The focus on the grand movements also produces a rather masculine historical narrative of Mizrahi resistance, as it concentrates on the men active in these radical movements. Reading Shoshanna's autobiography, the word heroism often came to my mind. Yet this is not a heroism acquired in battle, but rather it is born of Shoshanna and her mother's insistence on maintaining a sense of normalcy in unendurable conditions: to give birth to a child in a transit camp, to care for the child's health, to survive as a widow. This experience was shared by Mizrahi women of different communities, and Shoshanna's story brings to light their efforts. It is indeed a travel narrative, yet curiously it is called *'Al Em he-Derech* (In the Middle of the Road). After so many years in Israel, so many losses and tragedies, and so many achievements, Shoshanna feels, I think, that in some ways her journey never ended; she remained stuck in the middle of the road, between Baghdad and Bat Yam.

NOTES

1. Ella Shohat, "Area Studies, Transnationalism, and the Feminist Production of Knowledge," *Signs* 26, 4 (Summer 2001), 1269–1272.

2. On Iraqi Jewish history, see: Reuven Snir, *'Arviyut, yahdut, zionut: Ma'vak zehuyot bi-yetziratam shel yehudei 'iraq* (Jerusalem: Yad ben tzvi, 2005); Nissim Kazzaz, *He-Yehudim be-'iraq ba-me'a ha-'esrim* (Jerusalem, Yad Ben Zvi, 1991); Nissim Rejwan, *The Jews of Iraq: 3000 Years of History and Culture* (Boulder: Westview Press, 1985); Avraham Ben Ya'qov, *Yehudey bavel mi-sof tekufat ha-ge'onim ve-'ad yemeynu* (Jerusalem: Yad Ben Zvi, 1965); 'Isam Jum'a Ahmad al-Ma'adidi, *al-Sahafa al-yahudiyya fi'l 'iraq* (Cairo: al-dar al-dawliyya li'l istithmarat al-thaqafiyya, 2001); Mir Basri, *A'lam al-yahud fi'i 'iraq al-hadith* (Jerusalem: Manshurat rabitat al-yahud al-nazihin min al-'iraq, 1986); Khaldun Naji Ma'ruf, *al-Aqaliyya al-yahudiyya fi'l 'iraq bayn sanat 1921 wa 1952* (Baghdad: Markaz al-dirasat al-filastiniyya, jami'at Baghdad; Wizarat al-ta'lim al-'ali wa'l-bahth al-'ilmi, 1975-1976); Sylvia G. Haim, "Aspects of Jewish Life in Baghdad under the Monarchy," *Middle Eastern Studies* 12, 2 (1976), 188–208.

3. Yehouda Shenhav, *The Arab Jews: A Postcolonial Reading of Nationalism, Religion, and Ethnicity* (Stanford: Stanford University Press, 2006); Ella Shohat, *Taboo Memories, Diasporic Voices* (Durham: Duke University Press, 2006); Ella Shohat, "Sephardim in Israel: Zionism from the Standpoint of Its Jewish Victims," *Social Text* 19, 20 (1988), 1–35; Ella Shohat, "The Invention of the Mizrahim," *Journal of Palestine Studies* 29, 1 (1999), 5–20.

4. Shohat, "The Invention of the Mizrahim," 5–20. On Mizrahi feminism in opposition to the Ashkenazi one, see Smadar Lavie, "Mizrahi Feminism and the Question of Palestine," *Journal of Middle East Women's Studies* 7, 2 (2011), 56–88.

5. Orit Bashkin, "Representations of Women in the Writings of the Iraqi Intelligentsia in Hashemite Iraq, 1921–1958," *Journal of Middle East Women's Studies* 4, 1 (2008), 52–78; Orit Bashkin, "Iraqi Women, Jewish Men and Global Noises in Two Texts by Ya'qub Balbul," *Transnational Borderlands in Women's Global Networks: The Making of Cultural Resistance*, eds. Clara Román-Odio and Marta Sierra (New York: Palgrave, 2011); Sabiha al-Shaykh-Da'ud, *Awal al-tariq ila'l-nahda al-nisawiyya fi'l 'iraq* (Baghdad: al-Rabita, 1959); Noga Efrati, *Women in Iraq* (New York: Columbia University Press, 2012); Doreen Ingrams, ed., *The Awakened: Women in Iraq* (London: Third World Centre, 1983); 'Abd al-Hamid al-'Alwaji, *Al-Intaj al-nisawi fi'l 'iraq* (Baghdad: Wizarat al-I'lam, 1975); Shaul Sehayek, "Changes in the Social Status of Urban Jewish Women in Iraq as the Nineteenth Century Turned," *Women in Judaism: A Multidisciplinary Journal* 3, 2 (2003) available at: http://jps.library.utoronto.ca.proxy.uchicago.edu/index.php/wjudaism/issue/view/37

6. On Mizrahi identity in Israel and tensions between Mizrahis and Jews of European origins (Ashkenazi), see Shenhav, *Arab Jews*; Shohat, "Invention"; Pnina Motzafi-Haller, "Scholarship, Identity, and Power: Mizrahi Women in Israel," *Signs* 26, 3 (2001), 697–734; Shlomo Swirski, *Israel, the Oriental*

Majority (London: Zed Books, 1989); Moseh Lissak, *ha-'Aliyah ha-gedolah bi-shenot ha-hamishim, kishlono shel kur ha-hitukh* (Jerusalem: Mosad Bi'alik, 1999); Hannan Hever, Yehouda Shenhav, and *Pnina Mutzafi Heller*, eds., *Mizrahiyim be-Israel, 'iyun bikorti mehudash* (Jerusalem: Van Leer/Tel Aviv: Ha-Kibbutz ha-me'uhad, 2002); Oren Yiftachel and Avinoam Meir, *Ethnic Frontiers and Peripheries: Landscapes of Development and Inequality in Israel* (Boulder: Westview Press, 1998); As'ad Ghanem, *Ethnic Politics in Israel: The Margins and the Ashkenazi Center* (London: Routledge, 2010); Oren Yiftachel, *Ethnocracy: Land and Identity Politics in Israel/Palestine* (Philadelphia: University of Pennsylvania Press, 2006); Gai Abutbul, Lev Grinberg, and Pnina Motzafi-Haller, eds., *Kolot Mizrahiyim: likrat siah Mizrahi hadash 'al ha-hevrah veha-tarbut ha-Yisre'elit* (Tel Aviv: Masada, 2005); Sammy Smooha, *Israel: Pluralism and Conflict* (Berkeley: University of California Press, 1978); Aziza Khazzoom, *Shifting Ethnic Boundaries and Inequality in Israel: or, How the Polish Peddler Became a German Intellectual* (Stanford: Stanford University Press, 2008); Sami Shalom Chetrit, *Intra Jewish Conflict in Israel: White Jews, Black Jews* (London; New York: Routledge, 2010).

7. Naïm Kattan, *Adieu, Babylone: roman* (Montréal: La Presse, 1975); Nissim Rejwan, *The Last Jews in Baghdad: Remembering a Lost Homeland* (Austin: University of Texas Press, 2004); Shim'on Ballas, *Be-Guf Rishon* (Tel-Aviv: Ha-Kibbutz ha-me'uhad, 2009); Sasson Somekh, *Baghdad, Etmol*, 3rd ed. (Tel Aviv: Ha-Kibbutz ha-me'uhad, 2004). The first edition appeared in December 2003. English translation: Sasson Somekh, *Baghdad, Yesterday, The Making of an Arab Jew* (Jerusalem: Ibis, 2007); Anwar Sha'ul, *Qissat hayati fi wadi al-Rafidayn* (Jerusalem: Manshurat Rabitat al-jami'iyin al-yahud al-nazihin min al-'iraq fi isra'il, 1980); Salman Darwish, *Kull ishi hadi fi'l 'iyada* (Jerusalem: Manshurat rabitat al-jami'iyin al-yahud al-nazihin min al-'iraq fi isra'il, 1981); Mir Basri, *Rihlat al-'umar: min difaf dijla ila wadi al-tims* (Jerusalem: Rabitat al-jami'iyin al-yahud al-nazihin min al-'iraq fi isra'il, 1991); Ahmad Nissim Susa, *Hayati fi nisf qarn* (Baghdad: Dar al-shu'un al-thaqafiyya al-'amma, 1986); Ariel Sabar, *My Father's Paradise: A Son's Search for His Jewish Past in Kurdish Iraq* (Chapel Hill, N.C.: Algonquin Books of Chapel Hill, 2008); Marina Benjamin, *Last Days in Babylon: The History of a Family, the Story of a Nation* (New York: Free Press, 2006); Sami Zubaida, "Being an Iraqi and a Jew," in *A Time to Speak Out—Independent Jewish Voices on Israel, Zionism and Jewish Identity*, eds. Anne Karpf, Brian Klug, Jacqueline Rose, and Barbara Rosenbaum (London: Verso, 2008); Ezra Drori, *Mi-Bavel la-carmel* (Haifa: Carmel, 2005); Jonah Cohen, *Hilla 'Al gedot ha-perat* (Carmiel: Jonah Cohen, 2004); Judah Asia, *Ha-Geshamrim shel hayayi* (Tel Aviv: Dahlia Asia Pelled, 2005); Avraham Kahila, *Hayinu ke-holmim* (Jerusalem: Research institute of the Zionist-Pioneer Underground in Iraq, 2007); Badri Pattal, *Halomot be-tatran, Baghdad* (Jerusalem: Carmel, 2005); Salim Fattal, *Be Simta'ot baghdad* (Jerusalem: Carmel, 2003).

8. Examples of such texts include: Shoshana Arbeli Almozlino, *Me-ha-Mahteret be-bavel le-memshelt Israel* (Tel Aviv: Ha-kibbutz ha-me'uhad, 1998); Tikva Agasi, *Mi-Baghdad le-Israel* (Ramat Gan: Kolgraph, 2004).

9. Shoshana Levy, *'Al Em ha-derekh* (Tel Aviv: Sh. Levi, 2001).

10. Ibid., 19.

11. Ibid., 50.

12. Ibid., 31.

13. Ibid., 36.

14. Ibid., 39.

15. Yehuda (Gurji) Barshan, *Yehudi be-zel ha-islam* (Ramat Gan: Havazelet, 1997), 35.

16. This school was established in 1923 to provide a modern secular education to members of the community. Its principal was the Jewish intellectual Ezra Haddad.

17. Barshan, *Yehudi be-zel ha-islam*, 39.

18. Orit Bashkin, *New Babylonians: A History of Jews in Modern Iraq* (Stanford: Stanford University Press, 2012), 59–99.

19. Shoshanna explains in the text that the cinema owner knew her father and thus they did not have to pay.

20. Levy, *'Al Em ha-derekh*, 39, 46.

21. Walter Benjamin, *Charles Baudelarie, A Lyric Poet in the Era of High Capitalism* (London: Verso, 1973), 37–66.

22. On the development of the city in the 1920s, see 'Abbas Baghdadi, *Lila nansa Baghdad fi'l 'ishrinat* (Beirut: al-mu'assasa al-'arabiyya li'l dirasat, 1998).

23. David Naggar, *Bab al-sheikh* (Tel Aviv: Kobbi Ran, 2007), 74.

24. Arabic written in Hebrew characters.

25. Yosef Me'ir, *Hitpathut tarbutit hevratit shel yehudey 'iraq me'az 1830 ve 'ad yemenu* (Tel Aviv: Naharayim, 1989), 35–36, 550–551, 557; Bashkin, *New Babylonians*, 59–99, 64–75.

26. Levy, *'Al Em ha-derekh*, 60.

27. Ibid., 60.

28. Ya'qub Iliyahu 'Aqabiya, ed., *Al-Ta'ifa al-isra'iliyya fi mawakib shuhada' al-huriyya* (Baghdad: Matab'at al-Rashid, 1948).

29. On communism in Iraq and the Jewish role in it, see Bashkin, *New Babylonians*, 141–182; 'Abd al-Latif al-Rawi, *'Usbat mukafahat al-sahyuniyya fi'l 'Iraq, 1945–1946: dirasa wa watha'iq al-yasar al-'iraai wa'l mas'ala al-filastiniyya* (Damascus: Dar al-Jalil, 1986); *Manshurat 'usbat mukafahat al-sahayuniyya* (Baghdad: Mabta't dar al-Hikma, 1946); Al-Shurta al-'amma, *Mawsu'a siriyya khassa bi'l hizb al-shuyu'i al-'iraqi* (Baghdad: Matba'at mudiriyyat al-tahqiqat al-jina'iyya, 1949); Hanna Batatu, *The Old Social Classes and the Revolutionary Movements of Iraq* (Princeton: Princeton University Press, 1978); Tareq Y. Ismael, *The Rise and Fall of the Communist Party of Iraq* (New York: Cambridge University Press, 2007).

30. Bashkin, *New Babylonians*, 182–228; Abbas Shiblak, *The Lure of Zion: The Case of Iraqi Jews* (London: al-Saqi Books, 1986), 67–71, 103–127; Yehouda Shenhav, "The Jews of Iraq, Zionist Ideology, and the Property of the Palestinian Refugees of 1948: An Anomaly of National Accounting," *International Journal of Middle East Studies* 31, 4 (1999), 605–630; Moshe Gat, *The Jewish Exodus from Iraq, 1948–1951* (London: Frank Cass, 1997).

31. On Zionist activities in Iraq, see Shiblak, Gat, and Shenhave, "The Jews"; Haim Cohen, *Ha-Pe'ilut ha-zionit be-'iraq* (Jerusalem: Ha-sifriya ha-zionit, 1969).

32. Esther Darwish Tzorani, Speech in Second Zionist conference, 2 December 1944, reprinted in Sha'ul Sehayek, *Haluzot ba-mahteret: hishtalvut bahurot bi-tenu'at he-haluz ha-mahtartit be-'iraq* (Or Yehudah: Merkaz moreshet Yahadut Bavel, ha-Makhon le-heker Yahadut Bavel, 2000), 78–79; Evelyn Salton-Zlikha, "Until When Shall We Wait?" *Derech Ha-haluz* (May 1945), reprinted in Mordechai Bibi, *Ha-Mahteret ha-zionit ha-haluzit be-iraq* (Jerusalem: Yad Ben-tzvi, 1988), 2:564–565.

33. The state received 684,000 newcomers; 50 percent were Europeans and 50 percent were characterized as Asians and Africans. In this group were 124,000 Iraqi Jews. Most arrived in 1950–1951, though 9,000 Iraqis had arrived before and during 1948. Most of them were young; about 39 percent were under 15 and 32 percent were 15 to 29 years old. See Esther Me'ir-Glitsenshtain, *Ben bagdad le-ramat gan: Yots'ey 'iraq be-yisra'el* (Jerusalem: Yad Ben-tzvi, 2008), 75–77.

34. Meir, *Ben bagdad*, 107–108.

35. Levy, *'Al Em ha-derekh*, 79.

36. DDT—dichlorodiphenyltrichloroethane, an insecticide with which the newcomers were sprayed for supposed health reasons upon their arrival to Israel.

37. Levy, *'Al Em ha-derekh*, 80.

38. Oz Almog, *The Sabra, the Creation of the New Jew* (Berkeley: University of California Press, 2000).

39. Levy, *'Al Em ha-derekh*, 83.

40. On the nationalization of holidays in Israel, see Yael Zerubavel, "Transhistorical Encounters in the Land of Israel: On Symbolic Bridges, National Memory, and the Literary Imagination," *Jewish Social Studies* 11, 3 (2005), 115–140; Anita Shapira, "Ben-Gurion and the Bible: The Forging of an Historical Narrative?" *Middle Eastern Studies* 33, 4 (1997), 645–674; Orit Bashkin, "Hanukka in the Zionist Discourse according to Seffer Ha-Mo'adim (The Book of Festivals)," *Zemanin* 16, 61 (Winter 1997/8).

41. Eli Amir, *Tarnegol Kaparot* (Tel Aviv: Or 'Am, 1989).

42. Levy, *'Al Em ha-derekh*, 86. On Mizrahis in the Kibbutzim, see also Dani Zamir, *'Adot ha-Mizrah ve-ha-Kibbutz* (Haifa: University of Haifa, Ha-Merkaz ha-universita'i ha-kibbutzi, 1983).

43. Levy, *'Al Em ha-derekh*, 90.

44. Ibid., 94.

45. Ibid., 95.

46. Meir, *Ben bagdad*, 205–206.

47. Ibid., 306–310.

48. Margalit, letter to her parents, February 1946, 8, reprinted in Sehayyek, *Haluzot ba-mahteret: hishtalvut bahurot bi-tenu'at he-halutz ha-mahtartit be-'iraq* (Or Yehudah: Merkaz moreshet Yahadut Bavel, ha-Makhon le-heker Yahadut Bavel, 2000), 109.

49. Central Zionist Archive S20/613, Association of the Youth from Aram Naharim, brochure dated 17 September 1950.

50. Arieh Gelblum, *Haaretz*, 21 April 1949.

51. In 1954 the number dropped to 43,553 Iraqis in 60 camps. Meir, *Ben bagdad*, 111–112.

52. Ibid., 122–123.

53. The reference here is to the last verse in Proverbs 31 and to a hymn celebrating the virtues of the woman of valor often recited on Friday nights.

54. Levy, *'Al Em ha-derekh*, 88.

55. *Haaretz*, 8 May 1955; *Haaretz*, 4 May 1953, 5 May 1953; *Maariv*, 5 May 1953 in Central Zionist Archive S71/109 [Ma'abarot].

56. *Davar*, 17 August 1955, in Central Zionist Archive S71/109 [Ma'abarot].

57. *Haaretz*, 5 August 1955, in Central Zionist Archive S71/109 [Ma'abarot].

58. Levy, *'Al Em ha-derekh*, 98.

59. Ibid., 99.

60. Ibid., 100.

61. Ibid., 101.

62. Ibid., 101.

63. Ibid., 107.

64. Tom Segev, *1967—Ve Haaretz Shinta et Panieh* (Jerusalem: Keter, 2005).

65. The metaphor of the slaughtered lamb appears in the Bible (Isaiah 53: Psalms: 44:23) and in prayers. In 1943, Jewish rebels in Lithuania called the Jews not to go to their deaths as lambs to the slaughter; in Israel the expression was evoked in the early years of the state to depict the manner in which Jews went unresistingly to their deaths.

66. The major organization was Yad le-Banim ("Commemoration of [the] Sons"), which was established by a woman who lost her son in 1948 and received financial support from the government and local municipalities. In 1991 the widows who were active in the organization withdrew and established their own group because they felt that their needs were not being met within the organization.

67. Levy, *'Al Em ha-derekh*, 110.

68. Ibid., 114.

69. Chaim Nachman Bi'alik, *Im Yesh et nafshekha lada't, Shirim, 1890–1897* (Tel Aviv: Devir, 1983).

70. Central Zionist Archive S84/135, Committee of Babylonian Jews in Jerusalem, 1/June/1951, memo on the 'Aliya from Iraq.

71. Central Zionist Archive DD1/2901, a letter by Y. A. B. Ini, Chair, association of 'Olim from Aram Naharim.

72. Central Zionist Archive S20/613, Jewish Agency, letter to the director of the department of Eastern Jews from the communication bureau of the Babylonian community dated 27 April 1950; 3 July 1949.

73. Tom Segev, *The Seventh Million: The Israelis and the Holocaust* (New York: Hill and Wang, 1993), 255–309.

74. While 41 percent of all Iraqi men had received an elementary education prior to their arrival in Israel, 26 percent had graduated from high schools and 7.5 percent had a degree higher than that. Among the women, the rate of illiteracy was about 60 percent. Meir, *Ben bagdad,* 78, 189–191.

75. Adriana Kemp, "Medabrim Gevulot, havnayat teritoriya politit be-Israel 1949–1957," Tel Aviv University, Ph.D. dissertation, 1997.

11

An Artistic Perspective

The Women of Bahram Beizai's Cinema

HAMID DABASHI

As the Ma'arefi family is getting ready in Tehran for the wedding of their young daughter Mahrokh, the bride's elder sister Mahtab Ma'arefi, her husband Heshmat Davaran, and her two children get into a rented car in the northern part of the country to drive south for the occasion. Their luggage packed in the car, just before getting into the car, Mahtab Ma'arefi looks straight into the camera and with a disarmingly blank face says, "We are going to Tehran to participate in my younger sister's wedding. We will not reach Tehran. We will all die."

With that simple line, something extraordinary happens, not only in the creative career of the widely admired Iranian filmmaker Bahram Beizai, but in the vast and variegated spectrum of Iranian cinema.

Women at Work

Bahram Beizai was born in 1938 in Tehran to a prominent Iranian literary family. As both a playwright and a filmmaker he has had a long and illustrious career in both the pre- and post-Islamic Revolution eras. From the late 1960s he has been at the forefront of Iranian cinema—overcoming much censorial hardship to produce a magnificent body of work at the core of the Iranian New Wave.[1]

A strong female character often sets the mood for his films. All the women in Beizai's cinema work and they are located right in the middle of a material constellation of reality. As early as "Thunder Shower" (*Ragbar*, 1971), Beizai places women's dignity in their working habitat. Atefeh the lead character works in a tailor's workshop. Her mother, despite her old age, weaves handmade sweaters to help out with the expenses, and the owner of the tailor shop is also a woman. These three women are not defined by their dependence on any other breadwinner. They are autonomous, earthly, real, tangible, and their dignity is conditioned labor.

Rooted and confident in their workplace, Beizai's women have an active, even aggressive, role in their own destiny. In the central event of "Thunder Shower," an emerging affection between Atefeh and the new schoolteacher, Mr. Hekmati, Atefeh is a major actor. Atefeh has another suitor, the local butcher, who is wealthy, powerful, determined, and influential. By marrying him, Atefeh would have secured a comfortable life for herself and her mother and young brother together. Her attraction to Mr. Hekmati is gradual, logical, and yet palpably affectionate. Even more importantly, she is an equal partner in making that affection possible, real, and trustworthy. The reality of Atefeh is embraced by the realism of her mother and her employer, both of them women, both of them straight from the streets and alleys of Iranian reality. Even the neighborhood butcher contributes to the realization of Atefeh as an active moral agent in her life. If we agree with Shahla Lahiji's assessment that "these three women [i.e., Atefeh, her mother, and her employer] are caught in the *cul-de-sac* of enduring social traditions, personal emotions, fear of [an] unknown environment, and the world outside,"[2] they are still active moral agents, alert and aware, in their worldly affairs.

Laboring women are equally central to "The Crow" (*Kalagh*, 1976). The old, stately Mother used to be a nurse; her daughter-in-law Asiyeh is now a teacher to deaf children. Again, the dignity of working, the social location of full membership in the world, is the bracing grace of these women. It is crucial to keep in mind that Beizai does not concoct this working status for the women in his films. He is extraordinarily realistic in these depictions. His "realism" in fact is not only rooted in the immediate historical experiences of his society but also in his mythological reconstitution of the prehistorical nuclear family where women have been at the center of the community of labor. Throughout his cinematic career, Beizai has always operated on the borderline between myth and reality. Even in his most visibly modern and urban films, such as "Thunder Shower" and "The Crow," Beizai sees life as the site of a "ritual" that collapses myth and reality and one in which myth animates actions. From these earliest works, the cross-fusion of *mythos* and *logos* in the work of Beizai has been evident. As forms of cognitive categories, myths for Beizai constitute a material, historical, and evolving character.[3]

The most significant aspects of "The Crow," however, are Beizai's imaginings of women in a multidimensional, multitemporal way—a strategy that breaks the apparent solidity of the subject in any patriarchal context. The Mother in "The Crow" is narrating her memoir to her daughter-in-law, Asiyeh, while a picture of her youth has mysteriously appeared in the "Lost" section of the daily paper. Meanwhile, Asiyeh is expecting a child, which could very well be a girl. Among the Mother, her daughter-in-law Asiyeh, the picture of the Mother's youth, the narration of her memoir, and the expected child there thus emerges a composite picture of one single woman: at once old (the Mother), young (Asiyeh), unborn (Asiyeh's fetus), past (the mother's memoir), present (Asiyeh's writing that memoir), visual (the Mother's youthful picture), and verbal (the Mother's narration of her memoir). If myth is the symbolic structuring of the world in a meaningful way, Beizai has a Lego-like attitude toward myths that has been constitutional in the social formations of a culture. In "The Crow" in particular, he dismantles the fixated subjectivity of the feminine in temporal and narrative terms. The breakdown of the feminine subject and its cinematic reconstitution is one particularly effective way of not only screening their historical formations but, equally important, negotiating a new composition for that subjectivity.

The Mythically Pregnant Reality

Beginning with a historically disenfranchised segment of his society, namely women, Beizai's access to what he perceives as the mythological roots of contemporary social ills thematically expands to include far more universal implications of the problem. His art, as Theodor W. Adorno would call it, would thus strategically dwell on reality in a way that can begin to manipulate and change it. "Art's autonomous realm," Adorno suggests, "has nothing in common with the external world other than borrowed elements that have entered into a fully changed context."[4] The aesthetic context within which Beizai ritually choreographs and orchestrates myth and reality has an emancipatory angle on the self-same reality; it is not formed in pure artistic isolation, because, again as Adorno put it, "the development of artistic process . . . corresponds to social development"[5] in such a way that the two will have authoritative correspondences with each other. Beizai is attuned to the external world in which he lives and works. The elements of the world that he borrows and infuses into his art initiate a fateful negotiation with their own mythological underpinnings. In his art, Beizai's cinematic vision is *ambassadorial*, oscillating between the realm of the real and the domain of the mythical.

By the time Beizai makes "The Stranger and the Fog" (*Gharibeh va Meh*, 1973), he is completely at home with his richly implicative and pregnant mythological language, a language that despite its ascending allegorical suggestiveness has a profoundly earthly quality to it. The emerging affection in "The Stranger and the Fog" between Ra'na, the coastal woman of permanence, and Ayat, the maritime man of migration, is rooted in the twilight zone of land and sea, life and death, fact and fiction, reality and myth. The village of Ra'na, the young widow, is ethereal, somewhere in the north of Iran or perhaps nowhere at all. The village, on the edge of a maritime abyss, is as foggy as real, as imaginary as material. On that borderland of life and death, Ayat has to fight against the demons that have chased him from the sea into the security of the village with the same ferocity that Ra'na has to fight the ghosts of her dead husband's ancestors, who in turn haunt the villagers with the same intensity as does the fear of an invading army of sea monsters. The crucial aspect of this dual, circular, warfare is that Ra'na and Ayat fight it together, on two simultaneous fronts, from the land and the sea. Ayat is haunted by his fatal attraction to the sea, Ra'na by the ancestral gaze of a dead husband. The invading sea monsters, apparitions from Ayat's own perturbed fears of the unknown, are no less scary than the invisible ghosts that roam the village in the form of "traditions," "customs," "habits," and "manners." At the end, Ayat, Ra'na, and the entire village fight as much against the invading sea monsters as they do against the monstrous apparitions, a whole genealogy of fear, that they have themselves invented.

The chief protagonist of "The Stranger and the Fog" is neither Ayat nor Ra'na. It is the fog. It is the furiously foggy subjugation of the real, where the real can yield alternative visions of itself. The foggy disposition of "The Stranger and the Fog" exposes all the received wisdom that defines a culture. The symbolic structuring of the universe of imagination called culture is actively mutated under this hazy vision of the real. As a visual projection of the subconscious, Beizai uses the fog to melt away the presumed rigidity of the evident. The result is a spectacular loosening of the obvious. After watching the atmospheric mistiness of "The Stranger and the Fog," we no longer look at reality with the same submissive matter-of-factness. The authority of sight itself is compromised, reconstituted, negotiated anew, implicated in a whole new hermeneutics of subjectivity.

"If by abolishing the mythic universe we have lost the universe," in Georges Bataille's words, "the action of a revealing loss is itself connected to the death of myth. And today, because a myth is dead or dying, we see through it more easily than if it were alive: it is the need that perfects the transparency, the suffering which makes the suffering joyful."[6] Bataille here speaks of what Max Weber earlier in the twentieth century had termed the universal disenchantment of the world.[7] Both Bataille and Weber are responding to the predicament of instrumental rationalism as the greatest achievement of the dual projects of the European Enlightenment and its colonial Modernity. But what they say resonates with the world ravished by the consequences of colonialism. Our mythic universe and the terms of our enchantment, as the subjects of Beizai's visual reflections, were either actively forgotten or ferociously remembered under the dire consequences of colonialism and the colonized subject. The culture of "authenticity" that was created under these circumstances was conducive to a servile status vis-à-vis the colonial consequences of those projects.

Beizai, among other visionaries of emancipation from that predicament, has been at work not to abolish this received mythic universe but to reinvent it. In his cinema, we do not watch a "revealing loss" because we do not remember our own dreams, let alone lose them. For the colonial subject, there is no "revealing loss." For them, and as they see themselves in their active reimagination by Beizai, the world needed to be invented anew, this time with the postcolonial subjects in it. The colonial subjects were *invented out* of the world of the Enlightenment by the very inventors of the Enlightenment and Modernity, the author of *Was ist Aufklärung* chief among them. In Beizai, among a handful of other visionary theorists of our liberation, the postcolonial subjects are being invented back into something they can call their own "history," but this time with no Hegelian teleological illusion about the term.

In Beizai, we do not see through the dead or dying myth but through the resuscitated reinventions of myths. Bataille is correct that through a dying myth one can see the world as even more profoundly mythical. But that only happens if one has first benefited from the fruits, and not merely suffered the dire consequences, of the illusion of the myth. In the colonial outposts of the European Enlightenment, we have an entirely different stand vis-à-vis myth. We need, as Beizai intends, to reinvent them in ways that affirm our place in the world, that do not deny us our historical inflection. And ultimately, because our needs are of an entirely different sort, the need to be born into the world, we cannot have any conception of "joyful suffering." We have had too much "joyful suffering" in our neck of the woods. We called it "Sufism."

Remythologizing the Real

By "The Ballad of Tara" (*Cherikeh-ye Tara*, 1978), Beizai has thoroughly reimagined Iranian mythology in order to project a new angle on that reality. Without full command over the inner workings of Iranian mythological memories it is impossible to do what Beizai does, at once resuscitating them and manipulating them, to force them to yield to alternative modes of meaning, being, and activating. No one in the history of the Iranian performing arts comes anywhere near Beizai in his phenomenal command of Persian mythological culture and his ability to force it into a creative convulsion. The reason Beizai has become proverbial among his Iranian critics for the "incomprehensibility" of his cinema is precisely because of the deep-rootedness of these mythological referents in the mind of his Iranian audience. Beizai's attempt has invariably been to defamiliarize these myths in order to shake his audience into a renewed pact with them.

With a gaze fixated on contemporary realities, particularly the fate of Iranian women, but through women the entire crooked timber of trying to be an "Iranian" in the contemporary period, Beizai rattles the forgotten realities of antiquity into speaking their reason, breaking their conspiratorial silence, effacing the banality of their claim to sacred certitude and to authorial authenticity. Beizai opts for the archaic word "Cherikeh" not in a vain search for authenticity but in order to shock the familiar with the unknown, the comfortable with the mysterious, the overtly remembered with the actively forgotten. All these are effective strategies of alienating the world from its familiar habits of cozening itself into the habitual. Any number of other words—*Afsaneh, Ostureh, Hekayat, Qesseh*, and so on—would have equally conveyed the sense of a ballad. What "Cherikeh" does here is to force the lazy audience to pause and ponder, to dwell on the unknown, to distance itself from the habitual, even to distrust the received definitions and locations of our place-in-the-language we call home. "The main function of the myth," in the judicious words of Åke Hultkrantz, the distinguished scholar of myth who conducted extensive fieldwork among the Wind River Shoshoni Indians, "is to sanction the establishment and condition of the world and its institutions, thereby safeguarding the existence of people and society. In many cases, the very recitation of the myth is so filled with power that it influences—or is thought to influence—the course of actual events."[8] But myths as such have a habit of not just making the world possible, but of making it possible at the heavy price of a tyrannical subjugation of one race or one gender to another. Beizai's cinema provides a gendered and visual access to Iran's mythical universe and invites the creation of new, more just and more equitable myths for the world.

In "The Ballad of Tara," which immediately after "The Stranger and the Fog" is Beizai's most mythically narrated film, he opts for a cinematic redaction of the creation myth from a decidedly feminine perspective. Here, he draws on any number of distant Iranian mythological narratives in order to generate his own.[9] In this narrative, Tara is a woman, earthly, seasonal, in tune with the land, fertile in her attendance to the real. Tara is part of nature, embracing a fertile celebration of life, with two children, ready for any new season, with no sign of self-consciousness evident about her. The description of Susan Taslimi as Tara by Shahla Lahiji is quite poignant:

> The impeccable acting of Susan Taslimi as Tara is the indication of a perfect choice and of the remarkable capability of the actor in the cultivation and performance of her role. This capability is evident not only in her acting but also in her physiognomy. Susan Taslimi—with her Wheat-like complexion, elongated nose, set-back but penetrating, open and intimidating eyes, and then at times, with that affectionate look, bony and sculpted cheeks, the wrinkle of power at the side of her mouth, the thin line of thought on her long forehead, the tall stature, and then that authority in her demeanor and speech—is the very epiphany of Mother-Earth: that very mythological vision of woman that can very well belong to yesterday, today, or tomorrow, and [yet] at the same time remain thoroughly woman.[10]

Tara as earth, nature, and fertility appears at a moment when she has lost two of her men: a husband and a father. Meanwhile, she is being pursued by four men: by a half-crazed boy, by the brother of her murdered husband, whose name is Ashub, meaning "Chaos," and who loves her madly and is probably her husband's murderer, by Qelich who like her is earthly and digs water from the depths of the earth, and then by the Historical Man who is there to get the sword and yet falls in love with her. Located between these two manly brackets of dead and living attendants, whatever Tara has inherited from her masculinist ancestry she distributes to everybody in the village, much to their delight, even the sword that is brought back to her immediately because of the fear of its being haunted. She is given back the sword but she does not know quite what to do with it. She tries to cut wood, chop vegetables, or hold the door with it. She throws it out into the sea, much to the anger of the Historical Man, but the sea returns the sword back, much to her surprise. She discovers the use of the sword when a wild dog attacks her and her children and she kills the wild dog and thus finds out, much to her awe, the use of the sword. Among awe, delight, surprise, and anger, Tara defines the world, locates herself, and there places the reality of the earthly life in which she lives. She is the original point of departure for whatever exists, for whatever should, and does, matter.

In "The Ballad of Tara," as in all other films by Beizai, the lead woman protagonist has the dignity of place by the ennobling grace of work. Tara is a farmer. Her children, her domestic animals, her farm, and the retinue that holds these together are at the center of a universe over which she presides. In this premoment of History (when history has not started yet), only work matters. The sword is of no use in this pre-moment. Tara tries to put the sword to work. But it is a useless, work-less, instrument. History not yet having begun, there is no use for the sword. When Tara and the Historical Man meet, he can only speak of death, destruction, and honor, while she tries to see if the man has any talent she can put to work.

The Historical Man is out to get her sword back to defend his honor, but while here in the premoment of History he falls in love with Tara and cannot leave to go back to History, until such time as he is assured that Qelich is in love with Tara and will actually take care of her children in her absence. Only then will the Historical Man go back to His-tory, having found a cause to reenter it. Thus, Beizai in effect holds His-tory hostage to a mythological renegotiation of it in the premoment of History. For the Historical Man, as he enters this premoment, honor precedes life, whereas Tara places life, in which dwells her love for the Historical Man, before any Historical constitution of manly "Honor." She has no use for such cultural abstracts, particularly when defined by useless men. Tara is *noble* in the pre-cultural materiality of the term. He speaks of honor in History, and of love in the material context of a life that is too real to collapse into any History. Central to this distinction is the function of the sword. She first tries to use it practically, or to sell it, or throw it away, or go harvesting with it. The sword, however, belongs to the lost honor of a tribe. But the people of the village have no use for the sword either. She kills a dog with the sword to protect herself and her children and thus learns the use of the sword and is petrified by it. She gives the sword back to the Historical Man so he can leave, but by then she is told that he cannot go back because he has fallen in love with her: history taken hostage by its own premoment.

Far more important than defining myth as "sacred tale" or "tradi-tional tale,"[11] it is important to see the act of myth making as a form of communal self-signification, a manner in which a world comes to self-consciousness. Outside such significations, the world atrophies into confusion and chaos. Beizai's cinema in general, and "The Ballad of Tara" in particular, is a singularly successful negotiation with the enduring parameters of the Persian mythologizing imagination. One of the crucial achievements of Beizai in "The Ballad of Tara" is to subvert time and narrative in a way that enables his story to find and demonstrate its own internal "logic." Consider the narrative elements of this ballad. The Historical Man has exited history and entered its premoment in order to retrieve his sword, and yet he is held back by a love affair. The Grandfather is dead and yet he speaks in person beyond his grave as the solitary sound of an authority that defies death and timing. Equally paramount in this premoment of History is a sword that always mysteriously reappears, against all logic, despite all resistance, in tune with a narrative logic that only a myth—or perhaps more accurately in Beizai's case, a "counter-myth"—can generate and sustain. Dialogues in "The Ballad of Tara" vary in accent and intonation, implicating no particular time or location, implicating all times and all locations. Not all the costumes are from Tavalish, the region in which the film was made. They are the visual regalia of a premoment in the world. The sights and sounds here do more than just express ideas, they actually define the terms, as they constitute the parameters of a different world, the world of the story, the realm of the unreal to which the real must yield. The stylized gestures are pantomime invitations into the sight of the unseen, the place of the premoment of being-in-the-world. In "The Ballad of Tara," Beizai enters the world of myth in order to force his audience to exit the routinized (experienced) world, alerted to a whole different consciousness of reality.

To achieve that reconstitution of the real cinematically, visuality becomes the central mechanism of Beizai's narrative, which must begin to teach its otherwise primarily auditory audience how to see. Foregrounding the visual possibility of colors and shapes as the constituent forces of the narrative results in an active stylization of colors and shapes, which in turn results in a formal stylization of the visual. Stylizing movements come next, aided admirably by an almost self-conscious stylization of the camera movement and angles. All these lead to the constitution of a visual world legitimately operative on its own terms, irreducible to the outside world, giving palpable reality to the film as the visual substitution of the real from which to reconstitute the real by contesting the real. No other Iranian filmmaker has this kind of command over the function of the visual or is so richly rooted in the Iranian visual memories, able to pull this off without collapsing into the museumization of the culture. To see Beizai's remarkable ability all one has to do is to see Shahram Asadi's "The Fateful Day" (*Ruz-e Vaqe'eh*, 1995) based on Beizai's script but which visually collapses into a museum piece of tourist attraction. Beizai is no museum curator. He is a puppeteer of our forgotten memories.

By renarrating the myth, Beizai in effect creates the visual site of a ritual, a sign of his lifelong dedication to and fascination with the Persian passion play (*ta'ziyeh*). Bringing the "ritual" to climactic closure is the scene where Tara picks up the sword and attacks the Historical Man receding into the sea. In the stunningly shot and acted final scene, Tara, sword in hand, attacks the sea and delivers her futile blows against wave after wave. The sheer futility of Tara's act and the stunning beauty of this scene is where Beizai rests his camera for the longest time, allowing the effect of the ritual to sink in. But Beizai opts to end on a different note. When the Historical Man leaves, Tara tells Qelich they should get married as soon as the next harvest.

Mythologies

In a short stroke against Mickiewicz's *Julius Caesar*, Roland Barthes catches the fabricated spontaneity of trying to pass the fake as the real. In a brilliant reading of the connotation of sweating as a sign of oral exertion, Barthes formulates a shortcut into what he calls "an ethic of signs."[12]

> Signs ought to present themselves only in two extreme forms: either openly intellectual and so remote that they are reduced to algebra, as in Chinese theatre . . . or deeply rooted, invented, so to speak, on each occasion, revealing an internal, a hidden facet, and indicative of a moment in time, no longer of a concept (as in the art of Stanislavsky, for instance). But the intermediate sign . . . reveals a degraded spectacle, which is equally afraid of simple reality and of total artifice. For although it is a

good thing if a spectacle is created to make the world more explicit, it is both reprehensible and deceitful to confuse the sign with what is signified. And it is a duplicity which is peculiar to bourgeois art: between the intellectual and the visceral sign is hypocritically inserted a hybrid, at once elliptical and pretentious, which is pompously christened "nature."[13]

The ethics of signs that Barthes proposes here open a whole new window on the workings of the mythic. Beizai's cinema is somewhere between the Chinese theater and Stanislavsky's art, as Barthes typologizes them here. His cinema is at once archetypal, or what Barthes calls openly *intellectual* and *algebraic*, and rooted in the moment. In fact, Beizai makes a cinematic virtue out of mythically impregnating the present moment. "Simple reality" and "total artifice" collapse in Beizai's cinema on the site of a "ritualistic" constitution of an angle on the real. Barthes is here rightly disgusted by the duplicity of Julius Caesar's pretension to being "natural." But in his anger he issues a manifesto in his ethics of sign that is theoretically limited. Barthes is correct that between "the intellectual and the visceral" Hollywood has "hypocritically inserted a hybrid, at once elliptical and pretentious." But he completely loses sight of the possibility of collapsing "the intellectual and the visceral," as Beizai does systematically in almost all his films, on the site of a mythic-ritual reconstitution of the real—with a female character always at the center of his remythologies. The reason that Barthes is theoretically blinded here is that the context of bourgeois art in which he launched his pathbreaking collection of essays in the late 1950s was, as indeed it still is in much European theorization of the aesthetic, oblivious to the functioning of the aesthetic in the colonial outposts of the Enlightenment project. Because no autonomous national bourgeoisie could have existed in this context, art was faced with an entirely contingent social formation of classes and their consciousness. As a result, art had a vastly different kind of creative disposition. In this particular case, the phenomenal cross-fusion of "the intellectual and the visceral," far from feigning "nature," cultivates an extraordinarily revolutionary angle on the real, forcing it to yield alternative meanings.

To see that proposition in practice, we can do no better than turn to "Bashu: The Little Stranger" (*Bashu: Gharibeh-ye Kuchak*, 1985), where Beizai brings Tara to History, as it were. This confluence of time and

narrative is crucial to our reading of Beizai's cinema.[14] By historiciz-
ing mythology and mythologizing history, Beizai visually crosses the
received borders of both and takes us into a third territory, at once historical and yet radically alerted to its self-inflicted wounds of perhaps
inevitable mythologizing urges. The site of the confluence between the
mythos and the *logos* in Beizai is his fascination with "ritual." "Ritual"
for Beizai is the performative microcosm of a universe in which both
the *logos* of history and the *mythos* of making it comprehensible collide.

In his *Absence of Myth*, Georges Bataille seeks to strike the chord that
captures the moment of the unmyth as itself mythical: "Night is also a
sun," and the absence of myth is also a myth: The coldest, the purest,
the only *true* myth."[15] "The world" itself being mythical and "the Myth"
worldly, as a filmmaker almost condemned to realism Beizai cannot but
underline that cross-fusion. What is thus evident in Beizai's cinema is
the fictive transparency of the real, the therapeutics of myth making in
the face of the fear of the real—with working women at the heart of his
recasting of world-making myths.

"Bashu" is the critical evidence that the binary opposition between
"History" and "Myth" does not hold for Beizai—for in his cinematic
cosmovision he has collapsed both and construed a third world in
which we become radically conscious of the *mythos* in the operative
energy of the *logos*.

Despite her extraordinary critical intelligence in reading Beizai's
women, Lahiji regrettably falls squarely into the trap of a patriarchal
definition of "motherhood," without pausing for a second to question
whether or not that power-based definition is remotely "instinctual."
There is nothing "instinctual" about a definition of "motherhood"
which is historically constituted. In haste to celebrate Na'i as the ideal-
typical "Mother,"[16] Lahiji completely forgets to consider that on more
than one occasion Na'i's attitude toward Bashu is inexcusably racist. In
their first encounter Na'i makes a nasty reference to the dark complexion of Bashu (he being from southern Iran), darker in complexion than
Na'i and her children who are from northern Iran), and says, "Are you
an animal or a human being?" She is at first very protective of her own
biological children and treats Bashu as if he were a dangerous animal
in her rice paddy. The leitmotif of racism is quite constant in "Bashu,"
resulting in one of the most glorious scenes in which Na'i ritually gives

birth to Bashu, but not before buying a whole bar of soap to wash his dark skin and make him white. Having failed to make him white, she says, "No way, he will not become white." None of these racist comments, however, has the slightest effect on Na'i's character. In the earthly self-confidence of his characterization of Na'i, Beizai knows only too well that she must share the racist presupposition of her village, the universe of her physical location and material imagination. (Yes, Na'i is a product of her racist environment but unlike the other villagers does overcome her initial knee-jerk reactions to Bashu's dark skin.)

Na'i is no "mother" in a limiting, patriarchally constituted sense. Na'i is earth incarnate. To her, Bashu, her own two children, the animals to which she attends, the shooting stems in the rice paddy are one and the same. Beizai could not possibly pose the most serious challenge to the Iranian performing arts, down to the very mythological foundations of Persian patriarchy, and yet accept and celebrate its constitution of motherhood as a trap in it.

Ritual Birth

To understand Na'i better and what Beizai does in his characterization of her, we need to see her in the context of the mythological motif and against the two opposing myth types of the world parents.[17] In the most familiar world parents myth type, which is A 625 in Thompson's motif-index, we have sky-father and earth-mother as parents of the universe. This myth type is found in a vast historical and geographical expanse that ranges from ancient Greece to India, Eastern Indonesia, Tahiti, Africa, and native North and South America. The less widely known world parents myth type, which is motif-index A 625.1 in Thompson's motif-index, is exactly the reverse of A 625, that is, we have the mother as sky and the father as earth.[18] Na'i is of course immediately identifiable as the mother-earth motif of A 625. However, Beizai does not leave the matter at that simple indexical level.

Throughout "Bashu," Na'i's husband is completely absent, and when he does appear at the very last sequence of the film, his most visible and symbolic phallic symbol, his right hand, is cut off, presumably in a war or work-related accident. We are never told. As a result Beizai has Bashu being "born" to Na'i by having her ritually give birth to him. Visually, this ritual birth-giving has a number of references. One is when Na'i washes Bashu at a river, and in Beizai's extremely accurate mise-en-scene Bashu's head is precisely located next to Na'i's vagina and womb when she is sitting and washing Bashu who is in the river. A second visual effect is when Na'i fishes Bashu out of a small brook with a net that she casts toward her. Bashu does not know how to swim and has just fallen off a branch over which he was frolicking. While all the village men are standing by completely paralyzed and impotent, unable to do anything, Na'i grabs her fishing net and casts it toward the drowning Bashu. Inside the pool-like brook, Bashu appears as if in Na'i's womb, more specifically in the plasmatic meconium of the fetus. The grayish-green color of the water is particularly reminiscent of the meconium—the dark green mass that accumulates in the bowel of the fetus during its fetal life and is then discharged shortly after birth. Na'i pulls Bashu out in a gesture that is remarkably similar to the labor that a mother goes through to "fish her child out of her womb." She saves and thus "gives birth to him," because otherwise he would have died with all those impotent men around, and then she holds him to her bosom exactly as if he were a newborn baby fresh out of her womb. Having been saved by the net that Na'i has cast into the small brook, Bashu is inside the net like a newborn baby bursting out of the plasmatic fetus. There are many more such birth-giving rituals, such as Na'i's hallucinatory, ritualistic dance to Bashu's magically therapeutic drumbeats that look like the twisting and turning of the body during the final stages of labor. It is right after this scene that we see Na'i washing the clothes she wore while she was sick (pregnant), as women do after childbirth, while dictating a letter to Bashu to be sent to her husband. "My son Bashu writes this letter," Na'i says proudly. "Like all other children, he is the offspring of earth and the sun." Bashu is conceived immaculately, with no need for any "husband." The only remote "contact" with the husband comes *after* the ritual birth of Bashu to Na'i.

Bashu's ritual birth to Na'i in the conspicuous absence of her husband leads us to the precise site of remythologization in which Beizai has narrated his version of world parenting, central to his cosmovision. To see Na'i's place as mother earth in that cosmovision and the revolutionary reimagination of the world through a reinvention of the world parent myth, we need to look at the originary myth itself prior to Beizai's reconstitution of it.

Let me begin by drawing attention to the splendid work of Professor K. Numazawa of Nanzan University of Nagoya, Japan, on the related motif of creation myth, Thompson motif-index A 625.2, on the specifics of "the Raising of the Sky."[19] Written by a Japanese scholar in German, published in Paris in 1946, and predicated on material from Japanese mythology, this study could not be further from Beizai's "Bashu," Beizai's knowledge of the Asian performing arts and his admiration for the late Akira Kurosawa notwithstanding. Precisely in this obvious unrelatedness dwells the universal claim that "Bashu" has over a range of mythological parameters at the heart of Beizai's cosmovision. The parameters of that cosmovision work through and for a specifically mythological reconstitution of the culture.

To achieve that objective, Beizai reaches for the most elemental and mythological parameters of the culture. In Numazawa's observations about the "Raising of the Sky" motif of the creation myth is already evident a theory of the link between agricultural communities and their mythologizing proclivities. The significance of agricultural communities, into which the setting of "Bashu" falls, is in their physical approximation to the earliest forms of human society. Myths that have to do with the origin of the universe, in which a mother-earth and a father-sky play the central role, take us directly to the communal context of patriarchal and matriarchal patterns of social formation. The myth of world parenting usually begins at a premoment of the world, a moment which is also central to both "The Ballad of Tara" and to "Bashu." What does the world look like at this premoment? "There is, common to nearly all the myths I have spoken of," Numazawa observes, "the idea that darkness filled the universe before the separation of the sky and earth, and that light appeared for the first time in the universe when the sky and earth had been separated. And with the coming of the light, everything on earth which had been hidden in the darkness appeared for the first time."[20]

Now consider the fact that until the very last sequence of the film, we do not see Na'i with her husband. He is present by virtue of Na'i's speaking of him; her neighbors, some of whom are her husband's relatives, remind her of him; and of course her two children are presumably the result of her marriage to that man. The husband arrives *after* the ritual birth of Bashu to Na'i. So the narrative moment of "Bashu" is an untime of the world, namely, the father-sky has left but his marks are on the mother-earth, and thus the world is evident. And yet there are many nights and days, that is, the death and resurrection of the world, without the father-sky ever being around. Numazawa again: "This is precisely what we see every morning at the break of dawn. The breaking of dawn starts with the union of the sky and earth in the darkness of the night. This union is the union of father sky and mother earth, and all things that appear with the rising of the sun are born of these two."[21]

But we never see Na'i sleeping with any man. No sign of the father-sky in sight. The repeated emphasis of Na'i's sleeping patterns, in which she has to keep an eye on the rice paddy, are visually emphatic. She sleeps alone, in the dark. Now consider the fact that Beizai's intuitive grasp of this myth, at once critically intelligent and creatively subversive, leads him to have a whole(?) son being born to Na'i *in the absence of a husband.* Now consider Numazawa again:

> The myths in which father sky leaves mother earth in the morning show clearly traces of the custom of visit marriage (Besuchsehe). When morning comes, the man, like Uranos, must leave the woman. Therefore the myths have merely transferred what happens every morning to the first morning of the beginning of the universe—in other words, to the morning of the creation of all things.[22]

The Japanese practice of "the visit marriage," which we see in its patriarchally reversed mode in the Shi'i practice of "*mut'ah*" or "temporary marriage," is far closer, as Numazawa suggests, to the original matriarchal practice where the husband is only there to occasion the birth of the child and then go away. But in Beizai's case, what is remarkable is the ritual elimination of the father. By Bashu being born to Na'i through a ritually staged immaculate conception, even the "temporary marriage" is rendered "ritually" superfluous. But Na'i and Bashu become parent and child not simply through a cinematically staged ritual but far more effectively by "working" together. "Work" is constitutional to the emerging parental relationship between Na'i and her son Bashu. At first Bashu does not work, and the neighbors ridicule her for giving shelter to a useless boy. Then she makes him work, which results in her neighbors harassing her for turning the boy into a slave! From this bit of social satire, Na'i and Bashu emerge into a parental relationship that is occasioned by work. When after her illness Na'i gets up as usual one night and sees Bashu already awake and in charge of protecting the rice paddy, the young boy has already been born into work and into her womb. Now get ready for a startling revelation from a Japanese scholar who could not possibly have seen "Bashu" in 1946 when he wrote his *Die Weltanfänge in der Japanische Mythologie* or the shorter version of it in 1953:

> A principal feature in so many myths, particularly those whose motif is the banishment of heaven, is agriculture, specifically agriculture whose chief product is rice. The central figure in these myths is a woman, and the principal animals are cows and pigs. In the social system one may see the prevalence of visit marriage (Besuchsehe), the earliest form of marriage in the matriarchal cultural sphere that developed out of the status that women had acquired economically in the course of social development. From such facts one may conclude that the myths we have been discussing are products of the matriarchal cultural sphere.[23]

The location of an agricultural community, the pivotal importance of a rice paddy, the centrality of a woman in the story, omitting the pigs from the domestic animals for obvious reasons but adding Na'i's economic autonomy, all these are the startling evidence of a conscious constitution of "Bashu" on a universal mythological motif that anchors its narration on the centrality of the idea of mother-earth before launching its cosmovision toward a radical reconstitution of the myth in liberating Na'i and the entire gender she represents from mental, moral, mythological, cultural, historical, and political bondage. No other filmmaker comes even close to Beizai in his ambitious thrust into a radical reconstitution of Iranian culture.

Alan Dundes has suggested an Oedipal explanation for the myth type that Numazawa has examined, the myth in which a male offspring of world parents would want to separate his parents by pushing the sky-father off the earth-mother.[24] This is quite suggestive in the case of "Bashu," particularly in light of the last sequence when the father returns with his right hand, the most visible phallic symbol, cut off. The first time we see the father is when Beizai masterfully draws his figure from a scarecrow that Bashu has made. The father comes and stands in front of the sun, blocks the sunlight, creates a momentary night, and asks Bashu who made that scarecrow. While sitting, Bashu has a conversation with the father, not knowing that he is the father, while in his shadow is an extension of the scarecrow. After this conversation, during which Bashu gives the father a cup of water to drink, Bashu hears from his friends that Na'i's husband has returned. On his way to Na'i, for some inexplicable reason nervous and even frightened, he picks up a stick and runs toward the rice paddy where Na'i resides. When Bashu gets there, Na'i is already engaged in a quarrel with her husband, objecting to his objection that Bashu must leave. Bashu comes hurriedly, stands between Na'i and the father, and automatically raises the stick to attack him and protect the mother. The angle of Beizai's camera here is punctilious. From the corner of the father's right side, we see his amputated right hand, Bashu's raised stick, and then Na'i safely behind her son. The scene is too powerful and too clear to need any further elaboration. Beizai has by then rendered the scarecrow-figure of the father phallically castrated, visibly redundant, and socially irrelevant. It is the beginning of a whole new definition of family, father, mother, son, and the power relationship that is to hold them together.

Urban Legends

"The fact that a universe without myth is the ruin of the universe," Bataille suggests, "—reduced to the nothingness of things—in the process of depriving us equates depravation with the revelation of the universe."[25] In the colonial frontier apparently myths die harder—perhaps because we keep reinventing them, sometimes for the right reasons. What Beizai has done in his long and illustrious career is precisely to keep all of us at bay from a collapse into a universe without myth. The old myths that refuse to die continue to haunt us. We are at the mercy of falling into the abyss of nothingness. Beizai's career, however, has been directed to have the nothingness of things signified or mythologized, into breaking loose from the old, lazy, overbearing, and domineering myths we have received. His cinema has been always at work to forge a new revelation of the universe in which we, as Iranians, as colonials having been written out of the history of our own world, can be born again. To be born again, in terms that will finally enable us in our unique destiny, Beizai has always gone for the juggernaut. Here is another example.

Under the calm, even prosaic veneer of "Perhaps Some Other Time" (*Shayad Vaqti Digar*, 1988), Beizai has a far more ambitious agenda, even more ambitious, I venture to say, than that attained in "The Stranger and the Fog," "The Ballad of Tara," and "Bashu" put together. "Perhaps Some Other Time" is predicated on a suspicion. Modabber suspects his wife Kian of having an illicit love affair, while Kian is trying to conceal a succession of inexplicable nightmarish memories, perhaps even symptomatic of schizophrenic paranoia. While pregnant and fighting to conceal her psychological predicament, Kian finds out that she is not the natural child of her parents and that they have adopted her. Meanwhile, Modabber is going mad with his suspicion. He finally locates Mr. Ranjbar, the antique dealer whom he suspects of having an affair with his wife. Kian is desperate to conceal her psychological problems from her husband. Modabber is desperate to find out the truth about his wife's fidelity. They give each other the wrong signals, add to each other's confusion, and lead each other to false conclusions. Finally, Modabber finds out that Ranjbar is married to a woman who looks remarkably similar to his wife. She turns out to be the lost twin sister of his wife, and Kian finds out that her recurring nightmarish images go back to her early childhood when her mother, destitute and desperate, abandoned her on a street corner to be picked up by a caring couple.

In "Perhaps Some Other Time," through a very simple narrative, Beizai examines the function of "evidence" and the mechanism of gathering it in the constitution of Truth and Falsehood. The place of women in this film is of an entirely different order and has nothing to do with Beizai's concern about the fate of women in Iranian society. Here, he is after something far more universal, far more significant, and he achieves his end in a far more ingenious way which implicates the question of masculinity/femininity in an entirely different way. For me, "Perhaps Some Other Time" is infinitely more mythical than "The Ballad of Tara" and "The Stranger and the Fog" put together. The urbanity of its simple appearance is too deceptive for those who are accustomed to see the working of the mythical in rural settings, archaic clothing, or antiquated dialogue.

Both Modabber and his wife Kian begin with a visual representation: Modabber with a video shot of his wife, Kian with the nightmarish images the meaning of which she cannot fathom. But, and here is the rub, Modabber is watching something that he is not watching, while Kian is watching something that she does not know she is watching. He watches a complete stranger to him, the lost twin sister of his wife, but he thinks he is watching his wife. She sees in her dreams the real images of her infancy, but she does not have the complete data and the interpretative framework to realize what it is she is watching. Modabber begins to interpret the video images he watches on the false exegetical premise of marital infidelity. Kian begins to accumulate data, piece by piece, from her dreams and from her husband's suspicious behavior, and yet does not have that exegetical premise to interpret them. Hermeneutically, he is deductive, she inductive. Logically, he operates a priori, she a posteriori. He collects indubitable data just to end up proving himself wrong. She collects dubious data just to prove herself right. It is only here that we see the manner in which Beizai has passed historical judgment on the masculine proclivity to violent abstractions and grand metaphysics, and conversely the feminine proclivity to material fact and always provisional, substitutional propositions.

The two character type, mythical images that Beizai construes and examines here are those of the woman as "food-gatherer" and of man as "animal-hunter." Kian gathers the data of her early childhood with the sedentary patience of an archaic Woman. Modabber hunts for Absolutist Abstractions and Certainties, caring very little for the facts. Kian is after no Absolutist Abstraction. She just wants to accumulate/gather enough data/food to make sense of/feed her perturbed imagination/household. Modabber cares very little for the facts. He simply wants to hunt for/Abstract a final explanation/Absolute Certainty that will determine his wife's infidelity/establish the Truth. Kian lives in and by reality. Modabber is a metaphysician par excellence. "Perhaps Some Other Time" is Beizai's manifesto against a whole history of phallogocentricism.

By the brilliance of one cinematic strike seeking to alter, or at least visibly and narratively challenge, the age-old authority of a phallogocentricism that for millennia has managed to conceal itself behind a metaphysical culture to which veiling is second nature requires not only a comfortable command but a critical intimacy with the mythological workings of a culture. That "changeability is one of the specific characteristics of myth"[26] is an insight that can indeed be gained after long and arduous examination of myths in their cross-cultural, and trans-historical settings. Professor Th. P. Van Barren, an Egyptologist from the University of Groningen, supports his assertion via examples of mythological behavior in settings as diverse as Tahiti, among the Anuak (a Mitotic tribe on the Upper Nile), among the Papuans of the Want oat region in Northeast New Guinea, and in Ethiopia. But to initiate mythical changes that are as rooted in the contemporaneity of our circumstances as they are directed toward an emancipation of our future requires a critical intelligence of an entirely different order. What is gathered in Beizai's cinema is the unusual combination of a scholar and an artist. His exceptionally detailed knowledge of both Iranian mythology and of the Persian performing arts is squarely at the service of his creative imagination, and all of this geared toward a radical, surgical break from the historical bondage to myths that have so far occasioned our entrapment and slavery to symbolics and the institutions of power.

Meanwhile the Ma'arefi Family . . .

After the opening sequence of "Travelers," Mahtab Ma'arefi, her husband Heshmat Davaran, and their two children get into their car, head south toward Tehran, get into a fatal accident, and (just as she had told us on Beizai's camera) die. Meanwhile, Mahtab Ma'arefi's sister Mahrokh and her entire family are getting ready for her wedding. The sad news of the tragic accident arrives. The wedding preparation turns into mourning. But against all the evidence, the Grandmother of the family refuses to believe that her daughter and her entire family have perished in a fatal automobile accident and insists that the wedding preparations proceed as planned. While the whole family is stricken with sorrow, she persists in her optimism. Finally, at the crucial moment when the wedding was to take place and Mahtab was to arrive with her family bringing with her the auspicious mirror for her sister's ceremonial marriage, the Grandmother insists that the bride should go and change into her wedding gown. Against all indications and her own better judgment, but unable to refuse her Grandmother's wish, she goes upstairs and changes into her wedding gown. As she descends the stairs, suddenly the door opens and . . . in comes Mahtab Ma'arefi with the promised mirror in her hands and her entire family behind her.

"The Travelers" is the logical culmination of the work of arguably the most visually perceptive Iranian filmmaker. "The Travelers" is narrated with haunting precision within the double-bind of two impossibilities, two negations of the ordinary, two suspensions of the rational, two framings of the common. Thus framed and folded, "The Travelers" is visualized on a timing and a scale, a tempo and a movement, that actively suspends and transforms every shred of reality into a visual narrative of compelling power and poise. From the very first shot of a mirror laid down on the grass, and from the very first sequence of the Davaran family getting ready for their trip to Tehran, that visual narrative informs an aesthetically transformed reality, a transformation that holds everything in suspense from the beginning to the end of the story.

How are we to understand that suspense? All those who have written on "Travelers" have tried in one way or another to grapple with the central tension of the narrative, namely, the startling announcement in the very first sequence of the film and its precise reversal at the end.[27] How are we to understand that? Is Mahtab Ma'arefi joking with the audience? Is she mad? What sort of a film is this for a lead actor to face the camera and tell the audience that she (not as Homa Rusta the actor, but as Mahtab Ma'arefi the character) and her entire family are going to die in an automobile accident? Then how come they all come back to life at the end of the film? Did we not in fact see that she and her family actually got into an accident and according to all evidence, including a police report, they all perished? The central tension of the film, then, is the fact that a whole family dies and withers away early in the film and yet they are all somehow miraculously resurrected at the end.

The resurrection of the dead: that is at least one central creative tension in "Travelers." Either all the dead were miraculously resurrected back to life by means of some deed, or else the expecting family, the Grandmother in particular, wished them back to life. In either of these two cases, the element of "hope" is central in a resurrection which is not in the realm of the beyond and after but in the realm of the here and now. How are we to deal with that? Resurrection of the dead? Well, to begin with Muslims have a theory of resurrection in the belief that they will all be brought back from the dead on the day of judgment, face God, and be punished or rewarded for things they have done in this world. Muslims are not alone in their belief in resurrection. Christians believe that Christ was resurrected from the dead too. For Shi'ism in particular, "bodily resurrection" (*Ma'ad-e Jesmani*), as it is called, is a central doctrinal issue. Muslim jurists have written volumes on the subject, mystics have theorized upon it, even philosophers, including Avicenna, have grappled with the doctrinal proposition.

One of the most recent philosophical discussions of the issue of "bodily resurrection" in a specifically Shi'i context, but equally applicable to Islam at large, is by the nineteenth-century Iranian philosopher Shaykh Ahmad Ahsa'i (died 1826). Right from the heart of the "School of Isfahan" and under the influence of the monumental Mulla Sadra Shirazi (died 1640), Shaykh Ahmad Ahsa'i dealt with the issue of "bodily resurrection" in the rich philosophical language that Mulla Sadra virtually invented in the seventeenth century and which has all the material elements for an Islamic theory of the body. In his treatment of the issue of "bodily resurrection," Ahsa'i makes a distinction between *jism* (the body) and *jasad* (the corpse). This distinction is not only central to Ahsa'i's own theory of "bodily resurrection," it is one of the most crucial perspectives on an Islamic theory of the body. "What seems most likely to me," Ahsa'i asserts, "is that originally, or as time went on, the word *jasad* in the Arabic language was taken to mean the body (*jism*) of the living being insofar as the spirit (*ruh*) is absent from it."[28] *Jism*, as opposed to *jasad*, is that "which is animated by the *pneuma*, the spirit (*ruh*), as when speaking of 'the body of Zayd.'"[29] The domain of existing beings whose physical bodies have this dual aspect is not limited to human beings. Even metals can be "represented as inanimate bodies without the spirit (*ajsad*), the spirit being for them the Elixir."[30] The extension is rather comprehensive. Even "if the astronomers . . . use the word *jism* . . . it is because the celestial spheres are in a subtle state comparable to that of the spirits, or else because astronomers regard them from the point of view of their eternal interdependence with the souls by which they are moved."[31] Ahsa'i's assumption that celestial spheres are in the form of *jism* and not *jasad*, that is, they are living things rather than dead masses of matter, or that they have "interdependence with the souls by which they are moved," is a crucial astronomical observation for which the credit should really go to Aristotle. In *Generation and Corruption*, *De Caelo*, as well as *Generation of Animals*, Aristotle believed that the sun is the efficient cause of all events, that the planetary spheres and the planets are responsible for all worldly events, and that the generation of everything, including the generation of animals, is "controlled by the movements of these heavenly bodies."[32] From Aristotelian sources, the idea that the planets and planetary spheres have not just a body but also a soul that animates and enlightens them and thus makes them authoritative over human affairs gradually entered Islamic astronomical beliefs. Al-Kind, for example, one of the greatest commentators on Greek philosophy in the earliest stages of Islamic philosophy, believed that "the planets are rational (*natiqat*), spiritual beings capable of intelligence and speech, and [themselves] cause (*fa'ilat*) and administer (*mudabbirat*) everything in this world by the order of the prime Creator who controls all."[33]

Bodies are thus either dead (*jasad*) or alive (*jism*) and bodies have a range of multifaceted modes of existence ranging from the stars down to human beings. In their living status as *jism*, bodies move, rationalize, speak, and live. *Jasad* in particular is used as opposed to *ruh*, or the "soul" which animates the body. The presence or absence of the "soul" is the distinction between a "corpse" and a "body." Then comes Ahsa'i's most startling observation:

> Now you should be informed that the human being possesses two *jasad* and two *jism*. The first *jasad* is the one which is made up of elements that are a prey to time. This *jasad*, this flesh, is like a garment that a man puts on and later casts off again; this body in itself has neither enjoyment nor suffering; it is subject neither to fidelity nor to rebellion . . . . As for the second *jasad* . . ., this body survives, for the "clay" from which it was constituted survives "in the tomb," when the earth has devoured the elementary terrestrial body of flesh . . . whereas the "body of celestial flesh" survives and retains its perfect "shape."[34]

This theory of the dual body generates an entire new vista on the whole notion of "bodily resurrection." The Second (celestial) Body of which Ahsa'i speaks is not subject to timely erosion and corruption as the First (terrestrial) Body is. We die and we are placed in the tomb with our First Body weakened and dead but our Second Body intact. The First Body soon decomposes and its constituent elements join their origin—fire to fire, earth to earth, and so on—but the Second Body which is celestial in nature and disposition survives even in the tomb. Here, Ahsa'i's eschatology is aided by a theory of optics that is very important for our purpose. The obvious question is why we ordinarily do not "see" this Second (celestial) Body when the First (terrestrial) Body has dissolved? Or even more simply put, why do we not see dead people? Ahsa'i's answer rests on his theory of optics.

Ahsa'i's theory of optics, on the basis of which we see the terrestrial body and do not see the celestial body, is very simple. The reason we see Mr. Zayd in his terrestrial body, that is, when he is alive, but do not see him in his terrestrial body, that is, when he is dead, is not because that body is constitutional to his being. It is only because that body "is homologous to the opacity that exists in silica and potash."[35] What exactly does this mean?

When these [terrestrial bodies, i.e., silica and potash] are fused together, liquefied, they turn into glass. The glass is certainly the same silica and the same potash that were completely dense and opaque. But after the fusion, the opacity disappeared. This means that opacity is not a property of the earth itself. The earth itself is subtle and transparent; its opacity is caused by the clash between the elements. When water is still and pure, you see everything in its depth. But if you stir it up, you can no longer distinguish anything in it so long as it is in movement, because of the collision between its parts and the rarefaction of the element of the air. What then happens when the four elemental Natures come into collision! This *jasad*, this body of flesh made of terrestrial elements, is comparable to the density that makes silica and potash opaque, although this is not a part of their essence, of their ipseity.[36]

If we have followed Ahsa'i so far, he is almost home free in terms of proving why we cannot see dead people. If we agree with him that the only reason we see living terrestrial bodies is that the composition of elemental matters in them has caused their opacity and thus visibility, then all he has to do, which he does, is to change the direction of the camera (as it were) and say that the reason that we do not see the celestial body is that our own bodily organs, our eyes in this case, are made of such opacity that we cannot see a thing when dissolved from that opacity. The Second—subtle, celestial—Body "is invisible to earthly beings, to the people of this world, on account of the opacity that darkens their fleshly eyes and prevents them from seeing what is not of the same kind as themselves."[37]

There is thus no mystery about "Travelers" at all: all Beizai has really done at the end of the film—with the figure of the Grandmother as the solitary source of insight beyond the materiality of all evidence—is to turn his camera into an instrument of vision with which we overcome the opacity of our elementally constituted and limited organ of perception. Put very simply, with Beizai's camera we see things that we ordinarily cannot see, which is the very rudimentary definition of art: to see things otherwise invisible. The fusion of Beizai's cinematic cosmovision and Ahsa'i's dual theories of "bodily resurrection" and its preliminary theory of optics creates a visual condition in which we can see the Ma'arefi's family in their "true," ("celestial"), significant body, in the flesh and bone of their moral significance, the corporeal veracity of their very being-in-the-world.

"When God wishes to bring his creatures back to life," Ahsa'i stipulates, "he causes a rain coming from the ocean situated below the Throne to spread out over the Earth, the water of this rain being colder than snow. . . . "[38] For mortals who have the gift of being able to show the way out of a deadly entrapment in the real, that rain is a shower of light—we call it "cinema."

NOTES

1. This is my third, most comprehensive, encounter with the mythic dimensions of Bahram Beizai's cinema. A shorter version of this essay was part of my chapter on Beizai (along with an extended interview) in my *Close Up: Iranian Cinema, Past, Present, Future* (London: Verso, 2001), 76–11. I have also dealt extensively with his *Bashu: The Little Stranger*, in my *Masters and Masterpieces of Iranian Cinema* (Washington, D.C.: Mage, 2007), 252–277.

2. See Shahla Lahiji, *Sima-ye Zan dar Athar-e Bahram Beiza'i: Filmsaz va Film-nameh-nevis* (Tehran: Roshangaran Publishers, 1993), 38. This is a pioneering and comprehensive study of the place of women in Beizai's cinema from the

perspective of a feminist activist who has championed the cause of women's rights in Iran under intolerable conditions.

3. For a short discussion of the various theories of myth, see Lauri Honko, "The Problem of Defining Myth," in Alan Dundes, ed., *Sacred Narrative: Readings in the Theory of Myth* (Berkeley: University of California Press, 1984), 41–52.

4. Theodor W. Adorno, *Aesthetic Theory*, newly translated, edited, and with a translator's Introduction by Robert Hullot-Kentor (Minneapolis, Minn.: University of Minnesota Press, 1997), 5.

5. Ibid.

6. Georges Bataille, *The Absence of Myth: Writings on Surrealism*, translated and with an Introduction by Michael Richardson (London: Verso, 1994), 48.

7. See Max Weber, "Science as a Vocation," in H. H. Gerth and C. Wright Mills, translated and eds., *From Max Weber: Essays in Sociology* (New York: Oxford University Press, 1946), 155.

8. See Åke Hultkrantz, "An Ideological Dichotomy: Myth and Folk Beliefs among the Shoshoni," in Dundes, *Sacred Narrative*, 165.

9. On the quantitatively reducible number of variations on a single myth, see, for example, the astonishing discoveries of Anna Birgitta Rooth, professor of ethnology at the University of Uppsala, about the North American creation myths that all the 300 myths that she had collected could squarely be divided into no more than eight archetypes. See Anna Birgitta Rooth, "The Creation Myth of the North American Indians," in Dundes, *Sacred Narratives*, 166–181.

10. Lahiji, *Sima-ye Zan* 49. My translation.

11. See, for example, G. S. Kirk's "On Defining Myths," in Dundes, *Sacred Narratives*, 53–61, as an articulation of such choices.

12. See Roland Barthes, *Mythologies*, selected and translated from the French by Annette Lavers (New York: Hill and Wang, 1972), 28.

13. Ibid., 28.

14. In one way or another most readers of Beizai fall into this trap. For good examples, see Lahiji, *Sema-ye Zan*, 48–60; Baqer Parham, "Negahi beh Film-ha-ye Bahram Beizai," in Anonymous, ed., *21 Sal: Az Amu Sibilu ta Mosaferan. Moruri bar Athar-e Bahram Beiza'i beh Bahaneh-ye Jashnvareh-ye Vinnale* (Vienna: Markaz-e Esha'eh-ye Iranshenasi, 1995), 38–48; Zhaleh Amuzegar, "Raz-ha-ye Ostureh dar 'Mosaferan,'" in Zaven Qukasian, ed., *Dar-bareh-ye "Mosaferan"* (Tehran: Roshangaran Publishers, 1371/1992), 29–33. The unexamined binary opposition between myth and history is central to all these readings of Beizai. In the absence of critical attention to the place and function of the mythical in Beizai's cinema, Parham, for example, comes to the outlandish conclusion that "Bashu" is "parenthetical" to Beizai's cinema! See Anonymous, *21 Sal*, 39.

15. Bataille, *The Absence of Myth*, 48.

16. See Lahiji, *Sema-ye Zan*, 54–60. Lahiji has a similarly "motherly" reading of "Perhaps Some Other Time" in *Sema-ye Zan*, 66. In both these cases, Lahiji's

laudable social concerns about the fate of Iranian mothers dull her critical reading of Beizai's cinema.

17. These are motif-index A 625 and motif-index A 625.1 in Stith Thompson's *Motif-
Index of Folk Literature* (Bloomington: Indiana University Press, 1960).
18. See Alan Dundes's editorial note in Dundes, *Sacred Narratives*, 182.
19. For the full version of Professor Numazawa, see K. Numazawa, *Die Weltanfänge
in der Japanischen Mythologie* (Paris: Lucerne, 1946). For a short version of it, see
Dundes, *Sacred Narratives*, 182–192.
20. K. Numazawa, "The Cultural-Historical Background of Myths on the Separation of Sky and Earth," in Dundes, *Sacred Narratives*, 191.
21. Ibid.
22. Ibid., 192.
23. Ibid.
24. Ibid., 183.
25. Bataille, *the Absence of Myth*, 48.
26. Th. P. Van Baaren, "The Flexibility of Myth," in Dundes, *Sacred Narratives*, 222.
27. The best collection of essays on Beizai's "Travelers" is to be found in Qukasian,
Dar-bareh-ye "Mosaferan."
28. Shaykh Ahmad Ahsa'i, "Physiology of the Resurrection Body," in Henry Corbin,
Spiritual Body and Celestial Earth: From Mazdean Iran to Shi'ite Iran (Princeton: Princeton University Press, 1977), 180. Except for minor modification,
I use Corbin's translation of his extract from *Kitab Sharh al-Ziyara*. Corbin's
book contains excellent excerpts from the works of Suhrawardi in the sixth/
twelfth century to Sarkar Agha in the fourteenth/nineteenth, on the issue of
"body," which is of concern to me here. But I dissociate myself completely from
Corbin's outlandish interpretations of these texts in the first part of the volume.
29. Ahsa'i, "Physiology of the Resurrection Body," 180.
30. Ibid., 181.
31. Ibid.
32. For the centrality of all these Aristotelian references in Islamic astronomy, see
George Saliba, "The Role of the Astrologer in Medieval Islamic Society," *Bulletin
d'Études Orientales* 44 (1992), 45–67. For more detailed accounts, see George
Saliba, *A History of Arabic Astronomy: Planetary Theories during the Golden Age of
Islam* (New York: NYU Press, 1994).
33. L. V. Vaglieri and G. Celantano, "Trois Epitres d'Al-Kindi," *Annali, Instituto Ori-
entale di Napoli* 34 N.S., 24 (1974), 523–562, 537, as quoted in George Saliba, "The
Development of Astronomy in Medieval Islamic Society," in Saliba, *A History of
Arabic Astronomy*, 55.
34. Ahsa'i, "Physiology of the Resurrection Body," 182–184.
35. Ibid., 183.
36. Ibid.
37. Ibid., 184.
38. Ibid., 185.

Afterword

Common Ground, Contested Terrain

JOAN W. SCOTT

These days when one thinks of Jews and Muslims it is as irreconcilable enemies with little in common beyond mutual dislike for one another's politics and religious practices. At least in public discourse, the "clash of civilizations" has framed the relationship of the two groups, with Jews identified as belonging to Europe and "the West," and Muslims seen as the representatives of the "East." From the Western side, the contrasts usually offered are between modernity and tradition, reason and aggression, civility and terror, freedom and oppression, democracy and theocracy. On the Muslim side, the contrasts employed are most often between morality and materialist excess, modesty and promiscuity, collective identity and rampant individualism, nationalism and colonialism. Despite the long history of anti-Semitism, which depicted Jews as unassimilable "others" in the countries of the West, Jews are now placed on the side of the West. This is true whether they are being denounced as agents of Western imperialism or defended as the embodiment of Judeo-Christian culture. Some of the enflamed rhetoric has to do with the politics of the state of Israel as it justifies its settler colonialism in terms of a civilizing mission; some of it is the result of the post 9/11 emphasis on security as the ultimate good provided by nation-states; some of it is a consequence of the Manichean logic of the war on terror.

Feminists have not been exempt from participation in this discourse. Across the divide, discussions have been difficult, whether the issue has been the fate of Palestine or the right to wear headscarves in public schools. If feminists are said to share a commitment to women's emancipation, there have nonetheless been bitter struggles over the meaning of the term, including whether religious practice (any? all? which?) can be reconciled with the exercise of free agency. Attempts by secular and religious (Muslim) feminists (in France, in Turkey) to find common ground have foundered on the issue of homosexuality, an unacceptable practice in the eyes of the religious women, a healthy sign of sexual democracy for their secular counterparts. In contrast, efforts to bring Muslim and Jewish feminists together have often been hampered less by religious differences than by political ones, stemming from or leading back to the turmoil in the Middle East and particularly to the way in which Israel figures in those politics.

In this tumultuous context, the conference that initially inspired this volume of essays was a courageous and welcome intervention— not because it took up or took sides in the conversation as I have been describing it, but precisely because it did not. Instead, it offered an alternative way of thinking about Islam and Judaism and about the feminisms related to these intertwined traditions. The emphasis, even in the more literary presentations, is on history and on the complex relationships between Islam and Judaism that a historical approach reveals. Although the essays are not technically formal exercises in deconstruction, their combined effect is nonetheless that—a dismantling or displacement of the binary construction that represents Muslims and Jews as opponents in a global war to the death; an insistence on the variability and multiplicity of groups and identities within each of the opposing categories; a refusal to deal in reductive categorizations that serve only to mask the interdependence and interconnections between the divided terms. We are invited to think of Islam and Judaism together, as the similarities and differences between them emerge in specific contexts, and as they are revealed in a variety of texts, from ancient medical prescriptions to contemporary cinematic productions.

These "kindred religious traditions"[1] share a common history "extending from the Euphrates and Iraq all the way to early modern Spain. The origins of the legal systems in both societies have roots in the ancient Middle East and the histories of the two communities illustrate that they were in constant contact through long periods of time."[2] These "people of the book" share a tradition in which law takes written and oral form and in which the local interpretation of texts takes the place of the centralized orthodox pronouncements more typical of Catholicism. Of course, the interpretations have a history. In Lisa Fishbayn Joffe's account of family courts in Mandate Palestine, the assignment of cases relating to women and children to religious authorities worked to the disadvantage of wives in matters of inheritance and remarriage, and of young women on the question of the age of marriage. At that moment British administrators sided with conservative religious authorities against the demands of feminists both in Britain and in Palestine. More recently, in Israel, Muslim women have strategically turned to shariʿa family courts instead of Israeli civil courts on matters of divorce, child custody, and the like because they find that those courts offer "a more progressive interpretation of Islamic law" on questions of women's rights. There is, at the moment, greater flexibility for women in shariʿa courts than for orthodox Jewish women in rabbinic courts, the result not of some intrinsic difference between the religions, but because of the positioning of the different groups in Israeli society.[3]

The kindred traditions have shared stories that are nonetheless differently inflected, as Lori Lefkovitz's deft reading of the Joseph story points out. For Islam, Yusuf is a more "consistently virtuous hero" who "embodies a more secure masculinity," while the Hebrew Yosef is "positioned ambivalently, [as] a site of projective anxiety about masculinity."[4] These tales reveal less about some inherent gender typing specific to each religion than they provide insight into the history of religious representations as they are articulated in moments of contest and/or consolidation.

On the question of women there are overlapping accounts as male medical or religious authorities confront the enigma of sexual difference. Marion Katz's nuanced study tracks male appropriation of women's experience of menstruation in early Islamic law while Charlotte

Fonrobert shows us how rabbinic legal texts grappled with the assignment of meaning to androgynous bodies that defied the binary logic of
masculine/feminine, male/female. In both instances we see not a case
of prior knowledge (or existing orthodox belief) conferred by religion
on experience, but the ways in which religious doctrine, religious outlooks, are formulated in interaction with the materiality (in this case)
of bodies. Women and their reproductive bodies are also an issue in
contemporary Iran. Soraya Tremayne's chapter indicates that the use of
reproductive technologies is regulated in the interests of state population policies in conjunction with (but not determined by) Shi'a religious teaching. "Modernity and globalization," she writes, "combined
with cultural practices and religious beliefs, have redefined the boundaries of interaction between men and women in unexpected ways."[5] In
her piece, theocracy is not immune to changes that sometimes work
to the benefit of women as child bearers and child rearers. The point is
that no single religious determinism is at work.

It is instructive to pair Catherine Warrick's chapter on honor killings
in Muslim communities with Andrea Siegel's on domestic violence as it
was represented in early Zionism. In the Warrick chapter we learn that
"there are striking similarities . . . between honor killing and the more
familiar Western phenomenon of 'crimes of passion,'" although there
are also differences.[6] Honor killings are usually carried out by fathers or
brothers against a daughter or sister who has shamed the family; crimes
of passion are usually enacted by husbands or lovers against a woman
who has committed adultery or simply broken with her partner. In
either case the laws relating to these crimes are "secular in origin." Their
social meaning may be related to religion (in the case of honor killings), but they are not based in Islamic law. "That honor killings still
find some accommodation in Arab legal systems is evidence not of the
fundamental 'Islamicness' of these systems, but of the power of cultural
claims; where cultural authenticity is at issue, as in postcolonial states,
the state has a tactical interest in making use of cultural elements to
bolster its own legitimacy."[7] Even so, honor killings have become evidence to their critics of the religious pathology of Muslims. Andrea Siegel's piece illustrates how the stereotype of aggressive, murderous Arabs
was created in Zionist literature in the nineteenth and early twentieth
centuries. The fiction Siegel analyzes offers a more complicated vision

of the relationships between Arabs and Jews than the outcomes or morals of the stories. Jewish women fall in love with Arab men; Arab men are neighbors and collaborators with Jews on the land—these are relationships entertained and then rejected in the fictional accounts. At the end, the depiction of virtuous Jews—women and men—is achieved in contrast to representations of aggressive, violent Arabs, perpetrators of domestic violence. And in this way were "created boundaries between Arab and Jew, contributing to the Jewish self-separation process from the Palestinian Arabs that arguably continues to this very day."[8]

Orit Bashkin's chapter challenges the idea that Jews can be talked about as a single category. She reads the autobiography of an Arab Jew (a Mizrahi) who migrates with her family from Iraq to Israel to show how complicated and varied were identities of Jews of many different origins and cultures in the new Zionist state.

> The autobiography exposes a few circles of identity: the Jewish, as a member of a minority group in Iraq who was forced to migrate to Israel; the Iraqi, an identity formed in Baghdad, its schools , and its politics, and preserved in Israel; the Mizrahi; and the Israeli. . . . Shoshanna finds little in common with certain Ashkenazi women in the kibbutz. . . . When characterizing her identity, she never uses the phrase "Arab-Jewish"; the word "Arab" is used to depict the Muslim and Christian inhabitants of Iraq. In Iraq, religious identity—that is, being Jewish—is of paramount importance, whereas in Israel, the word Mizrahi is utilized in a binary with Ashkenazi, native Israeli, while the concept "Iraqi" accentuates the group of Jews with whom she identifies most.[9]

So much for the clear opposition between Jews and Arabs or Jews and Muslims. Although there is no companion piece to Bashkin's in this volume, a similar description of the complexities of Muslim identity (Sunni, Shia, Middle Eastern, Asian . . .) could be developed (and indeed has been elsewhere). Two clearly distinct, opposing entities (the Jewish and the Muslim) exist only in the polemics of ideologues and politicians!

Finally, what of feminism? Susannah Heschel's essay finds points of convergence for Muslim and Jewish feminists: the struggle to achieve equality within their respective religious frameworks; the need to counter "Orientalist" representations at once historical and contemporary; the difficulty of arguing that change is possible within religious traditions dismissed by secular feminists as inherently and unalterably patriarchal; the temptation to assert the singular superiority of one's religion against all others. But she insists as well on points of difference, thus refusing a universalizing and essentializing notion that assumes a commonality of womanhood that transcends all the differences of history and politics. Jews were long wanderers in diasporic exile; the state of Israel was meant to solve the national question. But Heschel suggests that "the national question remains profoundly unresolved today." And, as Bashkin's essay reminds us, there is surely even disagreement about what a common Jewish feminist identity (Ashkenazic? Sephardic? Mizrahi?) might mean. Muslim women, Heschel says, "were long accustomed to living under Muslim rulers."[10] It is only recently that migrations to Europe and the United States have "posed new challenges to the transnational nature of Islamic identity." Still, the situation for women of Islamic faith differs profoundly depending on where they reside and it is hard to imagine a single transnational Islamic feminism emerging any time soon. Rather, feminist efforts of both Jews and Muslims seem to be more local and piecemeal, whether they involve rereadings of the Old Testament or the Qur'an. The fractured nature of these feminist religiously based movements is not a sign of weakness or incoherence. Rather it is symptomatic of the complex histories that at once unite and divide us.

The achievement of this book, it seems to me, is to demonstrate how rich and diverse are the commonalities and differences among us. Commonalities not based on sameness but on shared and interconnected histories. Differences, the fruit of those same histories, the results of processes of change in which we (women, feminists, Muslims, Jews) are both cause and effect. An appreciation of this complex history undermines the easy and misleading invocations of "axes of evil" and "clashes of civilization," replacing them with more nuanced understandings of how individual and collective identities are formed, how they are instantiated by custom and by law (secular and religious), how they are resisted and transgressed (feminism being a prime example), and how they change.

NOTES

1. This term is used by Lori Lefkovitz in her essay "Not a Man: Joseph and the Character of Masculinity in Judaism and Islam," in this volume.
2. Amira Sonbol, "Jewish and Islamic Legal Traditions: Diffusion of Law," in this volume.
3. Lisa Fishbayn Joffe, "Legislating the Family: Gender, Jewish Law, and Rabbinical Courts in Mandate Palestine," in this volume.
4. Lefkovitz, "Not a Man."
5. Soraya Tremayne, "Gender and Reproductive Technologies in Shia Iran," in this volume.
6. Catherine Warrick, "Dishonorable Passions: Law and Virtue in Muslim Communities," in this volume.
7. Ibid.
8. Andrea Siegel, "A Literary Perspective: Domestic Violence, the 'Woman Question,' and the 'Arab Question' in Early Zionism," in this volume.
9. Orit Bashkin, "An Autogiographical Perspective: Schools, Jails, and Cemeteries in Shoshanna Levy's Life Story," in this volume.
10. Susannah Heschel, "Jewish and Muslim Feminist Theologies in Dialogue: Discourses of Difference," in this volume.

Agunah: A halachic term describing a Jewish woman who is "chained" to her marriage. It may refer to a woman whose husband is incapacitated, on a journey, or in an unknown location. In contemporary usage it most often refers to a woman whose husband is unable or unwilling to grant her a divorce, or a *get*.

Fatwa: A term in Islamic legal discourse that refers to the legal opinion of a scholar of Islamic law, either by an officially sanctioned jurist (most often a *qadi*) or a *mufti*. In order to be considered a *fatwa*, the ruling must be given in a formal setting and cover an aspect of Islamic law that has not been addressed by previous jurists.

Fiqh: This is the term for Islamic jurisprudence. It refers to the expanded code of conduct in Islam as discussed in legal opinions and rulings of Islamic jurists. Within Sunni Islam, there are four major schools, or *madhhabs*, of interpretation, while in Shi'i Islam there are two.

Get: A Jewish document certifying a divorce. It is presented by the husband to his wife, freeing her from all laws of adultery, and it returns to her all rights formerly held by the husband according to a Jewish marriage.

Hadith: Most often translated as "tradition," *hadith* are the reports of the deeds and sayings of the Prophet Muhammad. They form part of the basis of Islamic legal interpretation, and they were gathered into large compendiums in the eighth and ninth centuries C.E., after which they were evaluated for their authenticity and sorted into three distinct categories, *sahih* (authentic), *hasan* (good), and *da'if* (weak).

Halacha: This term refers to the entire body of Jewish law, including biblical, Talmudic, and rabbinic law, as well as custom and tradition. It can be translated, in a similarity to the Arabic term *sunna* (from which Sunni is derived) to mean "the way of walking" or "the path." Customarily it does not differentiate between religious and civil duties.

Ijtihad: This term refers to the efforts of an Islamic legal scholar to interpret the Qur'an and hadith through analogical reasoning in order to provide a sound juridical decision. For those qualified to conduct it, known as *mujtahid*, it is considered a spiritual duty.

Ketubah: A Jewish marriage document certifying the responsibilities of the groom in relation to the bride.

Madhhab: A school of Islamic jurisprudence (*fiqh*). There are four primary schools in Sunni Islam (Hanafi, Shafi'i, Maliki, and Hanbali) and two in Shi'i Islam (Ja'fari and Zaidi).

Marja-e taqlid: A term in Shi'i Islam meaning "a source of emulation." It most often refers to a religious authority, such as the Grand Ayatollah in contemporary Iran, and is granted the power to make legal decisions within the confines of Islamic law.

Midrash: This term refers to the body of stories told by rabbinic sages to explain difficult or obscure passages in the Hebrew Bible. They provide exegetical interpretations of the stories in the Hebrew Bible in order to fill in gaps that lend obscurity to religious, moral, and legal teachings.

Mishnah: The first major redaction of Jewish oral tradition, and the first major work of rabbinic literature. It is a foundational source for rabbinic law, first compiled between the years 200 and 220 C.E.

Qadi: This term refers to an Islamic judge who has the authority to provide legal rulings to Muslims. They are meant to rule based on a consensus reading of one of the prevailing *madhhabs* of Islamic jurisprudence, or *fiqh*.

Talmud: This term refers to the compendium of rabbinic law encompassing both the *Mishnah* and the *Gemara*. Among many other things, including Jewish lore and tradition, it is the source from which *halachic* law is derived.

Ulama: This term refers to the class of Islamic legal scholars (sing: 'alim) through any period of Islamic history. Ulama were often engaged in a number of intellectual tasks but were primarily concerned with the interpretation and execution of Islamic law.

Waqf: This Islamic term refers to a pious endowment meant to provide special funds for the service of the Muslim community. Most often, a *waqf* was the primary source of funding for mosque construction. Since *waqf* land was not allowed to be taxed according to Islamic law, it was often a way for wealthy individuals to avoid taxation and at the same time demonstrate their importance in the surrounding community.

Orit Bashkin is Professor of Modern Arab History at the University of Chicago. She received her Ph.D. from Princeton University (2004) and her B.A. (1995) and M.A. (1999) from Tel Aviv University. Her publications include twenty book chapters and articles on the history of Arab Jews in Iraq, on Iraqi history, and on Arabic literature. She has also edited a book *Sculpturing Culture in Egypt* with Israel Gershoni and Liat Kozma, which included translations into Hebrew of seminal works by Egyptian intellectuals. She is the author of the following books: *The Other Iraq—Pluralism, Intellectuals and Culture in Hashemite Iraq, 192–1958* (2009, paperback, 2010), *New Babylonians: A History of Jews in Modern Iraq* (2012).

Hamid Dabashi is the Hagop Kevorkian Professor of Iranian Studies and Comparative Literature at Columbia University. He has written twenty-five books and edited four, contributing chapters to many more. He is also the author of over one hundred essays, articles, and book reviews in major scholarly and peer-reviewed journals on subjects ranging from Iranian studies to world cinema and the philosophy of art. A selected sample of his writings can be found in *The World Is My Home: A Hamid Dabashi Reader*, 2010, coedited by Andrew Davison and Himadeep Mupidi.

Charlotte Elisheva Fonrobert teaches in the Religious Studies Department at Stanford University where she serves as the director of the Taube Center for Jewish Studies. She is the author of *Menstrual Purity: Rabbinic and Christian Reconstructions of Biblical Gender* (2001), which was awarded the Salo Baron Prize for best first book in Jewish Studies, and was a finalist for the National Jewish Book Award in Jewish Scholarship. Together with Martin Jaffee, she edited *The Cambridge Companion to the Talmud and Rabbinic Literature* (2007), and with

Amir Engel the American edition of Jacob Taubes's essays, *From Cult to Culture* (2010).

Susannah Heschel is the Eli Black Professor of Jewish Studies at Dartmouth College. She is the author of *Abraham Geiger and the Jewish Jesus* (1998) and *The Aryan Jesus: Christian Theologians and the Bible in Nazi Germany* (2010), as well as numerous articles and edited books.

Lisa Fishbayn Joffe is Director of the Project on Gender, Culture, Religion and the Law at the Hadassah-Brandeis Institute of Brandeis University. She writes on issues of gender, multiculturalism, and colonialism in Jewish family law and African customary law. Her publications include *Gender, Religion and Family Law: Theorizing Conflicts Between Women's Rights and Cultural Traditions*, with Sylvia Neil (2012).

Firoozeh Kashani-Sabet is the Robert I. Williams Term Professor of History at the University of Pennsylvania. She is the author of *Frontier Fictions: Shaping the Iranian Nation, 1804–1946* (1999) and *Conceiving Citizens: Women and the Politics of Motherhood in Iran* (2011), which won the 2012 book award from the *Journal of Middle East Women's Studies*. She is also author of the novel *Martyrdom Street* (2010). Since 2006, she has been the Director of the Middle East Center at the University of Pennsylvania.

Marion Katz is Associate Professor of Middle Eastern and Islamic Studies at New York University. Her publications include *Body of Text: The Emergence of the Sunni Law of Ritual Purity* (2002), *The Birth of the Prophet Muhammad: Devotional Piety in Sunni Islam* (2007), and *Prayer in Islamic Thought and Practice* (2013).

Lori Lefkovitz is Ruderman Chair of Jewish Studies and Professor of English at Northeastern University where she directs the Jewish Studies Program and the Humanities Center. Her most recent book, *In Scripture: The First Stories of Jewish Sexual Identities*, was a finalist for the National Jewish Book Award (2010). She is coeditor (with Julia Epstein) of *Shaping Losses: Cultural Memory and the Holocaust*, editor of *Textual*

Bodies: Changing Boundaries of Literary Representation, and author of *The Character of Beauty in the Victorian Novel*.

Joan W. Scott is Professor Emerita in the School of Social Science at the Institute for Advanced Study. Her most recent book is *The Fantasy of Feminist History* (2012). Her other publications include *Gender and the Politics of History* (1988), and *The Politics of the Veil* (2007).

Andrea Siegel is Acting Director of the Jewish Communal Leadership Program at the University of Michigan School of Social Work and Lecturer in the University's College of Literature, Science and the Arts. She has taught at Pepperdine University and at SUNY Purchase College. Siegel completed her Ph.D. at Columbia University in 2011; she is a recipient of the Wexner Foundation Graduate Fellowship, the Ralph I. Goldman Fellowship in International Jewish Communal Service at the American-Jewish Joint Distribution Committee, and was a 2012–2013 Fellow at the Frankel Institute for Advanced Judaic Studies at the University of Michigan. Her article, "Rape and the 'Arab Question' in L. A. Arieli's *Allah Karim!* and Aharon Reuveni's *Devastation*," a companion piece to the chapter included in this volume, was published in the Spring–Fall 2012 issue of *Nashim*. Her scholarly interests include service-learning pedagogies, gender in Hebrew culture, interfaith encounters in Jewish texts, and medical humanities.

Amira Sonbol specializes in the history of modern Egypt, Islamic history and law, women, gender, and Islam and is the author of several books, including *The New Mamluks: Egyptian Society and Modern Feudalism* (2000); *Women, the Family and Divorce Laws in Islamic History*; *The Creation of a Medical Profession in Egypt: 1800–1922* (1996); *The Memoirs of Abbas Hilmi II: Sovereign of Egypt* (1998); *Women of the Jordan: Islam, Labor and Law* (2003); *Beyond the Exotic: Muslim Women's Histories* (2005). Professor Sonbol is editor-in-chief of *HAWWA: The Journal of Women of the Middle East and the Islamic World* published by E. J. Brill. She teaches courses on the history of modern Egypt, women and law, and Islamic civilization.

Soraya Tremayne is a social anthropologist, the Founding Director of the Fertility and Reproduction Studies Group, and a Research Associate at the Institute of Social and Cultural Anthropology, University of Oxford. She is the founding editor of Fertility, Reproduction and Sexuality Series at Berghahn Books. She has also served as the Director of International Gender Studies (formerly the Centre for Cross-Cultural Research on Women) at the Department of International Development Studies, Queen Elizabeth House, University of Oxford. Her publications include *Managing Reproductive Life: Themes in Fertility and Sexuality*, ed. (2001); A. Low and S. Tremayne, eds., *Women as Sacred Custodians of the Earth? Women, Spirituality and the Environment* (2001); M. Unnithan-Kumar and S. Tremayne, eds., *Fatness and the Maternal Body: Women's Experiences of Corporeality and the Shaping of Social Policy* (2011); M. Inhorn and S. Tremayne, eds., *Islam and Assisted Reproductive Technologies: Sunni and Shia Perspectives* (2012).

Catherine Warrick is Associate Professor of Political Science at Villanova University and the associate director of Villanova's Center for Arab and Islamic Studies. Her publications include *Law in the Service of Legitimacy: Gender and Politics in Jordan* (2009). Her research on Islamic law in Western countries has been supported by a grant from the National Science Foundation and a Fulbright Scholar award.

Beth S. Wenger is Professor of History and Chair of the History Department at the University of Pennsylvania. Her most recent book is *History Lessons: The Creation of American-Jewish Heritage* (2010). She is also the author of *New York Jews and the Great Depression: Uncertain Promise* (1996), which won the Salo Baron Prize in Jewish History from the American Academy of Jewish Research, as well as *The Jewish Americans: Three Centuries of Jewish Voices in America* (2007), which was named a National Jewish Book Award Finalist.

9/11 (September 11), 19, 20–21
1967 War, 296, 297–298

Abbasid Empire, 31
Abbasi-Shavazi, M. Jalal, 140
'Abd al-Fattah al-Tamimi, 194
Abdullah bin Salam, 57
Abdullah bin 'Umar, 54
Abel, 166–167
Absence of Myth (Bataille), 323
Abū Ḥanīfa, 76, 78, 90
Abu Huraira, 51–52
Abu Musa al-Ash'ari, 50
Abū Yūsuf, 76, 77–78, 82, 101n12
Abu Zahra, Muhammad, 54, 55
Adam, 57
Adelson, Leslie, 36
Adler, Rachel, 32, 34
Adorno, Theodor W., 314
adultery: crimes of passion, 186, 189; "death penalty for adultery," 193–194; French law, 187, 190; Islamic law (sharia or shari'a), 51, 53, 193–194; Qur'an, 51; zina, 193
Afghanistan, 50
Africa, 206–209, 210
Age of Marriage Act (Mandate Palestine, 1929), 235n137
Agudath Israel (Union of Israel), 204
agunah or agunot, 40, 215, 219, 234n103, 234n112, 248, 349
Ahad Ha-am, 245, 254
AḤmad ibn Ḥanbal, 92, 93
Ahmadinejad, Mahmoud, 147n14
Ahmed, Leila, 22, 31
Ahsa'i, Ahmad, 334–337
'A'isha, 36, 74, 89, 95
'Al Em Ha-Derech (In the Middle of the Road) (Levy), 271, 304
Alexander, Elizabeth Shanks, 121n10
Alexandria, 63, 64
Al-Husayn bin Salam, 50

Ali, Ayaan Hirsi, 20
alimony in rabbinical courts, 217
Allegorized Commentary (Philo), 163
Allen, Woody, 163, 164, 175
Alliance Israélite Universelle, 275–276
Almozslino, Shoshanna Arbeli (Irbili), 299
Altneuland (Old New Land) (Herzl), 242
Amin, Qasim, 22
Amir, Elie, 286
Amoraic period, 215
Andalusia, 50, 79, 88
androginos, 112–119; capital crimes, 115; circumcision, 124n44; definition, 6, 107; dissimilarity to men or women, 113; as a "figure" *(Denkfigur)*, 110, 116; gender ambiguity, 114, 116, 120n7; male personal pronoun, 107; men, similarity to, 112–113; Mishnah, 122n26; queer theory, queer identity politics, 109; rabbinic logic of gender duality, 107; *seder androginos*, 115–119; *tumtum*, 114; valuation of, 124n42; women, similarity to, 112–113
anti-feminism, 28
anti-Jewish attitudes, 21–22, 23–24, 280, 281
anti-Muslim attitudes, 19–21, 23–24, 197–198
anti-Semites, 21, 213
anti-Semitism, 26, 288–289, 341
Anwar, Zainah, 32, 33
Arab Agency, 210
"Arab Jew," 239–240, 269, 279, 289, 302
Arab Question *(ha-she'ela ha-'aravit)*, 9, 239, 243–246, 256
Arab riots (1920-1921), 246
Arab Spring, 38
Arab world: honor crimes, 4, 187, 188–189, 192–193; honor killings, 198; state criminal law, 184
Arabic language, 277, 278–279, 303–304
Arab-Israeli conflict, 46, 342
Arabiyyat, Abdul Latif, 195
Arab-Jewish binationalist Zionism, 242–243

Arab-Jewish relations: gender, 239; history, 49–50; Iraq, 239–240; Palestine, 9; Zionist literature, 242–244, 249–250, 251–252, 253, 262
"Arabness," 252
Arabs, Palestinian, 255
Ardebil, Iran, 128, 131
Arieli, L. A., 244, 248–250, 254–255, 262
Aristotle, 335
Asadi, Shahram, 321
Aseneth, 169–170
Ashari school of law, 34
Ashkenazi: holy Jewish towns, 265; intellectuals and bureaucrats, 270; Israel, 270; Levy, Shoshanna, 10, 287–288, 293, 296; Mizrahi Jews (Mizrahim), 270, 288; Ottoman Empire, 218; Palestine, 265n33; women, 345; Zionism, 256; Zionist literature, 249, 251, 252, 261–262, 267n61
Asia, 187
assisted reproductives technologies (ARTs): Muslim Middle East religious leaders, 135–136; reproductive technologies in Shia Iran, 127–128, 135–145
'Aṭā (ibn abī Rabā), 86
Attah, Mohammad, 28
Avicenna Research Centre, 128, 141
Aviel, Jacob, 291–292
al-Azhar, 194
Azur, Israel, 293–294

Babylonian Talmud, 117, 119n4, 123n49, 125n49
Bach, Alice, 161
Baghdad, 276–281, 284–285, 286, 299
Baghdadi Jewish writers, 279
al-Bājī, 90–91
Bakr, Salwa, 184
Bal, Mieke, 161, 168
"Ballad of Tara, The" (Cherikeh-ye Tara) (film), 316–321, 326
Barlas, Asma, 32
Barshan, Gurji, 275
Barthes, Roland, 321–322
Bashkin, Orit, 9–10, 239–240, 345, 346
"Bashu: the Little Stranger" (Bashu: Gharibeh-ye Kuchak) (film), 322–329
Bat Tsiyon (Daughter of Zion) (Burla), 244, 255–262
Bat Yam, Israel, 296
Bataille, Georges, 315, 323, 329

bayd, 75
al-Bayhaqī, 90
Bayuda bint Mymuna, 65
Bebel, August, 260
Bedouin, 211, 226
beit din, 215, 216
Beizai, Bahram, 311–339; archetypical films, 322; "Ballad of Tara, The" (Cherikeh-ye Tara), 316–321, 326; "Bashu: the Little Stranger" (Bashu: Gharibeh-ye Kuchak), 322–329; birth, 311; career, 311–312; celestial bodies, 334–337; "Cherikah," use of, 317; cosmovision, 326, 337; "Crow, The" (Kalagh), 312–313; Enlightenment, 316; evidence-gathering theme, 330; female characters, 10, 240, 312, 313, 319, 322, 331; history or History, 319, 320, 338n14; Iranian culture, reconstitution of, 328; Iranian/Persian mythology, 316–317, 320, 332; Modernity, 315; mythological motifs, 10, 313–320, 323, 324–326, 333–337, 338n14; performing arts, 326, 332; "Perhaps Some Other Time" (Shayad Vaqti Digar), 330–332; phallogocentricism, 331–332; racism theme, 323–324; rationalism, 315; reality, 313–316, 320–321, 333; resurrection of the dead, 333–337; ritual birth, 324–329; "Stranger and the Fog, The" (Gharibeh va Meh), 314–315, 317; suspicions theme, 330; "Thunder Shower" (Ragbar), 312, 313, 332–337; "Travelers," 332–333; "Travelers" opening scene, 311; visuality, 320–321
Ben Gurion, David, 32, 246, 295
Benard, Cheryl, 20
Benjamin, Walter, 278
Ben-Tsiyon, Simkha, 251
Bentwich, Norman, 220, 222
bet din (Jewish court), 31
Biale, Rachel, 46
Bi'alik, Haim Nachman, 300
Bible, 156–168; elder brothers, 167–168; Genesis, 166–167; Joseph (Yosef, Yusuf), 7, 156–157, 158–162, 163, 165–167, 169, 172, 175; menstruation, 74; Pauline gender utopianism, 115, 118; radical readings, 34–35; sexism, 34
birth control, 130–131, 146n9
Blackstone, William, 187
Borochov, Ber, 243
Brenner, Yosef Hayim, 248

Britain, 205–212; Africa, 206–207; child marriage, 235n137; Colonial Office in the British Parliament, 225–226; customary elites, negotiation with, 207; customary law, 207–209; ethnic strife, pacification of, 221; indirect rule, colonial policy of, 205–212, 217; Mandate Palestine (1920-1947), 205–212, 229n33; Mandate system, 209–210; marriage, age of, 225; Palestine, 209, 212; property law, 207; religious rights, Jewish women's, 27; "repugnancy proviso," 208, 211; slavery, 211; trial by ordeal, 211; Wathba (1948), 280–281

Brokhes, Zalmen, 244, 250–255, 262

Brooten, Bernadette, 33

Buber, Martin, 241–243, 250

Buddhism, 25

al-Bukhārī, 53, 86–87, 88

Burla, Yehuda, 244, 255–262, 267

Cain, 166

Cairo, 50, 53

Calder, Norman, 101n12

"Castration or Decapitation?" (Cixous), 36

celestial bodies, 334–337

Cemse Allak, 50

"Chava" (Sholem Aleichem), 247–248

child marriage, 206, 224–225, 226, 235n137

chillul hashem, 213

Christ, 168

Christian Europe, 21–22

Christian feminists, 17, 33

Christianity: Buddhism, 25; child marriage, 225; Iran, conversion to in, 142; Islam, 2, 21, 22, 35; Judaism, 22, 35; patriarchy, 33; veiling, 19; Zoroastrianism, 31

Christians, 21, 65, 211, 269, 334

Cignani, Carlo, 159

Citizenship, Faith, & Feminism (Feldman), 2

civil courts: Israel, 212, 214, 216, 223–224, 343; Jewish courts, 212–213; Mandate Palestine (1920-1947), 218–219, 226–227; rabbinical courts, 212

"Civil Democratic Islam" (Rand Corporation), 20

civil law, 154, 186

Cixous, Helene, 36

Clarke, Morgan, 136

"clash of civilizations," 341–342

colonialism: consequences, 315; European, 24; inequality, 219–220; Israel, 341; Mandate system, 209–210; Middle Eastern discourses about, 268; resistance to, 15; veiling, 41

courts: civil (see civil courts); Gentile, 212–213, 215–216; rabbinical (see rabbinical courts); religious, 216, 218–219, 226; shari'a (see shari'a courts)

crimes of passion, 185–187; adultery, 186, 189; criminal penalties, 186; criminal responsibility, 185–186; definition, 184–185, 199n4; French Penal Code, 186–187; honor killings, 154, 188, 190; Islamic law (sharia or shari'a), 7; Jordan, 186; Judaism, 7; law, 185; masculine honor, 189; premeditation, 190; privileging in law, 185, 190–191; provocation-leading-to-rage-leading-to-homicide-model, 187; provoked fury, 186, 188, 189; reasonable man/woman/person standard, 186–187, 200n12; theoretical neutrality, 186, 199n7; victim's role, 186; Washington State, 199n9; West, the, 184

"crisis in Islamic masculinity," 176

"crisis in masculinity," 175

"Crossing the Styx" (Arieli), 244, 248–250, 254

"Crow, The" (Kalagh) (film), 312–313

culture in producing law, 47–50, 56

Dabashi, Hamid, 10, 240

Daly, Mary, 34

dam, 117

Damascus, 94–95

Daniel Deronda (Eliot), 246

Daughter of Zion (Burla), 9

Daughters of Abraham (Haddad and Esposito), 2

David, 163

democracy: American frontier, 243; Arab Spring, 38; Islamic world, 21, 40; Jewish women, 280; sexual, 342; theocracy, 341

Denkfigur, 110, 116

Der Mabl (The Flood) (Sholem Aleichem), 256

Diaspora Jews, 165, 169, 170, 171, 265n33

Die Welt (newspaper), 241

Die Weltanfänge in der Japanische Mythologie (Numazawa), 328

Dina, 169–170

divorce, 58–61, 214–217; agunah, 40, 215, 234n103, 248, 349; agunot, 219, 234n112; Gentile courts, 215; *'idda,* 65, 85; Islamic law (sharia or shari'a), 18, 33, 58–59; Islamic law of menstrual purity, 85–86, 89; Israel, 154, 205, 212, 233n94; Jewish law (halacha or halachic law or halakhic law), 18, 32, 33, 215; Jewish women, 214–216; Mandate Palestine (1920-1947), 154; Ottoman Empire, 65, 214–215; paternity, denial of, 58–61; qadi, 215; rabbinical courts, 217; spouses cursing one another, 58–61; Talmud, 33

Docherty, Susan, 164, 170–172
domestic policy, 242, 243
domestic violence: correlates, 175; Jewish families, 244; Zionism, 9, 239, 244; Zionist literature, 9, 239, 254, 257, 262
duf'a, 79
Dundes, Alan, 328

East, the, 246, 292
Ebadi, Shirin, 133
education: Iranian females, 131–133; Iraqi females, 276; Jewish women, 22–23, 38, 248; Levy, Shoshanna, 274–276, 294; mission schools, 248
Egypt: Alexandria, 63, 64; Cairo, 50, 53; honor killings, 194; Ikhshidid dynasty, 62; Islamic law (sharia or shari'a), 32; Joseph (Yosef, Yusuf) in, 156, 163, 170–171, 172; Maliki or Mālikī or Malikite school of law, 81; marriage contracts, 61; Muslim feminists, 22; stoning, 53
Egyptian Penal Code, Article 237, 188
Eliot, George, 246
El-Or, Tamar, 28, 38
English common law, 187
Enlightenment, 15, 316. *See also* Jewish Enlightenment *(Haskalah)*
Epstein, Yitzhak, 245
equality: Jewish feminists, 18, 23, 27, 30; male imitation, 30; Muslim feminists, 18, 23; religious, 23
erotic desire in Islamic law (sharia or shari'a), 36–37
Esau, 167–168
Esposito, John L., 2
Esther, 172
ethnicity and gender, 177
"Eurabia," 24, 25

Europe: civil law, 186; colonialism, 24; colonized bodies within, 22; feminist organizations, 23; gender identity, 40; Islamic threat, 21–22; "Islamization of the West," 25; Judaism, 26; Muslims, 40–41, 346; self-understanding as Christian, 24
European Jews, 21, 23–24, 25
European legal codes, 204
Eve, 57
Eve and Adam (Evam, et. al.), 2
Ezer, Eliyahu, 281

Fadlallah, Muhammad Hussein, 194
family law: Islamic law (sharia or shari'a), 195–196; Israel, 4, 8, 154, 212; Judaism, 30; male elites, 153–154; Mandate Palestine (1920-1947), 8, 154, 204, 206, 210–212, 216, 226; menstruation, 30; Muslim feminists, 18; Ottoman Empire, 206; Palestine, 4; patriarchy, 153; rabbinical courts, 8, 212; Turkey, 211
family life: Iran, 7, 128; religious law, 49; reproductive technologies in Shia Iran, 7, 72; Zionism, 239
family planning: Ahmadinejad, Mahmoud, 147n14; Iran, 129, 130–131, 133; Islam, 130; Islamic law (sharia or shari'a), 146n9
family size in Iran, 134, 147n14
family values in Islam, 26
fasting in Islamic law of menstrual purity, 73, 97
"Fateful Day, The" *(Ruz-e Vaqe'eh)* (film), 321
Fāṭima bint 'Abbās ibn Abī'l-Fatḥ, 95
fatwa: definition, 349; honor killings, 194; Islamic law of menstrual purity, 92, 97; issued by women, 30; masturbation, 137; third-party gamete donation, 138–139; virginity, hymenoplasty to restore, 149n34; web page about, 67n16
Fausto-Sterling, Anne, 120n6
Feldman, Jan, 2
femicide law, 190–192
feminism, 17–45; Christian feminists, 17; "clash of civilizations," 342; feminist organizations in Europe, 23; honor killings, 181–182; Iraqi feminists, 280; Islam, 11; Jesus, 34; Jewish feminists (*see* Jewish feminists); Judaism, 11; modesty, 39; Muslim feminists (*see* Muslim feminists); piety, 32; plumbing and electricity, 27; second-wave American Jewish, 108–109,

121n18; women's rights, 23
Fiedler, Leslie, 171
fiqh, 57, 63–64, 349, 350
flâneur, 278
Fonrobert, Charlotte, 6, 71–72, 74, 343–344
For Love of the Father (Stein), 28
foreign policy, 242
fornication, 51, 60
French Penal Code, 186–187
Freud, Sigmund, 171, 173–174, 178n3
fuqaha', 48, 52, 56, 57, 99

Geiger, Abraham, 25
gender: Arab Question, 239; Arab-Jewish
    relations, 239; ethnicity, 177; gendering
    through textual editing, 56–57; God,
    27; "hir," 107, 122n26; Islamic studies, 3;
    mouths, 36; Pauline gender utopianism,
    115, 118; religion, 39; third-person gender-
    neutral pronouns, 107; "ze," 107, 122n26;
    Zionism, 239
"Gender: A Useful Category for Historical
    Analysis" (Scott), 244–245
gender ambiguity, 114, 116, 120n7
Gender and Nation (Yuval-Davis), 262
*Gender and Timebound Commandments in
    Judaism* (Alexander), 121n10
gender duality, 106–125; Babylonian Tal-
    mud, 117; Jewish commandments, 108;
    Jewish feminists, 110–111; Jewish gender
    categories, 106; Mishnah, 6, 108, 111–117,
    118, 119n1; one person (*see androginos*);
    as organizational principle of Jewish
    law, 71–72, 106–107, 109–110, 111, 115, 117,
    118; rabbinic logic of, 106–107; "redness"
    ('odem), 112, 116–117; Seder Nashim,
    115–116, 119; Tosefta, 109, 111, 115; "white-
    ness" (loven), 112, 116, 117
gender inequality, 219–220, 223
gender relations: globalization, 344; Islam,
    126; Jewish law (halacha or halachic law
    or halakhic law), 109; Mishnah, 109;
    modernity, 268; reproductive technolo-
    gies in Shia Iran, 7, 139, 141–142
Gentile courts, 212–213, 215–216
Geonic or Gaonic period, 18, 33, 215–216
Geonim, 33
get, 40, 215, 349
al-Ghamidiyya, 55
al-Ghazali, 130, 146n9
Ghorbaninejad, Masoud, 179n14

ghusl, 83
Ginsberg, Allen, 171
globalization, 126, 344
God: access to, 3; gender, 27; homoeroti-
    cism, 29; Jews, 40; law proclaimed by, 32;
    messengers of, 153; Muslim feminists, 35;
    orgasms from believers' suicides, 28; as
    phallus, 29; Qur'an, 99; rights, 33; veil-
    ing, 28
Goitein, S. D., 49, 50
Golan Heights, 297
Goldziher, Ignaz, 25–26
Goshen, 176–177
Gratz, Rebecca, 23
Great Britain. *See* Britain
Great Rabbinical Court, 223
Greek Orthodox Church, 233n94
Greenberg, Blu, 31
Griffin, Nick, 198

Haaretz (newspaper), 289, 291–292
Haddad, Yvonne Yazbeck, 2
haditha: authenticity of, 52; chains of attri-
    bution/reference, 26; definition, 349, 350;
    Islamic law (sharia or shari'a), 47, 48–49,
    51; Islamic law of menstrual purity, 77,
    82, 88, 90, 92, 98, 101n12, 104n51; Jews in
    early Islam, 54–55; a learned man's ink,
    41; menstruation, 36; *mula'ana*, 59–60;
    Qur'an, 48; science of, 48; stoning, 51–52,
    54–55, 56; withdrawal, 146n9; women's
    actions, precedents for, 35
Haham Bashi, 217–218
Haifa, 304
halacha or halachic law or halakhic law. *See*
    Jewish law
halitza, 222, 223, 234n112
Hallaq, Wael B., 193
Halle-Wolfssohn, Aaron, 247–248
Hamdi, Abd al-Hamid, 258
Hanafi school of law, 32, 76, 84, 90, 96,
    202n33
Hanbali school of law, 92, 202n33
Handley, William, 243
al-Hanooti, Muhammad, 194–195
haredi women (ultra-Orthodox Jewish),
    30–31, 38
Hayd, 77–78, 93, 94
Ha-'ezrah (journal), 251
"He," 33, 112–113, 119n2. See also *androginos*
Hebrew Bible. *See* Bible

Hebrew language, 10, 107, 247, 263n7, 270, 271, 274
"Hebrew law," 219
Hebron/El Khalil, Mandate Palestine, 255, 265n33
Hélie-Lucas, Marie-Aimée, 195
hermaphrodites, 125n46. See also *androginos*
Herzl, Theodor, 241–243
Heschel, Susannah, 5, 15–16, 32, 345–346
heterosexuality, 29, 37
"hir," 107, 122n26
Hizbollah, 194
Holocaust, 288–289, 301
holy edits, 47
Holy Letter, The, 37
homoeroticism, 28–29
honor killings, 181–202; Arab world, 4, 187, 188–189, 192–193, 198; common good, 184; community identity and cohesion, 181; conflation of honor and community identity, 197–199; conflation of honor and passion, 182, 184–192, 189–190; crimes of passion, 154, 188, 190; criminal responsibility, 182, 183–184, 188; criticisms of, 199; cultural preservation, 195, 198; "death penalty for adultery," 193–194; defenders of, 195–198, 201n29; definition, 187; Egypt, 194; fatwa, 194; female chastity, enforcement of, 197; femicide law, 190–192; feminist commentators, 181–182; human rights, 191; individual interests, 184; Islamic law, 7–8; Islamic law (sharia or shari'a), 154, 181, 183, 192–195; Islamic religious leaders, 184, 197; Islamists, 8, 183; Jordan, 154, 194, 200n20, 201n22; law, 185; legal treatment of, 182; murder, 182; private actors, 193–194; privileging in law, 185, 190–191; public opinion, 196; rights, implications for, 190–191; sexual relations, 187; state statuary law, 183; Syrian attitudes, 196; toleration of, partial, 192; traditional social norms, 181, 183–184; Turkey, 50; violence against women, mitigating, 182; the West, anti-Muslim attitudes in, 154, 184, 192–193, 197–198; women's morality, control over, 8, 182, 183, 195
Hoodfar, Homa, 135
Horovitz, Josef, 26
Hosea, 34
Hourani, Albert, 22

hudud, 53
Hultkrantz, Åke, 317
human rights, 32, 191, 203
Hurwitz, Sara, 31
Hussain, Safiya, 50
"Hypocrisy and Light Mindedness" (Halle-Wolfssohn), 247–248

Ibn Abd al-Wahhab, Muhammad, 53. *See also* Wahhabism
Ibn al-Jawzi, 73
Ibn al-Mājishūn, 81
Ibn al-Qāsim, 87
Ibn al-'Arabi, 89
Ibn Ḥajar al-Haytamī, 97–98
Ibn Ḥazm, 88, 100
Ibn Hisham, 62–63
Ibn Qayyim al-Jawzīya, 95–96
Ibn Qudāma, 102n22
Ibn Taymiyya, 52–53, 54, 92–96, 98, 100
'idda, 84–91; divorce, 65, 85; Islamic law of menstrual purity, 84–88, 93, 94, 100; women's interest in, 85
identity politics, 109, 268
IDF (Israeli Defense Forces), 285, 294–295, 297–298, 302
ijtihad, 137, 147n20, 350
Ilan, Tal, 35
'ilm al-rijal, 48
Imru al-Qais, 259
"In the Shadow of the Hermon" (Brokhes), 244, 250–255
infidelity in Islamic law (sharia or shari'a), 58–61
inheritance, 57–58, 123n29, 206, 221–223
Inhorn, Marcia, 136, 139
intersexuality. See *androginos*
Iran, 127–134; Ardebil, 128, 131; art and literature of, 240; Christianity, conversion to, 142; civil code, 127; contraceptive use, 129, 130–131; economic crisis, 127; education, female, 131–133; education, higher, 132; family life, 7, 128; family planning, 129, 130–131, 133; family size, 134, 147n14; infertility rate, 127–128; Islamic law (sharia or shari'a), 127; Islamic Penal Code, 53; Islamic Revolution (1979), 126–127, 129; marriage, 129, 132–133, 148n32; Ministry of Women's Affairs, 128–129; modernization, 127; National Census (1986), 129; population growth, 127,

129–130; population policies, 7, 128–133, 142–143, 145; reproductive technologies in (see reproductive technologies in Shia Iran); single-sex schools, 131; stoning, 50; Tabriz, 140; Tehran, 128, 132; urbanization, 134; women's suffrage, 280; Yazd, 128, 131

"Iranian ART Revolution" (Abbasi-Shavazi), 140

Iranian Jews, 302–303

Iranian Revolution (1963), 50

Iranian women: empowerment of, 133–134, 143–144, 145; fertility treatments, who seek, 144; kin groups, 140–141, 143; labor force participation, 135; literacy rate, 135; politics and art on, influence of, 240; virginity of, importance attached to, 149n34

Iraq, 276–286; anti-Jewish attitudes, 280; Arab-Jewish relations in, 239–240; art and literature of, 240; Baghdad, 276–281, 284–285, 286, 299; Baghdadi Jewish writers, 279; cultures in, 270; female Jewish education, 276; Islamic law of menstrual purity, 76; Jewish women in, 280; Judaism, 303; Mandate for, 210; marriage contracts, 61; military coup (1936), 281; Palestine War (1948), 281–282; stoning, 196; Torah, 275; Wathba (1948), 280–281; Zionism, 282–283; Zionism, demonstrations against, 280; Zoroastrianism, 31

Iraqi feminists, 280

'Irāqī Ibrāhīm (al-Nakha'ī), 86

Iraqi Jewish girls, 270

Iraqi Jewish intellectuals, 239–240, 269

Iraqi Jewish women, 270, 271. See also Levy, Shoshanna

Iraqi Jews: Hebrew language, 270; Israel, 282, 288, 289, 291, 294, 296–297, 300–301; kibbutzim movement, 288; Levy, Shoshanna, 300–301; Mandate Palestine (1920-1947), 300–301; nationalism, 269–270; transregional connections, 273; Woman Question, 240; Zionism, 282. See also Levy, Shoshanna

Iraqi women, 240

Isaac, 168

Ishmael, 167–168

Islam, 1–6, 21–34; birth control, 146n9; body, theory of, 334–336; Buddhism, 25; Christianity, 2, 21, 22, 35; civil and religious practices, 4; family planning, 130;

family values, 26; fatwas, 30; feminism, 11; gender relations, 126; globalization, 126; God, access to, 3; God's messengers, infallibility of, 153; Golden Age of, 50; heterosexuality, 29, 37; human rights, 32; Jewish conversion to, 33–34, 50; Judaism, parallels to, 1–5, 26, 35, 343; legal framework, 6; legal interpretation, 4, 5; legalism, 21; male scholars and judges, 17; menstruation, 5–6; modernity, 126; modernization, 41; Moorish architecture, 26; mosque movement, 27–28, 38; Muftiyah, 30–31; Orientalism, 19, 23–24; patriarchy, 10, 31–34, 57–58; piety, 28; prayer, 3; preservation of, 48; rabbinic literature, 26; rigidity, 126; sexism, 20, 27; toleration for monotheists, 214; West, the, 21; women's rights, 32, 33; women's sexuality, 36; women's status in, 5

Islam and New Kinship (Clarke), 136

Islamic Action Front, 195

Islamic feminism. See Muslim feminists

Islamic identity, 17, 40–41

Islamic jihad. See jihad

Islamic law (sharia or shari'a), 46–65; adultery, 51, 53, 193–194; Ashari school of law, 34; chains of attribution/reference, 26, 48–49, 51; crimes of passion, 7; criminal codes in the Arab world, 184; "death penalty for adultery," 193–194; divorce, 18, 33, 58–59; drunkenness, 53; erotic desire, 36–37; extramarital sex with/by married woman, 193–194; family law, 195–196; family planning, 146n9; fornication, 51, 60; fuqaha', 48, 52, 56, 57, 99; haditha, 47, 51; Hanafi school of law, 32, 76, 84, 96, 202n33; Ḥanbalī school of law, 92, 202n33; holy edits, 47; honor killings, 7–8, 154, 181, 183, 192–195; hudud, 53; infidelity, 58–61; Iran, 127; Israel, 233n93; Jewish law (halacha or halachic law or halakhic law), 18, 33, 46–47; lashing, 54, 193; li'an, 58–60; male scholars, 5–6, 17; Maliki or Mālikī or Malikite school of law, 32; Mandate Palestine (1920-1947), 218; marriage, age of, 129, 133, 224; marriage contracts, 61–65; married vs. unmarried women, 56–57; menstrual purity (see Islamic law of menstrual purity); mula'ana, 58–61; narrative, 48–49; nasab, 136; oral precedents, 47–48, 49;

Islamic law (*continued*)
origins, 46; paternity, denial of, 58–61; patriarchy, 32; powers granted by individual governments, 32; Qur'an, 47, 51; religious change, 49; reproductive technologies in Shia Iran, 72, 135; sexual activity, 61; shari'a courts, 228n18; sorcery, 53; spouses cursing one another, 58–61; stoning, 50–58, 193; sunna, 51, 59; Sunni law, 81, 193; theft, 53; tribalism, 53; United States, 18; Western law, 49; women, 46; women's bodies, control over, 71; women's rights, 228n18; written word, 49
Islamic law of menstrual purity, 5–6, 71, 73–105; ablutions, 75, 79, 83; ambiguous bleeding, 75–76; application of, 80; biomedicine, 98; chronic bleeding (*istiḥāḍa*), 75–80, 93; divorce, 85–86, 89; duration, length of bleeding, 80–81, 86, 92–94, 96, 98, 102n22; empirical evidence, 82–83; fasting, 73, 97, 100n2; fatwa, 92, 97; haditha, 77, 82, 88, 90, 92, 98, 101n12, 104n51; Hanafi school of law, 76, 84, 90, 96; Ḥanbalī school of law, 92; *ḥayḍ*, 77–78, 93, 94; '*idda*, 84–88, 93, 94, 100; Iraq, 76; irregular, intermittent bleeding, 73–74, 76–79, 101n19, 103n40; *Kitāb al-Ḥayd (Book of menstruation)*, 76–77; *Kitāb al-Umm* (al-Shāfiʿī), 78, 81–84; Maliki or Mālikī or Malikite school of law, 79, 81, 84, 87, 90; menopause, 93–94; *Mudawwana* (Mālik ibn Anas), 79–81, 87, 103n40; Muhammad, Prophet of Islam, 75–76, 77, 78, 94; normal or regular flow, 73; prayer, 73, 75, 76, 79, 80, 83, 100n2; *qar'*, 89; Qur'an, 86, 88, 89, 92, 98; ritual purity, as issue of, 75–84; sexual relations, 73, 75; al-Shāfiʿī, 78, 81–84, 87–88, 89–90, 91, 95; thirteenth century and beyond, 91–98; twentieth century, 98; women's knowledge/authority, 74, 88–92, 94–97, 99, 102n22, 136; *wudū*, 75
Islamic Penal Code, 53
Islamic Republic of Iran. *See* Iran
Islamic Revolution (1979), 126–127, 129
Islamic studies, 2, 3, 11, 25–26
Islamic world, democracy and, 21, 40
Islamists, 8, 183
"Islamization of the West," 25
Islamonline.net, 194
Islamophobes, 21

Islamophobia, 3, 18, 26
isnad, 48
Israel, 283–304; 1967 War, 296, 297–298; anti-Semitism, 26; art and literature of, 240; Ashkenazi intellectuals and bureaucrats, 270; Azur, 293–294; Bat Yam, 296; Bedouin, 226; child marriage, 226; civil courts, 212, 214, 216, 223–224, 343; colonialism, settler, 341; creation of, 214; divorce, 154, 205, 212, 233n94; family law, 4, 8, 154, 212; gender inequality, 223; gender relations, 303; Golan Heights, 297; Greek Orthodox Church, 233n94; Haifa, 304; health system (Kupat Holim), 283; identity politics, 268; Iraqi Jewish women, 283; Iraqi Jews, 282, 288, 289, 291, 294, 296–297, 300–301; Islamic law (sharia or shari'a) in, 233n93; Jewish feminists, 342; Jewish law (halacha or halachic law or halakhic law), 32, 204–205; Jewish studies, 3; Judaism, 303; kibbutzim movement, 288; Knesset, 217, 298–299, 300; Labor Union (the Histadrut), 283; levirate marriage, 234n112; Mansi, 290; marriage, 154, 205, 212; marriage, age of, 226; Ma'oz Haim kibbutz, 289; Middle Eastern Jews, 285; Mishmar ha-ʿEmek kibbutz, 284–288; Mizrahi Jews (Mizrahim) in, 270, 271, 289, 296–297, 301–302; Muslim feminists, 342; Muslim women, 223–224; Orthodox women, 2; rabbinical courts, 204–205, 212, 224; religious courts, 226; shari'a courts, 223–224, 233n94, 343; Sha'ar ha-ʿAliya transit camp, 283; Spouses (Property Relations) Law (1973), 232n81; Succession Law (1965), 232n81; technology, modern, 273–274; Tel Aviv, 293; Tiberias transit camp, 291–292; transit camps (ma'abarot), 290–292, 300; ultra-Orthodox, political power of, 204; Wadi Salib riots (1959), 304; widows, 222, 234n112; wills, 232n81; women's equality, 154; women's inheritance rights, 223; women's rights, 224, 272, 343
Israeli Muslim women, 223–224, 343
Israeli women, 227, 240, 294. *See also* Levy, Shoshanna
istiḥāḍa, 75–80, 93
istikbar, 34

Jabotinsky, Vladimir, 245
Jacob, 167, 170

Japanese mythology, 326
jasad, 334–335, 336
Jerusalem, Mandate Palestine, 265n33
Jesus, 33, 34
Jewish Agency for Israel, 204
Jewish Agency for Palestine, 210
Jewish Antiquities (Hellenistic text), 164
Jewish Chronicle (newspaper), 247
Jewish courts, 212–213
Jewish Enlightenment (*Haskalah*), 22, 243,
    247–248, 263n7
Jewish feminists, 108–111; Arab-Israeli con-
    flict, 342; cultural conflict, 15; equality, 18,
    23, 27, 30; exclusion of women from Jew-
    ish man's religious life, 108–109; exclu-
    sion of women from producing rabbinic
    intellectual culture, 110; future of, 118;
    gender duality, 110–111; Israel, 342; male
    imitation, 30; Muslim feminists, 17–18,
    26–27, 35, 345–346; niddah, 30; origins,
    22–23; patriarchy, 31–34; public wor-
    ship, 18; rabbinic literature, 27; religious
    change, 41; religious rights, 23; religious
    texts, 35, 37–38, 39
Jewish holidays, 285–286
Jewish identity, 17
Jewish law (halacha or halachic law or hal-
    akhic law): agunah, 40, 215, 234n103,
    248, 349; bet din (court), 31; chains of
    attribution/reference, 26, 48–49; divorce,
    18, 32, 33, 215; gender duality (*see* gender
    duality); gender inequality, 219–220;
    gender relations, regulation of, 109;
    Gentile courts, 212–213, 215; holy edits,
    47; Islamic law (sharia or shari'a), 18, 33,
    46–47; Israel, 204–205; levirate marriage,
    222; male scholars, 5–6, 17; marriage,
    32; marriage, age of, 224; married *vs.*
    unmarried women, 56–57; menstruation,
    71, 123n36; narrative, 48–49; non-Jewish
    courts, 214; oral precedents, 49; origins,
    46; Orthodox religious authorities,
    204–205; Palestine, 212; powers granted
    by individual governments, 32; religious
    aspect of, 219; religious change, 49; ritual
    purity, 74; sexual relations, 61; tolera-
    tion of by dominant legal authorities,
    212; Torah law, 214; Tosefta, 109, 111, 115;
    women, 46; women's bodies, control
    over, 71; women's inheritance rights, 221;
    written word, 49

Jewish maleness, stereotype of, 163, 164,
    175–176
Jewish studies, 2, 3, 11, 37
"Jewish Woman's Zion" (Buber), 241–243
Jewish women: agunah, 40; agunot, 219,
    234n112; democracy, 280; divorce,
    214–216; education, 22–23, 38, 248;
    Enlightenment, 15; foreign literature,
    exposure to, 247; Gentile courts, 215–216;
    haredi (ultra-Orthodox Jewish), 30–31,
    38; Iraq, 280; irreligion, charged with,
    246–257; Islam, conversion to, 33–34;
    maskilim, 247; Muslim women, 1–2; New
    Jewish Women, 256; non-Jewish courts,
    215; non-Jewish men, 247–248, 251, 262;
    Orthodox, 2, 3, 31; as Rabbah, 31; reli-
    gious law, 16; religious rights, 27; rights,
    15; self-representation, 4–5; statuses, 239;
    tefillin, 30; United States, 2; weaving
    wool, 35; widows, 221–223, 234n112; Zion-
    ism, 241–242, 267n61, 283
Jews: "Arab Jew," 239–240, 269, 279, 289, 302;
    Arab Palestinians, 255; Ashkenazi (*see*
    Ashkenazi); assimilation, 341; customs,
    17; Diaspora Jews, 165, 169, 170, 171; early
    Islam, 54–55; East, the, 246; European,
    25; exile, 40; God, 40; haditha on, 54–55;
    holy Jewish towns, 265; infantile dread,
    174; Iraq (*see* Iraqi Jews); Islamic studies,
    25–26; Kurdish, 291, 302; Mizrahi (Miz-
    rahim) (*see* Mizrahi Jews); "Muscle Jew"
    or "muscular Jew," 176, 180n29; Ottoman,
    213; Ottoman Empire, 25; Palestinian,
    218; Sabras, 285; Sephardi, 218, 256–257,
    261, 262, 265n33; shari'a courts, 213; Turk-
    ish, 302–303; United States, 2; West, the,
    246, 341; the West, 3
jihad, 19
jism, 334–335
Joffe, Lisa Fishbayn, 8, 153–154, 343
Jordan: crimes of passion, 186; honor crimes,
    187; honor killings, 154, 194, 200n20,
    201n22; personal status law, 32
Jordanian Penal Code, Article 98, 190
Jordanian Penal Code, Article 340, 188, 190
Joseph (Yosef, Yusuf), 7, 153, 155–180; Abel,
    166; Allen, Woody, 163; angelic status,
    157; arrogance, 166; beauty, 157, 159, 162–
    165, 167, 169; Biblical stories, 7, 156–157,
    158–162, 163, 165–167, 169, 172, 175; boast-
    fulness, 163; boyhood, 156;

Joseph (*continued*)
  brother (Judah), 157; brother (Reuben), 157; brothers, 156, 162, 163, 165, 166, 167–168, 172–173, 176, 180n19; business wisdom, 165; circumcision, 163; coat, 156, 163, 165–166; communal unconscious, 158; Diaspora Jews, 165, 169, 170, 171; Divine will, 166; as dreamboat, 175; dreams, 156, 162, 165, 174; effeminacy, 162; Egypt, 156, 163, 170–171, 172; father (Jacob), 155, 163, 165–166, 167–168, 170, 171, 174; Freud, 173–174; hard work, 165; heroism, 163; hubris, 166; imprisonment, 158; infantile dread, 174; Iranian television, 163, 164; Islamic stories, 153, 162; Jewish maleness, stereotype of, 163, 164, 175–176; Jewish stories, 153, 162–163, 172, 177; "Joseph and the Amazing Technicolor Dream Coat," 157, 163; Klein, Melanie, 173–175; literary descendants, 171; loyalty, 165; lust, 166; magnanimity, 173; manliness, 162; Mann, Thomas, 161, 163, 168; marriage, 169–170; masculinity, 7, 153, 155, 157, 162, 165, 175, 343; megalomania, 168; Midrash, 156–157, 158–159, 163, 166–167, 170, 178n7, 180n19; moral strength, 162; Moses, 172; Muhammad, Prophet of Islam, 164; omnipotence, 174; Pharaoh, 156, 164–165, 169, 170, 172, 176–177; physical strength, 162; piety, 158; Potiphar, 156, 165, 169; Potiphar's wife (Zuleika), 157, 158–162, 165–166, 168–170, 177, 179n14; Qur'anic stories, 7, 153, 156, 157, 160–162, 164, 165–166, 168–169, 170, 174–175; as role model, 171–172; self-consciousness, 165; self-control/restraint, 157, 164, 174; sexual desirability, 157; sin, 178n7; sister (Dina), 169–170; slanderer, 166; slavery, 156, 172, 176; suffering, 176; Talmud, 178n7; as teen idol, 163; virtue, 157; wife (Asenath), 169–170; willfulness, 160–161; worry, 165, 176; Zaphenath-paneah, 169
Joseph and Aseneth (Hellenistic text), 164, 170
"Joseph and the Amazing Technicolor Dream Coat" (musical), 157, 163
Joseph and Zuleika (Persian story), 160–161
Josephus (Flavius Josephus), 49
Judah, 157
Judaism, 1–6, 26–34; Christianity, 22, 35; Christians, 21; civil and religious practices, 4; commandments, 108; crimes of passion, 7; de-eroticization of, 29; Europe, 26; exclusion of women from Jewish man's religious life, 108–109; exclusion of women from producing rabbinic intellectual culture, 110; family law, 30; feminism, 11; God, access to, 3; heterosexuality, 37; Islam, parallels to, 1–5, 26, 35, 343; Israel, 303; legal framework, 6; legal interpretation, 4, 5; legalism, 21; Levy, Shoshanna, 303; male scholars and judges, 17; marriage, 57, 65; mashgichim (religious supervisors), 32; Moorish architecture, 26; niddah, 30; Orientalism, 19, 23–24; patriarchy, 10, 31–34, 110; piety, 28; prayer, 3; preservation of, 48; Rabbah, 31; rabbinic literature, 26; sexism, 27; stoning, 54–55; tefillin, 30; women rabbis, 30; women's sexuality, 30, 36; women's status, 5, 21
Judeo-Christian tradition, 2, 11n1, 341
Jüdischer Frauenbund (Jewish Women's Organization), 23
Julius Caesar (Mickiewicz), 321

Kabak, Aaron Abraham, 256
kafir, 56
Kafka, Franz, 171
Kaplan, Amy, 242
Katz, Marion, 5–6, 71, 136, 343
Kemp, Adriana, 304
ketubah or Ketubot or katb al-kitab, 33, 35, 61–62, 221, 223, 350
khabīr, 99
Khadīja bint ʿAlī al-Anāsrī, 95
Khamenei, Ali, 133, 138
Khatami, Mohammad, 133
Khomeini, Ruhollah, 129, 131, 137
khul, 224
Kitāb al-Aṣl (anthology), 76–77, 101n12
Kitāb al-Ḥayd (Book of menstruation), 76
Kitāb al-Umm (al-Shāfiʿī), 78, 81–84
Klausner, Yosef, 246
Klein, Melanie, 173–174, 175, 178n3
Knesset, 298–299
Knesset Israel (Hebrew People Living in the land of Israel), 217, 298–299, 300
Kook, Abraham Isaac, 245
Kurdish Jews, 291, 302
Kurds, 269
Kurosawa, Akira, 326

Kutty, Ahmad, 194
Kuwait, Muslim women in, 2

Lafraie, Najibullah, 179n9
Lahiji, Shahla, 312, 318, 323
law: African, 207; civil law, 154, 186; crimes
    of passion, 185; criminal codes in the
    Arab world, 184; culture in producing,
    47–50, 56; customary law, 207–209;
    European legal codes, 204; family law
    (see family law); femicide law, 190–192;
    French law, 190; "Hebrew law," 219; his-
    torical change and production of, 66;
    honor killings, 185; Islamic (see Islamic
    law (sharia or shari'a); Islamic law of
    menstrual purity); Jewish (see Jewish
    law (halacha or halachic law or halakhic
    law)); legal frameworks, 6; legal in-
    equalities, 191; legal interpretation, 4, 5;
    legalism, 21; Mandate system, 209–210;
    personal status law, 32, 220; political
    rule-of-law norm vs. moral norms, 185;
    privileging of a particular set of homi-
    cides, 185, 190–191; property law, 207;
    rabbinic (see Jewish law (halacha or hala-
    chic law or halakhic law)); "reasonable
    man/woman/person" standard, 186–187,
    200n12; "repugnancy proviso," 208, 211;
    social norms, 191–192; state criminal law,
    184; succession law, 221–222; traditional
    practices, "authentic," 183; trial by ordeal,
    211; Western law, 49; wills, 217, 232n81
Lawal, Amina, 50
Layish, Aharon, 226
Leah, 170
Lebanese Penal Code, Article 562, 188
Lebanon, 210
Lefkovitz, Lori, 7, 153, 343
legal pluralism, 203–204
Levada (Alone) (Kabak), 256
levirate marriage, 112, 123n32, 123n33, 222,
    234n112
Lévi-Strauss, Claude, 24–25, 39
Levy, Shoshanna, 271–310; 1967 War, 296;
    ability to study, 294; 'Al Em Ha-Derech
    (In the Middle of the Road) (autobiog-
    raphy), 271, 304; Arabic language, 277,
    278–279, 303–304; as Arabic speaker,
    9–10; Ashkenazi, 10, 287–288, 293, 296;
    aunt (Farha), 273; aunt(Hanna), 272;
    Azur, Israel, 293–294; Baghdad, 276–281,
    284–285, 286, 299; Bat Yam, Israel, 296;
    birth, 9, 271; brother (David), 290–291;
    brother (Ephraim), 277; brother (Jo-
    seph), 277; companionship, 299; edu-
    cation, religious, 274–275; education,
    secular, 275–276; education in Israel, 294;
    father (Hesqel), 274, 277–278, 282, 284,
    293; Germany (1985), 299, 301; grand-
    mother (Khatun), 272, 273; grandmother
    (Simha), 272, 273; Hebrew language, 10,
    274; heroism, 291, 304; herring, 286–287;
    Holocaust survivors, identification with,
    299, 301; husband (Mishal), 296–297,
    298; identities of, 240, 302; IDF (Israeli
    Defense Forces), service in, 294–296;
    Iraqi identity, 274, 279, 301, 302; Iraqi
    Jews, affiliation with, 300–301; Israel,
    leaving Iraq for, 282; Israel, life in, 9–10;
    Israeli identity, 300–301; jail, 295; Jewish
    holidays, 285–286; Judaism, 303; Knesset
    appearance, 298–299; Kurdish Jews, 302;
    Labor Party, 299, 301; Mansi, Israel, 290;
    marriage, 296; Me'ir, Yosef, 299; Mish-
    mar ha-'Emek kibbutz, 284–288; Mizrahi
    identity, 10, 240; Mizrahi Jews (Mizra-
    him) in Israel, tensions between, 297;
    Moroccan Jews, 293, 294, 302; mother
    (Nazima), 272, 273–274, 284, 290–291;
    mysticism, 299; nursing, 293; Palestine
    War (1948), 281–282; politics, awareness
    of, 280; sexual openness of others, 295;
    Shabbat dinner, 285–286; Sha'ar ha-'Aliya
    transit camp, 283, 290; sister (Farha),
    272; sister (Gurgia), 272, 273, 275; sister
    (Nazima), 272, 273; teaching career, 298;
    teaching seminary, 293–294; Tel Aviv,
    293; uncle (Ezra), 281–282; uncle (Iliya),
    272; uncle (Rahamin), 281–282; Wathba
    (1948), 280–281; widows' organizations,
    involvement in, 298–299; Woman Ques-
    tion, 279; women in her family, 271–274
Lewis, Bernard, 20
Libson, Gideon, 18, 33
li'an, 58–60
lobola, 208

madhhab, 63, 65, 147n20, 349, 350. See also
    Islamic law (sharia or shari'a)
Magnes, Judah, 245
Mahmood, Saba, 20, 27–28, 38–39
Mahmud b. Ahmad, 65

Maimonides (Moses Maimonides), 50
Ma'iz, 52, 55
Makhlout-Obermeyer, Carla, 146n9
Malamud, Bernard, 171
male scholars and judges, 5–6, 17
Mālik ibn Anas, 53–54, 79–81, 87, 88, 102n22
Maliki or Mālikī or Malikite school of law:
    Andalusia, 88; Egypt, 81; Islamic law of
    menstrual purity, 79, 81, 84, 87, 90; patri-
    archy, 32; *zina*, proof of, 202n33
Mandate Palestine (1920-1947), 203–236,
    244–245; 1929 "events," 255, 261; Age of
    Marriage Act (1929), 235n137; Beersheba
    district, 211; Bentwich, Norman, 220–221;
    Britain, 205–212, 229n33; British colonial
    policy of indirect rule, 205–212, 217;
    child marriage, 206; Christians in, 211;
    civil courts, 218–219, 226–227; collusion
    between authorities and religious elites,
    224; divorce, 154; family law, 8, 154, 204,
    206, 210–212, 216, 226; gender inequality,
    223; Gentile courts, 212–213, 215; Great
    Rabbinical Court, 223; Hebron/El Khalil,
    255, 265n33; Iraqi Jews, 300–301; Islamic
    law (sharia or shari'a), 218; Jerusalem,
    265n33; Jewish widows, 221–223; Jews,
    violence against, 255; Knesset Israel (He-
    brew People Living in the land of Israel),
    217; legal pluralism, 203–204; levirate
    marriage, 222; marriage, 154; marriage,
    age of, 224–226; military occupier,
    229n33; Palestinian Jews, 219; patriarchy,
    221–227; personal status law, 220; rabbin-
    ical courts, 8, 154, 205, 212–220, 216–217,
    219, 223, 226; religious courts, 218–219;
    "repugnancy proviso," 211; Safed, 255,
    265n33; shari'a courts, 216; succession
    law, 221–222; Succession Ordinance
    (1923), 222; Supreme Muslim Council,
    218; Tiberias, 265n33; ultra-Orthodox,
    political power of, 226; ultra-Orthodox
    Jews, 218–219; women's inheritance
    rights, 206, 221–223; Women's Organiza-
    tion for Equal Rights, 234n1–3; women's
    rights, 206, 220–221, 226–227
Mandate system, 209–210
Mandates for Palestine and Iraq, 210
"Manifest Domesticity" (Kaplan), 242
Manji, Irshad, 20
Mann, Thomas, 161, 163, 168
Mansi, Israel, 290

Mansour, Hamza, 195
marja', 137, 139
marja-e taqlid, 147n20, 350
marriage, 56–66; Africa, 208; agunot, 219,
    234n112; beauty, 169; child marriage, 206,
    224–225, 226; *fiqh*, 57, 63–64, 349, 350; in-
    fidelity, 58–61; Iran, 129, 132–133, 148n32;
    Israel, 154, 205, 212; Jewish law (halacha
    or halachic law or halakhic law), 32; Jo-
    seph (Yosef, Yusuf), 169–170; Judaism, 57,
    65; levirate marriage, 112, 123n32, 123n33,
    222; Mandate Palestine (1920-1947), 154;
    married *vs.* unmarried women, 56–57;
    Mishnah, 121n12; premodern Muslim,
    62–63; rabbinical courts, 217; religious
    law, 49; Seder Nashim, 115–116, 119;
    spouses cursing one another, 58–61; tem-
    porary marriage, 137, 148n22, 327; visit
    marriage, 327, 328
marriage, age of: Britain, 225; Iran, 129, 132,
    133; Islamic law (sharia or shari'a), 129,
    133, 224; Israel, 226; Jewish law (halacha
    or halachic law or halakhic law), 224;
    Mandate Palestine (1920-1947), 224–226
marriage contracts, 61–65
masculinity: "crisis in Islamic masculinity,"
    176; "crisis in masculinity," 175; Joseph
    (Yosef, Yusuf), 7, 153, 155, 157, 162, 165, 175,
    343; "muscular Jew," 176; Potiphar, 162
mashgichim (religious supervisors), 32
maskilim, 247, 263n7
Masorti movement, 219
"Master of Dreams" (Fiedler), 171
Mathes, Bettina, 19, 24
ma'abarot, 290–291
Ma'oz Haim kibbutz, 289
Mehran, Golnar, 131–132
Meir, Esther, 288, 290
"men" *(anashim)*, 110
menstrual impurity in Judaism, 123n36
menstrual purity. *See* Islamic law of men-
    strual purity
menstruation: Bible, 74; family law, 30; ha-
    ditha, 36; Islamic law (sharia or shari'a)
    (*see* Islamic law of menstrual purity);
    Jewish law (halacha or halachic law or
    halakhic law), 71, 123n36; menstrual im-
    purity in Judaism, 123n36; Mishnah, 74;
    niddah, 30, 37; Qur'an, 36; religious law,
    6; women's sexuality, 36
"Merciful God" (Molodowsky), 177

Merguerian, Karen Gayane, 160
Mernissi, Fatima, 29, 31, 37
Me'ir, Yosef, 299
Mickiewicz, Adam, 321
Middle East, 187, 269
Middle Eastern Jewish women, 270. *See also*
    Levy, Shoshanna
Middle Eastern Jews, 285
Middle Eastern women, 269
Midrash: definition, 178n6, 350; Genesis
    Rabbah, 156, 166–167; ha-Gadol, 178n6;
    Israelite men, enslaved, 177; Joseph (Yo-
    sef, Yusuf), 156–157, 158–159, 163, 166–167,
    170, 178n7, 180n19; Potiphar's wife (Zu-
    leika), 158–159; Tanchuma, 178n6
Mir-Hosseini, Ziba, 32, 34
Mishmar ha-'Emek kibbutz, 284–288
Mishnah, 111–117; *androginos*, 122n26; defini-
    tion, 350; gender duality, 6, 108, 111–117,
    118, 119n11; gender relations, 109; inheri-
    tance, 123n29; Kiddushin, 108, 111–117;
    levirate marriage, 123n32; marriage,
    121n12; menstruation, 74; "orders" of,
    121n12; valuation of people, 124n42; wives
    weaving wool, 35
mishpat ivri, 219
misogyny, 35
mitzvah, 258
Mizrahi Black Panthers, 304
Mizrahi identity, 271, 296–297, 304, 345
Mizrahi Jews (Mizrahim): Ashkenazi, 270,
    288; Israel, 270, 271, 289, 296–297, 301–
    302. *See also* Levy, Shoshanna
modernity or Modernity, 126, 316, 317
modernization, 22, 41, 127
modesty, 39
Molodowsky, Kadya, 177
Moorish architecture, 26
Moroccan Jews, 293, 294, 297, 302
Moses, 172
mosque movement, 27–28, 38
Motsa, Palestine, 261
Mubyī al-Dīn al-Nawawī, 91–92
Mudawwana (Mālik ibn Anas), 79–81, 87,
    103n40
Muftiyah, 30–31
Muhammad, Prophet of Islam: daughter
    (Fatima Zahra), 164; father (Abdallah),
    62; Fāṭima bint 'Abbās ibn Abī'l-Fatḥ, 95;
    infidelity, 58–61; Islamic law of menstrual
    purity, 75–76, 77, 78, 94; Joseph (Yosef,

Yusuf), 164; Lévi-Strauss, Claude, 24–25;
    mother (Amina), 62; paternity, denial
    of, 58–61; sayings (*see* haditha); stoning,
    51–52, 54; widow ('Ā'isha), 36, 74, 89, 95;
    wife (Khadija), 63, 164
Muhammad ibn al-Ḥasan al-Shaybānī,
    76–78, 81, 82–83, 101n19
Muhammad ibn Sīrīn, 87, 99
Muhammad Pīr 'Alī al-Birgivī, 96, 97
mula'ana, 58–61
"Muscle Jew" or "muscular Jew," 176, 180n29
al-Museimi, Hayat, 195
Muslim feminists, 20–23, 31–38; 9/11, 20–21;
    Arab-Israeli conflict, 342; cultural conflict,
    15; Egypt, 22; equality, 18, 23; family law,
    18; God, 35; Israel, 342; Jewish feminists,
    17–18, 26–27, 35, 345–346; origins, 22–23;
    patriarchy, 31–34; Qur'an, 34–35; religious
    change, 41; religious rights, 23; religious
    texts, 35, 37–38, 39; United States, 20
Muslim men, 176
Muslim men: fatwas issued by, 30; infer-
    tility, 136–137; Islamophobia, 18; Islam's
    sexism, 20; Israel, 223–224, 343; Jewish
    women, 1–2; Kuwait, 2; mosque move-
    ment, 27–28, 38; as Muftiyah, 30–31; op-
    pression of, stereotypes of, 176, 197–198;
    Qur'anic studies, 28, 41; religious law, 16;
    rights, 15; self-representation, 4–5; sexu-
    ality of, control over, 136; statuses, 239;
    United States, 2; veiling, 19, 24, 41
Muslim world, 187
Muslims: customs, 17; Europe, 346; jihad, 19;
    resurrection theory, 334; United States,
    2, 40–41
Mu'tazilite school of law, 34
myth, 313–320, 324–326, 332–337; agricul-
    ture, 328; Bataille, Georges, 315, 323,
    329; Beizai, Bahram, 10, 313–320, 323,
    324–326, 333–337, 338n14; celestial bod-
    ies, 334–337; changeability, 332; colonial
    frontiers, 329; creation myth, 317–318;
    death of, 315, 329; earth-mother, 324, 326;
    history, 338n14; Hultkrantz, Åke, 317;
    Iranian/Persian mythology, 316–317, 320,
    332; Japanese mythology, 326; main func-
    tion, 317; myth making, 319–320; parents
    myth type, 324–326; reality, 313–316;
    resurrection of the dead, 333–337; sky-
    father, 324, 326; Thompson's motif inden
    (Stith Thompson's), 324, 326

*al-nafs*ā, 81
Naggar, David, 279
Najmabadi, Afsaneh, 160
narrative, 48–49
nasab, 136
Nazi Germany, 21
Neriya-Ben Shachar, Rivka, 28
niddah, 30, 37
Nigeria, 50
Nordau, Max, 180n29
North Africa, 79
Numazawa, K., 326, 327, 328

Orientalism, 19, 23–24, 245–246
Orientalist stereotypes, 292
"Orientalizing," 177–178
Orthodox Jewish women, 2, 3, 31
Ottoman Empire, 214–218; Ashkenazi, 218; chief rabbi, 217–218; Christians in, 65; courts, religious, 204; courts, shari'a, 204; courts, state, 204; decline of, 24; divorce, 65, 214–215; European legal codes, 204; family law, 206; Jews, 25; legal pluralism, 204; military power, 21–22; millets, 65; qadi, 218; religious courts, 218; Sephardi, 218
Ottoman Jews, 213
Ottoman Law of Family Rights, 211

Pakistan, 50, 187
Palestine: Arab riots (1920-1921), 246; Arab-Jewish relations in, 9; Ashkenazi, 265n33; Britain, 209, 212; child marriage, 224; English law, 212; family law, 4; Jewish immigration waves, 210, 243, 245; Jewish law (halacha or halachic law or halakhic law) in, 212; Mandate Palestine (*see* Mandate Palestine); Motsa, 261; Rehovot, 246; religious courts, 216; Zarnuka, 246
Palestine Jewish Women's Equal Rights Association, 225
Palestine Order in Council (1922), 217
Palestine Order in Council, Article 51, 218
Palestine War (1948), 281–282
Palestinian Arabs, 210, 246, 255, 259–260
Palestinian Jewish Orientalism, 245–246
Palestinian Jews, 214–215, 218, 219
Palestinian Muslims, 246
Pappenheim, Bertha, 23
paternity, denial of, 58–61
patriarchy: Africa, 207; Christianity, 33;

family law, 153; Hanafi school of law, 32; inheritance and wealth, 57–58; Islam, 10, 31–34, 57–58; Islamic law (sharia or shari'a), 32; Jewish feminists, 31–34; Judaism, 10, 31–34, 110; Maliki or Mālikī or Malikite school of law, 32; Mandate Palestine (1920-1947), 221–227; Muslim feminists, 31–34; origins, 33; Qur'an, 32–33; women's minds, 36
Peretz, Y. L., 247
"Perhaps Some Other Time" *(Shayad Vaqti Digar)* (film), 330–332
personal status law, 32, 220
Peskowitz, Miriam, 35
phallogocentricism, 331–332
Pharaoh, 156, 164–165, 169, 170, 172, 176–177
Philo, 163
piety: feminism, 32; God's orgasms from believers' suicides, 28; Islam, 28; Joseph (Yosef, Yusuf), 158; Judaism, 28; mosque movement, 27–28; social change, 39; ultra-Orthodox Jewish women, 28
Plaskow, Judith, 32
Pliny, 125n46
Politics of Piety (Mahmood), 38–39
population policies in Iran, 7, 128–133, 142–143, 145
position, 170–171, 178n3
Potiphar, 156, 162, 165, 169
Potiphar's wife (Zuleika), 157, 158–162, 165–166, 168–170, 177, 179n14
Powers, David S., 85
prayer: Islam, 3; Islamic law of menstrual purity, 73, 75, 76, 79, 80, 83, 100n2; Judaism, 3
public worship, 18

qadi, 215, 218, 224, 349, 350
qadiman, 81
al-Qaraḍāwi, Yūsuf, 98–99
qar', 89
al-Qubruzi, Wassili, 64–65
queer identity politics, 109
queer theory, 109, 174
Qur'an, 32–35, 54–61, 160–170; abrogation of, 54; adultery, 51; Allah's prophets, infallibility of, 158; *aya* (verses), 54, 56–61; birth control, 146n9; bracketed phrases added to, 56–57; embryo donation, 138; fornication, 51; God, 99; haditha, 48; husbands disciplining wives, 176; Islamic

law (sharia or shari'a), 47, 51; Islamic law of menstrual purity, 86, 88, 89, 92, 98; Joseph (Yosef, Yusuf), 7, 153, 156, 157, 160–162, 164, 165–166, 168–169, 170, 174–175; menstruation, 36; Muslim feminists, 34–35; paternity, denial of, 58–61; patriarchy, 32–33; rabbinic literature, 26; reproductive technologies in Shia Iran, 138; stoning, 52, 55, 56; Sura 12, 156, 164, 179n14; Surat al-Nisa' ("Chapter on Women"), 57; Trust, 89

Qur'anic studies, 28, 41
al-Qurṭubī, 85

Rabbah, 31
Rabbi Yosé, 156–157
Rabbi Yossi (Jose b. Hanina), 107
rabbinic law. See Jewish law (halacha or halachic law or halakhic law)
rabbinic literature, 26, 27, 31
rabbinical courts: alimony, 217; civil courts, 212; divorce, 217; family law, 8, 212; Israel, 204–205, 212, 224; levirate marriage, 234n112; Mandate Palestine (1920-1947), 8, 154, 205, 212–220, 216–217, 219, 223, 226; marriage, 217; wills, confirmation of, 217

Rabī', 83–84
Rachel, 167, 168, 170
Radler-Feldman, Joshua, 245
Rand Corporation, 20
Rapoport, Yossef, 85–86
Raz-Krakotzkin, Amnon, 32
Rebecca or Rebekah, 57, 167
"redness" ('odem), 112, 116–117
Rehovot, Palestine, 246
religion: free agency, 342; gender, 39; holy edits, 47; homoeroticism, 28–29; human rights, 32; women's rights, 32
religious change: Islamic law (sharia or shari'a), 49; Jewish feminists, 41; Jewish law (halacha or halachic law or halakhic law), 49; Muslim feminists, 41
religious courts: Israel, 226; Mandate Palestine (1920-1947), 218–219; Ottoman Empire, 218; Palestine, 216
religious law: civil law, 154; family life, 49; human rights, 203; Jewish women, 16; marriage, 49; menstruation, 6; Muslim women, 16
religious orthodoxy in women, 2

religious rights: Britain, 27; Jewish feminists, 23; Jewish women's, 27; Muslim feminists, 23; United States, 27; women, 22–23
religious texts: bracketed phrases added to, 56–57; Jewish feminists, 35, 37–38, 39; modesty, 39; mosque movement, 27–28; Muslim feminists, 35, 37–38, 39; Muslim women, 28, 41; political undertones, 35; rabbinic literature, 26, 27, 31; study of, 27–28, 37–38, 39, 41
Rembrandt, 159
reproductive technologies in Shia Iran, 126–149; ancient religious laws, 72; assisted reproductive technologies (ARTs), 127–128, 135–145, 147n20; birth control, 130–131; consequences, 7, 72, 139–140, 141, 143; contraceptive use, 129, 130–131; embryo donation, 138; empowerment of Iranian women, 133–134, 143–144, 145; family life, 7, 72; family planning, 129, 130–131; fertility treatments, 139–141, 144; gender relations, 7, 139, 141–142; in vitro fertilization (IVF), 72, 137; infertility, men's, 72, 138, 140, 141; infertility, stigma of, 72, 140, 144; infertility, women's, 136–137, 145; Islamic law (sharia or shari'a), 72, 135; Khamenei, Ali, 133, 138; Khatami, Mohammad, 133; Khomeini, Ruhollah, 129, 131, 137; kin groups, 140–141, 143; marja, 137, 139; masturbation, 137; population policies, 7, 128–133, 142–143, 145; Qur'an, 138; religious authorities, 6–7, 127, 130, 137, 139, 142–143; resistance to, 7; "Shia egg," desire for, 139; stoning, 142; temporary marriage, 137; third-party gamete donation of sperm and eggs, 6, 72, 127, 135, 136–139, 140–141; violence, men's, 141–142; women's reproductive decisions, 133
"repugnancy proviso," 208, 211
Reuben, 157
ritual birth, 324–329
ritual purity: Islamic law of menstrual purity, 75–84; Jewish law (halacha or halachic law or halakhic law), 74
Rohani, Sadeq, 149n34
Roth, Henry, 171
Roth, Philip, 171
Royan Institute, 141
ruh, 334
al-Rumi, Marusa bint Dimitri, 64–65

Sabras, 285
Ṣadr al-Din ibn al-Wakīl, 95
Safed, Mandate Palestine, 255, 265n33
Sahih International, 56–57
Saiving, Valerie, 39
Salafi movement, 53
Salahshoor, Farajollah, 164
salat, 73
Saleh, Su'ad, 30–31
Salinger, J. D., 171
Samuel, Herbert, 225
Samuel ben Nahman, 157, 178n7
Samuel ibn Adiya, 259
Saqr, 'Atiyya, 194
Sarah, 57, 167
Saudi Arabia, 50, 53, 199n3
sawm, 73
Schechina, 213
Schuessler-Fiorenza, Elisabeth, 35
Schwartz, Delmore, 171
Scott, Joan Wallach, 10–11, 244–245
secularization, 32
seder androginos, 115–119
Seder Nashim, 115–116, 119
Sedgwick, Eve Kosofsky, 173
Sephardi, 218, 256–257, 261, 262, 265n33
Sexing the Body (Fausto-Sterling), 120n6
sexism, 20, 27, 34
sexual democracy, 342
sexual relations: extramarital sex with/by mar-
    ried woman, 193–194; honor killings, 187;
    Islamic law (sharia or shari'a), 61; Islamic
    law of menstrual purity, 73, 75; Jewish law
    (halacha or halachic law or halakhic law),
    61; witnesses to, need for, 193
sexuality: erotic desire, 36–37; fornication,
    51, 60; heterosexuality, 29, 37; intersexu-
    ality (see *androginos*); niddah, 30, 37;
    tumtum, 6, 114, 117, 124n42; women's (*see*
    women's sexuality)
al-Shāfi'ī, 53–54, 78, 81–84, 87–88, 89–90,
    91, 95
Shami, Yitzhak, 256
sharia or shari'a. *See* Islamic law
shari'a courts: Islamic law (sharia or shari'a),
    228n18; Israel, 223–224, 233n94, 343;
    Jews, 213; Mandate Palestine (1920-1947),
    216; Ottoman Empire, 204; Palestinian
    Jews, 214–215; women's rights, 228n18
al-Shawkānī, 98
Sha'ar ha-'Aliya transit camp, 283, 290

Shenhav, Yehouda, 269
Shia, 146n9, 147n20, 148n22, 334. *See also*
    reproductive technologies in Shia Iran
"Shia egg," desire for, 139
Shirazi, Sadra, 334
shirk, 32, 33
Shi'is, 269
Shohat, Ella, 268–269
Sholem Aleichem, 247–248, 249, 256
Shoshan, Simon, 48–49
Shurayh, 86
Siegel, Andrea, 9, 239, 344–345
signs, 321–322
al-Siryani, Maryam bint 'Abdel-Ahhad, 65
slavery, 156, 172, 176, 211
Smith, Anthony, 246
Smuts, Jan, 209
social change, 39, 261
Somalia, 53
Sonbol, Amira, 5, 32, 228n18
Soraya, stoning of, 50, 55
Souaiaia, Ahmed, 47
South Africa, 209, 222
Spain, Andalusia, 50, 79, 88
Spain, Christian, 25
Spain, Muslim, 25
Spouses (Property Relations) Law (Israel,
    1973), 232n81
Stein, Ruth, 28, 29
stoning: Iraq, 196; Islamic law (sharia or
    shari'a), 50–58, 193; Judaism, 54–55; re-
    productive technologies in Shia Iran, 142
"Stranger and the Fog, The" *(Gharibeh va
    Meh)* (film), 314–315, 317
Strassfeld, Max, 119n2, 120n7
succession law, 221–222
Succession Law (Israel, 1965), 232n81
Succession Ordinance (Mandate Palestine,
    1923), 222
Sudan, 50
al-Sufur (Unveiling) (newspaper), 258
Sufyān al-Thawri, 76
Sulaymān ibn Yasār, 88–89
Sunday School movement, 23
sunna, 51, 59
Sunni law, 81, 193
Sunnis, 91, 136–137, 146n9, 269
Supreme Muslim Council, 218
Supreme Shari'a Appeals Court, 224
Syria, 31, 53, 91, 194, 196, 210
Syrian Penal Code, Article 192, 189

Syrian Penal Code, Article 242, 190
Syrian Penal Code, Article 548, 188, 189

al-Tabari, 53
Tabriz, Iran, 140
takfiriyyin, 56
Taliban, 53
Talmud: Babylonian Talmud, 117, 119n4, 123n49, 125n49; chains of attribution/ reference, 26; definition, 350; divorce, 33; inferior courts recognized by, 214; Joseph (Yosef, Yusuf), 178n7; non-Jewish courts, 215; sexism, 34
talmud Torah, 110
Taslimi, Susan, 318
Tawhid, 32–33
technology, 273–274
tefillin, 30
Tehran, 128, 132
Tel Aviv, 293
temporary marriage, 137, 148n22, 327
Thompson's motif index (Stith Thompson's), 324, 326
"Thunder Shower" *(Ragbar)* (film), 312, 313, 332–337
Tiberias, Mandate Palestine, 265n33
Tiberias transit camp, 291–292
Tohorot, 116
Torah, 54–55, 213, 275
Torah law, 214
Tosefta, 109, 111, 115
Transjordan, 210
Transvaal Supreme Court, 208
"Travelers" (Beizai), 332–333
Tremayne, Soraya, 6–7, 72, 344
Tristes Tropiques (Lévi-Strauss), 24–25
"Truth from the Land of Israel" (Ahad Ha-am), 245
Tucker, Judith, 194
tumtum, 6, 114, 117, 124n42
Tunis, 53
Turkey, 50, 211
Turkish Jews, 302–303
Turkmans, 269

ulama, 54, 350
United Kingdom, 141–142. *See also* Britain
UN Population Award (1998), 130
United Nations Population Fund (UNFPA), 133
United States: Islamic law (sharia or shari'a), 18; Jewish women, 2; Jews, 2; Muslim feminists, 20; Muslim women, 2; Muslims, 2, 40–41; religious rights, Jewish women's, 27
urbanization, 134
ustaz, 274

Vambery, Arminius, 25
Van Barren, Th. P., 332
veiling: Christianity, 19; colonialism, 41; God, 28; Muslim women, 19, 24, 41; West, the, 24; Zionist literature, 258–259
visit marriage, 327, 328
von Braun, Christina, 19, 24

Wadi Salib riots (1959), 304
Wadud, Amina, 32, 34
Wahhabis, 54
Wahhabism, 53
waqf, 218, 350
Warrick, Catherine, 7–8, 153–154, 344
Was ist Aufklärung (Kant), 316
Washington State, 199n9
Wathba (1948), 280–281
weaving wool, 35
Weber, Max, 315
Weil, Gustav, 25
West, Nathaniel, 171
West, the: anti-Muslim attitudes, 197–198; crimes of passion, 184; honor killings in the Arab world, 154, 184, 192–193, 197–198; Islam, 21; Jews, 246, 341; Jews in, 3; state criminal law, 184; veiling, 24
What Went Wrong? (Lewis), 20
"whiteness" *(loven)*, 112, 116, 117
wills, 217, 232n81
Woman Question: Arab Question, 9; Iraqi Jews, 240; Levy, Shoshanna, 279; Zionist literature, 9, 243–244, 246–248, 256
women: Ashkenazi, 345; Iranian (*see* Iranian women); Iraqi, 240; Iraqi Jewish, 270, 271 (*see also* Levy, Shoshanna); Islamic law (sharia or shari'a), 46; Israeli, 240 (*see also* Levy, Shoshanna); Israeli Muslim, 223–224, 343; Jewish (*see* Jewish women); Jewish law (halacha or halachic law or halakhic law), 46; Middle Eastern, 269; Middle Eastern Jewish, 270 (*see also* Levy, Shoshanna); Mizrahi, 10, 240, 301 (*see also* Levy, Shoshanna); Muslim (*see* Muslim women); religious orthodoxy, resurgence in, 2;

women (*continued*)
rights (*see* women's rights); sacred texts, 3–4; sexuality of (*see* women's sexuality); status of, 5, 21; veiling (*see* veiling); violence against, 141–142, 175–176, 182
"women" *(nashim),* 110
Women and Jewish Law (Biale), 46
"Women and Law" (seminar), 46
Women's Equal Rights Law (Israel, 1951), 223
Women's Organization for Equal Rights, 234n1–3
women's rights: feminism, 23; institutions, 203; Iraqi Jewish women, 270; Islam, 32, 33; Islamic law (sharia or shari'a), 228n18; Israel, 224, 272, 343; Jewish Enlightenment *(Haskalah),* 22–23; Jewish women, 15; Mandate Palestine (1920-1947), 206, 211, 220–221, 226–227; modernization, 22; Muslim women, 15; religion, 32; religious rights, 22–23; shari'a courts, 228n18
women's sexuality: Islam, 36; Judaism, 30, 36; menstruation, 36
women's suffrage, 280
World Health Organization (WHO), 127–128
wudū, 75

Yazd, Iran, 128, 131
Ya'ari, Meir, 255
Yemenite Jews, 296–297, 302–303
Yusuf-e Zahra (Zahra's Yusuf), 162–163
Yuval-Davis, Nira, 262

Zāhirism, 88
Zalmona, Yigal, 255
Zaphenath-paneah, 169
Zarnuka, Palestine, 246
zavim, 114
"ze," 107, 122n26
Zierler, Wendy, 171, 180n19
zina, 60, 61, 193, 202n33
Zionism, 241–267; Arab and Muslim Palestinians as an ancestry group, 246, 253; Arab ideal, romantic, 251; Arab Question, 239; Arab-Jewish binationalism, 242–243; Ashkenazi, 256; demonstrations against, 280; domestic violence, 9, 239, 244; egalitarianism, 267n61; family life, 239; folk culture, search for, 246; gender, 239; Hebrew literary scholarship, 244; Herzl, Theodor, 241–243; Iraq, 282–283; Iraqi demonstrations against, 280; Iraqi

Jews, 282; Jewish studies, 3; "Jewish Woman's Zion" (Buber), 241–243; Jewish women, 241–242, 267n61, 283; Middle Eastern Jewish women, 270; national language, 242; Orthodox *vs.* secular struggle, 8; Palestinian Jewish Orientalism, 245–246; pioneer ethos, 259; types of, 245
Zionist literature, 248–267; *Altneuland* (Old New Land) (Herzl), 242; Arab Question *(ha-she'ela ha-'aravit),* 9, 239, 243–246, 256; Arab-Jewish couples, 251–252, 255, 258–261; Arab-Jewish relations, 242–244, 249–250, 251–252, 253, 262; Arabs as means to new cultural authenticity, 253; Ashkenazi, 249, 251, 252, 261–262, 267n61; Ashkenazi-Sephardi relations, 256–257; *Bat Tsiyon (Daughter of Zion)* (Burla), 244; changes in family life due to immigration, possibility of, 250; "Chava" (Sholem Aleichem), 247–248; commitment to progress and social change, 261; "Crossing the Styx" (Arieli), 244, 248–250, 254; *Daniel Deronda* (Eliot), 246; *Der Mabl (The Flood)* (Sholem Aleichem), 256; domestic policy, 243; domestic violence, 9, 239, 254, 257, 262; "In the Shadow of the Hermon" (Brokhes), 244, 250–255; intra-Jewish relations, 253; Jewish female migrants to Palestine, 248–255; Jewish men's dress, 252; Jewish self-separation from Arabs, 244, 255, 345; Jewish women and non-Jewish men, 247–248, 251, 262; Jewish women's dress, 252; *Levada (Alone)* (Kabak), 256; nationalist narrative, a woman's, 261–262; New Jewish Women, 256; Old Yishuv, 251, 255, 257–258, 260, 262, 265n33; Palestinian Arab nationalism, 259–260; Sephardi, 256–257; veiling, 258–259; Woman Question, 9, 243–244, 246–248, 256; women's rights, 260; Zionist pioneer ethos, 259
Zornberg, Avivah, 180n19
Zoroastrianism, 31
zov, 117
Zuleika (Potiphar's wife), 157, 158–162, 165–166, 168–170, 177, 179n14
zulm, 33